Public
Relations
Writing

Wadsworth Series in Mass Communication
Rebecca Hayden, Senior Editor

General

The New Communications by Frederick Williams

Mediamerica: Form, Content, and Consequence of Mass Communication, 3rd ed., by Edward Jay Whetmore

The Interplay of Influence: Mass Media & Their Publics in News, Advertising, Politics by Kathleen Hall Jamieson and Karlyn Kohrs Campbell

Mass Communication and Everyday Life: A Perspective on Theory and Effects by Dennis K. Davis and Stanley J. Baran

Mass Media Research: An Introduction by Roger D. Wimmer and Joseph R. Dominick

Communication Research: Strategies and Sources by Rebecca B. Rubin, Alan M. Rubin, and Linda J. Piele

The Internship Experience by Lynne Schafer Gross

Journalism

Media Writing: News for the Mass Media by Doug Newsom and James A. Wollert

Exercises for Practice in Media Writing by Doug Newsom and James A. Wollert

Excellence in College Journalism by Wayne Overbeck and Thomas M. Pasqua

When Words Collide: A Journalist's Guide to Grammar and Style by Lauren Kessler and Duncan McDonald

Exercises for When Words Collide by Lauren Kessler and Duncan McDonald

Interviews That Work: A Practical Guide for Journalists by Shirley Biagi

News Editing in the '80s: Text and Exercises by William L. Rivers

Reporting Public Affairs: Problems and Solutions by Ronald P. Lovell

Newswriting for the Electronic Media: Principles, Examples, Applications by Daniel E. Garvey and William L. Rivers

Free-Lancer and Staff Writer: Newspaper Features and Magazine Articles, 4th ed., by William L. Rivers and Alison R. Work

Magazine Editing in the '80s: Text and Exercises by William L. Rivers

This Is PR: The Realities of Public Relations, 3rd ed., by Doug Newsom and Alan Scott

Public Relations Writing: Form & Style, 2nd ed., by Doug Newsom and Bob Carrell

Creative Strategy in Advertising, 2nd ed., by A. Jerome Jewler

Broadcast and Cable

Stay Tuned: A Concise History of American Broadcasting by Christopher H. Sterling and John M. Kittross

Writing for Television and Radio, 4th ed., by Robert L. Hilliard

Communicating Effectively on Television by Evan Blythin and Larry A. Samovar

World Broadcasting Systems: A Comparative Analysis by Sydney W. Head

Broadcast/Cable Programming: Strategies and Practices, 2nd ed., by Susan Tyler Eastman, Sydney W. Head and Lewis Klein

Broadcast and Cable Selling by Charles Warner

Advertising in the Broadcast and Cable Media, 2nd ed., by Elizabeth J. Heighton and Don R. Cunningham

Strategies in Broadcast and Cable Promotion by Susan Tyler Eastman and Robert A. Klein

Modern Radio Station Practices, 2nd ed., by Joseph S. Johnson and Kenneth K. Jones

Modern Radio Production by Lewis B. O'Donnell, Philip Benoit, and Carl Hausman

Audio in Media, 2nd ed., by Stanley R. Alten

Television Production Handbook, 4th ed., by Herbert Zettl

Television Production Workbook, 4th ed., by Herbert Zettl

Directing Television and Film by Alan A. Armer

Sight-Sound-Motion: Applied Media Aesthetics by Herbert Zettl

Electronic Cinematography: Achieving Photographic Control over the Video Image by Harry Mathias and Richard Patterson

Public Relations Writing

Form & Style

Second Edition

Doug Newsom
Texas Christian University

Bob Carrell
University of Oklahoma

Wadsworth Publishing Company
Belmont, California
A Division of Wadsworth, Inc.

Senior Editor: Rebecca Hayden
Editorial Assistant: Naomi Brown
Production Editor: Gary Mcdonald
Print Buyer: Karen Hunt
Interior & Cover Designer: Andrew H. Ogus
Copy Editors: Suzanne Lipsett, Lorna Cunkle
Compositor: G & S Typesetters, Inc.

Printed in the United States of America

4   5   6   7   8   9   10—90   89   88

ISBN 0-534-06096-X

Library of Congress Cataloging-in-Publication Data
Newsom, Doug.
   Public relations writing.
   (Wadsworth series in mass communication)
   Rev. ed. of: Writing in public relations practice.
c1981.
   Includes bibliographies and index.
   1. Public relations.   2. Persuasion (Psychology)
3. Public relations—Authorship.   I. Carrell, Bob.
II. Newsom, Doug. Writing in public relations
practice.   III. Title.   IV. Series.
HM263.N493   1986   659.2   85-26366
ISBN 0-534-06096-X

Dedicated to all public relations writers
who care about communicating clearly and effectively

Preface

Public relations professionals are presumed to be *effective* writers—wordsmiths—whose fact-finding skills are exceeded only by their ability to mold information into any format for presentation in any medium, mass or specialized.

In addition to presenting information, public relations specialists use the language to perform specific tasks. The effectiveness of their work is measured—sometimes specifically, sometimes generally—in terms of their audiences' perception, awareness and understanding of the PR specialists' messages and of the action audiences take in response to those messages.

PR writers must translate complex information with the expertise of master teachers, write with the parsimony and expressive symbolism of poets and sculpt their writing so that it survives the whittling of countless editors, not all of whom will be professionals.

This book is for those who realize that the education of a professional public relations writer never ends but rather is continually beginning. This book represents a new beginning.

Part One covers expectations, the achieving of results and the research techniques that are the backbone of strong communication. Our first chapter is an overview of the variety of writing tasks public relations practitioners face and the communication skills those tasks demand. Since all public relations writing tasks have a specific purpose, the second chapter gives writers some insight into various communication theories that will help them become more effective. And because public relations writing often tries to influence perceptions as well as inform, the chapter also addresses ethical considerations. Chapter 3 is devoted to the research that must precede writing. This research is of a kind most often associated with the social sciences. If done well, such research provides a firm basis in fact for good, purposeful writing.

Part Two deals first with problems all writers face and then with problems specific to PR writing. PR writers work with all kinds of people. They often work with people who have something to say and know they need to communicate with audiences but don't know how. Some think they have something to say but don't. Still others think they know how to present their information but don't. Mix and match these any way you wish and you'll arrive at some of the interpersonal problems a PR practitioner routinely faces. An essential part of communicating is simplifying the complex and presenting information in a form that both respects the language and takes advantage of its flexibility. We deal with these aspects of PR writing in Chapters 4, 5 and 6.

Audiences for public relations writers fall into two broad categories, general and specialized. The general audiences, discussed in Part Three, are often referred to as "the public." Professional writers, though, must have a clearer picture of a medium's audience than the vague term *general audience* suggests. To communicate with "the public," mass media are used. For professional writers this means preparing news releases and feature stories for print media, writing in a variety of formats for broadcast media and developing advertising copy and crafting speeches and scripts for slide presentations and films. Chapters 7 through 10 cover these public audiences.

Specialized audiences are the topic of Part Four, Chapters 11 through 15. This category of audiences includes, among others, internal audiences, those who share the institutional image. Principal communication tools for specialized audiences are annual reports, institutional magazines, employee publications, newsletters and brochures, backgrounders and position papers, plus memos and letters.

At the request of writers who used the first edition of this book, we have covered crisis communication in its own chapter (16), although in practice communication during a crisis draws on the information presented in all the other chapters. In the new chapter we cover the advance preparations for a crisis as well as communication during and after a crisis.

The last section, Part Five, is a project that will give you practice in all types of PR writing. In the course of completing this project you will see how all the pieces fit together and, we hope, come to work on real projects with confidence. The project can be done as a semester project or it can be done as a series of exercises based on the assignments at the end of each chapter.

This edition has a new co-author. Tom Siegfried, who was teaching with Newsom at TCU when the first edition was written, is now with the *Dallas Morning News* and asked to be relieved of the text updating. Because many readers of the first edition asked for more emphasis on ad copywriting, Bob Carrell, whose primary field is advertising, agreed to help with the second edition.

When the first edition was published, PR writing was just appearing as a course. It is developing into a standard offering of the typical PR curriculum.

We have collected some materials for instructors such as syllabi and test questions. These are available from the publisher on request. (Send your requests to the attention of the senior editor, mass communication texts.)

Both of us are university teachers of research and writing skills in all mass media. We also practice these writing techniques as consultants for a number of clients, profit and nonprofit, some of whom have permitted research and writing from their institutions to be used in this text. We appreciate this.

Also we are grateful for the incisive criticism of users of the first edition of this text, and we owe special thanks to Bill Baxter of Marquette University, William Ehling of Syracuse University, Nancy M. Somerick of the University of Akron, and Rita J. Winters of Anderson College and *The Muncie Star*.

Reviewers of the first drafts of this second edition also helped us to sharpen the new material, and we'd like to express our appreciation publicly to Carolyn Cline of the University of Texas at Austin and Douglas P. Starr of North Texas State University.

Our special appreciation goes to senior editor Rebecca Hayden, whose steady hand and critical eye always improve our efforts.

D.N. & B.C.

Contents

Illustrations

Public
Relations
Writing

Part One

Writing and PR

Knowing how to find facts and how to communicate effectively is essential in all public relations jobs, as is the ability to write for all media.

1
Public Relations and the Writer

Controversy continues about what public relations is or isn't. Some people think public relations is mostly writing, in the form of new releases or advertising. Others think it is smiling at your customers and asking how the family is doing. Some business executives assume all you need for good PR is a good product and a money-back guarantee. Others think the goal of PR is getting the company name in the news media (or keeping it out of the media) as much as possible.

Unfortunately, all of these conceptions of public relations are misconceptions. Much of the confusion arises because the term *public relations* has two senses—a literal sense and a professional sense. In the literal sense of "relating to the public," good public relations is just getting along with people. This is not to suggest that PR is a field for those who "like people." In the professional sense, PR involves the ways an organization's operations and policies affect people—the face-to-face interaction of employees with customers or clients and the organization's participation in the affairs of the community.

PR is the brokering of goodwill between an institution and its publics. So, good public relations in the literal sense is essential to the overall public relations effort for any organization. But it is not enough. Good policies and good performance are worth little if people don't understand the policies and don't know about the performance. Achieving this understanding and knowledge is the task of public relations in the professional sense.

Public relations in the professional sense involves communication skills, expertise in dealing with the media and a knowledge of mass communications, the dynamics of public opinion and the principles of persuasion. At the heart of professional public relations is communication—in particular, writing.

Yet professional public relations is more than writing. It is not simply preparing publicity releases or writing advertising copy. Professional public relations is an art and a science that involves analysis and judgment, and counseling and planning—in addition to writing. In this chapter we'll try to clarify the nature of PR (in the professional sense) and examine the writer's role in it.

Defining Public Relations

Even people who practice public relations don't all agree on just what PR is. Each practitioner probably has a slightly different definition, depending on his or her particular PR experience. Definitions have been composed, though, that express the meaning of PR to the satisfaction of most professionals. One accepted definition was adopted in 1978 in Mexico City during the First World Assembly of Public Relations Associations and the First World Forum of Public Relations:

> **Public relations practice is the art and science of analyzing trends, predicting their consequences, counseling organization leaders, and implementing planned programs of action which will serve both the organization's and the public interest.**

It's a broad definition, but it's a useful one. By examining it more closely, we can get a better understanding of what PR is and where the writer fits in.

Analyzing, Predicting and Counseling

The central part of this definition of PR outlines the main roles of the professional public relations person: "analyzing trends, predicting their consequences, counseling organization leaders." These roles fall into the management context, in which personnel help to frame, implement, adjust and communicate policies that govern how an institution interacts with its publics. It is by means of PR that a firm acts with responsibility and responsiveness—in policy and information—to the best interests of the institution and its publics.[1]

Doing this job well requires a broad educational background, expertise in many areas and, most of all, good judgment. Unlike the corporate attorney or accountant, the PR practitioner has no body of laws or procedures to refer to that prescribes behavior under given circumstances. Instead, the public relations person must know human behavior and combine that knowledge with specific information both about people within the institution and people outside that the institution deals with. For example, the PR director for a bank must consider the views of bank officers and bank employees as well as those of customers, the community, legislators and government regulatory agencies. The PR person for the local school district must be aware of the feelings of students, parents, voters and the regional accrediting agency. Any institution has many audiences, and the PR director must be able to advise management about the possible impact on those audiences of various policies and actions.

In addition to analyzing audiences and counseling management on the effects of policy, the PR person must be alert for signs of change. The right policy today will not necessarily be the right policy tomorrow. People's attitudes and opinions evolve, and the composition of the audience changes. The capable PR person notes trends in public opinion and predicts the consequences of such trends for the institution.

Usually, the PR director also serves as spokesperson for the organization and overseer of the entire public relations program. The PR person at the top of the department spends little time on basic PR techniques such as writing. The basics are handled by entry-level people, the staff writers.

Frank Wylie, a former president of the Public Relations Society of America, describes the division of PR labor this way. Senior level public relations people are likely to spend 10 percent of their time with techniques, 40 percent with administration and 50 percent with analysis and judgment. At entry level it's 50 percent techniques, 5 percent judgment and 45 percent "running like hell."[2]

Advertising, Publicity and PR

Much of the "running like hell" is done to carry out those "planned programs" of action mentioned in the definition of PR. These programs are the most visible part of public relations practice. Since they include publicity, and sometimes advertising, many people confuse public relations with publicity or advertising.

For that matter, advertising and publicity are themselves often confused. *Advertising* is media time or space purchased to display a message prepared (or approved) by the purchaser. The content of an ad is controlled by the buyers of the time or space. *Publicity* is information supplied to a news medium without cost. The decision to use that information and its final form are controlled by the medium.

People hired for public relations jobs often help design and write copy for ads, but advertising is usually a separate program, either a complement to the public relations program or subordinate to it. Ads for products and services (marketing-type advertising) are almost always handled exclusively by advertising agencies and their copywriters. Another type of advertising—image, identity or institutional advertising—may be written by someone in a PR department. Such ads are usually message-oriented rather than sales-oriented. They are used either to build an organization's image or to communicate views on some public issue.

Most business executives understand the difference between advertising and publicity, but many still think publicity is synonymous with public relations. It's true that publicity is usually handled by PR people, but public relations involves a much wider spectrum of responsibility, including policy making. A publicist merely disseminates information. A public relations person, as we discussed, is involved in the analysis, counseling and planning that precede the dissemination of information. Or, as PR authority Edward L. Bernays says, "Publicity is a one-way street; public relations is a two-way street."[3] PR incorporates publicity, press agentry and public information, with the emphasis dependent on the type of institution.[4]

The Two-Way Street

The last part of the Mexico City definition of PR speaks of serving "both the organization's and the public interest." Publicists who simply transmit their organization's views to the media are not likely to serve the public interest. As Bernays says,

> Public relations is not a one-way street in which leadership manipulates the public and public opinion. It is a two-way street in which leadership and the public find integration with each other and in which objectives and goals are predicated on a coincidence of public and private interest.[5]

This means that the task of PR people is not simply communicating management's view to the public. The task also involves communicating the views of the public to management. The objectives of an institution and its PR program must be designed with the needs and desires of the public clearly in mind.

Going one way, the PR person analyzes public opinion and the needs of the community, and opens channels of communication that allow such information to flow into the institution. Using this information, the PR person advises management on the policies that are likely to be of mutual benefit to the institution and the public—or at least acceptable, if not beneficial, to the public.

Then—going the other way down the PR street—the PR person opens channels of communication that reach out from the institution to the public. These channels are used to interpret the institution's policies and actions to its various audiences. Communication in this direction is largely the responsibility of the PR writer.

Publics, Channels and the Role of the Writer

It is a simple thing to say that the task of PR writers is communicating with the public. But in practice there is nothing simple about it. It's not as though there were one single "public" to write for. Rarely is a PR message important to everybody in the "public."

If a gas company wants to say it's not asking for a rate increase to build corporate offices, it is likely to aim its message at home owners and regulatory agencies at the state and federal level; it won't be concerned with middle-school students. Those students might be a very important audience, though, for the theme park advertising its new ride. A welfare agency announcing new food stamp rules would be most interested in getting the message to low-income families. A mayor raising money to help a downtown renovation project would be likely to appeal to the city's business leaders.

Home owners, legislators, students, business leaders—all are examples of publics. A *public* is any group of people tied together by some common factor. And as public relations writers soon discover, there are many, many such groups. As some PR people say, and as we've acknowledged through usage in this book, the *public* in public relations should really be *publics*.

The Public in Public Relations

In his book *The Mass Media*, Stanford professor Bill Rivers describes the endless variety of publics in this way:

> There are as many publics as there are groups with varying levels of income, education, taste, and civic awareness; as many as there are groups with different political allegiances, different religions and so on. What concerns and convinces one public may seem trivial to another. Furthermore, the definition of each public is never static; it changes as the issues change. When California is voting for a governor, a Los Angeles college student becomes one member of a large and diverse public that includes a San Francisco stevedore and excludes a college professor at the University of Maine. But, when higher education in the United States is the issue, the college student is one member of a public that includes the professor but excludes the stevedore—except that the stevedore's working partner may have a daughter who attends the University of Idaho . . . and so on in bewildering variety.[6]

Obviously, each one of us belongs to many different publics (see Figure 1-1). If you're a student, you're naturally a member of a public important to the university or college you attend. If you're about to graduate, you belong to a public important to prospective employers in the community. If you've just been married, you're part of a public important to real estate firms eager to sell you a house. If you belong to the local chapter of the Sierra Club, you're part of a public important to politicians and energy companies.

Just as each individual belongs to many publics, each institution must communicate with many publics—from customers and suppliers to employees and stockholders. A PR writer for a university must write for faculty, students, administrators, alumni, financial benefactors, community leaders, legislators and sports fans. The PR writer for a political candidate tailors messages to fund raisers, voters, reporters and precinct workers.

The variety of publics is so vast that PR people often find it useful to divide the publics they deal with into two broad classes: internal and external. *Inter-*

1-1

A Person—A Member of Many Publics Simultaneously

Human being
Stockholder
Employee
Art collector
Neighbor
Music lover
Car owner
Churchgoer
Driver
Consumer
Taxpayer
Parent
Voter
Sports fan
Citizen
Brother/sister
Media user
Aunt/uncle
Son/daughter
Public transportation user

nal publics are groups within the organization (such as employees or the board of directors). *External publics* are groups outside the organization (such as the media, your company's customers or the state legislature). The distinction between the two is not always clear-cut; stockholders, for example, though essentially an external public can have close ties to the institution. One definition of internal publics is "all those who share the institution's identity." (Some examples of publics and the media used to reach them are suggested in Example 1-2.)

Target Audiences

On any one project it is impossible to direct attention equally to all publics. Therefore, PR people must select audiences that are most important for the communication effort. They may include the group that a new policy will affect the most, or the groups whose opinions are especially important. In any event, the groups considered most important for a communication effort are called the *target audiences*.

How do PR people select target audiences? Only by knowing the

1-2

Internal and External PR

	INTERNAL	EXTERNAL	
		Direct	Indirect
PUBLICS	Management (top and middle)	(Marketing communications)	(Institutional communications)
	Staff and employees (union and employee organizations— non-union)	Customers	Potential customers
	Stockholders	Sales representatives	Potential investors (stockholders)
	Directors	Traders and distributors	Financial community
		Suppliers	Special community of institution
		Competitors	Government (local, state, federal)
			Community (environmental)
MEDIA	Personal (person to person/person to group)	Personal (person to person/person to group)	
	Audio/visual (films, slides, videotape, mass media, specialized media available to external audiences such as externally distributed slide presentations, etc.)	Audio/visual (specialized media: films, slides, videotape, closed circuit TV computer networks)	
	Publications (mass and specialized, including controlled and uncontrolled publicity as well as institutional and commercial advertising)	Publications (specialized media: books, magazines, newspapers, newsletters)	
	Direct mail (personalized, institutional and sales promotion)	Direct mail	
	Exhibits (mass and specialized externally displayed and product packaging, graphics, including point of sale promotions)	Exhibits (including posters and bulletin board materials internally displayed as well as personalized items such as pins, awards, etc.)	
		Critics (individuals and institutions)	

characteristics of the members of the various publics. They discover these characteristics through advance research, which is essential. PR people must, for example, collect certain statistical data about members of their publics—facts such as members' age and sex, where they live, how they make a living, the amount of money they earn, their educational level and such. Such statistics about groups are called *demographics*. Almost any survey form you fill out has places for such information.

But demographic information alone does not tell writers all they need to know about a public. Statistics such as age, sex and income are not useful in predicting whether a person would be likely to subscribe to the magazine *Dog World*, for example. Dog lovers come in all ages, both sexes, and most income groups, groups that might seem totally unrelated if judged by demographics alone.

In fact, what PR people call *psychographics* is frequently more important to the PR writer than demographics. Psychographics classifies people by what they think, how they behave and what they think about—their special interests, such as dogs. Psychographic information is not merely helpful to the PR writer—it is often necessary. Consider the public relations director responsible for a university's alumni association magazine who admitted, with some dismay, that she didn't know how to appeal both to an 80-year-old graduate of the engineering school and a 22-year-old sociologist. She did a research study that revealed a psychographic pattern binding all the alumni to the institution. This information suggested the sort of articles that would interest alumni. The PR director was then able to make informed decisions—and she now felt a great deal of confidence in her choices. (See 1-3 for another way of looking at psychographic categories for publics.)

Channels

To reach different publics, the PR writer must choose channels of communication carefully. To get the message across, the channel must be one that the target audience will receive and believe. For example, the amusement park that wants middle-school students to try its new ride would be foolish to run an ad in *Harper's* magazine. Few middle-school students even know that *Harper's* exists. They would not receive a message placed in that medium. But they do listen to radio and watch TV, so programs in those media are the channels that the amusement park would probably use.

The channel must also be appropriate for the message. Radio is not a good channel for conveying messages on complex subjects such as a university's endowment. These subjects are better suited to a magazine, a channel that readers can spend time with. Radio, though poorly suited for discussing endowments, works just fine for telling students the dates for fall registration.

Channels may be individuals or media and mass or specialized. Each medium has characteristics that make it suitable for sending a particular message to a particular audience at a particular time.

People may be channels—for example, in person-to-person meetings or person-to-group interactions such as speeches or meetings. When communication media are mentioned, you are likely to think of publications and audiovisuals. Publications may be books, magazines, newspapers, newsletters or reports. Audiovisuals may be films, videotapes, slides or television—mass or closed circuit. But people, publications and audiovisuals aren't the only channels of communication. Another channel is the direct mail of personalized letters or institutional or promotional pieces. Exhibits are another channel. They encompass anything from a trade-show display to a campaign button.

Specialized Media   Media designed for a particular audience are called *specialized*, to distinguish them from media for general audiences. Specialized media include the internal publications that institutions produce to communicate with employees, staff, management and others close to the institution, such as directors and stockholders. Also included in specialized media are audiovisuals intended for internal use only, such as closed-circuit television and training films, or videotapes and computerized message boards. Specialized media are usually controlled by the institution using them. The newest specialized media are the electronic information networks of personal computer users. For example, PR personal computer (P.C.)

Source: From Ed Zotti, "Brave New Typologies," *Public Relations Journal*, May 1985, p. 30. Copyright 1985. Used with permission.

Brave New Typologies

The Values and Lifestyles Program (VALS) devised by SRI International divides people into four types, which are expanded to include nine categories:

Need Driven

Survivors. 4 percent of the adult population. Elderly, poorly educated, barely hanging on economically. Tend to be conservative Democrats.

Sustainers. 7 percent. High unemployment, low income, but better off than Survivors. Distrustful; seldom vote. Live for the moment, but not without hope for the future.

Outer Directed

Belongers. 37 percent. The middle Americans—largest of the nine categories. Conservative (conforming), family-oriented, want to preserve status quo. Tend to be Democrats.

Emulators. 8 percent. Social climbers. Competitive, into conspicuous consumption. Appearances are everything. Distrustful, apolitical.

Achievers. 22 percent. Success-oriented—"the driving force of the economy." Materialistic, hard-working, affluent. Include many business leaders. Tend to be Republicans.

Inner Directed

I-Am-Mes. 3 percent. The punk rockers of the world. Young, liberal views, but rarely politically active. Individualistic to the point of narcissism. Into trendy products.

Experientals. 6 percent. Physical fitness buffs. Seek "intensity" in all things. Adventuresome, liberal.

Societally Conscious. 12 percent. Sixties activists grown to adulthood. Liberal, politically active. Leaders of single-issues causes. Into natural living.

Above It All

Integrated. 2 percent. Combine best features of inner- and outer-directed lifestyles—*i.e.*, affluence, sensitivity. Tolerant, self-assured.

It's worth pointing out that VALS isn't the only research program that's taken a look at lifestyles. Prizm, a service of Claritas Corporation, is a geodemographic system with a psychographic component. It identifies geographic "clusters" with similar demographic and behavioral characteristics, which are identified with names like Sun-Belt Singles and Coalburg & Corntown. ClusterPlus, a project of Donnelley Marketing Information Services and Simmons Market Research Bureau, offers similar capabilities.

Such systems often take greater account of regional differences than VALS does. For instance, Market Opinion Research in Detroit, which has done lifestyles research for a number of newspapers, has identified a group it calls the Winter Affluents in Palm Beach—active, wealthy, elderly folks who go to Palm Beach to play golf, go sailing, and so on. In Omaha, there are the Agribusiness Actives—entrepreneurial, risk-taking farmers (many of whom unfortunately gambled on rising land prices in the seventies and are now broke).

Says Barbara Bryant, senior vice president at Market Opinion, "we develop our categories according to the people we find, rather than making the people fit into the categories."

For more information about VALS, contact SRI International in Menlo Park, CA, (415) 859-3882. **—E.Z.**

users have a special channel, PRSIG (PR SIGnature), on one of the nation's largest computer networks, CompuServe.[7]

Mass Media   The mass media include magazines, books, newspapers, radio and television. Since neither the circulation nor the audience of such a medium is controlled by the institution, mass media are usually used for communication with external publics. PR writers using mass media to reach general audiences must remember, however, that such media are seen by internal publics as well. For example, some women airline employees complained about an advertising campaign they said not only projected the female flight crew as sex objects but also sounded sexually suggestive. French police did not like billboards portraying them as "helpful" rather than as crime fighters facing danger.

The Role of the Writer

PR writers must be knowledgeable not only about publics and channels, but about all aspects of their institution as well. The PR writer for a social work agency must understand welfare eligibility rules and federal funding guidelines. A writer for the highway department must know about everything from road-building materials to traffic laws. PR writers must know enough about the financial aspects of a business to prepare the right message for security analysts and to develop an annual report that the stockholders can read and the auditors will approve.

In addition to a broad knowledge of their company's business, PR writers must have the ability to research specific subjects to determine what is and what isn't important. They must be able to borrow ideas from other fields—psychology, social psychology, sociology and political science, for example—to help put that research in perspective. PR writers must be alert to changing patterns of thought and behavior in society and must fully comprehend the issues of the day.

Finally, and most important of all, the PR writer must be an expert in communication. If you want to be a PR writer, you must know how to write effectively in many different styles and for all media. You must understand the principles of good writing and be familiar with the vast body of scientific research on communication, persuasion and public opinion. Your goal is to be an efficient, effective communicator. No matter what message you communicate, what audiences you communicate with or what media you use to reach those audiences, you have to know which words will work and why. You are critical to the PR function.

Preparing you for these varied writing tasks is what this book is all about.

Conclusions

* Definitions of PR vary primarily because the term has two senses: the literal—getting along with people—and the professional—the brokering of goodwill between an institution and its publics.

* PR in a professional sense involves communication, half or more of the beginning PR person's work.
* PR, publicity and advertising are not synonymous terms. PR is analyzing, predicting, counseling and communicating—sometimes through advertising or publicity or both.
* Advertising is media time or space bought to carry the purchaser's message.
* Publicity is information supplied to various media to be used at their editors' discretion, and in a final form determined by the medium.
* PR communication is a two-way street, a place for incoming as well as outgoing messages.
* Publics are people tied together by some common factor(s).
* Factors binding people together as audiences may be demographics—statistics such as age, sex, geography and psychographics—interests and attitudes.
* Target audiences are the PR publics selected for specific messages.
* Channels of communication may be specialized or mass.
* A PR writer's role is to know about the institution for which that writer is working, the audiences or publics of that institution and the channels of communication through which to reach them.
* PR writers must be effective, efficient writers in *all* media.

Exercises

1. Find an article in a local newspaper that centers on one institution or one event sponsored by an institution. See if you can find some qualities that would suggest that the article is a publicity release. What are your reasons for thinking that this is a publicity release rather than a news story generated by the newspaper staff?
2. Find an example of institutional advertisement. List the ways in which it differs from a marketing (sales) ad. Describe the differences between the publicity release and the ad.
3. Study a copy of a public relations publication, such as your university's alumni magazine. How does that magazine's content (information and advertising, if any) differ from that of a consumer publication?
4. What types of public relations writing does a PR agency do? What types does your university's public relations office do? You should set up interviews to get this information and ask for examples to include as illustrations in your list of descriptions of these PR writing tasks.
5. Review the background on Ourbank in Part Five of the text. Identify Ourbank's publics. Use demographic and psychographic information to explain why each public is different from the others.

Notes

[1] Doug Newsom and Alan Scott, *This Is PR* (Belmont, Calif.: Wadsworth, 1985), p. 7.

[2] Frank Wylie, "The New Professionals," speech to the First National Student Conference, Public Relations Student Society of America, Dayton, Ohio, 24 October 1976. Published by Chrysler Corporation, p. 5.

[3] Edward L. Bernays, *Public Relations* (Norman, Okla.: University of Oklahoma Press, 1952), p. 5.

[4] James E. Grunig and Todd Hunt, *Managing Public Relations* (New York: Holt, Rinehart & Winston, 1984), pp. 22–24.

[5] *Public Relations*, p. 83.

[6] William L. Rivers, *The Mass Media* (New York: Harper & Row, 1975), p. 22.

[7] "The Division's Newsletter Is Available Via CompuServe," The Newsletter of the Public Relations Division of the Association for Education in Journalism and Mass Communication," Fall 1984 (Washington, D.C.: George Washington University, Division of Continuing Education and Summer Session).

Selected Bibliography

Edward L. Bernays, *Public Relations* (Norman, Okla.: University of Oklahoma Press, 1952).

Commission on Public Relations Education, "A Design for Public Relations Education," pamphlet distributed in 1975, published by the Public Relations Division of America and the Public Relations Division of the Association for Education in Journalism and Mass Communication through the Foundation for Public Relations Research and Education. A follow-up study was done in 1984–1985 by the same institutions.

Peter Davies, *Success with Words: A Guide to the American Language* (Pleasantville, N.Y.: Reader's Digest, 1983).

Doug Newsom and Alan Scott, *This Is PR*, 3rd ed. (Belmont, Calif.: Wadsworth, 1985).

Frank Wylie, "Public Relations: A Frontier Profession," reprint of a speech, "The New Professionals," by Wylie, Public Relations Director, U.S. Automotive Sales, Chrysler Corporation, to the First National Student Conference, Public Relations Student Society of America, Dayton, Ohio, October 24, 1976; published by Chrysler Corporation.

2
Persuasion

$\mathbf{A}$ nuclear engineer especially good at explaining technical matters once gave a talk to a civic club in a small town. He used dozens of slides, charts and graphs to describe the operation of nuclear power plants and to explain how safe they were.

At the end of his talk, an elderly lady thanked the engineer for his presentation. "I don't understand anything you said," she told him, "but I agree with you a hundred percent." The point: People rely on information and logic in forming their opinions but only up to a point.

A companion point is illustrated by another true story. In a midwestern state in the mid-1960s, a major department store was having its grand opening in a new mall. An in-store demonstrator in the housewares section was showing how eggs could be cooked in a coated skillet without a lubricant. A grandmotherly type in her seventies watched with rapt attention. When the demonstration was finished the crowd dispersed, but the woman approached the demonstrator and said, "I have read your ads and stories about that stuff and I saw you do it, but I just don't believe it." She had probably been frying eggs every morning for a half century, and no doubt every time she failed to use a lubricant in her skillet the eggs stuck to the pan. The point: Truth is sometimes stranger than fiction and more difficult to believe.

It is true that people are rational. But that only means they can think. People are also emotional. Were people driven only by logic, there would never be a need to persuade. The fact is, however, that people in economically advanced societies such as ours base most of their decisions and behaviors on emotion rather than logic. Most of us don't have to spend every waking hour just getting enough food, clothing and shelter so we can sustain life. As these things are easier to attain, we spend more and more time on their quality. That's where emotion comes in. And it is the context in which persuasion is most often used.

We all appreciate the idea that a free flow of information is necessary for enlightened self-government. At the same time, we enjoy enlightened self-interest, which is often motivated more by emotions than by logic. Nevertheless, we place great value on information. It is the stuff of which good public relations is made. But a lot of PR writing also attempts to persuade people to a particular point of view.

In order to be a persuasive writer, you need to have some idea of the arguments—both factual and emotional—that will work best with your audience. Common sense can give you some clues, but you'll do a much better job if you know something about the science of persuasion. Common sense is no substitute for what decades of research have revealed about how and why people form their opinions. As PR pioneer Edward L. Bernays puts it, "Like Columbus, you can sail west and reach new land by accident. But if you have charts, you can do better; you can arrive at a destination decided upon in advance."[1]

When engineers design bridges or buildings, Bernays points out, they apply a knowledge of physics and chemistry and other sciences. Doctors treat patients using a knowledge of the laboratory findings of biochemists and medical researchers. In the same way, PR people should apply the relevant findings of social sciences such as psychology, sociology and communication when they embark on an effort to persuade.

Knowledge of these disciplines will help the PR writer answer some of the many questions that come up time and again in persuasive writing. Should you give both sides of the story or only your side? If you give both, which side should you give first? Should you draw an explicit conclusion or is it better to let the audience figure it out for itself? Which should you give first, the good news or the bad news?

Other questions come up again and again. How effective are fear techniques? Should you make a point once or repeat it several times to make sure it sinks in? These are the sorts of questions that social scientists can help you answer.

Of course, research findings can only *help* you answer these questions. Research results can be valuable guides in planning persuasive communication, but they are not laws of nature. In many cases, the findings collected so far are not conclusive. At times, you have to rely on personal experience and knowledge of your audience.

Nevertheless, social science has found out a lot about the nature of persuasion, and it would be foolish not to put that knowledge to use. Research data is better than top-of-the-head speculation about the how and why of opinion formation.

Opinion Formation and Change

The first thing you need to know as a persuasive writer is that you are not going to gain many converts to your point of view, at least not immediately. The reason is simple. The few minutes a person gives to reading your message are not likely to change attitudes built up over a lifetime. However, if you're going to make headway at all, you need to know something about what attitudes and opinions are and how they form.

Opinion, Attitude and Belief

Some authorities see little or no need to distinguish among opinions, attitudes and beliefs, at least in theory. On the practical level of trying to understand how and why people behave as they do, however, it may be useful to you to make such a distinction.

In this context, opinions are temporal, fleeting and unstable. They can change on a whim. Attitudes are a little more stable and are less likely to change immediately. Beliefs, however, are very stable, and they are very resistant to change. To illustrate the different levels involved, suppose we get in a time machine and travel back to 1950. At that time, products made in Japan were generally believed to be of poor quality. Our opinions of products with the "Made in Japan" label were not charitable. With the introduction of import cars, a variety of electronic gear and camera systems of high quality, however, our attitudes began to change. Now we believe that many brands of products made in Japan in these categories set the standards of quality against which all others are judged. The point is that opinions can change with the wind. Beliefs can change but they are slow to do so. Attitudes fall somewhere between these extremes.

How did this change come about? As we began to experience products of higher quality from Japan, our opinions shifted to the extent that favorable attitudes began to be common and these eventually came together in support of a belief that the label "Made in Japan" deserved respect.

In many respects, opinions, attitudes and beliefs are closely linked, so it makes sense for us to discuss them as one, while using the term *attitude* to signify all three.

Models of Attitude Formation

There are many models of behavior that illustrate different perspectives on how attitudes are formed. But all these models have a lot of elements in common. Thus, if we concentrate on the main points, it will be enough for us to look at just one of them. M. Brewster Smith's "map" of attitude formation was first designed as a tool for studying political attitudes, but its main parts apply to attitude formation in general. Figure 2-1 is an adaptation of Smith's more elaborate model. It's easy to see that attitude formation is a complex process.

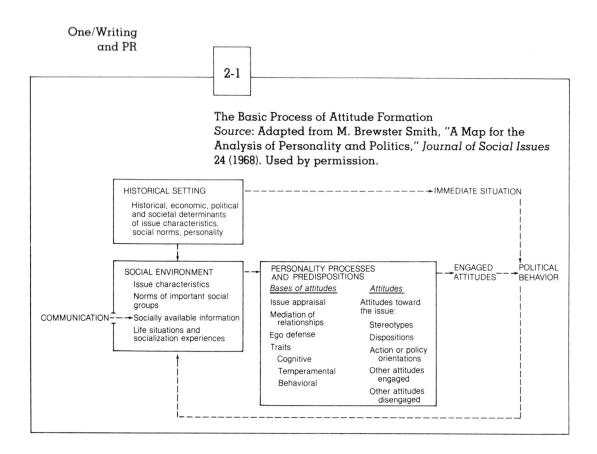

2-1

The Basic Process of Attitude Formation
Source: Adapted from M. Brewster Smith, "A Map for the
Analysis of Personality and Politics," *Journal of Social Issues*
24 (1968). Used by permission.

To begin with, an individual's personal background, or historical setting, plays an important role in his or her behavior. Where was the person born?
Where did he or she grow up? What were the social and economic conditions of the
day? These and similar factors help to shape personality. Historical factors also
shape the issues that persuasive writers deal with, not only those of their audience
but their own as well.

All of these considerations are part of the social environment in
which communication and persuasion take place. Individuals belong to groups with
social norms that affect their opinions. A person's life experiences also play a large
part in attitude formation. And, naturally, the characteristics of the issue at hand
are important.

One other major element of the social environment influences attitudes—available information. Here is the one door open to the persuasive writer.
The writer has no power to change a person's personal history or the norms of social
groups, although persuasive messages may be woven into those fabrics of experience. But you can't expect to change someone's life situation with your message or to
provide a significant new experience. However, as a writer, you can hope to add to
the information on which attitudes may be based.

If you look at the situation objectively, it does not appear to be encouraging. Why spend all the effort and resources necessary to shape and send persuasive messages if there isn't much hope for change? The fact is that providing information is your only chance at making an impact. Even if the impact is minimal, you have to try. That's why you need to understand the nature of persuasion.

The Nature of Persuasion

As a writer, you can look at persuasion in three basic ways. One is as a learning process, whereby you impart information and members of your audience seek information because they want to know something. Another way of looking at persuasion is to think of it as a power process whereby you attempt to "force" information on someone. The third broad view is that persuasion is simply an emotional process. No single perspective of persuasion is likely to be adequate, since, as we already know, the formation of attitudes is a complex process. But we can outline some aspects of the process that, when taken together, will give you some useful insights.

Aspects of Persuasion

One of the best outlines of this process appears in Otto Lerbinger's *Designs for Persuasive Communication*. Lerbinger describes five different "designs" of persuasion: (1) stimulus-response, (2) cognitive, (3) motivational, (4) social and (5) personality.[2]

Stimulus-Response   The concept of stimulus-response is the simplest approach to persuasion and, perhaps, the least useful. It is based on the idea of association. If two things are seen together many times, people tend to think of one when they see the other. Clearly, stimulus-response behavior does not involve any intricate thought on the part of the audience. It is useful only when a low level of response is acceptable. It seems to work as well with animals as it does with people, or perhaps even better. The classic illustration of this approach is Pavlov's experiments with dogs, in which a tuning fork was struck each time meat powder was fed to the dogs. Soon, whenever the tuning fork was struck the dogs began to drool in anticipation of food. Similarly, a cat owner (a non-scientist) discovered that she could call her cats from any hiding place by starting up the electric can opener. The cats associated the sound of the can opener with food and thus with dinner.

Obviously, this design is not a very good way to persuade someone regarding a complex issue. If, however, you simply want to establish an "association" between an idea and your organization in the public mind, stimulus-response may provide an adequate model to follow. For example, Avis has been successful in associating its name with the idea of trying harder.

Cognitive   The concept behind the cognitive design is that people can think and reason about what they read, see or hear. And they will come to the right conclusions if they are given the right information in an understandable way. "Right conclusion" is not necessarily the one you advocate, but it is the one that is "right" by the standards of individual members of the audience.

The cognitive approach can be effective in some situations. If a person has no personal stake in an issue, for example, or has no preconceived notions about it, the simple presentation of information may be effective. People like to think of themselves as fair and reasonable, and if you provide reasonable arguments, they will be likely to agree with you—other things being equal.

Of course, other things seldom are equal. You can't expect to dump your message (whether stimulus-response or cognitive) into people's heads without considering what is already in them. To persuade someone to take a certain position, you have to know what will motivate the person to take that position. This idea is the basis of the motivational design of persuasion.

Motivational Generally, the motivational design is based on the idea that showing a person how to change an attitude will fulfill a need. In essence, your message to the audience will offer some kind of emotional reward for accepting your message and responding to it as you suggest.

What are some needs that motivate people? A convenient outline of human needs was devised by the psychologist Abraham Maslow, who grouped human needs into a hierarchy ranging from the most basic to the least tangible (see Figure 2-2). At the bottom of the hierarchy are physical needs such as food, water, air and sleep. One step up is the general need for safety, or the need to be free from fear of harm. Then come social needs: the need to belong to groups, the need to associate with others, the need for love. Next come personal needs, such as the desire for self-respect, the desire to feel important, the need for status. At the top of the scale are the self-actualizing needs: the need to fulfill potential, to be creative and to have a rewarding life.

Whether these needs are being fulfilled, and in what measure, may play a major role in an individual's response to your attempts at persuasion. Persuasion that ignores these needs in order to concentrate on reason and logic is not likely to get very far. It is also important for you, as a writer, to identify the relevant needs of the members of your audience. Attempts at persuasion that do not meet their needs will fail.

Social Closely related to motivation is the focus on the social design of persuasion. This design takes into account an individual's background, social class and group norms. Often, group membership is the most important element in determining attitudes. On issues where attitudes are closely tied to social conditions, persuasion must be designed to address the social factors that influence the individual.

Essential to this design is the idea that we learn from society which values are best and worst and which patterns of behavior are most acceptable. The key point here is that if you are trying to persuade across major regional, ethnic or

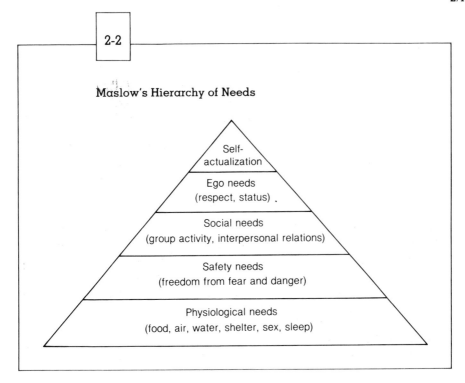

2-2

Maslow's Hierarchy of Needs

Self-actualization

Ego needs
(respect, status) .

Social needs
(group activity, interpersonal relations)

Safety needs
(freedom from fear and danger)

Physiological needs
(food, air, water, shelter, sex, sleep)

national boundaries, the same message is unlikely to be appropriate in every case. You'll have to prepare separate messages, based on different social influences.

Also, it is wise to remember that norms change. They are dynamic. It is necessary, then, that you continue to take the pulse of your public. What is the norm today may not be the norm tomorrow. You'll need to know when, why and how the norm changes so that you can adjust your messages to the new conditions.

Personality   Finally, you can't ignore the fact that each individual is unique. Personality characteristics can determine which arguments will work best with a given person or public. Of course, a persuasive message is frequently directed at a large group containing a number of different personality types, so the personality design cannot be used effectively in many instances. Even if your message is directed at a large group—that is, it is designed for the masses—you should always remember that it will be received separately by individuals. As a writer, you need to remain aware of how personality characteristics affect persuasibility.[3]

Steps in the Persuasion Process

There are many approaches to the act of persuasion, although most successful persuasion uses a combination of them. Once you have considered all the different approaches, how do you actually go about persuading someone?

To answer that, we must first identify the steps in the persuasion process. Social psychologist William McGuire lists six such steps: presenting, attending, comprehending, yielding, retaining the new position and acting.[4]

Presenting   You can't persuade anyone of anything unless he or she is at the right place at the right time to perceive a message. A person who does not own a television set will probably not see your announcement on TV. If he or she has a set but it is tuned to another channel, the result will be the same. In both cases, it will not matter how beautifully you have written the public service announcement. The same is true of the story in the newspaper about the benefit concert to help the hospital. If a person does not subscribe to the paper or does not buy one at the newsstand, your message is not going to penetrate and persuade that individual at all.

Attending   The non-viewer's next-door neighbor probably has a TV set, however, and he might see your announcement. But he might not pay the least attention to it. He might be looking straight at the screen but thinking about who's going to win the upcoming football game. If so, he's not getting your message either. He must *attend* to the message—that is, pay attention—if you're to have any hope of persuading him.

Comprehending   Suppose this guy's wife is paying attention. She is watching the screen and listening intently to the sounds. But she's Mexican-American and does not speak a word of English. She likes to watch football games even though she can't understand the announcers. But she can't understand the announcements either, so there isn't much chance that you'll persuade her. The point is, you have to use message symbols that your audience can comprehend. If you don't, your message, even if delivered technically as sent, will fail to communicate.

Yielding   In the house next door is another woman who sees the same message. She understands English, so she comprehended what your announcement said about the concert and its benefit to the hospital. And she happens to work at the hospital. But her reaction is somewhat neutral because she isn't very fond of the musical group. "They just try to make up for a lack of talent by playing and yelling louder," she says to herself. She got your message, but she did not yield to it. Although communication occurred, persuasion did not.

Retaining the New Position   Let's assume that this woman's husband isn't dreaming about the football scores after all, but sees the commercial and is impressed. "That looks like a great idea," he says. "I think we should go to the concert because it will not only be fun but it will help the hospital." But the concert does not happen for another month. By that time, he may have forgotten about the concert and the benefit to the hospital. Your attempt at persuasion has been successful in getting the viewer to accept it. But since the viewer didn't retain his new attitude, for all practical purposes this attempt at persuasion has failed.

This element, of course, represents one of the main arguments for sustained public relations programming. It is not enough to get the message through. The message has to be retained by the audience long enough for the desired action to occur.

Acting Now let's assume that the viewer didn't forget your message. Perhaps he saw the same announcement again and once more expressed a desire to go to the benefit concert. He may even have gone downtown with the intention of buying tickets, discovering when he got there, to his surprise, that his favorite pop singer was scheduled for a concert on the next weekend. So rather than buying the benefit concert tickets, he opted for the pop concert. Your announcement, then, did persuade him to a new attitude, but the persuasion was not successful enough to get him to act on it.

To be successful, persuasion must accomplish all six of these steps. You must get your message to the audience. More important, you must get someone to pay attention to it. And the message must be understandable—people are more likely to read things that are easy to understand. In any event, they aren't likely to come over to your side if they don't understand what your side is. But understanding isn't enough. Your arguments must be convincing. The audience must be willing to give in, or yield. Then they must remember that they gave in, and then they must act.

You'll need to consider all these steps when designing persuasive messages. Techniques that work well to achieve some steps might be useless for others. Some persuasive writing gets people to pay attention, but it might not be memorable. Messages designed only to produce yielding might not get the audience to act. For example, one research study tried to decide which persuasive methods were best for getting new mothers to go to the maternity ward for examinations. As it turned out, the best method depended on how the results were measured. One method got the most mothers to say they would come back a month later, but another method produced the most mothers who actually went back a month later.[5] Obviously, one method was good at inducing yielding, but the other was better for retention and action.

Persuasion and Communication

Persuasion is a special type of communication. To understand the persuasion process fully, then, we must understand something about communication. Like persuasion, the communication process can be divided into a number of elements.[*]

---

[*] McGuire calls the relationship between the steps in the persuasion process to those in the communication process the "matrix of persuasive communication."

As with persuasion, the communication process has many models. None of them is adequate in every situation all of the time. Some are clearly more relevant than others in certain situations. However, the principal paradigm of the communication process is by Harold Lasswell, who describes it like this: Who, says what, through what channel, to whom, with what effect?[6] By using this paradigm, we can say communication involves a source, a message, a medium (channel), an audience and an effect. Changes in the characteristics of any of these elements can cause differences in the communication's persuasiveness.

Source

At first glance it does not seem likely that you can change the "who"—the source of the message. You're stuck with who you are or whom you work for. But then again, it is sometimes possible to change some of your characteristics (or some characteristics of your firm). At the very least you can design your messages to take advantage of any helpful qualities that your organization has.

What qualities of the source of the message influence the effectiveness of persuasion? One of the most important is credibility. Usually, the more credible a source, the more persuasive it is.[7] This means that your organization must constantly strive to remain believable if your message is to be effective. And the best way to remain credible is to tell the truth—even when it hurts. Thus, even if you are trying to persuade, you must remember to be honest and accurate. What you write must correspond to your company's actions. If the organization is not acting the part of a good member of the community, it does not really matter much what you say, because your message won't be believed. As Lerbinger puts it, "The communicator realizes that what he says must correspond to the realities of a given situation. The management he represents cannot be doing one thing while he is saying something else."[8]

Credibility can be viewed as having two major elements: expertise and objectivity. The audience is more likely to believe you if its members think you know what you're talking about. But to believe you completely, they must also think you are telling the truth. If you have a vested interest in an issue, your objectivity will be suspect. McGuire says, "For maximum believability, the source must be perceived as not only knowing the truth but being objective enough to be motivated to tell it as he sees it."[9] Several research studies have confirmed that disinterestedness makes a source more persuasive to audiences. In fact, a source is most persuasive of all when arguing *against* his or her own best interests.

Credibility isn't the only source characteristic that can aid persuasion. Your audience is likely to be persuaded, too, by sources it likes. Of course, the audience's feelings about the source aren't always clear. Is an audience persuaded by a source because it likes the message or does it like the source because it agrees with message? In any event, being liked helps make persuasion more successful. So does being similar to the audience members in some way, especially when the similarity is ideological and not merely physical or social. Your persuasion, then, is more likely to be effective if you can establish some ideological similarities between yourself and your audience.

A third source characteristic that leads to effective persuasion is perceived power. Put simply, this means that your boss is more likely to persuade you than your neighbor is. Your boss has power over you; your neighbor does not.

Because many different source qualities affect persuasive success, it isn't always possible to predict what will happen when one of these qualities is changed. For example, if you work hard to appear to be an expert, your audience may very well perceive your expertise but may not agree with you as much as they would otherwise. By becoming more of an expert, you have become less similar to your non-expert audience. The increase in agreement produced by greater expertise can be more than offset by the loss of agreement caused by the decrease in similarity. In many cases, then, some intermediate level of expertise is probably best. Audiences tend to believe people who know more than they do, but not too much more.

Message

From the standpoint of the persuasive writer, the message element in the process is often the most important. At least, the message is the one element of communication over which the writer has complete control. In writing the message, you have to decide what things to say and how and when to say them. In doing this, you will be faced with any number of difficult decisions on fundamental questions. Here is what communication research says about some of these questions.

Should you give one side or both sides?

In general, studies show that it is better to give both sides of the story. One-sided arguments are frequently dismissed, especially if an audience is highly sophisticated or tends to oppose your point of view at the beginning. If the audience does not like you, or if the audience does not already agree with you on the issue at hand, it's usually best to give both sides. It's also better to give both sides if the audience is likely to hear the other side of the story.

Is there any time when stressing your side of the story only is a good idea? Possibly. If circumstances include *all three* of the following conditions: the audience is poorly educated; the audience is friendly to you; the audience probably will not hear any arguments from the other side. Only rarely, however, are all of these requirements met.

A related question is occasionally faced by PR writers: Should an issue be raised at all? Sometimes people (especially corporate executives) prefer to "let sleeping dogs lie" and not bring up a potentially controversial subject until somebody else does it first. This is usually a mistake. If there is any chance at all that someone will bring up an issue in the future, you should strike first with your side of the story. In fact, most research indicates that the first communicator has a significant advantage in winning over public opinion because of the inoculation effect. That is, the audience can be "inoculated" against the opponent's views, just as a person can be inoculated against a disease by an injection of a weakened form of the same disease. Thus, it is more effective, generally, to raise the issues yourself, before the opponent does.

A smart PR writer will supply a weakened form of the opposition arguments, and then refute them before the opposition can present its case. The audience will resist persuasion by the opposition at a later date. This strategy, studies show, works better than providing the audience with large amounts of propaganda designed merely to provide the persuader's point of view while ignoring the existence of conflicting opinions.

Which side should you give first?

If, as in most cases, you use both sides of the story, whose side should you give first? Unfortunately, the evidence on this question is not conclusive. Giving the opposition arguments first is apparently better when dealing with controversial issues, but not when dealing with non-controversial ones.

Which should come first, the good news or the bad news?

In general, give the good news first. This approach will probably get you the widest overall agreement with your message.

Should you make conclusions explicit or let the audience draw its own conclusions?

In essence, this question asks whether it's better to tell people what to think or to offer the facts and let them figure it out. It's true that a person drawing his or her own conclusions is likely to hold the new opinion more strongly. The problem is, the conclusion might not be the one you are after. Generally, then, it is safer to make the conclusion explicit, especially when the issue under consideration is complex.

There are exceptions to this general guideline, however. A highly intelligent audience can probably be trusted to form an obvious conclusion, based on the weight of evidence presented to it. In fact, such an audience may consider an explicit conclusion in such situations insulting. Sometimes an initially hostile audience reacts negatively to explicit conclusions. And when the issues are very personal, and members of the audience have a high ego involvement with your conclusions, it's definitely wiser not to make the conclusions explicit.

Do fear techniques work?

Research on this question seems to indicate that fear appeals do enhance persuasion, but only up to a point. Mild fear appeals appear to be more effective than strong fear appeals.

McGuire offers an explanation for this. Fear may be effective in passing the yielding step of persuasion. But high fear levels may work against other steps in the process, such as comprehension or remembering. If you scare people too much, they either won't get the substance of your message or they will put it out of their minds and forget it. Thus, as with expertise, some medium level of fear is probably the best approach. Keep in mind, though, McGuire's observation that the more complex the message, the less fear arousal is desirable.[10]

Is it better to use emotional or factual arguments?

Evidence on this question is simply not conclusive. Sometimes emotional appeals are the most persuasive, and sometimes factual ones are. It all depends on the issue involved and the composition of the audience. There are no good general guidelines to follow.

It is probably safe to say, however, that the best persuasive writing employs both factual and emotional arguments. Since information by itself seldom changes attitudes, some writers tend to rely on emotional presentations. But information is also important to persuasion, if only to provide people with the basis for justifying their attitudes based on emotion. Information can strengthen or weaken attitudes. It can blunt the enthusiasm of an audience opposed to your position. It can strengthen the opinions of those already on your side. Furthermore, providing information to supporters of your view gives them a way to verbalize their feelings—and to defend them. This reduces the chances that subsequent persuasion from the opposition will undo what your message has accomplished.

Medium

Although it may be a bit of an exaggeration, Marshall McLuhan's contention that "the medium is the message" certainly has application to the question of how the channel, or medium, can influence a persuasive outcome.

It should be obvious that the medium is important regarding both the presentation and attention steps in persuasion. As a writer, you must decide to use a medium that will get your message to the audience, and the medium has to be one that the audience will pay attention to. But research studies indicate that the medium is also important for other steps of persuasion.

One finding is that spoken communication is usually more likely than written communication to bring about yielding.[11] This does not mean that you should spend all your time writing speeches while ignoring print media. But it is useful to keep in mind that speech has more power to change minds than writing. The pen might be mightier than the sword, but the tongue can outdo both.

This is not an endorsement of "fiery oration," either. In fact, studies have been unable to show much difference between the persuasive effects of intense, enthusiastic speeches and more subdued ones. In both cases the spoken word wins out over the written word in persuasive power.

However, studies also show that the written word achieves better comprehension. This might seem strange, since comprehension is one of the steps in the persuasion process. But complete understanding is not always needed for successful persuasion. Remember the two stories at the beginning of this chapter? The spoken word diminishes understanding a little, but it increases yielding a lot.

These findings seem to recommend television and radio as media for carrying your message. But though the evidence shows that oral persuasion is more effective than written persuasion, it also shows that face-to-face encounters are more persuasive than messages in the mass media, especially in attempts to influence voting behavior.[12] Perhaps, this evidence suggests, spending a lot of money on media time and space isn't worth the price. But if mass media messages aren't effective, then the nation's businesses are wasting billions of dollars annually to promote their products, services and ideas via mass media. And there are reasons to believe that the media can play a role in persuasion, though perhaps an indirect one. It may simply be that the effects of the media are too difficult to isolate and to measure.

Studies show that the media can successfully convey information to people (though not in all cases, and not always to the extent that the communicator would like). And though information alone is usually not enough to get people to change their attitudes, it does, as we noted earlier, play a part. Even if most people are not persuaded much by the media, opinion leaders—that is, those who influence others in face-to-face contacts—do pay attention to the media and base their opinions at least in part on media messages.

The idea that opinion leaders transmit media messages to others is usually described as the "two-step flow" of mass communication. More recent research has cast some doubt on some of the details of this idea. For example, many people do receive input from the media, but they turn to opinion leaders for interpretations of facts more than for the facts themselves. Furthermore, the opinion leaders may receive information from sources other than the mass media.[13] Nevertheless, opinion leaders do provide a possible avenue for mass media to influence public opinion.

Another important influence of the media has been described as "agenda setting." Research seems to show that issues considered important by the population often are also issues that the media devote much time and space to. Thus, it has been suggested that even if the media don't tell people what to think, they do tell them what to think about. Of course, it is possible that the situation is the other way around—that people decide what's important first, and then the media begin to run stories on those subjects. Much recent work has established, though, that media coverage often comes first. So if your intent is merely to raise an issue, to bring it into the public consciousness, the mass media can be effective channels.

Given that the mass media can be used as channels for your messages, which media are best to use? That's a difficult question to answer. Since the media's measurable effects on attitudes are small, it isn't easy to tell if one medium is more effective than another. Looking at credibility alone, the evidence suggests that people are more likely to believe television than newspapers and newspapers than radio. But, although television is generally given the highest believability ratings, members of higher socioeconomic groups usually rate newspapers higher for accuracy and truthfulness.[14]

Looking at the question from the standpoint of complexity of the message, highly complex messages are generally more believable in print media. Messages charged with emotion appear to work best in broadcast media.

Audience

The greatest lesson of social science research on the question of persuasion is a lesson that all good writers should already know: Know your audience. Techniques that will work wonders persuading a football team may flop with a group of engineers. Most of the guidelines for preparing a message or choosing a channel depend on the characteristics of the audience.

The audience is made up of individuals. And all individuals, as receivers of your message, possess a common characteristic—they tend to forget things. This fact usually works to your disadvantage. Attitudes built up over a long period of time are hard to forget. If your organization has a long history of exploiting employees or making a poor product, and if the firm is perceived this way by your audience, you will have a difficult job writing credible messages. Before you can ever hope to be believed, the firm will have to clean up its act. And you will have to tell the "good news" often over a long period of time before the new truth about the firm will replace the old perceptions.

On the other hand, if your organization is generally perceived as a good place that is sensitive to employee needs, you'll be able to weather a damage suit filed by an employee with only moderate and temporary dents in your "white knight" armor.

The point is that the "retention" step in the persuasion process is a particularly difficult one.

But the human tendency to forget can also be helpful, especially to communicators with low credibility. If you are not a very credible source (because the audience believes you are biased), your message may not induce any immediate change. But months later, perhaps, the audience may show some agreement with your point of view. It is possible that they will remember your message but forget where it came from. Thus, the message, no longer associated with the low-credibility source, will now be believed, which is what you wanted in the first place. It just takes a while for it to happen.

This is sometimes called the *sleeper effect*, and whether it actually exists is a matter of some debate. Nevertheless, it's useful to know that even a low-credibility source can be effective in persuasion under some circumstances.

Loss of memory probably carries no such benefits for high-credibility sources, who want the audience to remember everything. High-credibility sources often repeat their messages over and over to make sure the point is retained. Research on this issue indicates that repetition (as with a commercial announcement presented many times) may indeed achieve greater effects, but only because it increases the chances that more people will hear the announcement.

On this point, however, it is wise to remember that people tend to forget information at about the same rate as they learn it. Hence, if you stop the flow of messages about your organization, you can expect awareness of your firm to drop, though it apparently never goes back to zero. This point, viewed from the stance of economy, is one that supports the idea of sustained programming, because it is more efficient to sustain awareness than to build it in the first place.

Effect

When you sit down to write a message about your firm to its public, you have some objective in mind. You want the audience to think about an issue in a certain way or you want the audience to do something. In other words, there is a motive, or intent, not only behind the message you want to convey but behind the way you will say it and deliver it. Thus, the overall "effect" question is, Did the audience do what you wanted it to do?

So you begin the process of writing with "an intended" effect in mind. It has to be "intended" because you don't know what the actual effect will be ahead of time. You can only guess—and hope. Nevertheless, you must ask yourself how your intended effect influences your success in persuasion.

The most obvious intention of any persuasive speaker or writer is to persuade. If the audience knows it is being persuaded, its resistance may increase. If, however, people merely overhear a message, without knowing the message is intended for their ears, they might be more susceptible to the argument.

This fact suggests that it might be helpful to disguise your persuasive intent. Some evidence supports this view, but some does not. At times the opposite effect can be seen. While there is little doubt that disguising the intent to persuade enhances yielding, such a disguise might hinder presentation, attention and comprehension. The benefits of making sure your audience gets the message may outweigh the disadvantages of letting your intent be clearly seen. [15]

A companion issue regarding intent is the matter of how extreme your appeal should be. Should you try to persuade people to change their minds just a little or a lot? This question has been the point of many research studies. It seems, generally, that increasing the level of intended change helps to increase persuasion, but only up to a point. If you ask for too much attitude change, effectiveness decreases. [16]

The Idea of Situation Theory

Because of conceptual problems regarding some methods by which some of the foregoing ideas have been tested, you will be wise as a writer to use them simply as guidelines, not gospels. Some conclusions are contradictory or, at least, inconclusive. James E. Grunig has proposed yet another theoretical perspective that may help us to better understand the effects of persuasion. Since it has not been subjected to adequate testing, it is too early to know if it will be useful to public relations writers.

Put simply, Grunig proposes a situational theory that says that "how a person perceives a situation explains whether he will communicate about the situation, how he will communicate, and whether he will have an attitude relevant to the situation." [17]

Grunig's theory is based on four independent and two dependent variables. Following are the four independent variables.

Problem Recognition A person must perceive something is missing or indefinite in a situation, which prompts him or her to stop and think about the situation. The importance of this variable to the public relations writer is that recognition of a problem or issue is requisite to increasing the chances that a person will respond to a situation or express a need for more information about it. This idea relates closely to the *attending* and *comprehending* functions cited earlier in this chapter.

Constraint Recognition If a receiver of a public relations message thinks his or her options to respond to the situation are limited by group, institutional, legal, economic or other external constraints, there is less need for information about the situation. Therefore, even if your message is loaded with relevant material it may have little impact because the receiver is resigned to a no or limited response. This idea relates to the *retaining* and *acting* functions discussed earlier.

Referent Criterion This variable simply presumes that a person brings to a situation some prior information that is relevant to the situation. If the situation is common, the prior information tends to lessen the person's need for additional information. This suggests that the person probably won't be very open to new information from a public relations writer. On the other hand, if the situation is new, related prior experience tends to serve initially as a guide to the seeking of information regarding behavior pertinent to the situation. This referent concept suggests that as a public relations writer you should be prepared to provide extensive information in new situations. This concept relates to Lerbinger's *designs of persuasion* mentioned earlier.

Level of Involvement This variable simply says that the more salient or important the issue is perceived to be, the more likely a person will be to respond to it. It seems not only to suggest *if* a person will respond but also *how*. Remember to attempt in every message to make its importance clear to the public.

The two dependent variables in Grunig's theory are *information processing* and *information seeking*. Although these are clearly related, they are distinctly different concepts.

Information Seeking This refers to deliberate acts by a person to get more information about the situation. A need is perceived and behavior is directed at fulfilling the need. The concept of information seeking tends to suggest behavior that has a higher threshold of involvement. Persons with these higher thresholds are much more eager to receive and accept your persuasive messages. As a public relations writer, you won't have to work as hard to communicate with these persons but they will probably demand a lot more salient material.

Information Processing On the other hand, information processing implies a much lower level of involvement because some—maybe a lot of—information is encountered and processed incidentally, if not accidentally, about the situation. The concept is based on the idea that information acquisition is unplanned but arises in the context of other behavior. For example, if there's nothing else to do, a person may switch on the television set and watch whatever appears on it, including your public service announcement on your community's blood drive. In order to reach this segment of your public, you will have to work especially hard to make your persuasive messages relevant. That's why we emphasize repeatedly in this book how important it is to know your audience. If you don't know your audience intimately, you'll probably not be very successful as a persuasive writer.

Conclusions

Because the results of research in persuasive communication are inconclusive or contradictory in some cases, the following conclusions should be interpreted as general guidelines, not rules, that may apply in many situations.

* Behavior is both rational and emotional. Effective persuasion uses appeals based on one or both characteristics.

* Attitude formation is a complex process. It involves our personal experience and history, social environment, personality characteristics, predispositions and communication.

* Persuasion can be viewed as a learning process, a power process or an emotional process.

* The communication-design aspects of persuasion include stimulus-response, cognitive, motivational, social and personality.

* The six steps in the process of persuasion are presenting, attending, comprehending, yielding, retaining and acting.

* As it involves the communication process, persuasion has five major considerations: source, message, medium, audience and effect.

* It is generally better to give both sides of an issue than just your side, especially if your audience is sophisticated.

* If there is a chance that the opposition will raise an issue, it is generally better for you to raise it and "inoculate" your audience against opposing views.

* When dealing with controversy, give your opponent's views first; then follow with your own.

* In general, tell the good news first, then the bad.

* It is safer to draw clear conclusions in your messages than to leave things to chance.

* Mild fear appeals appear to work better than strong ones, but a resolution to the fear should also be offered.

* Use both factual and emotional appeals.

* The spoken word is more persuasive than the printed word.

* Opinion leaders are generally effective persuaders.

* If you want to raise an issue for public debate, you have to get the attention of the media, for they set the agenda.

* You must know your audience very well in order to be able to shape effective persuasive messages to it.

* Attitudes built up over long periods of time are resistant to change. Even if you appear to be unsuccessful at promoting change in the short term, change might occur much later.

* A persuasive writer must know clearly what he or she wants to happen before writing the message. This intended effect may be quite different from the actual effect.

* If you ask for major attitude change, you will get more than if you ask only for a little, up to a point. However, asking for too much change diminishes your effectiveness.

Exercises

1. Much of persuasive writing depends on using words for their connotative meaning (the attitude or emotion they evoke) rather than their denotative meaning. In the following list of words, fill in the blanks with at least three alternatives:

Complimentary	Derogatory	Neutral
Investigator	Spy	( )
Captive	( )	Prisoner
( )	Bureaucrat	Government worker

2. Add two more sets of words to the examples in the list above.

3. Define the attitudes in the following passages and rewrite each passage with a "neutral" attitude:
   A. "From the averted faces and cold shoulders of the poll readers in Washington, the President escaped by steamboat to the smiles of welcome of Middle America" ("Cruisin' Down the River," *Time*, September 3, 1979, p. 16).
   B. "Some Jewish organizations and intellectuals who were previously identified with the aspirations of black Americans become apologists for the racial status quo" ("With Sorrow and Anger," *Time*, September 3, 1979, p. 16).
   C. These criminal defendants have a clear interest in making false and sensational charges in an effort to bargain for leniency.

4. Data indicate that customers are more concerned about the safety of deposits in banks in general than in their own banks. What psychological principles

might explain this? Ourbank has sufficient, documented information that some of its competitors are less prudent in their lending practices than is recommended. Since you and Ourbank's management have decided to promote Ourbank as *The Safe Place*, is it a good idea to play on the fear that some banks are not operating within recommended guidelines? Give a rationale for your answer.

Notes

[1] Edward L. Bernays, *Public Relations* (Norman, Okla.: University of Oklahoma Press, 1952), p. 130.

[2] Otto Lerbinger, *Designs for Persuasive Communication* (Englewood Cliffs, N.J.: Prentice-Hall, 1972).

[3] See, for example, Irving L. Janis, "Personality as a Factor in Susceptibility to Persuasion," in *The Science of Human Communication*, ed. Wilbur Schramm (New York: Basic Books, 1963), pp. 54–64.

[4] William J. McGuire, "Persuasion, Resistance, and Attitude Change," in *Handbook of Communication*, ed. Ithiel de Sola Pool et al. (Chicago: Rand-McNally, 1973), p. 221.

[5] Stanley Lehmann, "Personality and Compliance: A Study of Anxiety and Self-Esteem in Opinion and Behavior Change," *Journal of Personality and Social Psychology* 15 (1970): 76–86. Cited in McGuire, "Persuasion," p. 233.

[6] Wilbur Schramm, "The Challenge of Communication Research," in *Introduction to Mass Communication Research*, ed. Ralph O. Nafziger and David M. White (Baton Rouge, La.: Louisiana State University Press, 1963), p. 29.

[7] This is not always true, however. See B. Sternthal, L. Phillips and R. Dholakia, "The Persuasive Effect of Source Credibility: A Situational Analysis," *Public Opinion Quarterly* 42 (Fall 1978): 285–314.

[8] Lerbinger, *Designs*, p. 25.

[9] McGuire, "Persuasion," p. 231.

[10] Ibid., p. 234.

[11] William J. McGuire, "Nature of Attitudes and Attitude Change," in *Handbook of Social Psychology*, eds. Gardener Lindzey and Elliot Aronson (Reading, Mass.: Addison-Wesley, 1969), p. 225.

[12] Ibid., pp. 228–229.

[13] Everett M. Rogers, "Mass Media and Interpersonal Communication," in *Handbook of Communication*, ed. Ithiel de Sola Pool et al. (Chicago: Rand-McNally, 1973), pp. 292–298.

[14] McGuire, "Nature," pp. 230–231.

[15] McGuire, "Persuasion," p. 231.

[16] Elliot Aronson, Judith Turner and J. M. Carlsmith, "Communicator Credibility and Communication Discrepancy as Determinants of Opinion Change," *Journal of Abnormal and Social Psychology* 67 (1963): 31–36.

[17] James E. Grunig, "Communication Behaviors and Attitudes of Environmental Publics: Two Studies," *Journalism Monographs* 81 (March 1983), pp. 9–14.

Selected Bibliography

Elliot Aronson, Judith Turner and J. Merrill Carlsmith, "Communicator Credibility and Communication Discrepancy as Determinants of Opinion Change," *Journal of Abnormal and Social Psychology* 67 (1963): 31–36.

Edward L. Bernays, *Public Relations* (Norman, Okla.: University of Oklahoma Press, 1952).

Robert B. Cialdini, *Influence: Science and Practice* (Glenview, Ill.: Scott, Foresman, 1985).

James E. Grunig, "Communication Behaviors and Attitudes of Environmental Publics: Two Studies," *Journalism Monographs*, No. 81 (Columbia, So. Car.: Association for Education in Journalism and Mass Communication, March 1983).

Bernard C. Hennessy, *Public Opinion*, 5th ed. (Monterey, Calif.: Brooks/Cole, 1985).

Carl I. Hovland et al., *The Order of Presentation in Persuasion* (New Haven, Conn.: Yale University Press, 1957).

Otto Lerbinger, *Designs for Persuasive Communication* (Englewood Cliffs, N.J.: Prentice-Hall, 1972).

M. E. McCombs and D. L. Shaw, "The Agenda Setting Function of the Media," *Public Opinion Quarterly* 36 (1972): 176–187.

William J. McGuire, "Nature of Attitudes and Attitude Change," in *Handbook of Social Psychology*, 2nd ed., vol. 3, ed. Gardener Lindzey and Elliot Aronson (Reading, Mass.: Addison-Wesley, 1968), pp. 136–314.

William J. McGuire, "Persuasion, Resistance, and Attitude Change," in *Handbook of Communication*, ed. Ithiel de Sola Pool et al. (Chicago: Rand-McNally, 1973), pp. 216–252.

Ithiel de Sola Pool et al., *Handbook of Communication* (Chicago: Rand-McNally, 1973).

Ithiel de Sola Pool et al., "Public Opinion," in *Handbook of Communication*, ed. Pool et al. (Chicago: Rand-McNally, 1973), pp. 779–835.

Kathleen K. Reardon, *Persuasion: Theory and Context* (Beverly Hills, Calif.: Sage Publications, 1981).

Everett M. Rogers, "Mass Media and Interpersonal Communication," in *Handbook of Communication*, ed. Ithiel de Sola Pool et al. (Chicago: Rand-McNally, 1973), pp. 290–310.

Wilbur Schramm, "The Challenge to Communication Research," in *Introduction to Mass Communication Research*, ed. Ralph O. Nafziger and David M. White (Baton Rouge: Louisiana State University Press, 1963), pp. 3–31.

Wilbur Schramm, ed., *The Science of Human Communication* (New York: Basic Books, 1963).

David O. Sears and Richard E. Whitney, "Political Persuasion," in *Handbook of Communication*, ed. Ithiel de Sola Pool et al. (Chicago: Rand-McNally, 1973), pp. 253–289.

Mary J. Smith, *Persuasion and Human Action: A Review and Critique of Social Influence Theories* (Belmont, Calif.: Wadsworth, 1982).

M. Brewster Smith, "A Map for the Analysis of Personality and Politics," *Journal of Social Issues* 24 (1968): 15–28.

Brian Sternthal, Lynn Phillips and Ruby Dholakia, "The Persuasive Effect of Source Credibility: A Situational Analysis," *Public Opinion Quarterly* 42 (Fall 1978): 285–314.

Philip G. Zimbardo, Ebbe B. Ebbesen and Christina Maslach, *Influencing Attitudes and Changing Behavior*, 2nd ed. (Reading, Mass.: Addison-Wesley, 1977).

3
Research
for the
Public
Relations
Writer

We noted in the first chapter that writing is based on information. Information comes from research. The best information comes from the best research. PR professionals who climb the career ladder fastest and achieve the highest levels know how best to use research in their writing.

Research, then, is the key element in professional success. Research should be done by PR professionals at all levels. It is as important to the beginner as it is to a senior counselor, although the focus of research may change as you move up the career ladder.

Because most entry-level jobs in PR are related directly to the writing process, it is important that you learn as much as you can about research and how to use it as a writer. For this reason, you should review and remember the prewriting checklist in Figure 3-1.

Research in Public Relations

The question to ask now is, What kinds of research must I know about and be able to do?

There are six major categories of research with which you must be concerned.

3-1

Prewriting Checklist

1. Gather the facts of the matter and get them right.

2. Gather authoritative opinions and interpretations of the matter.

3. Evaluate facts and opinions for their pertinence. Discard those not directly related to the matter.

4. Synthesize the remaining facts and opinions into a cohesive body of information.

5. Organize the information for writing.

6. Develop a writing outline that moves logically from one point to the next.

7. Write. Edit. Rewrite.

1. Policy
2. Background material
3. Audience
4. Message
5. Media
6. Program evaluation

All six are important in every PR situation but rarely are they all equally important. Developing your sensitivity to the problem at hand will help you determine which one category or combination of categories is more important than the rest.

Categories of Research for the PR Writer

Policy "The company line" is a euphemism that hardly does justice to the full concept behind the term *policy*. Policy is a considered statement of purpose, position or direction that is expected to guide the behavior of those it covers.

Each firm or organization in both the public and private sectors has a set of policies. Anyone working for or with the firm or organization is expected to know the provisions of applicable policies.

Policy is of two general types—internal and external. Internal policy is that of your employer. It is a set of guidelines that directs and controls the collective behavior of the organization and the job behavior of each employee. Such policies may range from a firm's policy on benefits to a policy of public candor in the face of a community crisis.

External policy is policy that comes from a source outside the organization's immediate control but that bears on the organization's behavior toward its constituencies. For example, if you are writing the annual report for a publicly held company, there are certain Securities and Exchange Commission policies and requirements that you must know and observe. By the way, these are summarized in Appendix B. Review them.

It is critical that you know applicable policies in order to avoid problems. This may not only save your job but it may even get you promoted.

Some policies you may need to know are available to you only in oral form. Oral policy can be especially frustrating, for three primary reasons.

First, oral policy is easily distorted. What you believe today to be a clear understanding of the policy may be completely obsolete a year from now. Second, management may be unsure of itself and thus reluctant to put a decision into writing.

Third, management may have a hidden agenda. To understand this point, suppose you are about to write a series of releases for the local media about your country club's gala next month, the proceeds of which will go to the United Negro College Fund. Club policy does not bar blacks from membership but there are no black members in the club. And you are told, when you ask the club manager, that no blacks are invited or expected to attend the gala. Written policy may say one thing but unwritten policy may say something else.

If you find yourself relying more on oral than written policy, urge management to put oral policy into writing. If management resists this suggestion unreasonably, start looking for another job.

Background Material Successful public relations writing is based on a solid, fully developed body of facts. The kinds of facts necessary will vary, depending on the situation.

For example, suppose you are retained to write a brochure in support of a bond election to double the community's hospital bed space. What facts do you need to know before you begin to write?

For starters, here are a few: What has been the community's rate of growth over the last 20 years? How much is the community expected to grow in the next 20? What accounts for this rate of growth? What is the ratio of community patients to those outside the community? Why? Has this ratio changed in the last few years? Is the ratio expected to change in the future? Why? Is the interest rate on the bonds favorable? How do local financial leaders view the bonding program? Why?

The number of questions you might ask about this project may number into the hundreds. The number is not the issue. The point is that public relations planning, decision making and writing depend on the careful accumulation of facts and ideas.

As you begin the task of assembling background materials, you should assume the traditional role of the news reporter by asking who, what, where, when, how and why—especially why. As you ask these questions, you'll begin to build an elaborate, sophisticated, project-specific system of information that will help you handle assignments ranging in diversity from staging a small symposium to handling a crisis at a chemical plant.

One of the key points to remember about background materials is that even if the PR situation is new to you it is not new. Others have faced the same or a similar situation. Learn from their experiences.

Audience   As noted earlier, professionals in public relations are fond of talking about publics or audiences. These terms are used synonymously. It is rare in public relations that you will deal only with a single audience. Even when it appears that way, closer examination usually turns up two or more subsegments, each with its unique characteristics, concerns and needs.

Thus, the question is how can you identify the audience or subsegments of it? This requires research, perhaps at different levels of sophistication. To illustrate this point, consider this situation.

You are director of public relations for a new bank with a national charter in a metropolitan area. The bank's management is aware that deregulation allows savings and loans and investment firms, such as Merrill Lynch, to provide many financial services previously available only at banks.

Your management decides to "sell" the bank to certain types of potential customers, specifically those whose incomes are $40,000 or more annually. This rules out a lot of potential depositors from your target audience. And it focuses attention on specific segments of the community, such as physicians and dentists, attorneys, retailers, owners of manufacturing or service firms, and a variety of other professionals such as architects, designers and engineers.

In this situation you will first try to divide the target audience into segments by using demographic information—income, sex, education, occupation, marital status, home ownership and the like, as discussed earlier. Once the demographic profile is complete, the picture of the target audience comes into sharper focus. But does it tell you all you need to know? Perhaps. Perhaps not.

What you may need now is psychographic information—information about lifestyle, attitudes and behavior. Information of this type may give you important clues that your public relations program should communicate differently with, say, physicians and dentists than with retailers and manufacturers. For example, physicians and dentists may be more concerned with long-range financial planning, whereas retailers and manufacturers are more concerned with managing cash flow. Messages going to these two groups must be different.

Research helps you to understand to the fullest extent the needs of your audience and its components so that you can shape messages that speak to their distinct needs.

Message   What you say and how you say it may have a great deal to do with your success. Recall our discussion about audiences. If you are lucky enough to have a single audience with which to communicate, your job will be easier. But when you have several audiences, your job can be complex.

Whether it is one audience or several, you are generally well advised to first reduce your message to a single simple idea. Remember, though, that a single simple idea is not necessarily an insignificant or simple-minded idea. Reducing what you want to say to this level is necessary to help keep you on the right track as you shape your message.

There are different methods of constructing a message for maximum impact. And you would select an approach based primarily on your purpose for the message.

Is the purpose to change or reinforce behavior? If it is to change, you must remember to make a reward obvious to the receiver of your message. If it is to reinforce, your message must avoid information that contradicts current behavior.

Should you use a conclusion-drawing technique? In this method you select and present information that will lead your audience to draw the conclusion you want it to draw. Communication-research literature suggests that this is a good method of communicating with sophisticated audiences. However, this technique can be fatal if used with unsophisticated audiences.

There are many techniques of message presentation in addition to the ones discussed. You should review the communication-research literature and develop a personal understanding of these methods. What are they? How do they work? Under what conditions do they appear to work best? A good way to begin is to review Chapter 2.

Media   As you work your way through a public relations problem, you will have to make choices about which channels of communication to use and how to use them. Before you can make these decisions, however, you need to know the characteristics of the various media you may use. What are their technical qualities and requirements? What can they or can't they do? What are their emotional qualities? How do people react to them? How and why do people use them as they do? Should you use general or specialized media or a combination of the two types? These are serious questions, the answers to which are not easy, and the outcomes of which may involve large amounts of time and money. But you need to know, not guess.

Once you have chosen the media, you'll need to know whether they are effective and efficient in this particular PR program. This suggests that you'll need some plan for monitoring progress and, when the plan is complete, evaluating success. Four questions are important here. Did you reach your target audience? Was your message really heard and accepted? Was your message acted upon? Was the use of the media cost-effective?

Evaluation   Public relations programs have to prove their worth. This means that one of your tasks as a writer is to evaluate the cost-effectiveness of the program. You will need to know what worked well, what did not and why. Most of the techniques discussed earlier are used in this phase, too. It is simply a matter of employing questionnaires, interviews and secondary sources to evaluate what has been accomplished. Of course, such common pieces of physical evidence as how many people attended an event, how many people were exposed to your message, how many people responded to a special coupon offer and the like are critical in basic program evaluation.

Research for Storage and Retrieval

Public relations professionals would have more serious communication problems than they do if intensive spadework in policy, background materials, audience, message and media had to be fresh with each new program. However, professionals routinely accumulate pertinent research information, initiate research for later use and plan for future research needs.

Much of public relations research is borrowed from the social sciences, especially from behavioral areas. Useful research studies are accumulated and indexed for future use. Also, research about publics and about media is being continually reviewed and stored. Much of the information about publics comes from comprehensive studies done by the commercial media about their audiences. Other studies come from product and service institutions concerned about their own publics. Research on internal policies is mined from organizational sources, whereas external policies are gleaned from a variety of municipal, state and federal organizations, professional or associational groups and the like.

A particular PR situation may require some original fact finding. In conducting original research or in hiring a research firm to do it, the public relations practitioner must know clearly what is needed. Otherwise, the resulting information may be imposing but inadequate.

Organizing   Since public relations information comes from such a wide variety of sources, organizing it can be a problem. One common organizational pattern follows the lines of our earlier discussion. Information is categorized according to policy (pertinent internal and external guides), background material (substantive facts bearing on the situation), audience (facts about the people you want to reach), message (facts about successes of message types in similar situations), and media (the most effective ways of delivering your message).

Presenting   The organization of the research should reflect the ways in which it will be presented and used. In presenting this information, it is important to explain the implications of the findings when these are not obvious, and to suggest what bearing the research has on the situation. The information should also indicate what other research is needed to make the picture clearer.

Updating   Organization of the research should allow for easy updating, especially where ongoing research, such as periodic opinion measurement (as in an election campaign) is critical. Nowadays, much research information is stored in computers, and the PR professional must know enough about the method of storage to use the system effectively. What works best for computer-systems people may not always be what works best for the PR person trying to use the information.

Re-using Adding to or re-using research information is difficult if the information is not readily accessible. The retrieval process, therefore, is critical. PR professionals must work with information-systems people to tell them how the information will be used—what will be needed, under what conditions, when and in what form. For PR research needs, besides being re-usable, the system must be designed so that data is well organized, presented in a meaningful way and easily updated.

Sources for PR Writers and Researchers

Writers and researchers of all types, not just PR professionals, depend on research from two basic sources: paper and people. Of course, "paper" doesn't always mean books. It can mean magnetic tape or discs, film, video or audio tape, or some other form of storage. The important point to remember is that sources are either secondary (paper or other form of stored information) or primary (people).

Secondary Sources for Research

Every PR writer should have at least a working library in the office that contains a dictionary, thesaurus, appropriate reference volumes and bibliographies, and pertinent professional and technical journals and documents. Completing this working library is a file system where information can be placed for easy and immediate access. This office library will be your first line of attack when you need secondary information. See the list of selected references at the end of this chapter.

Your next stop for secondary information should be a regular library. But do as much research as you can in your office library so your queries at the regular library are as productive as possible. For example, you need to know the types of sources you want to tap. There are reference and bibliographic guides that can direct you to the sources you really need to review. One important reference work is Jacques Barzun and Henry F. Graff's *The Modern Researcher*, fourth edition. Another is William L. Rivers's *Finding Facts*. Both describe reference works so that you will know what to expect from them. Another help is a good reference librarian; such a person can help you cut many corners if you can succinctly describe the information you want. Some reference librarians will answer simple questions on the phone.

Library Most metropolitan areas have public libraries containing adequate resources for basic research. They also usually have cooperative agreements with other libraries to get information on loan. Colleges and universities have libraries that contain the scholarly material you may need. Some churches have substantial holdings of religious works, and many cities have law libraries. Some libraries have special collections—such as the History of Science Collection at the University of Oklahoma—that are open to qualified researchers.

Reference Works   The primary tools of both the reference librarian and the researcher in the library are collections of information and reference works. These are maps that enable you to find the treasures of information you seek. Standard reference works are encyclopedias, biographical dictionaries, dictionaries of quotations and concordances of the Bible and famous works, atlases and gazetteers, chronologies or other books of dates, handbooks and source books—including dictionaries of all kinds.

Bibliographies   One reference source that is especially important is the bibliography. In accumulating and categorizing bibliographies, authors provide you with paths through mazes of footnotes. Bibliographies usually identify reliable sources of information that you will want to tap. Many libraries now offer electronic access to stored bibliographies so that you can call up on a screen all the most likely sources. Hard (printed) copies are also available from material in these data banks.

Periodicals   One resource accessible in electronic systems is the *New York Times Index*. Using this data bank, you can track, call up and read any story that has appeared in the *New York Times* within a specific number of years. Since the *New York Times* makes an effort to be a newspaper of record, it is possible to do a great deal of research through this index alone. NEXIX/LEXIS, CompuServe, The Source, Dow Jones News/Retrieval Service and others are electronic data banks that may be tapped by public relations writers for research purposes. Many newspapers, in addition to *The New York Times*, such as *The Washington Post*, *The Daily Oklahoman* and the *Fort Worth Star-Telegram*, also provide data bank services that may be helpful. For commercial publications, the most useful index is the *Readers' Guide to Periodical Literature*. You can also find indexes that focus on highly specialized fields, such as law or medicine. Indexes also exist for most scholarly publications and even for a few newsletters issued by national institutions or organizations.

Other good references for events and issues of the day are *Facts on File* and the encyclopedia yearbooks.

Public Records   Government records at all levels—local, state and federal—are available to you unless they contain classified information. Some government agencies offer significant research assistance. For example, the Library of Congress is very helpful in locating information and will often offer advice to put you on the right trail.

Government Records   Most government offices are storehouses of information, and many government offices distribute their own materials. The federal government has its materials published by the U.S. Government Printing Office (GPO). A central store in Washington, D.C., contains information on every imaginable subject, as do GPO regional offices in cities with federal centers. Ask to be put on the GPO's mailing list. One source of information that is essential for PR people is the *Statistical Abstracts of the United States*, published annually by the U.S. Bureau of Census.

Public Access to Information   The Freedom of Information Act has opened many files of both public and private institutions to examination. This means that normally you now have access to any document—titles to property, budgets of state institutions, court proceedings and the like—that has been filed in a public place. A wealth of information exists in these documents.

Primary Sources for Research

When you must research primary sources, generally you have two ways of gathering information from people. One is the interview and the other is the questionnaire. Whether you're asking questions face to face or through a questionnaire, you must prepare yourself ahead of time so that you get the answers you want. Let's look at each of these methods in turn.

Interviewing   After you have done some fundamental research, you are ready to begin asking questions of people who might be knowledgeable in your subject. In any interview you may want to begin by asking yes/no questions but always use these as the basis for asking open-ended questions in the body of the interview. Find authorities through your research, develop questions for them and then follow up any leads they may give you.

Although some people seem to have a natural talent for getting information from others, every PR person should develop and practice interviewing skills. Like people who play musical instruments by ear, natural interviewers—and all others—become even better with practice.

Go to an interview prepared with questions on paper. Keep information in mind that you have gained from your research. Then, if the opportunity arises, you can follow a different line of questioning. Take notes and use a tape recorder, and try not to rely solely on one or the other. It is unquestionably ethical to advise your interviewee you wish to record the conversation and to seek consent. No federal law requires prior consent in a face-to-face interview but if the interview is recorded via interstate telephone without prior consent, it is illegal. A few states require prior consent to record intrastate telephone conversations. So be sure to check out legal provisions in the state where you work.

Listen to what the person is telling you and try to remember the information by putting it into the context suggested by your prior research. Encourage responses by asking relevant questions and by participating in the conversation. Avoid being judgmental. You are asking, not telling. Consult Figure 3-2 for an interviewing checklist.

Some of the important information you get from the interview will come from your keen observation of the behavior of the person you are interview-

3-2

Checklist for Interviewing

1. Research your subject before the interview.

2. Know something about the person you are interviewing.

3. Prepare a list of questions in advance.

4. Inform the interviewee in advance of the kinds of questions you will be asking.

5. Whenever possible use a tape recorder *and* take notes. Never put complete trust in a machine or your memory.

6. Ask for explanations if you don't understand something.

7. Ask specific questions. Vague questions elicit vague answers.

8. Ask one question at a time. Don't throw several questions into the same sentence and expect the interviewee to answer—or even to remember—them all.

ing. Watch for nonverbal communication cues, and note both physical characteristics and environmental factors that could be telling. In particular, note gestures that indicate personality characteristics and remember emotional emphases. The latter are particularly evident in the way something is said: the inflection of the voice, the expression on the face. Be cautious, however, about reading more into these details than is there. Be aware of your own bias and involvement with the subject so you don't misinterpret what you experience. To safeguard against misinterpretation, some researchers prefer to videotape interviews so that they can capture this information and isolate it later.

Questionnaires   The second means of getting information from people is the questionnaire. The questionnaire is a research workhorse. Drafting a questionnaire is difficult, however. Several simple questions are sometimes necessary to get a single piece of information.

It can be difficult to ask a question so that the respondent knows exactly what you mean by it. For example, a national survey once asked a question about "consumer movement leaders." Another researcher, attempting to replicate part of the study, used the same expression with different audiences and was asked by one respondent for a definition of "consumer leader." Did the researcher want to know about movement activists, government appointees or civil servants involved in consumer information, or corporate employees charged with responding to consumers? The question was invalid because it was being interpreted in different ways. One technique to safeguard against this is to pretest the questions before actually using the questionnaire.

All questions should be phrased in such a way that they are bias-free. Consider this question: Do you still drink too much? Even a negative response signifies that the respondent drank too much in some previous time, though in fact the respondent may have never indulged in liquor at all. Questions asked in this fashion are not only poor but also unethical.

To develop a questionnaire, begin by simply listing all the information you want to know. Then begin to draft questions that will get at the information. Next, consider your respondents. Who will be responding to these questions and under what circumstances? Some people get impatient with long telephone questionnaires, especially if the questions are on a topic that is personally uninteresting. A questionnaire that can be returned by mail gives the respondent the choice of answering on his or her own schedule. However, because you cannot control who responds to mail questionnaires, problems may arise regarding the representativeness of the sample.

The age and educational level of respondents may also be factors in how questions are phrased. Familiarity with the subject is another possible factor. The less familiar respondents are with the topic, the simpler the questions and the longer the response times need to be. It is also important to arrange questions in logical sequence so that answers develop naturally in the respondent's mind.

In writing the questions, it is also important to consider how the questionnaire will be administered and scored. If a questionnaire is to be used in a busy shopping mall, for example, or in a phone call, the respondent may not want to take time to answer long or involved questions. Open-ended questions are difficult to evaluate and score. How you ask a question affects the response and that, of course, determines whether the information you get from the questionnaire will be valid and useful.

Some open-ended questions and some interview responses are subjected to content analysis. This just means that words are counted to see how often they appear, and in what context. At least two national research agencies use in-depth interviewing and content analysis extensively. The system is to transcribe oral interviews and to enter these in the computer, as you would other open-ended responses. The computer can rank the words by their frequency of usage, and a social science software program can be used to analyze each word in relation to others. Subtle themes often emerge from such analyses, making it possible for researchers to determine accurately what people *mean* by what they say.

Caveats Much of the information you get from secondary and primary sources will be in simple statistical form that relies on your understanding of concepts like sum, mean (average), median and mode. If you are not adept with these terms now, get a mathematics book and study it until you are. Otherwise, you run the risk of

3-3

Checklist of Research Protocols

1. What is the name of the person(s) or organization who did the research? What was the date on which it was done? For whom and why was it done?

2. If a sample was used, what steps were taken to ensure randomness?

3. What steps were taken to validate the questions before they were asked of respondents?

4. What steps were taken to ensure the reliability of the research methods?

5. Is a copy of the questionnaire (or measuring instrument) included in the research report?

misinterpreting factual information and, thus, drawing poor conclusions and eventually misleading your public.

Research information that infers cause-effect relationships usually entails more sophisticated statistics and research methodologies. There are several good books you can consult for help in these areas. One is Frederick Williams's *Reasoning with Statistics*, second edition, a paperback designed for people who lack a statistical background but who need to know how to interpret and use information available only in statistical form. Another is *Introduction to Social Research*, third edition, by Sanford Labovitz and Robert Hagedorn, a paperback that treats research methodologies with clarity.

Whether you are using secondary or primary data, be skeptical about their meaning, especially if the compilers claim that it is based on a random sample. The term *random* has a very strict scientific meaning when applied to survey research. It means that every person in your public should have an equal and known statistical probability of being included in the sample. The key point to remember here is that only when the sample is truly random can the findings be generalized to the total public being researched.

There are certain research protocols you should look for in every piece of research data you use. These are listed in the form of questions in Figure 3-3. If answers to these questions are missing from the research report or if they are so vague you can't get a clear view of how the information was gathered, be wary of the data and any conclusions based on it. It is possible, of course, that the information is reliable, but you should still use it with caution. For a view of how a banking survey evolved, see Example 3-4.

3-4

Bank Consumer Research Survey

This questionnaire was developed for the management of a bank who
wanted to create a marketing and public relations plan, something the
bank had never had before. The immediate concern was management's
belief that, owing to a growing number of bank failures, the public was
becoming increasingly uneasy about the safety of banks. Since the client
had a demonstrable history of conservative debt-to-equity ratios—i.e., it
was very prudent in its lending practices and was thus an unusually sound
bank—management wanted to get that story out to its clients and potential
clients. The first group of questions emerged during the initial planning
conference for a scientifically random telephone survey of 398 respondents
in a market of approximately 100,000, served by seven banks (another bank
was chartered before the final report and plans were completed). The second version, composed of attitudinal questions, reflects early efforts to sort
out and form questions that could be asked *systematically*. The third version reflects the questions actually used. Note that Questions 1–9 were re-
formed so that they elicited information regarding the respondent's own
bank. Responses to these could then be compared to those about banks in
general, and attitudes held by customers of the client bank could then be
compared to attitudes of clients of the other banks. *Source: Courtesy Bob
Carrell.*

FIRST VERSION

Do you have more confidence in banks now than you used to have? Yes or
no? Why? Are you concerned about the soundness of the banking industry
in general? Yes or no? Why?

Do you believe that your deposits in your bank are safe? Yes or no? Why?
What do you think has been the primary cause of the many bank failures
lately? Have recent bank failures caused you to look more closely at the
soundness of the bank where you do business? Yes or no? Why?

SECOND VERSION

Please respond to the following questions with strongly agree, agree, neither, disagree or strongly disagree:

		SA	A	N	DA	SDA
1.	I believe banks are financially sound today.	1	2	3	4	5
2.	I believe banks lend money more cautiously today.	1	2	3	4	5
3.	Banks today do a good job of guarding deposits.	1	2	3	4	5
4.	I have a lot of confidence in banks today.	1	2	3	4	5

3-4 | continued

5. I don't worry about the safety of deposits in banks today. 1 2 3 4 5

6. I think banks are financially stable today. 1 2 3 4 5

7. The FDIC provides adequate supervision of bank practices. 1 2 3 4 5

8. Most people have more confidence in banks today. 1 2 3 4 5

9. I think it is a good idea to personally know a banker. 1 2 3 4 5

[To be followed by some marketing and demographic questions.]

THIRD VERSION

Bank Survey
February 1985

Number Phoned

Good morning/afternoon/evening. I'm [your name]. I am assisting with a telephone survey on the banking industry. Would you be kind enough to answer a few questions for me? If no, TERMINATE; if yes, ASK Q A.

___ ___ ___ -

1 2 3

___ ___ ___ ___ ___ b

4 5 6 7 8

A. First, are you 18 years of age or older? If yes, ASK Q B; if no, TERMINATE.

B. Do you currently bank in [name of town]? If no, TERMINATE; if yes, read the opening statement below and proceed with the interview:

The first group of questions I want to ask deals with your attitudes toward banks in general—not a specific bank or banks, but banks in general. I will read you a series of statements and I want you to respond to each statement by saying you strongly agree, agree, neither, disagree or strongly disagree:

[Circle appropriate response] SA A N DA SDA

1. Banks today are more financially secure than five years ago. 9- 1 2 3 4 5

2. Banks today are more cautious about lending money than five years ago. 10- 1 2 3 4 5

3. Banks today have a better record of guarding deposits than five years ago. 11- 1 2 3 4 5

4. I have more confidence in banks today than five years ago. 12- 1 2 3 4 5

3-4 | continued

5. I am less concerned today with the safety   13-   1   2   3   4   5
   of deposits in banks than five years ago.

6. I believe banks today are more finan-   14-   1   2   3   4   5
   cially stable than five years ago.

7. Laws and regulations are more adequate   15-   1   2   3   4   5
   today to protect depositors than five
   years ago.

8. The general public has more confidence   16-   1   2   3   4   5
   in banks today than five years ago.

9. It is more important today for people to   17-   1   2   3   4   5
   know their bankers personally than five
   years ago.

                                                 18-   b

10. Now, do you bank with more than one bank in [name of town]?

    Yes 19-1 [ASK Q 10a]   No 19-2 [ASK Q 10b]

    10a. Which do you consider to be   10b. With which bank do you
         your primary bank?   do business?

         Name of bank 20-1   Name of bank 21-1
         Name of bank 20-2   Name of bank 21-2
         Name of bank 20-3   Name of bank 21-3
         Name of bank 20-4   Name of bank 21-4
         Name of bank 20-5   Name of bank 21-5
         Name of bank 20-6   Name of bank 21-6
         Name of bank 20-7   Name of bank 21-7

[Sixty additional items, all of a marketing/perception nature, appeared in
the final version between Q10 and Q71. These dealt with the reasons respondents elected to do business with their present bankers, the types of
banking services they used and how often they used them, and the quality
of services they were getting. Questions 78 through 84 asked for key demographic information, which was used for cross-tabulations.]

Now, I want to ask you a short list of questions about your attitudes toward
[name of bank from Q 10 a or b]. I will read you a statement and I want you
to respond to it by saying you strongly agree, agree, neither, disagree or
strongly disagree with it:

[Circle appropriate response]   SA A N DA SDA

71. My bank is more financially secure than   6-   1   2   3   4   5
    five years ago.

| | 3-4 | continued |

72. My bank is more cautious about lending money than five years ago.	7-	1	2	3	4	5
73. My bank has a better record today of guarding my deposits than five years ago.	8-	1	2	3	4	5
74. I have more confidence in my bank today than five years ago.	9-	1	2	3	4	5
75. I am less concerned today about the safety of my deposits at my bank than five years ago.	10-	1	2	3	4	5
76. My bank is more financially stable today than five years ago.	11-	1	2	3	4	5
77. It is more important today for me to personally know my banker than five years ago.	12-	1	2	3	4	5

Verifying

When you start putting information together from all your sources, you will want to cross-check your sources. Check primary sources against each other. If you find areas of conflict, look for more primary sources so that the weight of information will clearly support your conclusions.

Also, check primary sources against secondary sources. People have fallible memories. In attempting to check out information, you'll often find conflicts among secondary sources. Historians, for example, sometimes spend years tracking down an elusive date for an event. Most PR researchers don't do that type of research, nor do they have the time for it, but it pays to be careful, especially now that so much information is highly specialized and technical. If authorities disagree, you need to know it and find out why. Check, and keep checking, until a pattern emerges.

Skepticism—A Requisite for All Research

Research involves digging, thinking and verifying and analyzing information. It is the act of deciding between the probable and the improbable, the true and the false, the likely and the doubtful, the acceptable and the unacceptable and the right and the wrong. These are vital decisions in any PR situation. They call for sustained reasoning, a dedication to knowing the truth and a determination to be satisfied with nothing less.

Questions to Ask

Every writer should be from the "Show Me" state, because skepticism is the hallmark of every successful writer, including those in public relations. Skepticism should not be confused with cynicism. It is a mindset that says "I will believe but you have to prove it to me." The cynic often rejects proof out of hand.

This skeptical approach is especially important to you as a PR writer, as it is with other writers in mass communication, even when it is your side of the story, because you are legally accountable for false information. You simply can't afford to take the word of any one person as "the truth." You should always insist on documentation and then cross-check the documentation just to be safe.

Probe with such questions as, Who says this is true? What documentation is available? Where is the evidence? Is there outside authority to substantiate this? What is the experience within the industry? Can I test this myself? What does other research suggest might be the case? What is my instinctive reaction to the credibility of all sources? Just remember that the only dumb question is the one not asked.

Answers Prompt Questions

When you begin researching secondary and primary sources, you'll discover that answers to your questions suggest more questions. These questions become an agenda for future research. The point is that if you expect to make it in PR, you'll need to dedicate yourself to being a good researcher who is always pursuing new questions.

Conclusions

* Research is vital to the PR writer.
* The focus of research for the PR writer is on applicable internal and external policy, relevant background material, appropriate publics, methods of message presentation, the most effective way of delivering the message and evaluating program success.
* Research information must be stored in such a way that it can be easily accessed, updated and used.
* The most common sources of secondary information are libraries, reference works, bibliographies, periodicals and government records, among others.
* Primary information is developed mostly through interviews and questionnaires. To get information by these means, you must prepare yourself carefully to ask good questions of the right people under the right circumstances.
* Gathering information is not enough. The data you collect has to be crosschecked and verified before you can base decisions on it. Be skeptical.

* It is the nature of research that answers to questions prompt still more questions.

* You can secure a place in public relations by becoming a skilled researcher.

Exercises

1. Compile a bibliography of at least 10 publications whose primary emphasis is on public relations.

2. Develop a bibliography of at least 10 reference sources on manufacturing in your state.

3. Analyze the bias in the following questions. Rewrite them as necessary to eliminate bias.
    A. Do you still believe smoking is not hazardous to your health?
    B. How often do you smoke?
    C. Do you believe that jogging does serious damage to the bone structures of the foot and joint?

4. Do research for and draft a questionnaire that probes the attitudes of the target audience toward physical fitness. The target audience is young men and women, ages 21–35, upwardly mobile in their professions, most with college degrees or some college, living in metropolitan areas. They lead very active social lives, but their careers are generally stressful.

5. Do the research necessary to write a backgrounder (see Chapter 14 for a description) for Ourbank on why more banks are failing. Do a draft copy of the research information. Save this draft for use later or turn it in as the instructor directs.

Selected Bibliography

Earl Babbie, *The Practice of Social Research*, 4th ed. (Belmont, Calif.: Wadsworth,

Jacques Barzun and Henry F. Graff, *The Modern Researcher*, 4th ed. (New York: Harcourt Brace Jovanovich, 1984).

Shirley Biagi, *Interviews That Work: A Practical Guide for Journalists* (Belmont, Calif.: Wadsworth, 1986).

John Waite Bowers and John A. Courtright, *Communication Research Methods* (Glenview, Ill.: Scott, Foresman, 1984).

Sanford Labovitz and Robert Hagedorn, *Introduction to Social Research*, 3rd ed. (New York: McGraw-Hill, 1981).

Philip Lesly, ed., *Lesly's Public Relations Handbook* (Englewood Cliffs, N.J.: Prentice-Hall, 1983).

William L. Rivers, *Finding Facts* (Englewood Cliffs, N.J.: Prentice-Hall, 1975).

Rebecca B. Rubin, Alan M. Rubin and Linda Piele, *Communication Research: Strategies and Sources* (Belmont, Calif.: Wadsworth, 1986).

Frederick Williams, *Reasoning with Statistics*, 2nd ed. (New York: Holt, Rinehart & Winston, 1979).

Roger D. Wimmer and Joseph D. Dominick, *Mass Media Research* (Belmont, Calif.: Wadsworth, 1983).

Selected Reference Materials

Michael Barone and Grant Ujifusa, *The Almanac of American Politics* (Washington, D.C.: National Journal, annual).

Federal Regulatory Directory (Washington, D.C.: Congressional Quarterly, annual).

Constant H. Jacquet, Jr., ed., *Yearbook of American and Canadian Churches* (Nashville, Tenn.: Abingdon, annual).

Matthew Lesko, *Information U.S.A.* (New York: Penguin, 1983).

Mona McCormick, *The New York Times Guide to Reference Materials* (New York: Popular Library, 1979).

National Directory of Addresses and Telephone Numbers (Hillsdale, Ill.: Concord Reference Books, 1984).

Rod Nordland, *Names and Numbers: A Journalist's Guide to the Most Needed Information Sources and Contacts* (New York: Wiley, 1978).

Official Congressional Directory (Washington, D.C.: U.S. Government Printing Office, annual).

United States Government Manual, The (Washington, D.C.: U.S. Government Printing Office, annual).

Washington Information Directory (Washington, D.C.: Congressional Quarterly, annual).

Nancy D. Wright and Gene P. Allen, compilers, *The National Directory of State Agencies* (Arlington, Va.: Information Resources Press, biannual).

Dictionaries

The American Heritage Dictionary of the English Language, New College Edition, William Morris, ed. (Boston: Houghton Mifflin, 1981).

The New York Times Everyday Dictionary, Thomas M. Paikeday, ed. (New York: Times Books, 1982).

Webster's Third New International Dictionary, Unabridged (Springfield, Mass.: Merriam-Webster, 1981).

Encyclopedias

An Encyclopedia of World History, 5th ed., William L. Langer, ed. (Boston: Houghton Mifflin, 1972).

National Geographic Atlas of the World, 5th ed. (Washington, D.C.: National Geographic Society, 1981).

The New Columbia Encyclopedia, 4th ed. (New York: Columbia University Press, 1975).

The World Almanac and Book of Facts, H. U. Lane, ed. (New York: Newspaper Enterprise Association, annual).

World Book Encyclopedia, 22 vols. (Chicago: Field Enterprises Educational Corporation, 1984).

Part Two

Writing Principles

PR writers are expected to have a fluent command of the language and a mastery of basic writing principles. But that is not enough. Chapters 4–6 discuss some of the finer points of writing to communicate.

4
Writing
for Clarity
and Interest

E very successful piece of nonfiction," says writer William Zinsser, "should leave the reader with one provocative thought that he didn't have before. Not two thoughts, or five—just one." [1]

Zinsser's book *On Writing Well* is full of excellent advice on how to produce good writing. It's worth reading. But all the advice in all the books about writing is worthless if you don't learn the most important point first: *Write so people will understand what you mean.* That is the one provocative thought you should take with you from this chapter.

Unfortunately, thousands of students and beginning writers never learn this lesson. They are taught all sorts of grammar rules and innumerable terms for tenses and cases, figures of speech and other rhetorical devices. Somehow all these details obscure the purpose of writing—communication. Good writing is writing that succeeds in communicating. Bad writing is writing that fails to communicate.

You won't be very successful in communicating if you simply pour words onto paper without giving them much thought beforehand, or with more concern for displaying your vocabulary than for communicating with your readers. You can't expect to flip on the typewriter or computer and rattle off page after page of high-quality prose. Writing well is harder than that.

For some, the ability to arrange words and express meanings clearly is a skill that comes naturally—a gift. For most of us, though, writing well is hard work. It is a craft that must be learned and practiced.

How do you produce prose that succeeds in communicating? There is no magic formula, but there are a few basic guidelines. This chapter discusses some of those guidelines.

Message, Audience, Medium

An important part of good writing is being properly prepared before you sit down at the typewriter. You must do the necessary research on the subject matter so you will understand the material, know what is important, and have in mind just what you want to communicate. You must know who will receive your communication, and you must know something about them. You must know how to reach the people at whom you are aiming your message, and you must know how different ways of reaching people affect the manner in which you prepare your material. In short, you must know your message, your audience and your medium.

Message

Most writing, whether for public relations purposes or otherwise, has one goal: to convey a message. The goal of any writer is to transfer his or her thoughts to the minds of other people via a piece of paper or some other visual, verbal or electronic medium. Step one, then, is deciding just what you want to say. If you don't understand what you're trying to say, neither will your audience.

This means you must know *exactly* what you are trying to say. Don't express your message in hazy, abstract terms. A psychologist points out that communication attempts often fail simply because the message is not "spelled out." [2] For example, an executive writes a memo asking for "more loyalty" in his department. What he really wants is somebody around to answer the telephone when he calls at 7:30 A.M.

Make sure you understand your message before you begin to write. If you can't write a short, simple sentence that summarizes the point you want to make, you probably need to do a little more thinking.

Audience

It is not enough, however, for you to understand your message. You must phrase it so the audience will also understand. You must know who your readers (or listeners) are (see target audience, Chapter 1), and you must know something of their characteristics, values and beliefs (see demographics and psychographics, Chapter 3). Otherwise, you won't be able to communicate effectively. In short, you must tailor your message to the audience.

Medium

As discussed earlier, part of tailoring your message to an audience is choosing the right media to reach that audience. In the same way, different media are appropriate for different types of messages. Choosing the right media is an important aspect of successful communication (see Chapter 1).

The choice of medium in turn affects the way you should frame the message. Articles written for magazines are done in an entirely different style from public service announcements on radio. You must use the style appropriate for the medium, being aware of the medium's technological advantages and limitations.

These three rules—know your message, know your audience and know your medium—will take you a long way toward successful writing. Both the substance and the style of what you write depend on them.

These rules, however, apply only to the planning stages of writing. Even if you know your message, your audience and your medium, your writing may fail. The execution is just as important as the preparation. So add two rules for successful execution: Write clearly so your readers will understand, and make what you write interesting so your readers will want to read it.

Clarity and Interest: Elements of Style

Clarity, of course, is the number one aim of writing style. If your audience doesn't understand what you've written, your efforts will have been wasted. But even if your writing is clear, a dull style can put your readers to sleep, and your message won't get across in that case, either.

Fortunately, the ability to write clear prose is not mysterious. It can be learned. Thanks to scientific research in the field of readability, the principles of clear writing are well known. You simply must learn them and practice them.

Readability

"If a person's motive is strong enough," writes readability expert Robert Gunning, "he will plow through any complexity of words, signs or hieroglyphs."[3] Sometimes the audience of a PR writer is intensely interested in the subject and will read through the worst writing to try to glean the slightest bit of new information. Usually, though, interest is not that great. And readers, bombarded from all sides with innumerable PR messages from different communicators, are likely to toss aside any messages that demand too much time or effort. Remember, the easier something is to read, the more likely it is that someone will read it.

What qualities make writing "easy to read"? This question has been the subject of a vast amount of research. And, especially as interpreted by writing consultants like Gunning and Rudolf Flesch, this research has revealed a number of elements that make writing readable. As early as 1935, researchers had identified more than 60 qualities affecting readability, and since then more have been found.

However, many are related to the two qualities usually considered the most important: sentence length and word length.

Sentence Length   The first principle of readable writing is to keep most sentences short. For the meaning to be clear, the reader must be able to grasp at once the relationship among the words in a sentence. Long, tangled sentences tend to obscure those relationships.

Of course, not *every* sentence should be short. An endless stream of short sentences makes for dull reading. And it is possible to write a long sentence that is also clear—just make sure that the sentence is properly constructed.

The key to readability, then, is *average* sentence length. An occasional long sentence is no problem. It is the never-ending series of long sentences that leaves readers dizzy. According to Gunning, modern prose read by the public has an average sentence length of about 16 words.[4] If your sentences are, on the average, much longer than that, your prose probably isn't as readable as it should be.

There are two major reasons why sentences are too long. One is the tendency of writers to connect independent clauses with coordinating conjunctions or to add details that could be left to later sentences. The other is simply the presence of a lot of words that don't need to be there. The cures are easy: Use more periods and fewer words.

Some long sentences, for example, can simply be cut in two with a period at the right spot. Take the following sentence-paragraph, for example:

> That may have worked out just dandy for the cigarette companies where advertising's influence on brand switching is the lowest of any major product category, but what about a company, or an industry, under fierce attack from many sides, including a press which itself has the opportunity to use time on radio and television to present the side of the story they wish to take?

The sentence is fairly clear. But it would be easy enough to put a period after "category" and give the reader a chance to breathe.

Other sentences need a little more work than just a period, especially sentences that are long because they don't stick to the point. Consider this example from a bank's PR magazine (the names have been changed to protect the guilty):

> The goal of the campaign, developed and implemented by the ABC Agency of Metropolis, is to communicate through all major media—radio, television, outdoor and newspaper—that Smallville National is the best bank to serve the people of Smallville because it is the largest.

This 44-word sentence is longer than it needs to be to make its point. It starts out well enough, promising to tell what the goal of the new ad campaign is. But along the way the sentence gets sidetracked into details about who designed the campaign and what media are to be used. Stripped of the unneeded details, the sentence might read like this:

> The campaign will tell people that Smallville National is the best
> bank for them because it is the largest.

Then details could be added in the following sentences:

> Ads will appear in all major media—radio, TV, newspapers
> and billboard. The ABC Agency of Metropolis developed the
> campaign.

Now, instead of one 44-word sentence, we have three sentences averaging just 13 words in length.

Sometimes sentences are too long simply because of extra words, not extra ideas (see Figure 4-1 for a list of redundancies). Writers frequently use three or four or five words where one will do. And words are often tossed in that aren't needed at all. Consider this sentence, for example:

> Students educated in the concept that PR is a management func-
> tion once on the job sometimes find the realities of PR practice
> demand a dismaying command of communication skills.

The phrase "educated in the concept" can be replaced with "taught"; "once on the job" can be deleted. With these simple changes made, the sentence becomes shorter and the message clearer.

Keeping sentences short is just the starting place in writing clearly, though. Short sentences won't make reading easy if the words within those sentences don't make sense. You can't write clear sentences if you don't use clear words.

Word Length A student with an exceptional vocabulary once turned in what he thought was an especially well written paper. The professor's comment scribbled across the top of the paper was simply: "Avoid sesquipedalianism." Since the student's vocabulary wasn't *that* large, he scurried to a dictionary to look up *sesquipedalianism*. He found it to mean the excessive use of long words.

The professor could easily have written "Don't use so many long words," and the student would have understood immediately. The point for PR writers is twofold. First, if you use long words, some readers won't understand them. Second, even if you use long words with well-known meanings, you make reading more difficult.

There is no need to say *precipitation* when you mean *rain*. There is nothing wrong with saying *use* instead of *employ* or *utilize*. *Fair* is just as good a word as *equitable*.

Some writers can't resist filling their prose with important-sounding phrases like "integrated conceptual analysis" or similar verbose nonsense. At least twice in every sentence they use words ending in *-ment*, *-any*, *-ial* and *-action*. Avoid such words when you can. They make reading more difficult and diminish the forcefulness of your statement. As PR writer Alden S. Wood points out, who would have responded to these words?

4-1

Dog Puppies

This is a list of redundancies. The word or words in parentheses should be deleted. *Source:* Reprinted with permission from Yvonne Lewis Day, "The Economics of Writing," *The Toastmaster*, August 1982.

(a distance of) ten yards
(a) myriad (of) sources
(absolute) guarantee
(absolutely) essential
(absolutely) sure
(actual) experience
add (an additional)
(advance) planning
(advance) reservations
all meet (together)
alongside (of)
(already) existing
(and) moreover
(as) for example
ask (a question)
(as to) whether
(as) yet
(at a) later (date)
at (the) present (time)
at some time (to come)
(baby) boy was born
(basic) fundamentals
(brief) moment
came (at a time) when
cancel (out)
(close) scrutiny
collaborate (together)
(completely) destroyed
consensus (of opinion)
continue (on)
(current) trend
(direct) confrontation

estimated (roughly) at
(every) now and then
(exact) opposites
(fellow) classmates
few (in number)
filled (to capacity)
(finally) ended
(first) began
first (of all)
(free) gift
gather (together)
had done (previously)
(hard) facts
(integral) part
(or) regardless
join (together)
last (of all)
(local) residents
(major) breakthrough
mean it (sincerely)
(midway) between
might (possibly)
my (personal) opinion
(old) cliché
(old) proverb
(past) history
protest (against)
refer (back)
(specific) example
(unintentional) mistake
written (down)

Retain your earth! Abstain from engagement in interpersonal ballistic relationships unless these relationships are initiated by the power incumbents. If, however, it becomes apparent that overt hostile interaction is to commence, let this commencement have its genesis in this geopolitical region.

The average sentence length in this paragraph is fewer than 14 words. But the words are so foggy that the meaning is completely lost. Fortunately, Captain John Parker didn't talk like that. Instead he uttered the famous command, "Stand your ground. Don't fire unless fired upon. But if they mean to have a war, let it begin here."

Why do long words make reading more difficult? One reason is that long words tend to be abstract. Readers comprehend more quickly if words are concrete—that is, if they evoke visual images. If an oil company says it's spending money on "petroleum exploration facilities," for example, the average reader won't have a very clear notion of what the company is buying. They will, however, if the company says "drilling rigs."

Also, long words are often unfamiliar to readers. Common words, which readers recognize immediately, are usually short. Why say "remuneration" when "pay" will do?

Readability Formulas   Short sentences and short words are the prime ingredients of clear writing. These ideas have been incorporated into various formulas to gauge the "readability" of a piece of writing (see Appendix A). These formulas—notably those devised by Gunning and Flesch—can be very useful to writers who want to check the clarity of their prose. Keep in mind, though, that a high readability score doesn't guarantee good writing. Readability formulas are actually nothing more than measures of structural simplicity, and, as Gunning points out, "nonsense written simply is still nonsense."[5]

Besides, clarity may be the first goal of writing, but it's not the only goal. Clear writing can be stilted and unnatural. Writing can be so simple that it's just plain boring. Clarity is worthless if the writing isn't also interesting, for writing that isn't interesting usually isn't read.

What makes writing interesting? Primarily, the subject matter. Some subjects are interesting to some people but not to others (which is why you should know your audience).

Here, though, we're concerned with style. The basic goals of style are, in addition to clarity, the logical development of ideas and a smooth transition from one idea to the next. Of course, style must also help maintain the reader's interest. Writing must be lively, with generous use of active verbs and vivid phrases. Interesting writing sounds natural, is not monotonous, and, in general, is "pleasing to the ear." Interesting writing uses personal words such as *you* and *people* to enhance human interest. Thus, along with the fundamental goal of clarity, good writers strive for naturalness, variety, euphony and human interest.

Naturalness

Reading is easiest if the style is conversational. Readability experts agree that one of the basic rules of readable writing is "write like you talk." Of course, you can't write exactly like you talk. There is a difference between the written and the spoken language. Spoken sentences are not carefully structured, and they often contain much repetition. In speaking, meaning can be shaded by intonation, inflection, facial expressions and gestures. You can't duplicate such features of the spoken language in your writing. But you can write prose that sounds natural, as though someone *could* have spoken it.

The following sentence, for example, is clear, but it sounds like a written, not a spoken, sentence:

> **Smith was not disturbed that Johnson had submitted his resignation. He said that the position held by Johnson was not of high significance.**

The same thing could have been written in a more natural, conversational manner:

> **Johnson's resignation didn't really bother Smith. He said Johnson's job wasn't very important, anyway.**

A good test of naturalness is to read aloud what you've written. If you stumble over phrases and your tongue gets twisted, the sentence is not easy enough to read. Try again. If you still have trouble writing sentences that sound natural, try this approach. Write what you want to say as you would say it in conversation. Then go back and rewrite the sentence with proper syntax, making sure the pronouns are in the right place and the meaning is clear.

Another guide to natural writing can be found in radio and TV newscasts. The style is conversational, but the words would make perfect sense if written.

A device that helps writing sound natural is the contraction. Use contractions freely. Everybody uses contractions in speech, and no matter what your old grammar school teacher used to tell you, there is absolutely nothing wrong with using them in writing. You suffer no loss of meaning when you use *don't*, *won't*, or *can't* instead of *do not*, *will not*, or *cannot*. Avoiding contractions does nothing but slow the reader down, and readers don't like to be slowed down.

Variety

Monotony can poison an otherwise good style. It's not enough to string a number of clear and natural-sounding sentences together if their structure is so similar that readers get bored. The style must push the readers along and keep them going. Readers shouldn't feel they have to force themselves through sentence after sentence.

Variety means following the rules wisely. For example, we already mentioned that not all sentences must be short. True, a series of long sentences makes it hard for a reader to follow the flow. And it's easy to get lost in a maze of adverbial prepositional phrases. But an occasional long sentence, if constructed properly, can improve the flow of the narrative. A compound sentence can take the reader from one idea to the next. An occasional inversion of subject and verb reduces monotony and can emphasize the action in the sentence. You need to be cautious with this technique to avoid altering meaning.

Use of the passive voice can aid variety. The passive voice can be appropriate if the object of the action is the most important thing in the sentence. But keep passive sentences to a minimum. Nothing is more boring than an endless stream of passive sentences.

Notice the improvement when we substitute the active voice for the passive in the following sentences:

Passive: Everything possible was done by company engineers to restore service.

Active: Company engineers did everything they could to restore service.

Passive: It was requested by the company president that the exhibit be kept open by the museum officials.

Active: The company president asked museum officials to keep the exhibit open.

Many writers aware of the need for variety in sentence structure go too far in trying to achieve variety in word choice. This leads to the use of three or four words to describe the same thing. For example,

When my books arrived, I took the hardbound texts from the package and placed the treasured volumes on my bookcase next to my other bound publications.

Usage experts call this pitfall "elegant variation." "There are few literary faults so widely prevalent," says one expert.[6] No doubt the problem stems from the widespread belief that you should never use the same word twice in one sentence. But no such prohibition exists in any rule book, and a single repetition is seldom as terrible as some writers think. Of course, repeating the same word several times can get boring. But you don't have to thumb through a thesaurus to find a synonym. Usually a pronoun works well enough: "I took the books out of the box and put them on the shelf with my others."

In other cases, there's no need to repeat the word at all: "Jones, Smith and Brown all won races; it was Jones's first win, Smith's third victory, and Brown's fourth triumph." But the vocabulary lesson is unnecessary. It's just as clear to say, "it was Jones's first win, Smith's third and Brown's fourth."

If there's no way to get around repetition, go ahead and use the same word again. It won't hurt you. And the reader won't have to figure out if you used different words because of some real difference or because you were trying to display your vocabulary.

As for the thesaurus, don't throw it away. But use it only when you are looking for a specific word, the exactly right word, which you know but just can't think of at the moment. It is rarely wise to pick a word you've never heard of or used before. Always use a dictionary to ensure the word you choose is applicable.

Euphony

The main reason so many writers worry about sentence variety and word repetition is that they want to achieve euphony in their writing. Indeed, there is nothing wrong with writing that is pleasing to the ear. Writing that is rhythmic, making appropriate use of figures of speech, is usually more enjoyable to read than straightforward stilted prose.

The only way to achieve euphony is to read good writing and develop an ear for it. If you discover a good style that is used successfully by someone else, don't worry about copying it. Just don't get carried away. As one observer puts it, a "concatenation of mellifluous phrases may indicate more polish than insight."[7] First make sure your thoughts are clear and your message is pleasing to the mind. Then worry about pleasing the ear.

Human Interest

If you are writing about people, your writing will naturally contain elements of human interest. But if your subject is something mechanical, impersonal or abstract, your task will be more difficult. How can you achieve human interest when writing about inanimate objects? The trick is to remember that you're writing *to* people even when you're not writing about them. When appropriate, address the reader as *you*. Use the pronoun *we* to refer to people in general when discussing common knowledge, as in, "We know today that the world is round." Rhetorical questions and direct quotations help make writing sound personal.

Rudolf Flesch has used these ideas to construct a "human interest" test for prose. The formula is described in Appendix A. Basically, Flesch's test is a way of merely checking to make sure that the writer has used an adequate number of personal words and personal sentences. If you don't want to be bothered with the formula, just look over your writing. If you don't find any rhetorical questions or direct quotations, and if you never use *we* or *you*, then your prose isn't likely to be very interesting.

In summary, refer to the checklist in Figure 4-2 in assessing a draft of your work.

4-2

Writing Checklist

1. Is the message clear? Have you said exactly what you want to say?

2. Have you identified important audiences? Does your writing speak to those audiences?

3. Is the style of writing appropriate for the intended medium?

4. Are your sentences instantly clear? Free from confusing constructions?

5. Are sentences, on average, fairly short? Have you avoided stringing long sentences together?

6. Is your writing concise, free from needless words?

7. Have you used common, concrete words? Words that evoke visual images?

8. Is your language natural? Can your writing be easily read aloud?

9. Is there variety in the sentence structure?

10. Are most sentences in the active voice?

11. Have you made sufficient use of personal words and sentences?

Conclusions

* Leave readers/listeners with *one* main thought.

* Write so people will understand what you mean.

* Know your message, your audience and your medium.

* Know *exactly* what you want to say.

* Tailor your message to your audience.

* Qualities of both the audience and the medium will determine your choice of a medium unless circumstances alone dictate the medium. In the latter case, you will have to adapt the style and content of your message to the medium.

* The principles of clear writing are readability, naturalness, variety, euphony and human interest.

* Readability depends primarily on the length of words and sentences.
* A conversational style is easiest to read.
* Vary sentence structure and word choice to avoid dullness.
* Write to please the ear, but not at the expense of clarity.
* Use personal words to involve the reader.
* Review your writing, using a checklist and test for readability.

Exercises

1. Apply one of the readability formulas in Appendix A to the first 100 words in this chapter. Show all your steps and math. Do the same with any other text. Compare the results.
   a. Discuss the advantages and disadvantages of readability formulas.
   b. Apply the formulas to some of your own writing, like a term paper. (Use in all of your PR writing.)
2. Apply any of the readability formulas in Appendix A to a story in today's newspaper. Then apply the same formula to a passage from a modern novel. Which is more readable? What are the implications of this result?
3. Rewrite the instructions in Exhibit A (in Figure 4-3) to make them easier to understand.
4. Rewrite the news release in Figure 4-4 to make it clearer and more interesting.
5. Apply one of the readability formulas to the first 100 words of the draft research information you did for the backgrounder in Chapter 3. Keeping in mind the people who may eventually read this information from Ourbank, what readability level should you strive for? Explain why.

Notes

[1] William Zinsser, *On Writing Well* (New York: Harper & Row, 1980), pp. 56–57.

[2] Kay Holmquist, "Feelings Poorly Defined, Says Psychologist," Fort Worth *Star-Telegram*, August 19, 1979, 19f.

[3] Robert Gunning, *The Technique of Clear Writing* (New York: McGraw-Hill, 1968), p. 1.

[4] Ibid., p. 51.

[5] Ibid., p. 44.

[6] H. W. Fowler, *Modern English Usage* (New York: Oxford University Press, 1965), p. 148.

4-3

Exhibit A
Source: Reprinted with permission of TCU Publications.

ADVANCE REGISTRATION
Spring Semester, 1985

Procedures

Advance registration for the Spring Semester, 1985, will be available to students in attendance at TCU during the Fall Semester, 1984. It will be conducted during the period beginning November 12 and ending December 4, 1984.

The following procedures have been established for students who wish to advance register:

1. **Undergraduates** must arrange for academic advisement. Academic advising is an integral part of the advance registration process. Students wishing to advance register must secure their registration forms from their advisor while being advised.

   Continuing Education (Evening) Students will be able to obtain their registration materials from the Office of Continuing Education, Room 212 Sadler Hall.

   Alumni and auditors wishing to register on a space available basis for tuition discount may NOT advance register. Full tuition is charged for all advance registration.

   Graduate students wishing to advance register may secure their enrollment forms at the following locations:

Non-degree, transient & MLA	SH 208
School of Business	DRH 210
School of Education	BB 201
School of Fine Arts	ELH 102
AddRan College of Arts & Sciences	RH 111

2. After receiving the materials, students should carefully read all instructions. Registration priority will be based on classification. A student's classification is determined by the number of hours earned plus the number of hours in progress.

3. Students should report to the Registrar's Office, Room 19 Sadler Hall, with their enrollment forms no earlier than the days reflected below:

Seniors (84 + hrs.)	Monday, Nov. 12
Juniors (54-83.5 hrs)	Thursday, Nov. 15
Sophomores (24-53.5 hrs.)	Tuesday, Nov. 20
Freshmen (0-23.5 hrs.)	Tuesday, Nov. 27
Others	Friday, Nov. 30

   (hours: 9:00 a.m. to 5:00 p.m.)

Advance Registration must be completed no later than 5:00 p.m., on Tuesday, December 4

Restrictions

Students whose current financial accounts are in arrears with the TCU Controller's Office will **not** have the privilege of participating in advance registration.

Conditions

Students who elect to participate in advance registration assume the financial obligations represented by the tuition and other costs connected with their enrollment. Students who decide not to attend the University must notify the Controller's Office in writing prior to January 3, 1985.

Satisfactory financial arrangements must be made in compliance with the instructions which will accompany their Registration Invoice mailed by the Controller's Office.

Changes in Schedule

Students who complete advance registration will be permitted to make changes in their schedules on Tuesday, January 15 in the Rickel Building. Those who wish to do so will be required to report on the following schedule:

Seniors	8:00 a.m.
Juniors	8:30 a.m.
Sophomores	9:00 a.m.
Freshmen	9:30 a.m.
Graduates, Post-Graduates and Special	8:00 to 9:30 a.m.

Changes in schedules may also be made beginning at 8:00 a.m. on Thursday, January 17, and extending through normal office hours on Tuesday, January 22. During this period changes will be initiated in the Office of the Registrar, Room 18, Sadler Hall. The last date for changes, other than drops, will be 4:30 p.m., Tuesday, January 22.

NOTE

Schedule Change Forms must be returned to the Registrar's Office for processing to be official. The date of return is considered the official date of the change. Courses dropped during 100% tuition refund period do not appear on the student's academic record.

News Release
Source: Reprinted with permission of the Gas Research
Institute.

NEWS RELEASE

Gas Research Institute/8600 West Bryn Mawr Avenue/Chicago, Illinois 60631/312·399·8100

September 6, 1983
Contact: Renee M. Schott
Technical Communications
312/399-8293

F. Richard Kurzynske
Manager, Environmental
Assessment and Control,
Utilization Research

APPLIANCE MANUFACTURERS SIGN LICENSING AGREEMENTS

Gas Research Institute (GRI), Chicago, has announced that two major

appliance manufacturers, Rheem Manufacturing Company and Ducane Heating

Corporation, have signed non-exclusive, royalty-free licensing agreements for

the use of a technology that will enable their natural gas furnaces to meet

new California environmental regulations. Effective January 1, 1984, the

regulations limit the allowable concentration of nitrogen oxides (NO_x) in

flue gas emissions to approximately one-tenth of an ounce per ten hours of

operation for a typical 100,000 Btu/hr furnace. Not all currently marketed

appliances comply with the new regulations.

4-4 continued

The application of this technology by Rheem and Ducane will immediately benefit the California consumer and the gas industry by ensuring the continued availability of gas furnaces, the lowest cost option for most space heating applications. Both manufacturers are adapting the technology to specific furnace units and plan to begin production during November for distribution in California beginning in January.

The technology, developed by the American Gas Association Laboratories with sponsorship by GRI, is a relatively simple, inexpensive burner modification using either ceramic or metallic inserts within the combustion area of a gas furnace or appliance in specific relationship to the flame. The inserts can be adapted easily to existing appliance product lines at a low cost. The insert lowers peak temperatures, producing a corresponding decrease in NO_x formation without a reduction in the energy utilization efficiency or a significant increase in carbon monoxide emissions. The insert materials were chosen based on such considerations as economics, availability, durability, and ease of manufacture.

Negotiations for similar licensing agreements are under way with several other furnace and water heater manufacturers having large California markets. Licensing agreements for this technology are available to interested gas equipment manufacturers through GRI.

GRI is a private, not-for-profit membership organization that plans, manages, and develops financing for a cooperative research and development program in gaseous fuels and their use. The research program, which is designed to benefit the regulated natural gas industry and gas consumers nationwide, consists of over 350 active research projects in four major areas: supply options, efficient utilization, enhanced service, and fundamental research.

[7]Kenneth E. Andersen, *Persuasion Theory and Practice* (Boston: Allyn and Bacon, 1971), p. 126.

Selected Bibliography

Jacques Barzun and Henry F. Graff, *The Modern Researcher*, 4th ed. (New York: Harcourt Brace Jovanovich, 1984).

Rudolf Flesch, *The Art of Readable Writing*, 25th anniversary ed. (New York: Harper & Row, 1974).

Robert Gunning, *The Technique of Clear Writing*, rev. ed. (New York: McGraw-Hill, 1968).

Lauren Kessler and Duncan McDonald, *When Words Collide: A Journalist's Guide to Grammar and Style* (Belmont, Calif.: Wadsworth, 1984).

William Zinsser, *On Writing Well*, 2nd ed. (New York: Harper & Row, 1980).

5
Simplifying
the Complex

In his first paper on the theory of relativity, written in 1905, Albert Einstein penned one of the simplest sentences you'll ever find in a scientific paper. In describing a point about time and simultaneity, Einstein wrote (in English translation),

> If, for instance, I say, "That train arrives here at 7 o'clock," I mean something like this: "The pointing of the small hand of my watch to 7 and the arrival of the train are simultaneous events."[1]

You can't get much simpler than that.

Einstein treasured simplicity in writing, and though his scientific papers did get technical in places, his writings for the general public were always clear and readable. Einstein could write simply on subjects like relativity because he understood them so completely himself. He could write clearly, without too many technical terms, because he knew his subject well enough to express the ideas in plain language and retain absolute accuracy.

PR writers are not likely to be as knowledgeable about any subject as Einstein was about physics. Yet they are still called on to translate complex subjects into language the general public can understand. There is nothing simple about nuclear power, pollution chemistry or petroleum economics. Medicine, urban affairs and social services can be as complex as advanced calculus. Yet such issues are becoming more and more important to the average citizen. PR people must be able to explain the implications of government and corporate actions in these areas, as well as interpret the latest research findings. It's advisable to have authorities check the final drafts to be sure your translations are accurate.

Millions of diet soft drink consumers, for example, are intensely interested in scientific research on the health effects of artificial sweeteners. Beverage companies, government agencies, universities and other institutions must be able to explain what's going on. Doing so is far more difficult than preparing a news release about the appointment of a new vice president. It takes special writing skills to simplify the complex without explaining it inaccurately.

Some authorities think it's impossible to explain complex things like scientific research to the general public. Even Rudolf Flesch, the ultimate advocate of simplifying the complex, advises writers not to try to give complete scientific explanations. You can describe the meaning of a discovery, he says, and indicate its importance. But a complete scientific explanation? Flesch wouldn't even try that with his own readability formula:

> Here I would have to get into statistical regression formulas and multiple correlation and whatnot, and nobody who hasn't had a course in statistics would know what I am talking about. . . . There is only one bit of advice I can offer in this business of giving laymen an exact scientific explanation: don't try.[2]

Not everybody agrees with this attitude. William Zinsser says "a complex subject can be made as accessible to the layman as a simple subject. It's just a question of putting one sentence after another."[3]

In practice, explaining deep scientific principles to nonscientists isn't often of much use—not because lay readers can't understand, but because most aren't really interested. If a reader is interested in a subject, however, a good writer can explain it. You can even explain statistics to people who haven't had statistics courses, *if* they are interested enough to follow what might be a fairly lengthy explanation.

Today, in many cases, people aren't "merely" interested in scientific explanations. They demand them. If your company is building a nuclear power plant near a town, you'd better be able to explain to the people who live there what that plant will do and how its safety systems will work. You won't get by with saying "Don't worry—it's safe."

And if the public doesn't ask technical questions directly, newspaper reporters and electronic journalists will. Today, the mass media deal with more technical subjects in greater detail than ever before. When reporters working on such stories don't understand something themselves, they often go to PR people for explanations. PR writers, frequently trained only in journalism or English and not in the technical fields they must try to interpret, often find themselves at a loss. When an activist group accuses your company of cheating on taxes, how do you explain the complexities of accelerated depreciation and the investment tax credit? How does the PR person for a factory suspected of polluting the air explain the difference between primary ambient air standards and secondary emission limits? How does the spokesperson for a nuclear plant explain the meanings of "10 picocuries of radio-activity"?

It isn't easy, but these things can be explained. You can simplify the complex, and you can simplify it accurately. But only if, like Einstein, you know your subject.

Know Your Subject

There is an old saying popular among newspaper editors to the effect that a good reporter can cover any story. If the reporter doesn't know much about the subject, he or she can simply call up an expert, ask a few questions and then explain it all to readers in words they'll understand. Or so the theory goes.

If this adage was ever true, it isn't any more. And it's no truer for PR writers than for reporters. Nevertheless, pamphlets on complex subjects are often written this way. An engineer produces a technical description of some process or machine in words peculiar to the profession. The copy is given to the PR person, who edits and rewrites to simplify the language but keep the facts as the engineer wrote them. In theory the PR person need know nothing about the subject—the engineer provides the facts. The PR writer just needs to know how to write clearly.

The problem is that you can't simplify complex writing unless you know what it means. You must understand it thoroughly yourself before you can explain it to somebody else. You must know more about the subject than you'll ever put in print. If you don't, you won't be able to tell when a statement as simplified can stand alone or should be qualified. And you won't know the difference between a correct statement and a false one.

Consider this example from a writer trying to describe the dangers of cigarettes in simple terms:

> Opening another front in its war on smoking, the federal government plans to publicize a new peril—carbon monoxide—to prod the cigarette industry to reduce its use of that substance in cigarettes as it has reduced tar and nicotine.

Simple enough, this sentence, but also sheer nonsense. Carbon monoxide is not a substance that exists inside tobacco, waiting to be unleashed. It is a gas created when carbon (in the tobacco) combines with oxygen (from the air) as tobacco burns. The writer simply didn't know much about the subject.

The same is true of the reporter who attempted to describe nuclear fast breeder reactors:

> The fast breeder gets its name . . . because the chain reaction is so much faster than in conventional . . . reactors.

Again, this is a readable simplification of a complex idea. It's also an incorrect simplification. The "fast" in fast breeder doesn't refer to the rate of the chain reaction (which would be measured by the number of atoms splitting per second) but to the speed of neutrons, small subatomic particles that fly around inside reactors and split atoms. In ordinary nuclear power plants atoms are split mostly by slow neutrons; in fast breeders, speedy neutrons do most of the splitting.

How can you avoid making such mistakes? You simply must research your subject before you begin writing, and research it thoroughly. Get help from experts on points you don't understand. Recheck any passage containing statements you're not absolutely sure of.

Finally, don't try to tell readers everything you know. That always takes you to fringe areas, where your knowledge gets a little shaky and errors begin to creep in. Statements perfectly consistent with what you know might be inconsistent with what you *don't* know. Besides, if you tell the readers everything *you* know, you're probably telling them a lot more than *they* want or need to know. Give readers just what they need to get the message.

For example, if you wished to continue the story of carbon monoxide in cigarette smoke, you might be tempted to write something like this:

> Carbon monoxide, a molecule of which consists of a carbon atom bonded to an oxygen atom, is dangerous because of its chemical affinity with hemoglobin. Hemoglobin, a complex chemical substance containing iron, serves as a transport mechanism for oxygen in the blood stream. Since the affinity of carbon monoxide with hemoglobin is greater than the affinity of oxygen with hemoglobin, carbon monoxide impairs the ability of hemoglobin to carry oxygen.

This explanation, while essentially accurate, is too long. Unless you're writing for medical students or biochemists, just say that carbon monoxide impairs the ability of the blood to carry oxygen through the body. *You* should know all about hemoglobin and oxygen transport. But you don't need to tell everybody about it. The more you know about a subject, the easier it will be to simplify, and the less likely you will be to make mistakes.

There is one danger, though, in knowing a lot about a subject. When you have written on the subject for a while, you may find yourself using the jargon of the discipline. This is the fatal flaw in most writing on technical subject matter. If you want the audience to understand what you write, avoid using technical terms. Instead, follow the golden rule of simplifying the complex: Use plain English.

Plain English

Most people know plain English when they hear it. It is everyday language, free from the long words and technical terms that plague the prose of scientists, engineers, economists, doctors, lawyers or writers in other specialized disciplines. All professions and trades have special vocabularies that members use when they communicate among themselves. Unfortunately, some members use the same words—the jargon of the field—when they try to communicate with people *outside* the discipline. It doesn't work. To write plain English, you must avoid jargon.

Avoid Jargon

Within any profession, jargon has its uses. A jargon term may stand for a complicated concept that would take paragraphs to describe in full. Once members of a profession agree on such a term, they can use it freely, since everyone within the discipline knows what it means. What communicators must realize is that people not trained in the field *don't* know what it and similar terms mean. See Figure 5-1.

Writers must also recognize three other types of jargon that cause problems. One type consists of common words that have special meanings to the members of a given group. Printers, for example, use words like *flat* and *signature* in an entirely different way from most people. Writers must make sure that readers understand when a common word is used with a special meaning.

Another type of jargon consists of fancy words used for common concepts, as when members of a given group use long or obscure words instead of short familiar ones that mean the same thing. Specialists, for example, often use technical terms to sound impressive. Consider the following sentence, written by an engineer explaining some of the drawbacks of solar-electric power plants:

> All solar-thermal systems must accept diurnal transients and rapid transients from cloud passage during daily operation.

He was trying to say that it gets dark at night and that clouds sometimes block out the sun. The idea wasn't any more complicated than that, and there's no reason to make it sound complicated.

A third type is institutional jargon. A good bit of it originates with the largest institution—the federal government. In 1981 Malcolm Baldridge, then Secretary of Commerce, decided to purge at least his area. He issued a memo outlawing certain expressions and discouraging the creation of new ones. He warned

> commerce staff to steer clear of "bastardized words, nouns and adjectives used as verbs, and passive verbs." Included were these miscues: finalized ("finished" is OK); impact a situation (you're on safe ground if you "control" it or "affect" it); parameters to work within ("specific limits" are acceptable); I share your concern (Who cares? You still have to say "yes" or "no").[4]

For more on "gobbledygook," see Figure 5-2.

Good writers never use fancy jargon words when common words will do the job as well. Sometimes, though, common words won't do the job as well. If a word has no plain English equivalent, and if it's essential to your subject, you have no choice but to use it. But make sure you explain to the readers what this new term means.

Jargon Avoided

The financial world is full of jargon, as anyone who has ever tried to read an economics or finance text can testify. But in less than 250 words the American Association of Retired Persons told its members how to follow their investment in the AARP investment program. *Source*: Reprinted with permission from *AARP News Bulletin*, Vol. 26, No. 6, p. 1.

Current value of investment program shares listed in most daily newspapers

The notice is to solve problem-calls.

Many members have been calling AARP to inquire about the current value of shares in the mutual funds that make up the AARP Investment Program from Scudder. The Association's Membership Division wants to point out that this information is being reported daily throughout the country in more than 2,300 newspapers that subscribe to the Associated Press and UPI wire services.

But notice how AARP members are made comfortable. "Anyone can do it."

Members who wish to check the current value of their holdings in the AARP Investment Program can find it as provided by the National Association of Securities Dealers under the heading "Mutual Fund Quotations" in the financial section of their local newspaper.

The AARP Investment Program from Scudder is easy to find, since the listing is alphabetical and the AARP funds head the list.

Where it is—heads the list titled "Mutual Fund Quotations."

Under "Mutual Fund Quotations" there are four columns. The first gives the name of the fund. The second is headed "NAV," which stands for "net asset value" per share and gives the current price of a fund share. The third column is headed "Offer Price," under which appears a figure that is the total of the "NAV" price plus sales charges, if any. For the AARP funds, the initials "N.L." appear in the third column, standing for "no load," which means there are no sales charges in connection with the purchase or sale of the AARP funds' shares. The figure in the last column, headed "NAV Chg," indicates the change in share price since the previous day of business.

How information is presented—four columns and what each means.

The total value of holdings in an AARP fund is calculated by multiplying the number of shares owned by the "NAV" amount.

How to get the total value of your holdings.

Gobbledygook Explained
Source: Reprinted with permission from *U.S. News & World Report*, February 18, 1985 (p. 57). Copyright 1985 U.S. News & World Report, Inc.

Gobbledygook, That "Normally Occurring Abnormal Occurrence"

College officials used to talk to one another. No longer. Today, they *articulate* with one another.

Gym classes once were in the physical-education department. No longer. At Rutgers University, they are in the department of *human kinetics.* In many schools, what was the library is now a *learning-resource center.*

Those are just a few examples of a language disorder known as "educationese," variants of which afflict business, science and medicine. Its governmental form is gobbledygook, a term coined in the late 1930s by a Texas congressman after he spent months reading official reports larded with bloated, empty words.

A more serious ailment is newspeak, euphemism gone bonkers to the point of standing truth on its head—such as the Ministry of Truth, which in the George Orwell novel *1984* propagated lies.

Plain-English advocates despair over such linguistic maladies. "They debase the language and obscure thought," charges Lt. Col. Robert Murawski, associate professor of English at the Air Force Academy.

Murawski, who advises the White House on clear writing, contends that "the real danger is not grammatical flubs but clotted expression that makes ideas needlessly complex."

Signs of improvement pop up from time to time. Last year, Navy Secretary John Lehman ordered the service to stop using certain terms that took root in the 1970s. A *Navy correctional facility* is once more a brig. *Unaccompanied officer personnel housing* is back to BOQ—bachelor-officer quarters. *Human resources* once again are people.

Commerce Secretary Malcolm Baldrige heartened purists when he ordered word processors in his agency programed to reject such terms as *task out* and *liaison with.*

"Gem" collectors. The bright spots, however, do not outweigh the assaults on clear communication, according to W. T. Rabe, head of the Unicorn Hunters, a plain-English group at Lake Superior State College in Michigan, and William Lutz, head of the English department at Rutgers University and editor of the *Quarterly Review of Doublespeak.* Rabe and Lutz offer these examples:

- *Predawn vertical insertion*, a White House coinage for the invasion of Grenada by parachutists.
- *Wood interdental stimulator*, Pentagonese for toothpick.
- *Experienced cars*, latest automotive euphemism to displace previously owned or used cars.
- *Normally occurring abnormal occurrence*, the nuclear industry's description of something that goes wrong all the time.
- A *therapeutic misadventure*, medical jargon for an operation that kills the patient.

Why do such linguistic atrocities persist? Sometimes, people want to make the common things they do seem more important. Thus, an elevator operator becomes a *vertical-transportation-corps member.*

Officials in government and industry use foggy phrases to hide harsh truths. An airline's report to stockholders referred to the "involuntary conversion of a 727." It was, in fact, a plane crash that killed three passengers. Medical experts and social scientists often create a jargon so abstruse that it discourages outsiders from second-guessing them.

"Pollution of the language keeps getting worse," complains Professor Lutz of Rutgers. "No one wants to talk directly any more."

By SUSANNA McBEE

Often, all you need to do is supply a simple definition when you introduce the word. But usually there's more to simplifying the complex than defining technical terms; in fact, dictionary definitions are frequently as confusing as the terms themselves. Remember, then, your purpose is not to build the readers' vocabularies but to convey an idea. Usually you can get the idea across more clearly by *describing* the new term than defining it.

Describe, Don't Define

Assume you're writing about the use of the chemical element lithium as an agent for treating psychological depression. It seems like a good idea to first define lithium. So you turn to the dictionary and find: "lithium: a soft, silver-white element of the alkali metal group. Atomic number 3, atomic weight 6.941." This is not a very useful definition. If this is all you tell your readers, they won't really know much more than they did before.

Instead, you could write, "Lithium is a silvery-white metal that is very light—in fact, it's the lightest metal known. It's also very soft and can be cut with a knife. Its name comes from the Greek word *lithos*, meaning 'stone.'" Now your readers will have a picture of lithium in their heads. You've removed some of the mystery behind the name and can go on to discuss the uses of lithium.

For the same reason, it does little good to define "kilowatt-hour" as "the amount of energy consumed when an electrical demand of one kilowatt is maintained for one hour." You're much better off if you describe a kilowatt-hour as the amount of electricity it takes to run a hand-held hair dryer for an hour, or as the energy needed to toast three loaves of bread. These are not good scientific definitions of a kilowatt-hour, but they are good descriptions—and they're much more likely to be understood.

Whether you use definitions or descriptions, though, you shouldn't introduce too many new terms. Using technical terms is a luxury to be indulged in sparingly. Don't expect a reader to assimilate several new terms at once. Of course, some writers operate on the "define and proceed" principle. This is a favorite method of textbook writers. They come to a new term—or five new terms, or however many they need—define them, and go on with the story, using the new terms freely. The unfortunate students find they must check back to the original definitions every ten seconds or so to keep track of what they're reading.

Textbook writers don't have much choice, however, since their purpose is often to teach a student the vocabulary of a new field. And this goal requires definitions. But PR writers have a different aim—to communicate a single message. You can't do that if you introduce new terms just to educate the audience. You have to convey the main part of your message in words the audience already understands. In other words, use plain English as much as possible.

If you're writing a medical brochure about interferon, a protein substance in the body that helps to fight disease, you must use the term *interferon*. But you don't need to give your readers a complete lesson in biochemistry. Avoid the temptation to use words like *fibroblasts* or *lipopolysaccharides*. Even if you define these terms, using them will obscure what you're trying to say about interferon.

What if such terms are essential to the discussion? The point is, they're probably not. At least the terms themselves aren't. Fibroblasts might be important, but you can just as easily say "connective tissue cells." Simply describe such things without naming them. It will be easier for you and the readers.

Of course, you can't describe technical terms without knowing what they mean. So whenever you're writing on a specific technical subject, keep a specialized dictionary on hand. If you're writing about geology, for example, you should have a dictionary of earth science or some comparable reference work at your fingertips.

What if you replace jargon with common words where possible and do a good job of describing any necessary technical terms, and the message is *still* too complex for the average reader? In that case, you simply must give readers enough background so they *will* understand. But you have to be careful not to give too much background at once. Take one step at a time.

One Step at a Time

You can confuse readers by telling them too much at once. A reader can accept one new fact if you use understandable words, but don't expect to transfer several new thoughts at the same time. The reader's mind will flash "overload" and stop taking in anything. It's like blowing a fuse when you plug too many appliances into the same outlet. The brain, like an electrical circuit, can stand only so much flow.

You have to introduce one new idea at a time. And you must do so in logical order. The first idea should help explain the second, the second the third and so on.

If you start with the simplest idea and proceed one step at a time, you can eventually take the reader to a high degree of sophistication. This is Isaac Asimov's description of how he wrote a book on mathematics:

> It was about elementary arithmetic, to begin with, and it was not until the second chapter that I as much as got into Arabic numerals, and not until the fourth chapter that I got to fractions. However, by the end of the book I was talking about imaginary numbers, hyperimaginary numbers, and transfinite numbers—and that was the real purpose of the book. In going from counting to transfinites, I followed such a careful and gradual plan that it never stopped seeming easy.[5]

Using the one-step-at-a-time approach, you can eventually explain almost anything. The important thing is to make sure the first step is in the right place. After you've identified the main points and put them in order, look at the first point. Will your audience know what you're talking about? Naturally, that depends on the audience. If you're explaining how a nuclear power plant works, your first point might be "splitting atoms gives off energy" or more technically "fissioning of atomic nuclei gives off energy." If your audience is composed of high school science teachers, it is probably safe to assume they know about atoms, and you can start with a description of how a nucleus can be split to release energy. But suppose you're explaining nuclear power to people who never went to high school but who live near the new nuclear power plant? In this case you'll have to start by describing atoms.

The key to success in using this method lies in identifying the steps. You must determine at the outset what the central points are. Many writers do this well enough, but somewhere between the start and the finish the central ideas get lost. Communicating the complex is bound to fail if only the writer knows what the central ideas are. Make the central points clear to the reader.

Make the Central Points Clear

Whether you're writing on a complex subject or a simple one, the objective is still the same—to convey a message. Messages must be supported with facts and figures, descriptions and explanations. You can't leave out important details. Too often, though, writers let details and descriptions obscure the message. The central point is buried in a paragraph of statistics or turns up at the end of a series of equivocal qualifying phrases. Don't lose track of your purpose. Make sure the main idea stands out.

Usually you do this by stating your main point clearly and forcefully at the outset, leaving the details to come later. It is much easier for readers to follow a chain of explanations if they know the point of the story ahead of time.

If you don't make the main point clear, your audience not only won't get the message, they also won't attach much importance to what you have to say. Take the case of an electric utility organization whose spokesman was asked to respond to a ruling by the Federal Power Commission. The utilities wanted the FPC to allow them to charge customers for the interest on money borrowed to build power plants while the plants were being built. Except for a few specific expenses, the FPC said no.

When wire service reporters asked the Edison Electric Institute for a comment, the organization's president responded with this:

> **We are disappointed that the Federal Power Commission, after long deliberation, has tentatively adopted such a restricted approach to construction work in progress. Inclusion of CWIP in the rate base with a commensurate rate of return is an important method of reducing the need for outside financing.**

If the reporters understood what he said, they certainly didn't care. They called upon an environmentalist group for its reaction to the FPC decision. That group's spokesperson said the decision was "a stunning victory for consumers" and then offered a dollar estimate of what the savings for consumers would be.

It isn't hard to guess which comment was in the lead paragraph of wire service stories that resulted. UPI led with the "stunning victory" quote and the utility statement didn't make it into the first five paragraphs, which is all that some newspapers carried. The Associated Press led with the environmental group's estimate of savings. The utility group showed up in paragraph nine.

Why? The environmentalists' statement is a dramatic, well-put reaction that has impact, clarity and simplicity. Their statement was written by somebody who knew how to write. The writer knew the point the environmentalists wanted to make, and made it. The utility statement sounds like it was written by a committee. Succeeding paragraphs continue in the same way, mixing important points with needless qualifications and elaborations. Because the main point was not identified and stated clearly, few people got the message.

Of course, failure to make the point clear was not the only problem with the utility's statement. It simply contained too many unfamiliar ideas. *CWIP*, *rate base*, and *rate of return* are not part of the working vocabularies of most readers. These are unfamiliar terms, and people don't grasp messages filled with words they don't understand. The solution is to explain the unfamiliar with things that *are* familiar.

Explain the Unfamiliar with the Familiar

Readers don't easily understand complicated explanations of things they know nothing about. But if you can tie your subject to something within the reader's experience, you can skip several steps of definition and description and get right to the explanation.

Simple analogies can work wonders in getting people to understand why things are the way they are. An electric utility often faces criticism because its large industrial users pay a lower cost for electricity (in cents per kilowatt-hour) than residential customers do. Utility rate setting is very complicated, but a writer for one company hit on an idea to explain the price difference using an analogy with tomatoes. When tomatoes, delivery trucks and catsup replace generators, transmission lines and transformers, readers can concentrate on the message instead of trying to understand unfamiliar terminology. (See Figure 5-3.)

Scientific subjects especially call for explanations in familiar words. It is possible, of course, to explain how a mass spectrometer measures the weight of various molecules by describing electromagnetic acceleration of molecule beams and mass-charge ratios. But most people have never seen a mass spectrometer and have only a hazy idea of what a molecule is. A *New York Times* writer solved this particular problem by describing the process with familiar ideas, beginning with a description of a cannon shooting iron balls of different sizes past a giant magnet.

> As the flying balls pass the magnet they are pulled toward it, and this causes their trajectories to curve in the direction of the magnet as they move past it. But since the balls are of differing

5-3

"Tomatoes Are Easier to Understand"
A PR writer for an electric utility company attempted to explain an unfamiliar subject—the setting of electric rates—by discussing a similar process using something familiar to most readers—tomatoes. This article appeared in a newsletter alongside a more detailed article that discussed electricity rate setting in more specific (though also readable) terms. *Source:* Reprinted with permission of Texas Electric Service Company, Fort Worth, TX.

TOMATOES ARE EASIER TO UNDERSTAND

To put cost-of-service principles into more familiar terms, let's forget about the electric utility business for a moment. Let's talk about tomatoes.

Acme Tomato Company sells and delivers tomatoes. The company charges 10 cents for each tomato. It also charges a 50-cent fee for deliveries to cover the expenses of the delivery truck and driver.

Acme has two customers. On one side of town is Harriet, a home-maker. She buys two tomatoes each day for husband Harvey's sandwiches. On the other side of town is Craig's Catsup Company. Craig buys 50 tomatoes each day to make catsup.

Acme delivers Harriet two tomatoes and charges her 70 cents. That's two tomatoes at 10 cents each plus the 50 cent delivery fee. That figures out to be 35 cents a tomato.

$$\frac{(2 \times 10\text{¢}) + 50\text{¢}}{2} = 35\text{¢ per tomato}$$

Acme delivers Craig's Catsup Company 50 tomatoes each day and charges him $5.50. That's 50 tomatoes at 10 cents each plus the 50 cent delivery fee. That figures out to be 11 cents a tomato.

$$\frac{(50 \times 10\text{¢}) + 50\text{¢}}{50} = 11\text{¢ per tomato}$$

That's quite a difference in the price of tomatoes — 35 cents compared to 11 cents. Just looking at the average price per tomato it would seem that poor Harriet is being overcharged.

That's clearly not the case. The cost of delivering tomatoes remains the same and must be paid, whether it's two tomatoes or 50 being delivered. If it's 50, the delivery cost is spread out thinly over the price of the tomatoes. If it's only two being delivered, it must still be lumped on.

But no one is overcharged, and no one subsidizes anyone else. Everyone pays for the cost of service.

It is the same way in the electric utility business as it is with Acme Tomato Company. A major part of the cost is "delivering" electricity to your house.

And that's why large industrial customers pay a lower average cost per kilowatt-hour. They simply have more kilowatt-hours to spread the delivery cost over. It's just easier to understand it if you're buying tomatoes.

weights, their trajectories are influenced differently by the magnet. The path of the lightest ball is most strongly curved by the magnet while that of the heaviest ball is least strongly curved.

The effect of this is to sort out the balls in order according to weight, and when they strike a target their distribution along a line exactly corresponds to their relative masses. The magnet has thus broken down a batch of assorted balls into the spectrum of their masses.

Molecules can be made to behave like such balls.[6]

5-4

Simplifying the Complex—Checklist

1. Have you researched your subject thoroughly? Do you understand its complexities and the precise meanings of the terms you use?

2. Does your writing stay within the range of your knowledge?

3. Have you told readers only as much as they need to know to understand the point?

4. Have you used plain English as much as possible? Avoided unnecessary jargon? Have you been sure to use common words whenever they can be substituted for technical terms?

5. Have you fully described all technical terms that you can't avoid?

6. Have you made sure all technical terms used are really necessary to communicate the message?

7. Have you taken the readers one step at a time? Have you started with a point your readers will understand?

8. Have you identified the central points you want to make? Are they made clearly and not obscured by explanation and detail?

9. Have you used familiar ideas to explain unfamiliar concepts?

The writer went on to describe the process with molecules, having provided the reader with a basis for understanding.

A natural science writer helped readers understand a known but seldom experienced natural phenomenon like the northern lights in this way:

> Scientists today believe that the Aurora Borealis is caused by the "solar wind" particles interacting with the earth's geomagnetic field beyond the upper atmosphere in the area called the magneto sphere. According to Syun-Ichi Akasofu of the University of Alaska's Geophysical Institute, the solar wind generates huge quantities of electricity in the magneto sphere. This energy accelerates particles into the upper atmosphere where they strike atoms of various gases, producing the characteristic colors and staining the sky with dancing light.[7]

In summary, use the checklist in Figure 5-4 in reviewing a draft of your work on a complex subject.

Conclusions

* Simplifying complex subjects is one of the toughest tasks PR writers face. But in modern-day society it must be done.

* Complex subjects *can* be simplified and made understandable, but doing so while maintaining accuracy is not easy.

* It's not enough simply to write short sentences and define technical terms. You must follow a number of important principles (see Figure 5-4).

* If you must interpret technical subjects, follow the rules of simplifying the complex.

* Use plain English, not the jargon of the discipline.

* When you must use technical terms, don't define them and proceed—*describe* them, so readers will have a clear notion of what you're writing about.

* Know your subject thoroughly, and be aware of what your readers don't know.

* Start at the beginning and proceed one step at a time.

* Know what message you want to convey.

* Identify the most important point and state it clearly—don't obscure the main idea with clouds of detail.

* If your important point is about something unfamiliar, use familiar ideas to explain it.

* If you follow these rules, along with the general principles of good writing, you should be able to explain anything important enough to deserve explaining.

Exercises

1. Rewrite in simple language this airline's effort to explain use of advantages from its frequent flyers' program:

> If you haven't accumulated the required number of segments or the necessary mileage for the Autumn '84 Award you desire, you may still have the opportunity to do so through the Segment Purchase Option and/or Mileage Exchange, now available to Autumn '84 Award winners. You can purchase one or two additional segments and/or you may exchange regular Advantage program mileage toward an Autumn '84 Award.
>
> Note: If you have qualified for the 50% Discount certificate and wish to purchase segments and/or exchange mileage to qualify for a "free" certificate, you must return the 50% Discount certificate in order to receive a "free" certificate.
>
> Autumn '84 Award winners who reach a qualifying mileage threshold, but do not have the number of segments required to earn that award, may take advantage of the Segment Pur-

chase Option. This option allows you to purchase one or two additional segments at $175 per segment. The segment(s) you purchase count toward the Autumn '84 program requirements only, and no mileage credit is associated with them.

Autumn '84 Award winners who reach the qualifying number of segments but miss an Autumn '84 mileage threshold by 3,000 miles or less, may choose to exchange regular program mileage for Autumn '84 mileage. Exchange mileage counts toward the Autumn '84 program requirements only. Regular program mileage exchanged will be deducted from your account. No segment credit will be associated with mileage exchanged.

The Segment Purchase Option and Mileage Exchange will be in effect for the period 12/1/84–3/31/85. Just use the attached Autumn '84 Segment Purchase and Mileage Exchange Card.

2. You have received this technical release (see Figure 5-5) from the marketing section of the Gas Research Institute. You are told that it contains all of the information needed for news releases. Write the following releases:
   a. One print release for an oil and gas trade industry journal that goes to all industry employees, including clerical help.
   b. One print release for the oil and gas pages (or business) of area newspapers.
   c. One print release for a weekly area business journal.

3. Assume you are preparing to write copy for an ad for Ourbank. The ad will appear in the newspaper and it will emphasize some fairly complex information about Ourbank. You are considering the use of these terms and phrases in the copy: *bank calls, demand deposits, time deposits, debt-to-equity ratio* and *statistically significant at <.05.* Don't write the copy but rather write a simple explanation of each of these terms and phrases and give them to your instructor.

Notes

[1] Albert Einstein, "On the Electrodynamics of Moving Bodies," *Annalen der Physik* 17 (1905): 891–929, reprinted in *The Principle of Relativity*, trans. W. Perrett and G. B. Jeffrey (New York: Dover, 1952), p. 39.

[2] Rudolf Flesch, *The Art of Plain Talk* (New York: Collier Books, 1962), pp. 158, 162.

[3] William Zinsser, *On Writing Well*, 2nd ed. (New York: Harper & Row, 1980), p. 114.

[4] *Public Relations Journal*, "Hacking Through the Paper Jungle" (August 1981): 26.

[5] Isaac Asimov, *Opus 100* (Boston: Houghton Mifflin, 1969), pp. 89–90.

[6] *New York Times*, August 28, 1979. © 1979 by The New York Times Company. Reprinted with permission.

[7] Bruce Brown, "Shedding Light on the Aurora," *National Wildlife* (February-March 1985): 51. Copyright 1985 by the National Wildlife Federation. Reprinted with permission.

Technical Release
Source: Reprinted with permission of the Gas Research Institute.

Gas Research Institute — October 1984

TECHNOLOGY PROFILE

Advanced Four-Burner Cooktop

Problem

Natural gas is now used for cooking in approximately 45% of the homes in the United States. In a conventional range, less than half of the air used for combustion is mixed with natural gas in the burner. The flame must draw extra air from the room when it is ignited, and combustion is completed above the burner. Because of this, present residential cooktop burners typically operate at efficiencies of 45%. Improved efficiencies and lowered emissions could be gained through the use of advanced burner technologies.

GRI Solution

GRI is supporting Thermo Electron Corporation in the development of an infrared jet-impingement cooktop burner. The advanced burner retains all the operating characteristics and marketable features of conventional gas cooktop burners, but improves efficiencies while reducing the products of combustion.

Benefits

The new burner has achieved a 50% improvement in fuel-use efficiency while significantly reducing NO_x emissions. Because the burner's fuel use is cut from 9000 Btu per hour to 6000 Btu per hour, almost 65% less unused heat will be released in the cooking process, resulting in a cooler kitchen. In addition, the burner provides more uniform heating across the bottom of cooking vessels.

Concept

In the infrared jet-impingement burner, the radiant and convective energy together transmit almost 75% of the heat available for cooking. As in all infrared burners, combustion occurs within or just above a one-half inch thick perforated flat ceramic tile. The tile is heated to about 1500°F and glows bright red, transmitting approximately 95% of its radiant energy. The high-temperature combustion products are then propelled by jets of air (jet impingement) through a high-temperature perforated glass plate to deliver the burner's convective energy to the bottom of the cooking vessel.

Project Status

In laboratory testing, a prototype of the infrared jet burner has achieved a 67% fuel-use efficiency and a turndown ratio of three-to-one. Because cooktop burners must supply widely varying heat levels, additional work on improving the burner's turndown ratio is continuing, with the project goal set for eight-to-one.

Caloric Corporation, the participating manufacturer in the project, has provided seven 30-inch freestanding ranges that have been modified by Thermo Electron for use in the six-month field test which began in July. The seven units have two standard burners and two infrared jet burners. Four of the prototypes have been placed in homes, and the remaining three have been placed with Thermo Electron and Caloric for extensive laboratory analysis.

Prospectus

The field test units will be monitored for energy consumption, emission concentrations, performance, reliability, and consumer response. Consumer response will be sought in the areas of improved comfort, uniformity of heating, appearance, turndown, and simmer performance. The units will be inspected and serviced at selected intervals.

GRI expects the advanced four-burner cooktop technology to be available for commercialization in mid-1985.

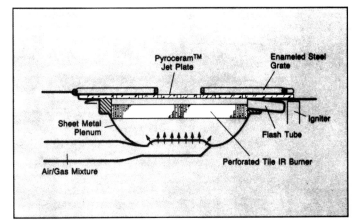

The new burner has achieved a 50% improvement in fuel-use efficiency.

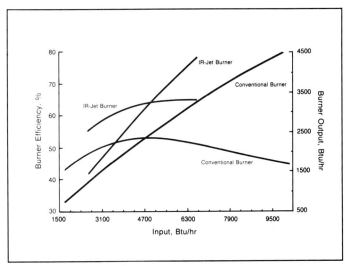

IR-jet burner performance.*

Selected Bibliography

Rudolph Flesch, *The Art of Plain Talk* (New York: Collier Books, 1962).

Rudolph Flesch, *The Art of Readable Writing*, 25th anniversary ed. (New York: Harper & Row, 1974).

Robert Gunning, *The Technique of Clear Writing*, rev. ed. (New York: McGraw-Hill, 1968).

William Zinsser, *On Writing Well*, 2nd ed. (New York: Harper & Row, 1980).

6
Grammar, Spelling, Punctuation

In the days when cigarette companies were allowed to advertise on TV, Winston produced a commercial that raised the hackles of grammarians across the country. The offending sentence: "Winston tastes good like a cigarette should."

English teachers howled. *Like* is a preposition, not a conjunction, they proclaimed. The correct way to express the thought is: "Winston tastes good as a cigarette should."

Later, Winston came out with a series of ads that took advantage of the grammarians' criticism. "What do you want," the new ads asked, "good grammar or good taste?"

PR writers might ask a similar question: "What do you want, good grammar or good writing?" The two are not the same. And despite what the grammar experts might say, you can't always have both.

"Language is for communicating," writes direct-mail expert Luther Brock. "Words are simply a means of expressing one's self and, in our business, of convincing people to do business with us."[1] Writing grammatically correct prose, he points out, isn't always the best way to communicate.

"Unfortunately," writes Brock, "traditionally correct language is dishwater-dull. Why? Because it is not a reflection of the way most people talk. And talk-language just about always outsells grammar-book language."[2] As Brock indicates, the purpose of writing is to get a message across to a reader. In many respects the rules of grammar help achieve that end. But sometimes they get in the way. When they do, the experienced writer may ignore them.

That doesn't mean you shouldn't bother to learn the rules, or that you shouldn't obey them most of the time.

But you should keep the rules in perspective. "Rules," says Robert Gunning, "are substitutes for thought."[3] That's true, but they still can be useful. In many cases it's easier to follow a rule than to waste a lot of time thinking. However, when it comes to making decisions about writing readable prose, rules are *no* substitute for thought.

Take the "like" versus "as" case. One of the main principles of good writing, says Gunning, is to "write like you talk." A lot of English teachers part company with Gunning here, some simply because the rules of grammar dictate that "write *as* you talk" is the proper way to state the principle. But Gunning responds with three good reasons for using *like* instead of *as*.[4] First, good writers have always used *like* as a conjunction (Norman Mailer, for a modern example, or John Keats if you prefer the old-timers). Second, "write as you talk" breaks the rule as it states it. When speaking, people say "write like you talk"—and everybody knows what they mean. That brings us to the third point, which is that "write as you talk" has two possible meanings. It can mean "write the same way you talk" or "write while you are talking." But this is ambiguous, and ambiguity, of course, is one of the worst of all possible writing sins.

Ambiguity and Grammar

Avoiding ambiguity is the main reason grammar exists. Many grammar rules help us keep the meaning clear. Dangling participles, for examples, are condemned by grammarians, and they should be—they can obscure the meaning of the sentence. (Sometimes a dangling participle sounds so silly that the true meaning is obvious, but in those cases the sentence is awkward and should be rewritten.)

That Versus Which

The common misuse of *that* and *which* is an example of how bad grammar can tangle meaning. Using *that* and *which* correctly is important, for it involves questions of both ambiguity and naturalness. In speaking, *that* comes more naturally. "I picked up the books *that* were on the table; where are the keys *that* I left on the shelf?" In writing, for some mysterious reason, people feel compelled to use *which*. "Attached are the copies *which* I promised to send you."

Rudolf Flesch, in *The Art of Readable Writing*, explains at great length why *that* is better in such cases.[5] His discussion is worth looking up and reading. Not only is *that* the more natural word, Flesch points out, but it prevents confusion about the meaning of the sentence. In the above examples the clauses beginning with *that* are restrictive; *which* should not be used to introduce a restrictive clause. When you say, "Bring me the books *that* are on the table," you want *only* the books on the table, none of the other books nearby. The clause is restrictive. When you say "Bring the books, *which* are on the table," you're not restricting the books, you're simply telling where they are. The comma is the clue (see p. 104). If the sentence reads correctly without the comma, you should use *that* instead of *which*. (In fact, try to avoid *which* clauses altogether. Clauses with commas slow readers down.)

Subject-Verb Agreement

Another rule that aids clarity is that the subject and verb in a sentence must agree. Subject-verb agreement helps us avoid confusion over who's doing what. There is a difference, for example, between "Growing vegetables is interesting" and "Growing vegetables are interesting."

Furthermore, merely misidentifying the subject is no excuse to break the rule. A headline in a major newspaper once said, "Workings of the SEC no longer is so mysterious." The subject is workings, not SEC; the verb should be *are* and not *is*. There is no excuse for making the mistake in less obvious cases either, as in "The general, along with his men, are marching tomorrow." The subject here is singular; the additional phrase does not make it plural. The corrected sentence reads "The general, along with his men, is marching tomorrow." If that sounds awkward, simply say "The general and his men are marching tomorrow."

Like any other rule, this one is no substitute for thought. When you write, "The data you need are on page 17," you are going out of your way to show that you know there is such a thing as a "datum." Most people would say "The data *is* on page 17," and there's no good reason not to. Your meaning will still be clear. *

The plain fact is that in modern American usage *data* can be construed either as a singular collective noun or as a plural. The *AP Stylebook* points out that in a sentence like "The data is sound," *data* clearly refers to a collective unit, and not to the individual bits of information that collectively make up the *data*. If you want to emphasize the individual entities in a collection of data, of course, it is correct (grammatically) to write "the data are."

Another awkward case of subject-verb agreement is the ubiquitous *none is*, which grates on the eardrums like a squeaky piece of chalk. "None of the boats is going out to sea today" sounds silly. Always using a singular verb after

---

*There is considerable difference of opinion on the propriety of using *data* with a singular verb. Wilson Follett's usage manual (published in 1966) says there's no reason not to use the plural verb with *data*. W. H. Fowler's *Modern English Usage* says data is often treated as a singular in the United States. Theodore Bernstein calls the use of *data* as a singular a "solecism," and points out that nobody tries to make it plural by way of *datas*. The *Harper Dictionary of Contemporary Usage*'s panel of experts, however, splits nearly 50–50 on the question of *data* as a singular.

none—no matter what the rest of the sentence says—is nonsense. Furthermore, any legitimate dictionary or usage manual says so. More often than not, the sense of *none* is plural. Theodore Bernstein, in *The Careful Writer*, says that the rule to follow is "Consider *none* to be plural unless there is a definite reason to regard it as a singular."[6] For example, when *none* is followed by a prepositional phrase with a singular object, the singular verb sounds better. "None of the cakes has been eaten" sounds awkward.

Myths of Grammar

Why do most people think *none* is singular and should always be followed by *is* or some other equally out-of-place singular verb? Even the *Oxford English Dictionary* says *none* is usually plural. Well, at some time in the ancient past a grammar teacher decided that *none* meant "not one" and that it should be singular. That teacher passed it on to a student who became a teacher who passed it on to another student and so on. And all of these teachers were steadfastly devoted to the cause of rules as substitutes for thought. These are the teachers who, as Rudolf Flesch puts it, "tell students from grade school through college that they'd better learn not to write 'it's me' and never split an infinitive; or they'll get shunned by society in later life and never get a decent job."[7]

Some of these grammar "pitfalls" are important; others are merely grammar myths. The old *it's me* or *it's I* question, for example, isn't worth the time it takes to quibble. Almost everybody uses *it's me* these days, and most experts accept it, even though a predicate nominative is supposed to use the subject form of the pronoun. Another contraction you hear is, "aren't I." Literally it is "are not I." This is still not generally accepted.

Also, few good writers would say "between you and I." This is not only grammatically wrong but, worse, it is stilted and unnatural. In this case the correct form is also the most natural one: "between you and me." The same is true for the common misuses of *myself* when *me* is the right word. "He sent a message to John and myself" is a self-conscious and awkward way of avoiding the use of *me*. *Myself* should be reserved for intensive or reflexive use, as in "I hurt myself" or "I myself will do it."

Split Infinitives

As for split infinitives, every good writer knows that infinitives should sometimes be split. Let the situation be your guide. If avoiding a split infinitive makes a sentence awkward, go ahead and chop the infinitive in two and get on with writing the story. Consider E. B. White's observation in *The Elements of Style*:

> The split infinitive is another trick of rhetoric in which the ear must be quicker than the handbook. Some infinitives seem to im-

prove on being split, just as a stick of round stovewood does."I cannot bring myself to really like the fellow." The sentence is relaxed, the meaning is clear, the violation is harmless and scarcely perceptible. Put the other way, the sentence becomes stiff, needlessly formal. A matter of ear.[8]

Keep in mind, though, that split infinitives sometimes cause confusion, especially if the insertion of several words turns the split into a gorge. "He wanted to quickly, skillfully, and perhaps even artistically complete the project" is widening the split a bit too far. Remember, clarity is the goal.

Sentence-Ending Prepositions

The split infinitive taboo originated with the fact that Latin infinitives are single words and thus can't be split. The same archaic logic led to the myth that you should never end a sentence with a preposition. Some people who remember nothing else at all from their grammar school days remember this "rule." But, in fact, this is just another example of somebody learning grammar from Latin in the Middle Ages and passing it down through the centuries until everybody says it's so but nobody knows why. In Latin it's very difficult to end a sentence with a preposition. Why allow English to do something denied in Latin?

Fortunately, some noteworthy language experts have ridiculed this rule to the point where few people still follow it. To writers, Winston Churchill's most famous line was not about blood and tears and sweat but about the rule against sentence-ending prepositions being nonsense "up with which I will not put." Nowadays, almost all usage manuals repudiate the "rule."

Using Usage Manuals

Once writers realize they are free from the chains imposed by grammar rules, some go off the deep end. If rules are made to be broken, why follow any of them? Well, not all rules should be broken. *Rules should be broken only when, by doing so, you can make the writing clearer, more natural, and easier to understand.* Feel free to dismiss the pedantry of critics who rank split infinitives on the same plane with arson or manslaughter. But do strive to use the language carefully and accurately.

It is no pedantry, for example, to insist that words be used in keeping with their proper meanings. *Allusion* is not the same as *illusion*, for example, and *imply* and *infer* are not interchangeable. *Parameters* are not *perimeters*, either. Countless other words are misused simply because they sound like others (see Table 6-1).

Many writers scoff at such criticism, saying, "The reader will know what I mean. Lots of people use the word that way." If you adopt this philosophy, you put yourself in the position of confusing the members of your audience who *do*

6-1

Commonly Confused Words
Here is a list of words commonly confused for each other. If
you don't understand the differences between the members of
each pair, consult a usage manual, the *AP Stylebook*, or *Words
Into Type* (see the bibliography on p. 109).

absorb, adsorb
adapt, adopt
adhesion, cohesion
affect, effect
all ready, already
allusion, illusion
apparently, obviously
appraise, apprise
arbitrate, mediate
baited, bated
canvas, canvass
cement, concrete
comprise, compose
continual, continuous
discreet, discrete
disinterested, uninterested
dual, duel
flaunt, flout
fortuitous, fortunate
imply, infer
principal, principle
compliment, complement
induction, deduction
naval, navel
pastor, minister
peddle, pedal
pore, pour
rebut, refute
rein, reign
stationary, stationery

know the correct meanings of words. The intelligent reader is left to wonder if the
writer is using this word correctly, in which case it means something else. Using
words imprecisely can lead to such ambiguity. Choose words carefully.

Even some grammar "rules" deserve a little thought before they are
rejected or accepted. Any given rule can be good for some situations—possibly even

most situations—though bad for others. How can you decide when to follow a rule and when not to? You must decide, of course, but it never hurts to get some advice. Check a few basic reference books. Besides a dictionary and a standard grammar handbook, you should have at least two language-usage manuals that discuss points of grammar and usage in depth. Such manuals analyze many of the tricky usage questions that writers stumble across.

Fowler's *Modern English Usage* is regarded by some as the ultimate authority and is perhaps the most respected of all usage manuals. But it is oriented more to English (as in England) than American English. Margaret Nicholson has "Americanized" Fowler, and her *Dictionary of American-English Usage* is available in paperback.* Another "American" manual is Wilson Follett's *Modern American Usage*. Bernstein's *The Careful Writer* is useful, and the AP and UPI stylebooks are valuable if you're writing news releases for newspapers.

Except for the wire service stylebooks, though, these other references are all more than a decade old and sometimes don't reflect the latest trends in usage. So you might want to consult a more recent manual, like the *Harper Dictionary of Contemporary Usage*. Strunk and White's *Elements of Style* was updated in 1979 (third edition), and although it is less comprehensive than the others mentioned, it is highly respected.

When you read over some of these manuals you'll find that usage rules aren't as restrictive as you've been taught. You'll be surprised to see what some language "purists" like Fowler and Follett have to say about split infinitives, for example. You'll also, no doubt, run across subtle but important usage matters that have escaped your attention until now.

Perhaps the most important lesson you'll learn from reading usage manuals is that there is considerable disagreement among the "experts" over what should or should not be allowed. The *Harper Dictionary* is especially instructive in this respect, for its editors made extensive use of a panel of 136 usage authorities, including many famous writers, editors and broadcasters.[9] The editors asked the panel to vote on various usage questions. The results appear in the manual along with selected comments from the panel members. For example, 80 percent of the panel members said they had no objection to using a preposition at the end of a sentence. (The surprising thing is that 20 percent did object.) As for *data*, the panel split down the middle—49 percent saw nothing wrong with *data is*, while 51 percent opposed that usage.

So don't let anybody tell you there is always a right and a wrong where grammar and usage are concerned. Gather some opinions, think about each problem and then make up your own mind. Just be sure that when you break a rule, you break it for a reason, and not because you didn't know.

---

* It is based on the first edition of Fowler (1926), however, and is somewhat dated.

Spelling

Rules of usage and grammar are largely a matter of sense and style. The important thing is expressing a thought clearly. The rules should serve that end.

Spelling, on the other hand, is largely a matter of convention. Sometimes a slight misspelling actually changes one word into another, and meaning can become confused. So it's a good idea to have a standard English dictionary around and follow the spellings it gives. If the dictionary gives two spellings, establish a rule and use it consistently—such as always using the first spelling given. *

Who cares about spelling? Well, the people who hire PR writers for one, so if you want a job, you'll take spelling seriously. There's no excuse for *not* spelling correctly. Just keep a dictionary within arm's length whenever you're writing. If you're not *absolutely certain* that a word is spelled correctly, look it up.

Face it. If your prose is riddled with spelling errors, your readers just might conclude that your facts are also suspect. (They might also conclude that you're not too bright.) Therefore, why should they believe what you've written or even read it at all? It's little consolation to say that most readers won't catch the spelling errors. Then only the educated people will think you're wrong.

Spelling errors do crop up now and again, even in prestigious publications. You can make every effort to eradicate mistakes, and some day a spelling error will appear in one of your finished products anyway. That's not a reason to be less diligent in your efforts. If you operate with the attitude that "just one error" isn't so bad, you'll end up with many. The old saying about "to err is human" should be applied as consolation only after the fact, not as a license ahead of time to make mistakes.

Sometimes mistakes result not from lack of diligence, but from overconfidence. Some people spell well, and spell so well that they're sure they can spot any spelling mistakes. Thus, they don't look up the words they should. To avoid such overconfidence, good writers and editors should occasionally test themselves on lists of commonly misspelled words. Even good spellers will find some surprises. The list that follows contains several misspelled words. Test yourself by counting the number of words that are spelled *correctly* in the list that follows. Most word-processing systems have spelling check capabilities. The only problem with relying on spelling check systems entirely is that if, for example, you have used *there* instead of *their*, the system will not find the error. The system will only find words that are misspelled as *thier* for *their*.

---

*The first spelling given is not necessarily always the preferred spelling. *Webster's New Collegiate*, for example, connects equal spelling variants with *or*, as in "peddler *or* pedlar." In these cases neither spelling is preferred; you must choose one and stick to it. If the spellings are connected by *also*, the second spelling is considered less common. Sometimes words connected by *or* are given in reverse alphabetical order; this indicates that the first spelling is slightly more common, though the second is equally correct. When writing news releases, be sure to follow the AP or UPI stylebook spelling rules.

6-2

Spelling Relief
Source: By permission of Johnny Hart and News America Syndicate.

badmitton

sacreligious

chaufeur

diarhea

embarass

Farenheit

flourescent

barbiturates

limosine

corollary

wierd

cemetary

mispelling

innoculate

pantomine

inocuous

perogative

excell

preceed

procede

comittee

comission

priviledge

knowledgable

sieze

satelite

If you counted two correct, you're right. Only *barbiturates* and *corol-lary* are spelled correctly. The rest are wrong.

If you knew that without any help, you're a pretty good speller and should have no trouble with the following test. Read the passage and circle the words that are spelled *incorrectly.* Assume that the piece is part of a feature story that is to appear in a newspaper, and follow AP or UPI stylebook spelling rules.

The scientists could not reach a concensus. One physicist argued that his experiments superceded earlier findings.

Beseiged by numerous complaints, the director of the labratory devised a stratagy to accomodate the researchers. He alotted each one 15 minutes to speak. One said everyone had benefitted from the experiments on liquefcation of nitrogen, but he saw no correllation between those results and the experiments on parafin.

"It would take a whole battallion of scientists to solve this dilemna," another scientist said. "We do high calibre work, but when you liquefy a miniscule amount of gas, there's no way to avoid all possible arguements about the results." Another suggested that a questionaire should be drawn up and sent out. "If we could get them all filled out, that would be quite an achievment," he said.

"That's an inovative idea," said the physicist. "I'd like to save my copy of the form as a memento of this occassion."

You should have circled 20 words. If you didn't find them all, a trip to the dictionary (or perhaps the AP stylebook) is in order. By the way, some dictionaries accept *bene-fitted,* but AP allows *benefited* only. Some dictionaries also accept *liquify.*

Punctuation

While grammar is mostly a matter of making meanings clear, and spelling is basi-cally a matter of convention, punctuation is a little of both. True, proper punctua-tion is usually just a matter of following the rules. But the underlying purpose of punctuation is to help make the meaning clear, and subtle changes in punctuation *can* change the meaning of a sentence. For example, the sentence "Woman without her man is an animal" can be punctuated "Woman—without her, man is an animal." Liz Carpenter, former press secretary to Lady Bird Johnson, likes to have people punctuate this sentence as a test for sexism.

Most reputable publications follow a fairly rigorous set of punctuation rules and apply them consistently. The virtue of consistency is simply that readers can pay attention to the message without being bothered by changes in the manner of punctuation. Sentences, for example, usually end with periods. Readers know this, and they don't have to think about it. They know that if a writer ends a sentence with some other mark, it is an intentional act to tell the reader something—as when a question mark is used to indicate a question.

Inconsistent punctuation calls attention to itself. Anything that calls attention to itself takes attention away from the message, and that hinders communication. When you're trying to communicate, there's no excuse for anything that will distract the reader, however slightly.

Sometimes punctuation conventions defy logic, but these conventions are so entrenched that violators expose themselves immediately as amateurs. The prime example involves the use of periods and commas with quotation marks. Whenever a period or comma follows a quotation, it is placed *inside* the closing quotation marks. Always. Without exception (at least in the United States). It doesn't matter whether the quote is a complete sentence or a title or a single word. For example:

John's article, called "The Hands of Time," is well written.

I didn't know he wrote an article called "The Hands of Time."

The rule still applies if single quotes are used inside double quotes:

He said he "wrote an article called 'The Hands of Time.'"

Other punctuation, like question marks or exclamation points, are placed according to the sense of the sentence:

Did he write an article called "The Hands of Time"?

He asked John, "What is the title of your article?"

If this seems trivial, it is. But many PR writers are their own editors. If you want your material punctuated correctly, you need to know the rules. And in the case of this particular rule, there is nothing to be gained by breaking it. It is followed uniformly (in the United States), and departures from the convention call attention to themselves.

There are many other punctuation rules where convention is not as binding. Often standard "rules" should be broken to make the reading easier or to make the meaning clear. People are taught in school, for example, to place commas before direct quotations, as in

John said, "What's going on here?"

Sometimes the comma is an intrusion, however, and can be dropped with no confusion:

"What did he say?" He said "Let's go!"

Not all rules should be so casually violated. Some are important for keeping the meaning clear; most rules of this type involve the comma.

There are dozens of rules regarding commas, and it doesn't hurt to know them. Most help keep sentences clear and prevent readers from stumbling over tricky passages or linking clauses to wrong elements. In general, comma rules are helpful.

Some writers overdo their use of commas, though, and stick one in wherever they can. Too many commas clog up the works, and make for slow reading. It's a better practice to use commas only when they are necessary to avoid confusion.

Avoiding confusion is the main reason for the careful use of commas with nonrestrictive clauses, for example. Restrictive clauses, which are necessary to make the meaning of a sentence clear, are not set off by commas. Consider these examples:

Restrictive clauses, which are needed for clarity, are not set off by commas.

All restrictive clauses are needed for clarity. Thus, the "which are needed" clause is merely explanatory and is not essential for the meaning of the sentence. It is a *nonrestrictive* clause and is set off by commas.

Not all clauses are needed for clarity. But the "that are needed" clause is essential to the meaning of the sentence—it *restricts* the types of clauses under consideration. It is therefore a *restrictive* clause and is not set off by commas.

Restrictive and nonrestrictive clauses are also called essential and nonessential clauses. They don't always use *that* and *which*. *Who* can be restrictive or nonrestrictive, and that makes proper punctuation all the more important. Consider these examples from the AP Stylebook:

Reporters, who do not read the stylebook, should not criticize their editors.

Reporters who do not read the stylebook should not criticize their editors.

The first sentence says that reporters—all reporters—do not read the stylebook. Therefore, they shouldn't criticize their editors. The second sentence says that some reporters—those who don't read the stylebook—shouldn't criticize their editors. There's a big difference.

Another comma error that can make sentences unclear involves appositives. An appositive is a phrase that stands for a noun and bears the same relationship to the rest of the sentence that the noun does. Example:

> Joe Smith, the captain of the football team, signed a contract
> today.

The appositive following "Joe Smith" is set off by commas. Note that the comma after *team* is essential. "Joe Smith, the captain of the football team signed a contract today" reads as though someone were telling Joe Smith (whoever he is) that the captain of the football team signed a contract.

Don't set off short titles with commas, however. "Team captain Joe Smith signed a contract" is perfectly correct. "Team captain, Joe Smith, signed a contract" is not. A similar problem sometimes comes up with restrictive appositives, when a descriptive phrase is needed for full meaning. "The American League baseball players, Rick Manning, Jim Rice, and Carl Yastrzemski, are outfielders" is not properly punctuated. This sentence makes them the only players in the American League. Omit the commas after *players* and Yastrzemski and the sentence is correct. Avoid too many related mistakes, such as the one made by a textbook author who wrote "In his novel, *The Deer Park*, Norman Mailer describes . . . ." There should be no comma after *novel*—Mailer has written more than one.

Many other punctuation rules are equally important, and it's impossible to cover all of them in a single chapter. Any conscientious writer takes punctuation seriously, though, and consults books like the *AP Stylebook* and *Words Into Type* for help on the fine points.

Of course, experts sometimes disagree about proper punctuation. Don't think that every rule should be followed in every instance. But make sure you know the rules. And when you break one, know why.

Conclusions

* Grammar, spelling and punctuation are important—not as ends in themselves, but as aids to clear communication.

* The PR writer's chief aim is to communicate, and following the rules of grammar and usage usually facilitates that task.

* Correct grammar and punctuation help to eliminate ambiguity.

* Consistent punctuation and spelling help direct the readers' full attention to the message, not to the mechanics.

* Occasionally, strict interpretation of grammar rules might result in awkward or confusing writing.

* In those cases, PR writers should ensure clarity even at the expense of traditional grammar rules. But such a step should never be taken lightly. You should know why the rule exists and why it should be broken in a particular situation.

* Conscientious writers take all construction seriously and consult reference books to be sure their decisions are well founded.

Exercises

1. Test your understanding of some basic punctuation principles by choosing the correct sentences from the list below. You might want to consult a handbook like *Words Into Type* or the *AP Stylebook* on some of these. Answers follow.

   1) a. Buy a case of Dr Pepper today.
      b. Buy a case of Dr. Pepper today.
   2) a. I wondered why he asked me, "Where have you been?".
      b. I wondered why he asked me, "Where have you been?"
   3) a. Have you ever asked "What should I do?"?
      b. Have you ever asked "What should I do?"
      c. Have you ever asked "What should I do"?
   4) a. She asked, "Who played the lead role in *Hello, Dolly!?*".
      b. She asked, "Who played the lead role in *Hello, Dolly!?*"
      c. She asked, "Who played the lead role in *Hello, Dolly!*"
   5) a. She asked, "Who wrote the words to 'The Star-Spangled Banner'?"
      b. She asked, "Who wrote the words to 'The Star-Spangled Banner'"?
   6) a. Have you ever exclaimed "My God!"?
      b. Have you ever exclaimed "My, God!"
      c. Have you ever exclaimed "My God!?"
   7) a. First, call your doctor. (If you don't have a family doctor, call the local health clinic.)
      b. First, call your doctor. (If you don't have a family doctor, call the local health clinic).
   8) a. First, call your doctor (if you have one.)
      b. First, call your doctor (if you have one).
   9) a. What should I do? he asked himself.
      b. What should I do, he asked himself.
      c. What should I do, he asked himself?
   10) a. "Will you come into my office?" he asked demandingly.
       b. "Will you come into my office," he asked demandingly.
   11) a. "Did you see that catch!?," I asked.
       b. "Did you see that catch!," I asked.
       c. "Did you see that catch!" I asked.
       d. None of the above.
   12) a. John Smith, author of "What's in a Name?," will arrive soon.
       b. John Smith, author of "What's in a Name?", will arrive soon.
       c. John Smith author of "What's in a Name?" will arrive soon.
   13) a. John Smith, state representative from Fort Worth, resigned.
       b. John Smith, state representative from Fort Worth resigned.
   14) a. State representative, John Smith, resigned from his job today.
       b. State representative John Smith, resigned from his job today.
       c. State representative John Smith resigned from his job today.

15) a. He didn't shout "Halt, thief!"; I did.
    b. He didn't shout "Halt, thief!;" I did.
16) a. Have you ever said, "Let's go for a walk."?
    b. Have you ever said, "Let's go for a walk"?
17) a. We can go to the beach, if it doesn't rain.
    b. We can go to the beach if it doesn't rain.
18) a. The spinning turbine is attached to a generator, which turns conductors in a magnetic field to generate current.
    b. The spinning turbine is attached to a generator which turns conductors in a magnetic field to generate current.

Answers

1) The correct answer is (a). This is a trick question—Dr Pepper is a registered trademark and has no period after the Dr.
2) (b) is correct. The period is not needed; furthermore, periods should never fall outside quotation marks.
3) No easy answer. Logic would seem to dictate the punctuation as in example (a), but in practice three punctuation marks in a row are seldom seen. Experts would say choose which of the questions you most want to emphasize. In this case (b) is probably the best choice.
4) (b) is correct. This is one of those rare cases where three punctuation marks do follow one another. The exclamation mark is part of the title and should not be dropped.
5) (a) is correct. The quotation is the question, so the question mark falls inside the quotation marks.
6) Another tricky one. (c) is wrong, (a) seems logical, but (b) is probably the correct choice to avoid an awkward appearance. The exclamation is more important than the interrogative.
7) (a) is correct. When a complete sentence is enclosed in parentheses, so is the period.
8) (b) is correct. When only part of a sentence is enclosed in parentheses, the period falls outside.
9) (a) is correct.
10) (b) is correct. While the sentence is phrased as an interrogative, there is no question—it is more a command than a request.
11) (c) is probably the best way to punctuate this. (a) and (b) are clearly wrong—the comma is not needed. Some might use exclamation and quotation together, but most would pick one.
12) (c) is correct. Commas are not needed in this construction.
13) (a) is correct.
14) (c) is correct.
15) (a) is correct. Semicolons always go outside of quotation marks.

16) (b) is correct.

17) (b) is correct. The "if" clause is essential to the meaning of the main clause. It is therefore a restrictive "if" clause and should not be set off by a comma.

18) (a) is correct. The "which" clause is descriptive, not defining. It merely gives more information about a generator; it does not make a distinction between generators in general and the generator under discussion.

2. Rewrite the following sentences eliminating jargon and needless words to make the resulting sentence clear and concise. Suggested revisions follow.

   a. Johnson supported his side of the issue by saying that contemporary revenue athletics, also known as big money sports, forces athletes to cheat in school because they have no time to study.

   b. As is the case with so many of the wars over the course of time, this war was largely a result of previous wars.

   c. If methods of communication had been comparable to those of the present century, there is little doubt that this war would never have begun.

   d. The interaction of petroleum liquid in aqueous media produces a heterogeneous, layered liquid mixture.

   e. Extent of labor and its propensity to fill time is peculiarly elastic; that is, the more time available for the completion of an assigned task, the longer it takes for the assigned task to be completed.

   f. We have encountered our military adversaries and successfully engaged them, taking control of their nautical vehicles.

   g. Whatever there is that needs to be done, this machine is able to accomplish it.

   h. Financial statements indicate that the company's financial situation was negatively impacted during the preceding twelve months.

Suggested Revisions

These revisions are only suggestions. Many other revisions are possible.

   a. Johnson said big money sports forces athletes to cheat in school because they have no time to study.

   b. As with so many wars, this war was largely a result of previous wars.

   c. If today's communication methods had been available, the war would never have started.

   d. Oil and water don't mix.

   e. Work takes up however much time is available.

   f. We have met the enemy, and they are ours.

   g. This machine can do whatever needs doing.

   h. The company lost money last year.

3. Write a news release from Ourbank that explains how to read and understand a bank call. (*Note to instructor*: Get a copy from the newspaper of the most

recent call of a bank in your community, duplicate it and distribute it to the
class.)

Notes

[1] Luther Brock, "In Direct Mail, Ignore Friends—Pay Attention to What Pays," *Southwest Advertising and Marketing* (December 1975): 20.

[2] Luther Brock, "Two Professionals Disagree on the Need for Purity in Language," *Southwest Advertising and Marketing* (March 1977): 11.

[3] Robert Gunning, *The Technique of Clear Writing* (New York: McGraw-Hill, 1968), p. 265.

[4] Ibid., p. 121.

[5] Rudolf Flesch, *The Art of Readable Writing*, 25th anniversary ed. (New York: Harper & Row, 1974), p. 163.

[6] Theodore Bernstein, *The Careful Writer* (New York: Atheneum, 1965), p. 288.

[7] Flesch, *Art of Readable Writing*, pp. 9–10.

[8] William Strunk and E. B. White, *The Elements of Style*, 3rd ed. (New York: Macmillan, 1979), p. 78.

[9] William Morris and Mary Morris, *Harper Dictionary of Contemporary Usage* (New York: Harper & Row, 1975), p. 166.

Selected Bibliography

Especially for grammar see:

R. Thomas Berner, *Language Skills for Journalists*, 2nd ed. (Boston: Houghton Mifflin, 1984).

Theodore Bernstein, *The Careful Writer* (New York: Atheneum, 1965).

Roy H. Copperud, *American Usage and Style: The Consensus* (New York: Van Nostrand Reinhold, 1980).

William R. Ebbitt and David R. Ebbitt, *Perrin's Index to English*, 6th ed. (Glenview, Ill.: Scott Foresman, 1977).

Wilson Follett, *Modern American Usage* (New York: Grosset & Dunlap, 1966).

H. W. Fowler, *A Dictionary of Modern English Usage*, 2nd ed. (New York: Oxford University Press, 1965).

Lauren Kessler and Duncan McDonald, *When Words Collide: A Journalist's Guide to Grammar and Style* (Belmont, Calif.: Wadsworth, 1984).

Michael Montgomery and John Stratton, *The Writer's Hotline Handbook* (New York: New American Library, 1981).

William Morris and Mary Morris, *Harper Dictionary of Contemporary Usage* (New York: Harper & Row, 1975).

Harry Shaw, *Punctuate It Right* (New York: Barnes and Noble, 1963).

Marjorie E. Skillin and Robert M. Gay, *Words Into Type*, 3rd ed. (Englewood Cliffs, N.J.: Prentice-Hall, 1974).

For newspaper style, see:

Christopher French, Eileen Alt Powell and Howard Angione, eds., *The Associated Press Stylebook and Libel Manual* (New York: Associated Press, 1980).

Bobby Ray Miller, *The UPI Stylebook* (New York: United Press International, 1977).

For readability, see:

Rudolph Flesch, *The Art of Readable Writing*, 25th anniversary edition (New York: Harper & Row, 1974).

Robert Gunning, *The Technique of Clear Writing*, rev. ed. (New York: McGraw-Hill, 1968).

International Association of Business Communicators, *Without Bias: A Guidebook for Non-discriminatory Communication* (New York: John Wiley and Sons, 1982).

William Strunk and E. B. White, *The Elements of Style*, 3rd ed. (New York: Macmillan, 1979).

William Zinsser, *On Writing Well*, 2nd ed. (New York: Harper & Row, 1980).

Part Three

Writing for General Audiences

Writing for "general" audiences requires an understanding of the components of that audience. You must also know the strengths and weaknesses of the media that may be used to reach them.

7
News Releases
for Print Media

The news release is probably the most frequently used tool for getting publicity. It is also frequently *misused* by PR people and often *not used* at all by the media. A business editor for a Texas daily once remarked that burning unused news releases as fuel could solve the energy crisis.

Why are news releases rejected? Most studies cite these reasons as most significant: poor writing, incompleteness, inaccuracy, poor timing and little local or no reader interest. A paper simply doesn't have the space to print all the releases it receives, nor does a magazine. But basically, it gets down to this: Most releases don't get used because the PR people preparing them don't know what they're doing. Many think they do. A recent study of news release quality measured writing, accuracy, completeness and timeliness as perceived by PR practitioners and media gatekeepers. The PR people considered their print and broadcast materials to be better written and sent on a more timely basis than the media representatives did. However, the media representatives rated the releases higher on accuracy and completeness than the PR practitioners rated the media's use of PR releases.[1]

Although some PR practitioners can recount stories of media errors, most editors keep files of releases that demonstrate glaring PR incompetence. One file contains a very nice piece of news release stationery that came to the editor saying "For Immediate Release." That's all it said; the rest of the sheet was blank. One release said "Do not use after Sept. 23." It arrived in the editor's mail on September 25. In another, the name of the firm was spelled one way on the letterhead and a different way in the body of the release. Of course, these examples are a little extreme. Many releases come to newsrooms correctly spelled and punctuated. The names and dates are all where they should be. But they still get thrown away. Why? Because they contain no news.

News

The first responsibility of the PR people preparing news releases is to know what news is. If a release doesn't contain news, it won't get printed. And if it contains valuable news, editors are quite likely to overlook poor writing, typographical errors and other blunders to get the story in the paper. It's essential to know what news is.

What Is News?

Different people have different definitions for news. Textbooks on beginning reporting and articles about the mass media in society construct elaborate definitions of what news is or should be. But for PR people, no esoteric or philosophical definition is necessary. A practical one will do: News is what newspapers print and what radio and TV stations broadcast on their news shows. News is *not* what *you* think it is or what the company president thinks it is. Realizing this will take you a long way toward writing effective news releases.

In the words of well-known PR consultant Philip Lesly,

> **The medium decides absolutely, in most cases, what it will use, when, and in what form. The editorial judgment or attitudes of the editors, however they may differ from those of the publicist and his organization, are the only determinants.**[2]

This is not a new idea. The best PR people have said the same thing for decades. Ivy Lee, one of the pioneers of public relations, once described how corporation executives would call on him to get their ideas printed in the newspaper. "They say you can get a thing on the front page of the newspapers," an executive would tell Lee. He would reply: "I cannot do anything of the kind. If you want a subject to get on the first page of the newspapers, you must have the news in your statement sufficient to warrant it getting the first page."[3]

Furthermore, Lee would point out, what good would it do if the paper *did* print something just because you wanted it to? If a piece has no news value, people probably won't read it. And if people are likely to read it, it *does* have news value. If readers will be interested, an editor will be happy to print it without coercion or tricks.

Finding News

A PR person, then, need not be concerned with thinking up ways to persuade an editor to use a release. If the release is newsworthy, it will be used. As a PR person, your job is to find news and put it in a form that will make the editor's job as easy as possible. To accomplish this, you must do two things. First, become familiar with the newspaper (or TV, radio station or other medium) you'll be sending releases to. In other words, if you want to know what news is, you have to read the papers. You have to watch TV newscasts. You should listen to radio news shows. You'll soon develop a sense for what is accepted as news and what isn't.

The second step is to become familiar with your own company or institution so that you'll be able to find the news within it. Presumably, you will work for an organization that does something worthwhile or that does things the public might find some value in knowing about. If you look around, you'll find things going on in the company that are similar to what the newspapers report about other companies. You'll find people who know things the public would like to know. You'll find research on topics that affect people's lives. You'll find unusual things that are simply interesting in themselves.

Of course, a PR writer's job is to get things into the paper that will benefit the organization. Just looking for things editors consider news, therefore, may not achieve your goals. But there is a broad area where public benefit and private benefit overlap. Generating a greater public understanding of your company and its activities is almost always beneficial, and if in the process the public is entertained and informed, then everyone benefits.

Getting News into Print

Once you find the news within your organization, your next step is to get it to the public through some medium—newspaper, TV, radio or possibly magazine. The news release is the tool most often used to do this.

How do you get your news into the paper? First, here's the wrong way. You *don't* go down to the editor with a story and say, "This is news and if you don't print it I'll cancel my subscription and cancel my advertising." You *do* make sure that what you have is newsworthy. You prepare the information in proper form so that it looks and sounds like news, and you give it to the editor to do with as he or she pleases. If you're right and it is news, the editor will print it. It probably won't appear exactly as you prepared it, but it will be used in some way or other. Example 7-1 shows how releases change form in the hands of an editor. The release is shown with the newspaper version, and the company's own version in an employee publication.

In writing a release, the first concern is newsworthiness. Make sure you're writing about something that is genuine news, not disguised advertising. If your news release is designed only to increase your company's sales without any concern for its value to the public, you're making a mistake. Buy an ad instead. As

7-1a

News Release and Published Version
Source: (a,c) Used with permission of ONEOK Inc.; (b) used
with permission of *The Daily Oklahoman.* © 1983.

December 13, 1983

For Immediate Release

ONEOK Inc. STOCKHOLDERS APPROVE PREFERENCE STOCK

OKLAHOMA CITY -- At their annual meeting today stockholders of
ONEOK Inc. approved the creation of three million shares of a new class of
preference stock. Stockholders also reelected the company's 13 directors.

The stockholders' meeting was held at the Sheraton-Century Center
hotel.

Stockholders were told that the preference stock is needed for
flexibility in future financing, but that "no outside long-term financing is
anticipated for fiscal 1984," according to ONEOK president J. E. Tyree.
"ONEOK Inc. has the strength to generate its own internal financial
requirements for the immediate future," he said.

In other action, stockholders ratified and approved amendments to an
Employee Stock Ownership Plan and an IRS 401(k) savings plan for employees.
Stockholders also voted to ratify and approve the continuing use of Peat,
Marwick, Mitchell & Co. as independent auditor for the corporation.

In his remarks, Tyree said that ONEOK Inc. had survived a "very tough"
fiscal year in 1983 but expects an earnings improvement in 1984.

He said that despite the problems of 1983, "the company continued to
build on a firm foundation and passed some important milestones."

Some of the milestones included reaching a billion dollars in assets
for the first time and finalizing purchase of a new headquarters building in
Tulsa.

Tyree also pointed out that a $43.4 million rate increase granted to
Oklahoma Natural Gas Company would produce a 5 percent increase in annual
revenues for the utility division, which is the most widely recognized
element of ONEOK Inc.

- over -

298-7

7-1a continued

Tyree said that ONEOK's nonutility division should improve its contributions to earnings in 1984. For one thing, he said, first revenues have been received from six offshore Louisiana oil wells in which ONEOK Exploration Company has a 10 percent interest as a partner in a group headed by Transco Energy Company of Houston. Also anticipated is an improvement for ONEOK Drilling Company, which now has seven of its ten rigs active.

"We believe that with or without improved national economic conditions, ONEOK will experience an earnings improvement in 1984," he said. "We also believe that the economy has leveled off and is showing some improvement, but we will continue to seek improvement of our earnings without waiting for an economic upturn." Earnings per share of ONEOK common stock were $2.51 for fiscal 1983, ended last August, versus $4.88 a year earlier.

"If the economic turnaround that we all hope for does come," Tyree concluded, "you may be assured we are extremely well positioned to take advantage of it."

The company's 12,434,635 shares of common stock eligible for voting at the annual meeting are owned by nearly 20,000 shareholders. Slightly more than 800 shareholders own the 180,000 outstanding shares of preferred stock. Common is traded on the New York and Midwest Stock Exchanges; preferred is traded over-the-counter.

#   #   #

For further information contact: Walt Radmilovich, Ed Wheeler, or Charlene Bassett, Oklahoma Natural Gas Company, P. O. Box 871, Tulsa, OK 74102, Phone (918) 583-6161.

298-7

7-1b

ONEOK Survives Tough Year, Things Looking Better for 1984

By Mary Jo Nelson

Despite a very tough fiscal year, ONEOK Inc. not only survived 1983 but is sound enough that its president and chief executive officer predicts no longterm outside financing will be needed next year.

ONEOK netted $30.8 million last year, down more than $25 million from the previous year's earnings of $56 million. Total operating revenues for the year were $1,058,838,000, down by $60.4 million from the previous year's $1,119,321,000.

Earnings for the year were $2.51 per share of common stock, compared to $4.88 the year before.

J. E. "Jim" Tyree, the chief executive, told to shareholders Tuesday, "We believe ONEOK has the strength to generate its own internal financial requirements."

Tyree's report came during the annual shareholders' meeting. It drew no more than a handful of investors in the holding company for Oklahoma Natural Gas Co. and Energy Companies of ONEOK.

Without opposition, ONEOK's 13 directors were re-elected to new terms on the board. Besides Tyree, they are C. C. Ingram, board chairman; J. D. Scott, president of ONG; Oral Roberts, Tulsa; W. M. Bell, Stanton L. Young and Dr. G. Rainey Williams, all of Oklahoma City; W. L. Ford, Shawnee; J. H. Glasser, Enid; A. G. Hays, Muskogee; J. A. McNeese, Ponca City; F. B. Muhlfeld, New York, and Dr. Douglas Ann Newsom, Fort Worth.

ONEOK relied on general improvement in drilling activity throughout the industry as "an encouraging sign," and Tyree said the key to success next year will be cost control paired with new, aggressive marketing.

ONEOK Drilling Co. now has seven active rigs, compared to none a year ago; a potential income of $7.6 million a year was reported from 133 completed wells that are shut in awaiting better market conditions, and ONEOK Exploration is shifting to oil production rather than natural gas, for which there is no market.

But if things look better for 1984, they were not easy this year, Tyree said.

"It was a disappointing year in many respects, but contained some future promise. Our company, like all businesses, was severely tested. Despite a drop in earnings, we not only survived a very tough fiscal year, but came out of it strong, lean and flexible," he said.

There were bright spots during 1983, Tyree said. They included acquisition of a new corporate headquarters building in Tulsa and a crucial decision by the Oklahoma Corporation Commission that permits ONG to buy shut-in natural gas and sell it at reduced rates to the state's five fertilizer manufacturers.

Tyree said this decision had kept the factories in business. The fertilizer plants buy about one-third of all gas sold by ONG and their financial collapse was foreseen as a potential disaster.

During 1984, the company plans to reduce its work force through attrition and a hiring freeze, Tyree said. He also foresees favorable settlement of most of the company's "take-or-pay" gas contracts.

At Tuesday's meeting, the shareholders—most of them voting by proxy—approved new plans for employee stock ownership and savings.

7-1c

NEWS LINE

Oklahoma Natural Gas Company, P. O. Box 871, Tulsa, Oklahoma 74102

VOL. XVII NO. XXI   TUESDAY, DECEMBER 27, 1983

Gas Usage Climbs Significantly As Temperatures Plunge

The big chill was the big news last week.

How cold was it?

It was so cold that—

- Our utility customers were using record amounts of gas; a record was set for the 24-hour period ending at 8 a.m. December 22, when 1.8 billion cubic feet of gas was delivered. This gas usage, prompted by sub-zero temperatures, broke the record set just two days earlier when 1.75 billion cubic feet of gas was sold.

- Consequently, customers' bills are going to be sharply higher.

- Oklahoma Natural was receiving all available gas purchases into our system and withdrawing substantial amounts of gas from storage.

- Asked if things were going well and if there were any major problems, Operations Manager *Jim Garrett* replied: "Yes and no. Yes, things are going well, and no, we've had no important problems other than one mishap at Clinton (details below)."

Record-breaking low temperatures, troubles for travelers and holiday shoppers, closed schools, and the prospect of a white Christmas—these were the topics people were thinking about and talking about last week.

Utility Sales Set Record; All Available Gas Being Purchased

Despite record high demand for gas, the Company's supply and delivery system was performing extremely well throughout ONG's territory. The 1,752,400,000 cubic feet of gas sold ONG's utility customers in the 24-hour period ended December 20 compares with 1,677,900,000 cubic feet in the previous 24-hour period, and with 1,675,500,000 on February 10, 1981. The 1981 date was the previous peak day, which still stands when total sales, including off-system pipelines are included. On that date sales totaled 2.02 billion cubic feet of gas. Total sales were 1.97 billion cubic feet on December 18, 1983, and 1.96 billion on December 19, 1983.

Last week gas was being withdrawn at a rate averaging about 875 millon cubic feet a day. By contrast, in the six days before Christmas a year ago gas was being injected into storage at a rate averaging 193 million cubic feet of gas a day. The low temperature in Tulsa on Decmber 23, 1982, was 60° and gas was injected into storage that day—272 million cubic feet. It was cooler Christmas day last year, when 111 million cubic feet of gas was withdrawn.

Gas was being taken from all purchase connections except the high-priced, deep well gas that has been shut in for some time.

Service Personnel Aid Customers With Operating Problems

Extra customer service personnel were on duty in Tulsa and Oklahoma City the cold and snowy weekend of December 17-18. Flurries of customer calls were received because of frozen meters or gas lines, problems with heating systems, etc.

Also, some gas purchase points were frozen off because of the extreme cold. At mid-week 300 million cubic feet of gas daily was not available for purchase because of freezing at wellheads; operators of the wells were trying to get their production back on, reported Gas Control Manager *Kenny Johnson*.

Stockholders Told That Earnings Improvement Is Seen In 1984

After a "very tough fiscal year" the Company expects an earnings improvement for fiscal year 1984. This was the message President and Chief Executive Officer *J. E. Tyree* brought to stockholders December 13 at the Company's annual meeting in Oklahoma City.

He said that despite the problems of 1983, "the Company continued to build on a firm foundation and passed some important milestones."

Some of the milestones included reaching a billion dollars in assets for the first time and finalizing purchase of a new headquarters building in Tulsa.

Tyree also pointed out that a $43.4 million rate increase granted to Oklahoma Natural Gas Company would produce a 5% increase in annual revenues for the utility division.

Tyree said that ONEOK's nonutility division should improve its contributions to earnings in 1984. For one thing, he said, first revenues have been received from six offshore Louisiana oil wells in which ONEOK Exploration Company has a 10% interest as a partner in a group headed by Transco Energy Company of Houston. Also anticipated is an improvement for ONEOK Drilling Company, which now has seven of its ten rigs active.

newspaperman Horace Greeley once said, "When you want an article inserted to subserve some purpose other than the public good, you should offer to pay for it."[4] Example 7-2 is more promotion than news.

Occasionally you'll get an editor to run something as news when an ad is called for. PR counsel Edward L. Bernays observes, "You may often crowd an article in, through an editor's complacency, that you ought to pay for; but he sets you down as a sponge and a sneak forthwith."[5] In the long run, it doesn't pay. Trying to pass off advertising as news simply makes editors angry, and they won't be inclined to treat your news releases favorably in the future. One PR agency even made the horrendous mistake of buying an ad in the city's largest paper while sending the same material as news release to a competing daily. Needless to say, the release wound up in the wastebasket—and so did the next releases from that agency.

How do you know if the release you want to send is newsworthy? There are several easy tests. Ask yourself, Is the information of general interest to readers not connected with your business? Is it about something that affects the lives of the newspapers' readers in some way (especially economically)? Is the substance of your release something unusual, out of the ordinary, or even bizarre? If you can answer yes to any of these questions, your release probably contains legitimate news, even if it also serves your own purposes.

Writing News Releases

How do you write legitimate news? The answer is simple—prepare the material as you would if you were a reporter working for a paper. A news release should be written in the same form and style, following the same punctuation and spelling rules, as the publication you want it to appear in.

If you've ever been a reporter, writing a news release should be as easy as writing a straight news story. If you haven't, you need to know something about the methods of writing news.

Approach

Every reporter has a personal method for approaching a story. But all methods should have the first step in common—identifying the most important thing about the story. In writing a news release the first step is the same. You must answer the question, What's the most important thing I have to say? The answer will determine what you should say in the lead.

Lead The lead—the first paragraph or perhaps the first two—is the most important part of the release. You can't write a good release without a good lead, and you can't write a good lead until you've answered the question about what's important.

Deciding what's important sometimes takes a little judgment. *Important* must be construed broadly. What you really want to isolate is the most signifi-

7-2a

Promotion

This is pre-event publicity to build up interest in the 150th state anniversary *and* a current event, the Great American Train Show. The purpose is to get people to the train show to buy seats on the sesquicentennial express so the antique engine can be maintained. Compare the release (a) with this story (b). *Source:* (a) Used with permission of *The Herald Banner;* (b) used with permission of the *Dallas Morning News.*

```
Ann Faragher
THE HERALD BANNER
P.O. Box 1047
Greenville, TX 75401
214-455-4220
```

The Texas Independence Express will steam its way around Texas during the 1986 Sesquicentennial Celebration, traveling more than 5,000 miles and stopping in 150 cities and towns. And, its backers think it might become a permanent tourist attraction in the state.

The Texas Independence Express is an officially sanctioned project of the Texas 1986 Sesquicentennial Commission and it is headed by a state-wide board of directors to organize, secure funding and direct the steam train excursion.

The Independence Express board is seeking sponsors for the passenger cars at $15,000 each and for the three dining cars at $10,000 each. These fees will help pay the necessary licensing and traffic costs of the train as it travels across the privately owned tracks of various railroad companies in the state.

Dan A. Catania, national director of the Railway and Locomotive Historical Society, was the moving spirit in organizing the Independence Express. He says the private owners of 10 antique passenger cars have offered the use of their rolling stock, all but one of them at no charge for the car.

A tentative budget shows it will take about $2 million to set the Express ready to roll and operate during the spring and fall months of 1986.

The initial fund raising activity to set the project into actual operation is the sale of engraved stock certificates for the Texas Independence Express in issue values of $1,500, $150 and $15. The stock will have no monetary value, though it will entitle the owners to discounts on purchases of tickets or souvenirs from the train, and the purchase price will be a tax deductible gift to a non-profit corporation, Catania said.

The first share of stock in the Texas Independence Express was purchased by Ann Faragher, editor of the Herald Banner and a member of the Express board.

The second purchaser was George Johnson of Greenville who specified he wanted Stock Certificate 13. Johnson is a retired Cottonbelt and Southern Pacific engineer who drove Engine 813 in the days of steam.

Stock certificates may be purchased by making checks payable to the Texas Independence Express and mailing them to P.O. Box 101986, Fair Park, Dallas, Texas 75201-1986.

7-2b

Antique train to chug through Texas for sesquicentennial

By Dale Hudson
Staff Writer of The News

The Texas Independence Express, an antique steam engine and train, will chug through the state next year as part of the official sesquicentennial celebration.

The engine, Texas and Pacific 610, will pull a train of antique rail cars featuring a crew of actors and musicians and a cargo of exhibits and sesquicentennial souvenirs. The crew will portray Texas heroes and pioneers.

The engine, 100 feet long and 16½ feet high, will travel to more than 100 Texas cities, said Dan Catania, a historical preservationist.

The steel engine's black exterior will be trimmed in forest green. A brass bell, red cab and steam whistle will more than announce its arrival, Catania said.

Catania said the engine is driven by 28 wheels and runs on 14,000 gallons of water and 5,000 gallons of oil.

Catania and a group of railway historians plan to get the engine on tracks by February 1986. More than 1.5 million people are expected to board the train during its sesquicentennial run, Catania said.

"Steam trains draw terrific crowds," said Ann Faragher, a member of the Express' board of directors.

Also called the "Texas Eagle," the engine was built in 1927, retired in 1952 and briefly reactivated in 1976.

It is stored at General Services Administration yards on Fort Worth's South Side, Catania said.

Before the engine was retired, it had traveled more than 1.1 million miles, many of them pulling World War II troop trains.

Express board members are raising funds for the journey by selling engraved stock certificates for $1,500, $150 and $15.

"We're seeking corporate and individual sponsors," Catania said.

Express board members will sell the certificates from a booth at the Great American Train Show in the Dallas Convention Center Saturday and Sunday, he said.

Funds from certificates will contribute to a $2 million budget, some of which will go the engine's maintenance, he said.

The 1986 tour will leave from Fort Worth in late February. Stops will include Abilene, El Paso, San Angelo, Del Rio, San Antonio, Austin, Longview, Greenville and Dallas, Catania said.

cant *and* most interesting aspect of your subject. And you have to keep in mind that *news* is what is happening *now*.

For example, if the release is about the opening of a new plant, the most important thing is the fact that the plant is *opening*. The action is the news. But is there something especially interesting about the plant itself? Is it the largest plant of its kind? The first? Will it provide a lot of jobs for the local economy? Once you've decided what's important and also what's interesting, you can write a lead.

The most important thing—in this case the action—should form the main part of the lead: "The plant is opening." The interesting thing about the story provides an "angle" for the lead: "The first plant of its kind is opening," according to X authority.

Sometimes you don't have to look for the most important aspect of the story if, for example, it's the appearance of someone noteworthy. That is your lead. Of course, that might suggest why public relations people planning special events always try to get celebrities there. The appearance of a well-known person becomes the focus for the news release.

Using the most interesting angle in the first sentence may cause you some problems in constructing the traditional newspaper lead, in which the who-what-when-where-why-how all appear in the first paragraph. Traditional leads are still the rule for most wire service stories, because the first paragraph is all some newspapers will use. However, that first sentence can get very long if you try to jam in all the essential elements. The rule is often relaxed, so that only two or three of the traditional elements appear in the first sentence, with the others following in the next sentence or two.

If you're writing a release for a wire service, try to get all of the elements in the first paragraph, or, at most, the first two. When writing for dailies in your area, study the papers' style. Are all the basic questions usually answered in the first paragraph? Or do a paper's staff writers tend more toward the attention-grabbing lead, with the details of time and place following in the next few paragraphs? The style of the papers you write for should determine style.

Naturally, if your lead sentence contains the most important and most interesting elements of your story, it probably already gives the who and what. You can sneak in the when, where and why later—but not too much later. The how usually comes last.

Once you've written a lead, read it over to make sure it does two things: states clearly what the release is about and grabs the reader's interest. In other words, the lead must give a quick indication of what the story is about and why it is important. And it must be interesting—both to catch the eye of the editor and to get the attention of the newspaper reader.

A local angle is essential in capturing the editor's attention. Most newspapers rely on the wire services for non-local news, and a release without a local angle is usually dumped. In fact, some editors cite the lack of a local angle as the single most important reason releases aren't used. Be sure to identify the local angle. Make it clear and get it high in the story, preferably in the lead. If you have no local angle to interest a given newspaper, don't bother mailing the release.

Amplifying the Lead   Once you have a lead that meets all these tests, writing the rest of the release should be easy. Simply amplify each of the elements introduced in the lead, giving all the details. Anticipate the questions that an interested individual might ask about your subject, and answer them in the body of the release.

Write in the style of the newswriter. Use short, concise sentences; short paragraphs; and common, concrete words. Avoid the jargon of your profession. If you must use a technical term, make sure to explain it fully. Above all, avoid editorial comment. Don't try to "sell" something in a news release. A release is not an ad. If a comment is necessary, be sure to enclose it in quotation marks and attribute it to a company executive.

Quotations   When using direct quotations, news-release writers have a great advantage over reporters—they can *create quotes*. A reporter using quotation marks must report exactly what was said. You, however, can take what you've written to the executive you're supposed to be quoting and ask for approval of the words you've attributed to him or her (see Figure 7-3).

Sometimes you won't know what to create for the quote and will have to go directly to the person to see what he or she wants to say. Often the person will scrawl something quickly on a memo pad or ask you to take something from an official statement already prepared on the subject. Such quotes are almost always awkward and lifeless. You will need to recast the words to make them sound like someone said them in conversation. For example, in writing a release about your company's reaction to a new government report, do not write something like this:

> Company President J. T. Person said, "We have not had time to adequately review the contents of the document in its entirety, nor have we ascertained the ultimate position we are likely to take on it, though, at this point in time, it seems not unlikely that we will find the conclusions, and the evidence supporting them, acceptable."

That doesn't sound a bit like spoken English. Instead, write something like this:

> "We haven't read the whole report yet," company executive J. T. Person said, "so we can't take a position now. But from what we've read so far, we think we'll like it."

As you write the release, keep in mind that you know much more about the subject than the editor or reader will. You cannot assume any previous knowledge on the reader's part—even things you are "sure" that "everybody knows." A good rule of thumb, to quote James Marlow, is "Always write for the fellow who *hasn't read yesterday's paper.*"[6]

That doesn't mean you write "down" to the reader. Assume that your readers are intelligent and capable of understanding something if explained in common English. But don't assume that they know anything about your subject to begin with.

7-3

Creating Quotes in an Announcement Release
This story is fairly typical of the form that attributes comments
to an official. This one comes from the PR wire, where copy is
not edited. The writer's creativity was somewhat on the ebb
with the lead sentence: "We are very excited about. . . ." This
is a "so what" quote. When you put words in the mouths of
officials, make them meaningful. The rest of the quote appears
to have come from an official release. The "excited about"
might actually have been real, but it shouldn't have been
used. The idea is to make every word count. Source: Used
with permission of the Datapoint Corporation.

12125812319

GRAND OPENING FOR DATAPOINT SHOWROOM AT INFORMART

SWN 034 FROM SOUTHWEST NEWSWIRE AT 214/748-1943

TO: BUSINESS DESKS

DALLAS, JANUARY 21, 1985--(SWN)--DATAPOINT CORPORATION (NYSE) TODAY
OPENED THE DATAPOINT (R) SHOWROOM AT INFOMART, THE NEW INFORMATION
PROCESSING MARKET SUPPORT CENTER IN DALLAS, TEXAS.

"WE ARE VERY EXCITED ABOUT INFOMART AND THE CONCEPT OF A PERMANENT
COMPUTER TECHNOLOGY SUPPORT CENTER," SAID HAROLD E. O'KELLEY, CHIEF
EXECUTIVE OFFICER. "WE THINK OUR PERMANENT SHOWROOM HERE WILL ENABLE
US TO MORE EFFECTIVELY REACH SPECIFIC TARGET MARKETS. DATAPOINT'S
SHOWROOM WILL INCLUDE ALL OF OUR LATEST PRODUCTS AND IT WILL ALLOW US TO
DEMONSTRATE OUR ARC (R) (ATTACHED RESOURCE COMPUTER(R)) LOCAL AREA
NETWORK. WE LOOK FORWARD TO HELPING BUYERS EVALUATE TECHNOLOGIES AND
FIND SOLUTIONS TO BUSINESS PROBLEMS."

7-3 | continued

THE RECENTLY ANNOUNCED DATAPOINT 3200, A 32-BIT COMPUTER WITH A

UNIX (TM)-LIKE OPERATING SYSTEM, IS CURRENTLY ON DISPLAY ALONG WITH

THE VISTA-PC (TM), THE DATAPOINT PROFESSIONAL COMPUTER. OTHER

CURRENT DATAPOINT PRODUCTS ON DISPLAY INCLUDE THE DATAPOINT LASER

PRINTER, AND THE VISTA-STATION-84(TM) AND VISTA-STATION-82 (TM)

WORKSTATIONS. IN ADDITION, THE DATAPOINT EXHIBIT INCLUDES A

DEMONSTRATION OF THE INTELLIGENT NETWORK EXECUTIVE (TM) LINKING IBM(R)

PCS INTO THE DATAPOINT ARC LOCAL AREA NETWORK. SPACE WILL BE RESERVED

FOR USE BY DATAPOINT ISOS FOR DEMONSTRATIONS OF APPLICATION

SYSTEMS FOR SPECIFIC VERTICAL MARKETS SUCH AS HEALTHCARE, BANKING AND

LEGAL.

DATAPOINT CORPORATION, A FORTUNE 500 INDUSTRIAL FIRM, MANUFACTURES,

MARKETS, AND SERVICES LOCAL AREA NETWORKS, MULTI-FUNCTION WORKSTATIONS,

AND DISPERSED COMPUTING AND OFFICE AUTOMATION SYSTEMS WORLDWIDE.

-0-

UNIX IS A TRADEMARK OF AT&T BELL LABORATORIES.

IBM IS A REGISTRED TRADEMARK OF INTERNATIONAL BUSINESS MACHINES

CORPORATION.

-30-

CONTACT: J. G. MILNE OR T. J. MOLDENHAUER, DATAPOINT, SAN ANTONIO,

512/699-4437.

Length Knowing how to write a release is important. But knowing when to end the release is equally important. If a release is too long, an editor may decide there isn't time to read it, and into the file it will go.

The essential points can usually be covered in one page. Sometimes an important event will call for two or three pages, however, so if you need that much space to cover the subject, use it. But even then, write the release so an editor can chop a few paragraphs off the bottom without damaging the story. (That's especially important for releases going to the wire services.)

Long releases with pages of generally irrelevant material are especially annoying. A common example is the release on an executive's promotion, a subject worth only two or three paragraphs. Frequently, however, such releases give pages of company history and information on the company's chief executive, who did nothing more than announce the promotion.

Keep the release brief, at least in most cases. If you really think more information might be needed—statistics or background, for example—attach a fact sheet to the release. (A fact sheet lists the basic elements of the institution and the event. See Chapter 8 media kit.)

Form and Style

The most important concern in a news release is not length, of course, but making sure your message gets across to the reader. If a subject deserves lengthy treatment, use the necessary space. And if the editor—and the newspaper readers—are to understand what you say, you must write in a clear, understandable way. It does no good to get your release printed if nobody understands what it means.

Unfortunately, most releases are written at a more complex level than the news stories of a typical daily paper (see Example 7-4). Readability expert Robert Gunning notes that the writing in most area papers is about on the level of *Reader's Digest*, whereas releases from business and industry are closer to the level of *Harper's*.[7] Even when people writing the releases are ex-reporters, Gunning observes, the writing is too complex—perhaps because the writers are now writing for bosses who are business executives, not city editors. But you must learn to write for the editors if you write news releases. *Don't* write for your boss. Write your releases for a city editor, just as you would write any news story if you were a reporter.

That doesn't mean you should give the facts in such a way that your story makes your company look bad (as a real reporter might do). But it does mean that you leave out *no* pertinent facts, however embarrassing they might be.

When you write a story, it's not enough to conform to newspaper style in the writing level and basic story structure. You must follow newspaper style to the finest detail, making sure that every comma and period is in the proper place.

For newspapers, this generally means adhering to the Associated Press or United Press International stylebook (the two are virtually identical). Most newspapers follow AP-UPI style, but many have special style rules that you should know. It's a good practice to ask editors for copies of their stylebooks. You can

7-4a

News Releases and Readability

The level of this release (a) is too high even for its sophisticated and specialized audience. Specialized audiences don't like to work any harder than anyone else to read news, although they will if the payoff is high enough. The one for this release isn't. See the edited version (b). The Clearing House release on state taxes (c) is exceptionally well done because it is direct, simple, clear, and comes with its own illustration—a map showing the major source of income for all of the states. *Source:* (a) Used with permission of the Gas Research Institute; (c) used with permission of the Commerce Clearing House News Bureau.

NEWS RELEASE

Gas Research Institute / 8600 West Bryn Mawr Avenue / Chicago, Illinois 60631 / 312·399·8100

September 6, 1983
Contact: Rebecca L. Busby
          Technical Communications
          312/399-8343

          Kenneth C. Kazmer
          Project Manager, Energy
            Systems Economics
          312/399-8147

          MARKET POTENTIAL LOOKS GOOD FOR
          ADVANCED COMMERCIAL WATER HEATER

    Thanks to its competitively short payback period, the high-efficiency

commercial water heater being developed with funding from Gas Research

Institute (GRI) should enjoy vigorous success when it reaches the market in

the mid-1980's, according to a market characterization study conducted by

Facility & Manufacturing Automation, Inc. The study confirms that the

hardware development goals of GRI's R&D program match the anticipated needs of

the market for commercial water heaters, which consume more natural gas than

any other commercial appliance.

    For analyzing the potential market penetration of advanced water heaters,

the study employed the design parameters of the high-efficiency (up to 93%)

prototype condensing water heater now being developed under GRI sponsorship by
Advanced Mechanical Technology, Inc. (AMTI). According to the results, the
AMTI water heater exhibits very competitive payback periods--less than 2
years--when compared with conventional models of both the storage (tank) and
instantaneous types. Even versus systems with efficiencies of 80% and no
first-cost premium, the advanced unit's payback period would remain below 3
years.

Preliminary data collected at four field test sites indicate that the AMTI
unit uses 20-25% less gas than conventional models, resulting in operating
savings of $500-$1400 per year, depending on hot water usage rates and local
gas prices. This strong economic advantage, coupled with continued strength
of demand in the replacement market, provides a very optimistic outlook for
this unit's successful commercialization in the mid-1980's.

The study's analysis of the commercial market by 15 subsectors determined
the characteristics of commercial buildings and water heating systems
currently in use. Market projections estimated from these data indicate that
sales for commercial gas-fired water heaters are likely to reach 286,000 units
by 1990 and 388,000 units by 2000. Replacement demand is expected to continue
to dominate the market, accounting for about 80% of sales throughout the
1982-2000 period.

The final report of the study, entitled "Commercial Water Heater Market
Characterization," is available as Report No. PB83-232736 (Price: $11.50)
from National Technical Information Service, U.S. Department of Commerce,
Springfield, Virginia 22161. Telephone: 703/487-4650.

GRI is a private, not-for-profit membership organization that plans,
manages, and develops financing for a cooperative research and development
program in gaseous fuels and their use. The research program, which is
designed to benefit the regulated natural gas industry and gas consumers
nationwide, consists of over 350 active research projects in four major
areas: supply options, efficient utilization, enhanced service, and
fundamental research.

NEWS RELEASE

Gas Research Institute / 8600 West Bryn Mawr Avenue / Chicago, Illinois 60631 / 312·399·8100

September 6, 1983
Contact: Rebecca L. Busby
Technical Communications
312/399-8343

Kenneth C. Kazmer
Project Manager, Energy
Systems Economics
312/399-8147

MARKET POTENTIAL LOOKS GOOD FOR
ADVANCED COMMERCIAL WATER HEATER

¶ A ~~Thanks to its competitively~~ should make a short payback period, ~~the~~ high-efficiency
commercial water heater being developed by Advanced Mechanical Technology, Inc. (AMTI), with funding from Gas Research

Institute (GRI), ~~should enjoy vigorous~~ a success ~~when it reaches the market~~ in

the mid-1980's. ~~according to a market characterization study conducted by~~
That is the finding of a study by
Facility & Manufacturing Automation, Inc., (FMAI). ~~The study confirms that the~~

~~hardware development goals of GRI's R&D program match the anticipated needs of~~

~~the market for~~ ¶ commercial water heaters, ~~which~~ consume more natural gas than

any other commercial appliance, but (insert here from page two)

~~For analyzing the potential market penetration of advanced water heaters,~~

~~the study employed the design parameters of the high-efficiency (up to 93%)~~

~~prototype condensing water heater now being developed under GRI sponsorship by~~

~~Advanced Mechanical Technology, Inc. (AMTI). According to the results,~~ ¶ the

7-4b continued

AMTI water heater ~~exhibits very competitive~~ shows a payback period[s] of ~~less than~~ (2)

years ~~,~~ when compared with conventional models of both the storage (tank) and

instantaneous types. ~~Even versus~~ When compared with systems with efficiencies of 80% and no

first-cost premium, the ~~advanced unit's~~ AMTI payback ~~period would~~ remain[s] below (3)

years.

~~Preliminary~~ data ~~collected at~~ from four field test sites ~~indicate that~~ shows the AMTI

unit uses 20-25% less gas than conventional models, resulting in operating

savings of $500-$1400 per year, depending on hot water usage rates and local

gas prices. ~~This strong economic advantage, coupled with continued strength~~

~~of demand in the replacement market, provides a very optimistic outlook for~~

~~this unit's successful commercialization in the mid-1980's.~~

[insert on previous page]

~~The study's analysis of the commercial market by 15 subsectors determined~~

~~the characteristics of commercial buildings and water heating systems~~

~~currently in use.~~ (¶) Market projections ~~estimated from these data~~ indicate ~~that~~

sales for commercial gas-fired water heaters are likely to reach 286,000 units

by 1990 and 388,000 units by 2000. Replacement demand is expected to continue

to dominate the market, accounting for about 80% of sales throughout the

1982-2000 period.

~~The final report of the study, entitled "Commercial Water Heater Market~~

~~Characterization," is available as Report No. PB83-232736 (Price: $11.50)~~

~~from National Technical Information Service, U.S. Department of Commerce,~~

~~Springfield, Virginia 22161. Telephone: 703/487-4650.~~

GRI is a private, not-for-profit membership organization that plans,

manage[s] and develops financing for ~~a~~ cooperative research and development

program[s] in gaseous fuels and their use[s]. The ~~research~~ program[s] ~~which~~ is

designed to benefit the regulated natural gas industry and gas consumers

nationwide ~~consists of over~~ GRI is involved in more than 350 active research projects in four major

areas: supply options, efficient utilization[, uses,] ~~enhanced~~ better service[s,] and

~~fundamental~~ basic research.

131

7-4c

7-10-85
FROM: Commerce Clearing House News Bureau   FOR IMMEDIATE RELEASE
       (Mort J. Sullivan)   (312) 583 8500
       4025 W. Peterson Ave., Chicago, Ill.   "Best Sources" Map
       60646   Enclosed for Reproduction

INCOME TAXES: TOP STATE REVENUE
SOURCE FOR 12TH STRAIGHT YEAR

Combined corporate and personal income taxes surpassed general sales taxes as the top revenue raiser of state tax dollars for the 12th straight year in fiscal 1984, Commerce Clearing House reports.

Income tax collections totaled $74.5 billion, while general sales and gross receipts tax collections -- the second largest source of tax dollars -- provided states with $62.6 billion.

Income taxes supplied the most revenue in twenty-eight states and the District of Columbia, while sales taxes proved to be the best source of revenue in twenty states in fiscal 1984. Severance taxes were the best source of revenue in Alaska and Wyoming.

Total state tax collections across the nation totaled $196.8 billion in fiscal 1984, an increase of 14.8 percent over the $171.5 billion collected in fiscal 1983.

Nationally, increases in state government tax revenues were noted in every category of tax except severance taxes (down 2.1 percent), with the largest percentage of increase occurring in individual income taxes, which were up 18.4 percent over collections for the previous fiscal year.

Corporate net income taxes experienced the second largest percentage of growth over fiscal 1983 figures (up 17.9 percent), while property taxes came in third (up 17.7 percent). Other taxes that registered increased collections in fiscal 1984 were general sales and gross receipts taxes (up 16.6 percent), motor fuel taxes (up 14.8 percent), motor vehicle license taxes (up 9.8 percent), alcoholic beverage taxes (up 5.7 percent), public utilities gross receipts taxes (up 4 percent), tobacco product taxes (up 3.7 percent), and insurance premimum taxes (up 3 percent).

(MORE)

7-4c continued

INCOME TAXES: TOP STATE REVENUE SOURCE FOR 12TH STRAIGHT YEAR - 2

Tax revenues increased in the District of Columbia and forty-nine
states from fiscal 1983 to fiscal 1984. Only one state-- Alaska -- registered
a decrease in revenues (down 3.6 percent) during this period, whereas nine
states showed a decline in revenues from fiscal 1982 to fiscal 1983.

In the states showing increased revenue collections, the percentages of
increase ranged from a low of 1.3 percent in Oklahoma to a high of 30.1 percent
in North Dakota. The median increase for all states from fiscal 1983 to fiscal
1984 was 14.9 percent, compared to a median increase of only 6.3 percent from
fiscal 1982 to fiscal 1983.

Nearly one-half of all state tax revenue was collected in the following
eight states; California ($25.6 billion); New York ($18.8 billion); Texas ($9.8
billion); Pennsylvania ($9.6 billion); Illinois ($8 billion); Michigan ($8.6
billion); Ohio ($8.0 billion); and Florida ($7.3 billion), CCH reported.

#

Best Sources of State Revenue in Fiscal 1984

©1985, Commerce Clearing House, Inc.

get a copy of the AP or UPI stylebook at a college bookstore or by writing directly to AP or UPI.

The stylebook will guide you on such matters as when to capitalize, how to abbreviate and what titles to use with specific people. The AP and UPI books describe certain punctuation rules that may differ from common usage. In AP-UPI style, for example, there is no comma between a name and Jr. or Sr., as in "Joe Zilch Jr."

As for spelling, AP and UPI have adopted *Webster's New World Dictionary of the American Language* as the standard guide for spelling (second college edition). Use the first spelling listed, or the spelling given with a complete definition if a word has more than one entry (like *T-shirt* and *tee shirt*). The stylebooks list exceptions to the dictionary spelling. If a word isn't in *Webster's New World*, check in *Webster's Third International* (and think again about whether you should be using such a word).

Since any written material you give to a newspaper will be edited at the copy desk anyway, you might wonder why it's necessary to pay strict attention to the details of newspaper style. In fact, it's *not* absolutely necessary but it's still a good idea. Even if your release is rewritten completely, the rewriter will notice if the original was in correct style—and will take particular note if it was in incorrect style. It's a matter of making a good impression. If your style is correct, an editor will know that the release was prepared carefully by someone who knew what he or she was doing. Correct spelling is even more important in this regard. If you don't bother to spell words correctly, an editor is likely to assume that you aren't very careful with the facts either. And if an editor can't trust your information, the release is worthless.

What about grammar? Some writers worry about grammar above all else, combing every line for a possible split infinitive or a *who* that should be a *whom*. Certainly good grammar is important, and awkward, obvious errors like subject-verb disagreements should not be tolerated. But don't worry more about grammar than about communication. The first concern must be the clarity of the message. If your sentences are clear and understandable, the grammar will take care of itself (see Chapter 6).

One more word about style. If you plan to send releases to papers other than local dailies (releases about financial news, for example, might go to the *Wall Street Journal*), you should know that these papers sometimes have completely different style rules. Some PR people send the same release to all papers, using the style applicable to the majority. You can get away with this, but it never hurts to tailor releases to individual publications. Remember that some papers—like the *Wall Street Journal* and the *New York Times*—have styles of their own.

The Electronic Transmission of Releases

Having the correct style is particularly important now that many PR practitioners are sending releases directly from their computers to the news medium's computer via modem. One practitioner predicts that the delivery of news releases by any other means (non-electronic mail, messenger or in-person delivery) will be obsolete soon. Once the release is in the medium's computer system, it can be called up for editing (or, of course, "killing").

Types of Releases

Once you know how to write a release, the next questions are why and when should you write one? The reason for writing releases depends on the type of company or institution you write for and what its goals are. Frequently the release is just one of many tools a company uses to get publicity. Sometimes releases are an important communications tool for explaining the company's position on major public issues. But remember also that PR people, as Boston University PR professor Otto Lerbinger puts it, "have an obligation to satisfy people's right to know about the operation of government units and the activities of corporations and nonprofit organizations that affect the public interest."[8] News releases are often necessary to meet that obligation.

Another reason for issuing releases is simply to keep the record straight. Tight-lipped corporations that maintain low profiles and seldom issue releases are frequently headed by executives who complain privately about the "unfair" treatment they get in the media, or who note the media's many mistakes in covering their companies. But they have no business complaining when a paper gets the facts wrong if they haven't provided that paper with the correct information. News releases are one way of helping papers get the facts right when they report about your business.

It's not only a matter of information. Besides getting publicity for your company, a good news-release program helps build good media relations. Reporters get paid to find news and write stories, and if you help them find news—real news—the reporters will be grateful.

When do you write releases? The rule is simple: When you have news, release it. Certain things call for news releases. Generally these correspond to a few basic types of releases.

Announcement Releases   These releases can announce a new product, the opening of a new plant, the company's latest financial results, or a new company policy. Generally these are routine items that don't require long releases. Just be sure the news is legitimate. In most cases the announcement of a new line of a familiar product is material for an ad, not a news release. The product has to be of a completely new kind—something really unique—to deserve a news story. A good test for the value of the information is "Who cares?" If the answer is "Only a few," it's not news. For a sample announcement release, see the one used in Figure 7-3.

"Created News" Releases   Often, a mere announcement isn't enough to attract much media attention. In this case, a company may try to "dress up" the announcement release by making sure something newsworthy is going on. The company might bring a well-known speaker to a company function, or stage a formal cere-

135

mony or other event like a concert or rally. This gives the news-release writer something more interesting or newsworthy to say.

Remember one thing, though. There should never be any confusion about what's really going on and who is responsible. If the company is behind an event, make that fact clear. Deception of any kind is always reprehensible, but it's twice as reprehensible in a news release.

Spot News Releases   Announcement releases can usually be planned. But sometimes things happen without warning. An electric utility's main power plant can break down, for example, threatening power shortages or higher costs for replacement power. An explosion can occur in a munitions factory; an airplane can be hijacked. Such occurrences are spot news, and when they happen, a news release is in order. You must fill them in as facts are available, issue news bulletins and a release incorporating as much information as you can provide.

In these cases the PR person must function like a reporter working on deadline, gathering the information quickly and writing the news bulletins as a release without delay. If media people aren't provided with information immediately, they will write their stories from whatever scraps of information they can find. And frequently in such a case the reporting is inaccurate.

A spot news release often has to be followed up the next day with a second release, explaining how the initial events were resolved.

Response Releases   Often news about a company reaches the media from sources other than the PR department. A consumer group may issue a report critical of the company, for instance. The government may announce an investigation into company pricing practices. A research group may publish a major study on your company's industry.

When these things happen, reporters call for a response. Companies with good PR organizations anticipate these calls and have response releases ready. Responses may be brief statements or full-fledged news releases with the company's position in detail (see Example 7-5).

In emergency situations, news releases aren't enough. PR people must sometimes use the telephone to transmit the latest developments to the media. See Chapter 16 on crisis communication.

Even if you are not asked for a response, you can offer one anyway as a way of communicating your company's views. For example, when President Reagan announced his "Star Wars" defense concept, defense industries were pushed to respond. And when his administration's next tax plan was advanced, the potential impact on tax shelters, especially oil- and gas-related ones, provoked those in the industry to respond.

Feature Releases   Not every story in a newspaper involves events that happened yesterday or today. Feature stories about topics of special interest are taking up an increasing share of newspaper space these days. All PR people can find feature material somewhere in their organizations—something going on in research and de-

7-5a

Responses

When a proposed piece of legislation didn't make it past the Oklahoma legislature, Oklahoma Natural Gas responded with a "We warned you, and now this is what is likely to happen" sort of piece in their utility bill stuffer (a) and a version in the employee publication (b). Another type of response followed with the request for a rate increase (c), and another piece appeared in the employee newsletter (d). *Source:* Used with permission of the Oklahoma Natural Gas Company.

VOL. 15, NO. 9   **Oklahoma Natural Gas Company**   **MARCH, 1985**

An Open Letter to ONG Customers

Senate Bill 137 died in a state Senate committee February 28, putting to an end the effort to head off legislatively an unnecessary increase in Oklahomans' gas and electric bills caused by federal law.

Many Supported Bill

Many of you supported the bill and asked your legislators to support it. Many others asked us for more information to help them make up their minds on the issue. Involvements like those are what the democratic process is all about.

By the same token, the people have spoken about SB 137 through their elected representatives—at least, those on the Natural Resources Committee of the Oklahoma Senate. Our idea that the unique gas pricing problem addressed by SB 137 could be solved through its passage, and the change in public policy that would bring, died when the bill died.

The Problem Remains

The legislative solution was not the only one possible. It was the simplest and fairest and quickest one that could have been put in force, and one far superior to all the alternatives.

There are other things that can be done to eliminate the problem of gas prices rising to levels far above what's realistic in today's marketplace. We are confident that a solution can be found.

It Must Be Joint Effort

And we are hopeful that gas producers, many of whom stoutly opposed SB 137, will cooperate in what must now be a joint effort toward achieving a solution to the problem that we share.

The burden is, in fact, a shared one. There's no such thing as a serious ONG problem that's exclusively ours, because it affects both producers and consumers if it's serious enough. This is a fact of overwhelming clarity which, we sincerely hope, will motivate the best efforts of everyone involved to find a way out—for all of us.

Free Tax Help

Taxpayers 55 years of age and older can get free assistance in the preparation of their income tax returns in some areas of Oklahoma.

Call your local library and inquire as to the days, hours, and sites for the service.

7-5b

NEWS LINE

Oklahoma Natural Gas Company, P. O. Box 871, Tulsa, Oklahoma 74102

VOL. XVIII NO. XXV   MONDAY, MARCH 4, 1985

In wake of Senate Bill 137's defeat . . .

What happens now to protect our customers?

ONG will take necessary steps to restrain price escalation

Pledging that Oklahoma Natural is ready to make renewed efforts to keep the cost of gas from escalating, Executive Vice President *Elmer Kamphaus* on Friday said "we will take whatever steps are necessary."

He stressed the following:

- "Since SB 49 expired we have been attempting to renegotiate contracts with producers, and obviously we will continue to do so. While we have contacted 550 producers, we've had responses from only 20%.

- "Senate Bill 137 was one of several ways the situation could have been remedied. I believe it was the surest and most direct way. We now accept the fact that there will be no legislative action. We will strive to achieve the necessary results even if it means the problem must be resolved through the courts. If so, we will assert any and all legal defenses we can to prevent a price escalation.

- "We do not intend to pay the higher rates. We are avoiding doing so by shutting in wells covered by contracts that call for the 50% escalation in costs.

- "All this said, let me emphasize that we are not anti-producer. In fact, we want and need the help of the producer. We share common problems and concerns. The energy business includes all components of exploration, production, transportation, and distribution. Together we must resolve the problems faced by the energy business today.

"We will succeed in meeting this challenge just as Oklahoma Natural has met all previous challenges," said Kamphaus. "This is because our primary resource is ONG employees, which was aptly demonstrated when ONGers rallied to support the SB 137 cause."

Gas price bill killed despite a strong case supporting it

Senate Bill 137, which would have extended the gas price protection provision of the old SB 49, was effectively killed in senate committee by a vote of 8-2 last Thursday despite a strong showing of support by employees and community and consumer groups.

"Oklahoma Natural employees are due tremendous thanks for their efforts to rally support for the legislation," said Executive Vice President *Elmer Kamphaus*, after testifying at the Senate hearing Thursday.

"Our message to all employees is: 'We may all feel disappointed and let down, but know that your efforts were not in vain; they showed the Oklahoma consumer that Oklahoma Natural was solidly behind a consumer issue.' "

"It's most important to remember that we demonstrated we were standing by our customers on this issue—and I believe that's a point that will be remembered by them," Kamphaus added.

"This is certainly not the end of the world. It is now time to undertake new strategy, to make a different thrust to achieve the results that are needed to keep gas costs at a reasonable level," Kamphaus emphasized. "Legislative action was the best solution, we thought, but it's not the only solution. And we are confident that we are going to solve the problem."

Oklahoma Natural took the lead in shaping the issue and presenting the case at Thursday's hearing held by the Senate Natural Resources Committee. More than 200 spectators attended the hearing, which was held in the senate chamber.

Speaking in favor of the legislation, in addition to Kamphaus and the bill's author, Senator *Lee Cate*, were *Leonard Benton*, Executive Director of the Oklahoma City Urban League; *Lu Patrick*, of the Tulsa Coalition of Older People; and *Jim Foster*, representing Agrico Chemical Company. In addition, petitions bearing 10,600 signatures favoring SB 137 were submitted to the committee by ONG.

The committee chairman, *Ray Giles*, who from the outset pledged to kill the bill, voted against it along with Senators *Dawson, Ford, Smith, Choate, Green, Sadler,* and *Landis*. Favoring the measure were Senators *Cullison* and *Howell*. Senator *Al Terrill*, a member of the committee, was not present for the vote.

Kamphaus, after pleading with senators that "the people's elected representatives and not the courts" should settle the energy issue, submitted to the committee a number of petitions and statements, among them one from 364 employees of Sheffield Steel in Sand Springs along with a joint statement from Sheffield managment and the United Steelworkers asking for senate support of Senate Bill 137.

Kamphaus said hourly and salaried employees of the steel company had just made payroll and benefit concessions to help Sheffield survive in the beleaguered steel industry. According to the statement, "If SB 137 is *not* passed, Oklahoma energy consumers would pay higher utility prices that in effect would subsidize users in other states whose rates would not go up for the same reason." Kamphaus quoted from the statement: "We are at a point in our (steel) industry where an advantage in utility costs for out-of-state competitors could seriously jeopardize the future of Sheffield and the jobs it represents."

Senator *Jerry Smith* of Tulsa made the motion to report "progress" on the bill, which was another way of tabling it and which had the effect of killing it for this session. It is now too late in this session of the Legislature for another measure to be introduced.

7-5c

June 17, 1985

ONG REQUESTS $61.1 MILLION RATE INCREASE

TULSA -- Oklahoma Natural Gas Company, a subsidiary of ONEOK Inc., today asked the Oklahoma Corporation Commission for a rate increase amounting to 7 percent of total utility revenues.

A company spokesman explained that the request was due to a serious revenue deficiency causing ONG to earn rates of return far below those authorized in late 1983, the time of the Commission's last rate order for the company.

The amount of the total increase requested was $61.1 million. Forty-eight percent--or $29.4 million of the requested increase--would be paid in increased federal and state taxes. The remainder, approximately $31.7 million, would help offset the impact of recent increases in operating and maintenance expenses, increased investment in property and equipment, and inflation.

In arriving at the amount of increase needed, the company is proposing a 16 percent return on stockholders' equity and a 15 percent return on rate base. The total rate base shown by the company is more than $568 million.

Oklahoma Natural documented the need for the increased rates in compliance with a state law that requires utility rate reviews every two years. Today's filing with the Commission follows up ONG's April 19 request for a review of its rates.

According to the Commission rules, ONG is required to submit a plan detailing how the increase could be applied to different customer classes, such as residential, commercial and industrial customers.

7-5c | continued

In information filed by the company, it is proposing rates that would increase the average residential customer's bill by approximately 92 cents per Mcf (thousand cubic feet) of gas. That increase would apply if the full $61.1 million increase is granted by the Commission and if the increase is applied in such a way that each customer class would be paying a share of the cost of providing service that's nearer a fair share than in the past.

Based on the 12 months ending February 28, 1985 (the "test year" being used in the information supplied by the company), the increase would raise the average Mcf cost from $4.62 to $5.54. Gas usage by the company's residential customers averages 95 Mcf annually.

The maximum increase for any residential customer, no matter how high the usage, would be $11.90 per month in what the company classifies as the six winter months and $4.90 per month in the six summer months.

The Commission will set hearings for the rate request at a later date.

ONEOK Inc. is a diversified energy company whose Oklahoma Natural Gas Company--serving about 650,000 residential, commercial and industrial customers--is the best-known element. ONEOK also is active in oil and gas exploration and production, natural gas liquids extraction and contract drilling.

#   #   #

For further information contact: Walt Radmilovich, Charlene Bassett, or J. A. Metcalf, Oklahoma Natural Gas Company, P. O. Box 871, Tulsa, OK 74102, Phone: (918) 588-7000. Or after office hours contact Walt Radmilovich at (918) 622-0439, Charlene Bassett at (918) 582-5406, or J. A. Metcalf at (918) 245-7793.

7-5d

NEWS LINE

Oklahoma Natural Gas Company, P. O. Box 871, Tulsa, Oklahoma 74102

VOL. XIX NO. VII   MONDAY, JUNE 24, 1985

Rate hearings to begin September 16
Pre-hearing dates set for July and August in rate case

An Oklahoma Corporation Commission order signed Friday has set September 16 as the opening hearing date on Oklahoma Natural's rate review request. The order reserves two weeks for the hearings; however, considerable work is still required before the actual hearings begin.

The Corporation Commission has established July 12 as the deadline for any intervention in the rate case, and interrogatories from those who wish specific questions to be considered must be submitted by July 19. The Company has until July 26 to object to any of the questions, which objections will be heard by the Commission on July 30. In the absence of any objection, the Company must provide the answers by August 16.

Written testimony from intervenors' witnesses must be submitted by August 26. This does not include testimony of the Corporation Commission staff, which will be filed on September 6.

A pre-hearing conference is set for July 22, at which lawyers for the Company, intervenors, and Commission staff agree as to the general procedures, order of witnesses, and time frame expected for the hearings.

On April 19 the Company filed its application with the Commission requesting an examination of its books and records in accordance with state law, which requires utility company rate reviews every two years. On June 17 testimony and exhibits were filed by the Company detailing the need for a 7% increase (which totals $61.1 million) in its rates.

Much of the rate increase requested—$29.4 million of the $61.1 million asked for—if granted, would go to pay federal and state taxes.

In its June 17 filing, ONG has requested that the bulk of the current rate increase be borne by residential customers. A large percentage of the rate increases granted in the last 15 years has been carried by industrial customers to the extent that, from a cost of service standpoint, industrial rates are now disproportionately higher than those paid by residential customers.

The ONG proposal would ask that residential customers pay 83.27% of the proposed increase; commercial customers, 15.91%; and industrial customers, 0.41%.

Documentation and testimony presented by the Company will demonstrate that the allowed rate of return on investment and on stockholders' equity needs to be raised. This is not a guaranteed rate of return but rather the upper allowed limit,'' according to the testimony of Company witness *J. A. Metcalf, Jr.*, Vice President, Controller and Assistant Treasurer. ''The Company almost never achieves this allowed maximum rate of return,'' Metcalf said.

If approved by the Corporation Commission, the rate increase for residential customers using an average of 95 Mcf annually would be about $11.90 a month in winter and about $4.90 a month in summer. This is the maximum increase, no matter how high the customer's usage.

Testimony of Company witness *E. H. Kamphaus*, Executive Vice President, details various programs instituted by ONG to help customers meet monthly bills and get maximum value from gas delivered to them.

ONG's last rate increase was granted in October, 1983.

Much of ONEOK Plaza leased as new firms move into building

Much of the space that is available in ONEOK Plaza, our headquarters building in Tulsa, has been leased, according to *Frank S. Chappelle*, Vice President, ONEOK Leasing Company.

He said that of the space available for occupancy—excluding space used by ONEOK Inc. and its subsidiaries—is already 70% occupied or leased.

The ONEOK Parking Company garage has less than 100 spaces left of the 1,160 total, he said.

A new tenant moved into the building this past weekend. This is the law firm of Pray, Walker, Jackman, Williamson & Marlar, which will use about 23,000 square feet. The accounting firm of Deloitte, Haskins + Sells, which will occupy about 16,800 square feet; Source Service Corporation, using over 1,200 square feet; and the law firm of Marsh and Armstrong, Inc., to occupy 10,600 square feet, are scheduled to move in the building about September 1, Chappelle says.

velopment, for example, like a new production process that improves efficiency or helps reduce pollution. Such feature stories can be prepared for newspapers as ordinary news releases.

Feature releases create a problem, however, if more than one newspaper in the same city covers your company. Newspapers don't expect special treatment when it comes to regular news—they know you give ordinary news releases to all news media. But features are different. An editor is not likely to use a feature if he or she knows some other paper might be running the same story. It's best to offer different features to different papers, or at least to develop a different angle of the story for each paper in the area.

Newspaper features have many of the same qualities as magazine articles, which are discussed in Chapter 12.

Bad-News Releases   Sometimes events occur that a company would like to keep quiet. The natural tendency in such cases is to issue no news releases at all and hope that the problem will go unnoticed. But more often than not, attempts to keep bad news out of the media backfire. Such stories often involve a company's regulatory agency. Since regulatory agencies are considered to be acting in the public's interest, you can be sure the agency will release a report. You've seen such stories: a restaurant gets a poor sanitation report from the city's health department; an industry is accused of contaminating a water supply; a nuclear plant gets a poor safety ruling from a routine inspection; a manufacturing plant is accused of exposing its workers to health hazards without warning them or protecting them. And what do you often see as the response of the accused? "No comment."

If your company has been attacked and you have made your own announcement release on the situation, the story will still be in the paper, and often prominently displayed, but it will be treated in a less sensational manner than if you issued no comment. If you hand over the facts to a reporter, the result will usually be a straight report. When a reporter has to dig the story out, however, he or she will make the article more dramatic, and the story will be more likely to linger on the front pages, with the reporter unveiling bits of information as they are uncovered. This is the classic treatment of a cover up. In recent years, more people have begun to realize that covering up a problem can become more of a problem than the problem itself.

Column Notes, Letters, Guest Columns and Photos   Sometimes the information you'd like to see in the paper doesn't fit the form of an ordinary news story (see Example 7-6). That doesn't mean you should forget about it. Most papers have special columns or sections that print unusual items, and these are often among the best read parts of the publication. Individual columnists might make use of readers' information. Or readers might want to write a "guest column." (You might want to write one under the by-line of your company's chief executive.)

Such items don't always follow the same form as an ordinary news

7-6a

Column Items

This is the type of material that can be put in columns, but there is a problem with this copy. An editor at the Portage, Wisconsin, paper received this release (a). It is for a city, but the piece didn't even name a town, and the newspaper serves a large community. The PR wire carried this Zale promotion (b), fairly typical of the type of story that gets the column treatment. The paper will run only the first three lines. Note the "throwaway" paragraph at the end. Source: Zale release used with permission of the Zale Corporation.

```
                    OPEN MEETING NOTICE
                        MARCH 1985


  March 5, 1985 - Tuesday - 7:00 P.M. - Public Hearing on rezoning of property
                                        at 634 Park Ave, Per the request of
                                        Joyce Borchert.

                     7:30 P.M. - Semi-monthly Council meeting - see
                                 posted agenda.


  March 6, 1985 - Wednesday - 7:00 P.M. - Monthly meeting of the Recreation and
                                          parks committeeat City Hall.


  March 7, 1985 - Thursday - 7:30 P.M. - Water and light commission meeting at
                                         water and light office.  See posted
                                         agenda.

  March 11, 1985 - Monday - 10:00 A.M. - Zoning Board of Appeals to hold a hearing
                                         on the request of James Bellin for a
                                         variance to construct a garage.


  March 13, 1985 - Wednesday - 2:00 P.M. - Board of Public Works at City Garage.
                                           Agenda will be posted.
```

7-6b

74251142299702125B1231905

Zale Announces New Assistant

Treasurer

SWN 009 FROM SOUTHWEST NEWSWIRE AT 214/748-1943

TO: BUSINESS DESKS

DALLAS, Jan. 21, 1985--(SWN)--Zale Corporation (NYSE-ZAL) today
announced the appointment of Richard A. Wiggins as Assistant Treasurer.

In his new position, Wiggins will be responsible for the treasury
function of the Corporation as well as Cash Control and Rent Control.
He will report to Walter H. Harvey, Vice President and Treasurer.

Wiggins, who joined Zale Corporation in 1978, was most recently
the Senior Vice President, Finance and Administration for the Company's
Diamond Park Fine Jewelers Division. Prior to joining Zale, his career
development included a variety of planning, budgeting and analytical
assignments.

Commenting on the appointment, Harvey said: "Rich's experience
in various corporate and divisional areas of responsibility make him a
valuable asset to the Treasurer's Department."

Zale Corporation, the world's largest fine jewelry retailer, has
sales of over $1 billion annually and more than 1,500 retail outlets
worldwide.

-30-

CONTACT: Jean Shanaphy Barrow, Vice President-Public Relations,
Zale Corporation, 214/257-4980.

release, but they can accomplish much the same thing. Study the newspapers your organization deals with so you'll know what outlets are available.

Photos are among the most effective publicity tools. Photos must tell a story to be worth using. They can accompany a release as an illustration or stand alone. In either case, they must interest the audience. Sometimes the single photos and their captions even qualify for what editors refer to as "wild art," photos that add reader interest to the page (see Example 7-7). Captions for photos that illustrate a story carry information that relieves the story of some detail. A caption for "wild art" only tells readers what they are looking at, and points out the picture's significance, if any.

The AP's rules for captions are worth remembering:

The caption's job is to describe and explain the picture to the reader.

The challenge is to do it interestingly, accurately, always in good taste.

A further challenge is to write the caption, whenever appropriate, in a spritely, lively vein.

An APME Continuing Study Committee put together Ten Tests of a good caption. They are:

1. Is it complete?
2. Does it identify, fully and clearly?
3. Does it tell when?
4. Does it tell where?
5. Does it tell what's in the picture?
6. Does it have the names spelled correctly, with the proper name on the right person?
7. Is it specific?
8. Is it easy to read?
9. Have as many adjectives as possible been removed?
10. Does it suggest another picture?

And rule No. 11, the Cardinal Rule, never, never to be violated:

Never write a caption without seeing the picture.[9]

Preparing and Delivering News Releases

With news releases, as with most things, substance is more important than form. But that doesn't mean that form is unimportant. There are some things you should know about form that will help you prepare releases in the most convenient way for the people who use them.

7-7

PR Photo
This picture is likely to catch the attention of readers just as it did the editors, so it's an interesting piece of "wild art" for the paper. *Source:* Courtesy of The Goodyear Tire & Rubber Company.

Technical Considerations

Leave space at the top of the first page where an editor can write instructions.

Double or even triple space your typing. Your copy needs to be easy to read and edit. A newsperson may edit the copy, but a newsclerk will probably type it into the system.

Make sure the name, address and phone number of the company organization all are on the news-release form. Also include the name and both office and home phone numbers of a person to contact for further information. A morning paper may be working on a story at midnight, and if a question comes up, the editor will need a number to call.

The release should have two dates: the actual date the release was sent to the media, and the date on which the release is cleared for use. If the release can be used at any time, "for immediate release" is sufficient to indicate release date. When necessary, specify "A.M. papers" or "P.M. papers" to indicate that the release can appear only in the day's morning edition or only in the day's evening edition. Remember, some morning papers have an early edition that appears the evening before the stated publication day. This is especially true for Sunday editions. Afternoon papers often issue a street edition that appears well before noon. If the time of the story's appearance in print is critical, be sure to specify which edition it can be used in, or fix a time after which a story may be used. (See Chapter 8.) (You should be aware that some newspapers ignore release dates, and many do not feel bound by them.)

Once the release has been typed, either on a typewriter, word processor or computer terminal, and is ready to be sent, go back one more time and check every fact, name, place, time and date. You can't afford mistakes. Nothing is more important than absolute accuracy. If you give an editor a release with just one false sentence, one misspelled name, or one wrong date that gets into the paper, that editor is going to have to apologize to somebody for your mistake. And the next time that editor receives a release from you, he or she will have to take extra time to check over the facts in your story. The editor who doesn't have the time—and editors usually don't—will probably throw your release away rather than risk more mistakes. Things might not go this way every time with every editor, but there's only one sure way to make certain they won't happen this way at all: Get everything right, every time.

Dealing with the Media

Once you have written a release and checked it for errors, a few important questions remain. Where should you send the release, and to whom? When should you send it? And, aside from preparing it properly, what can you do to make sure the release is used?

Ordinarily, you send releases to the daily newspaper. If your company serves an entire region, your release should be of interest to several daily papers. Nationwide firms may want to send releases to every city in which the company's plants or offices are. The military sends its news releases to the hometowns of the individuals involved in the stories. A computer program can handle this kind of distribution, filling in the name and appropriate information in blanks in a for-matted story. Stories going to international media are usually translated at the point of origin, except when agencies have international offices to handle translation and distribution.

Although most news-release publicity begins with daily newspapers, it is a mistake to stop there. Don't overlook wire services if the release will be of interest over a wide area. With news wire services, though, the release will not go to a paper in the form you prepared it—the wire editors will rewrite it. If you want to get the release to the paper as you wrote it, you can use one of several publicity wire services.[10]

The weekly papers that serve small towns, rural areas and, some-times, neighborhood communities within large metropolitan centers are another important place to send releases. Weeklies may have a low circulation, but they are well read by those who receive them. If you're trying to reach community audi-ences, weeklies can be much more effective than dailies. However, their newshole is small, so be concise.

Most releases should also be sent to the electronic media. But re-member that broadcast style is different from print style. A release prepared for a newspaper must be completely rewritten for TV or radio (see Chapter 8 on broad-cast writing). Since the electronic version will normally be much shorter than the print version, you should attach the print version to the release you send to radio and TV. This makes the details available to the electronic journalists if they need them.

It's helpful to know the right person to send a release to. Most TV and radio stations have a news director, and all releases should go to that individual. Newspapers are more complicated, however. Various section editors may be inter-ested in the news you have to offer, but sometimes their responsibilities overlap and it's hard to choose the right recipient.

A few simple guidelines may be helpful in such a situation. Releases specifically aimed at a single topic (like food or sports) should go to the section edi-tor. If a release contains strictly business or financial news, for example, it should go to the editor of the business section. If the news is of general local interest, the city editor is usually the right person for the release. (When you're in doubt about who should get the release, the city editor is probably the best bet.) If one reporter covers your company or organization all the time, send the release directly to him or her.

Sometimes it's appropriate to send a release to more than one person at the same paper—a reporter and an editor, for example. Some companies regu-larly send copies of releases to editorial writers, especially if the release addresses a controversial topic. Make sure, though, that if you send more than one copy of the release to a given paper, you indicate that you have done so on the release. To avoid duplicated story assignments, you must let an editor know that a reporter already has your release.

When should you send the release? On breaking news stories, as soon as possible—hand deliver the release if at all feasible, or call and connect from your electronic system to the medium's if the news contact wants your story. For announcements of upcoming events, mailing the story in three or four days in advance is usually sufficient. For a major story that should be released at a specific time, have the release arrive at the newspaper the day before the desired date.

Keep in mind that weekly papers have different deadline schedules from dailies. A weekly published on Thursdays might have a deadline as early as Monday. You must know the deadlines in order to deliver your release on time.

As for getting the papers to use your release, there is no substitute for a well-written release with genuine news value. All other considerations are secondary. But assuming that the release is properly prepared, there are things you can do to enhance the chances that it will get printed. One is to choose the proper release date. Setting the release time for Sunday helps your chances, since Sunday papers are large and have more space to fill. Monday is also good because news staffs are small on the weekend and newsmakers are not busy. Including a good picture with the release is also helpful, since editors are always interested in good art for page-design purposes. Perhaps the best way to get a release used, however, is to get it moved on the wire services. Newspapers use wire stories in preference to releases to save time in editing and typesetting.

One thing that won't help the release get used is printing it on colored paper stock. Many PR people use this technique to attract attention to their releases, but according to one survey, an overwhelming majority of editors disliked colored news-release paper—although most seemed to think that colored ink for the name on the letterhead was acceptable.

This chapter has covered primarily news releases to newspapers, but in practice you will be sending releases to a number of specialized news media like trade papers and internal publications. These publications are discussed in Chapters 12 and 13.

Conclusions

* News releases can be a valuable communication tool, but only if they are really *news*.

* In general, news media personnel do not consider news releases to be as well written and as timely as PR practitioners think they are.

* News media personnel evaluate releases on the basis of writing quality, accuracy, completeness and timeliness.

* To understand what news is most acceptable to the media you are trying to serve, you must study the media.

* You must understand your own institution to find the news within it.

* Use the news and advertising columns appropriately.

* The lead is the most important part of your news release.

* A local angle is important in getting the news editor's attention.

* In amplifying the lead, use short, concise sentences and be sure you cover the who, what, when, where, why and how of the story in the first two paragraphs.

* PR writers can develop quotes for stories and get them approved by the person to whom they are attributed—a luxury news writers don't have.

* News releases should be written in a simple, clear, direct style.

* The Associated Press or United Press International stylebook dictates generally accepted news style, though some media have their own styles.

* News releases are written to communicate announcements, information on special events, spot news, responses to events, features and reactions to bad news.

* Some information should be placed in forms other than straight news releases— for example, column notes, letters or guest columns.

* Technical considerations determine the form for the release.

* Some releases may be sent computer to computer.

* All news releases will be edited and some may not appear at all.

* Photos and their captions may be sent with a story as illustrations or alone as "wild art." In either case, they are good PR tools.

* Deciding where to send releases is critical.

* Releases should be prepared in a style and format appropriate to the medium.

* Before turning loose of a news release, PR writers should review all 12 items in the news media checklist (see Table 7-8).

* To help communicate PR messages and build good media relations as well, news releases must contain genuine news, be written in the proper form and style, and be truthful, complete and accurate.

Exercises

1. Prepare a news release from the copy in Example 7-9.

2. Would the information be more appropriate as a column item? If so, how would you write it?

3. Write a caption for the two photos in Example 7-10.
   a. The two artists are from the city ballet, and are rehearsing in the ballet association's downtown recital and rehearsal hall. This photo is being submitted as "wild art."
   b. Some workers in the company have been on strike, and a reporter was hit by a bottle thrown by a striker. You are using this photo in your corporate

7-8

News Release Checklist

1. Is the lead direct and to the point? Does it contain the most important and most interesting aspects of the story?

2. Has the local angle been emphasized?

3. Have who, what, when, where and why been answered in the first few paragraphs?

4. Are sentences short, concise? Paragraphs short? Words common and concrete?

5. Has editorial comment been placed in quotation marks and attributed to the appropriate person?

6. Are quotations natural, that is, do they sound as though they could have been spoken?

7. Has newspaper style (AP or UPI) been followed faithfully throughout the release?

8. Is spelling and punctuation correct?

9. Have all statements of fact been double-checked for accuracy?

10. Has the release been properly prepared, typed and double-spaced?

11. Is the release dated? Is release time indicated?

12. Are names and phone numbers for further information included?

magazine to illustrate a story about the strike. You can use any identification you wish for your caption. (In reality the strike pictured took place at the General Dynamics plant in Fort Worth, Texas, and the newsman hit was Russ Bauman from Channel 8, WFAA-TV in Dallas. The incident occurred on November 5, 1984. The strike involved 6,400 workers at the defense plant. Bottles were thrown at the firetruck shown in the picture and Bauman was filming when he was hit in the back of the head. He was taken to the hospital, but released: no concussion, only a big bump on the head.)

4. Write a series of news releases for the information in 7-11.
   a. the newspaper
   b. the Chamber of Commerce magazine
   c. a trade publication (malls)
   d. the PR wire

5. Write a news release to go with the position paper in Chapter 14.

7-9

Exercise 1 Information
Source: Used with permission of the Datapoint Corporation.

INFOMART Introduces State-of-the-Art Registration System

SWN 035 FROM SOUTHWEST NEWSWIRE AT 214/748-1943

TO: BUSINESS DESKS

DALLAS, Jan. 21, 1985--(SWN)--A proprietary registration system is an integral part of the new INFOMART(R) facility that opened today in Dallas, Texas. The system included 32 Datapoint(R) computer workstations and multiple badge generators and bar scanners in tenant showrooms. Part of INFOMART'S overall tenant service, the registration system enables INFOMART to gather demographic information on visitors to the market center. This information is then used in INFOMART's and tenants's marketing efforts to ensure that specific needs of visiting prospects are properly addressed. Data Management Group, a Datapoint OEM, developed the software working with the INFOMART MIS staff.

7-9 | continued

The Datapoint computers used in the registration process are linked to badge generators and bar code scanning badge readers. When an attendee registers, his or her responses to the registration form are keyed into a Datapoint workstation. Then, the attendee receives a coded badge that contains the attendee's name, title, company, address, and other information to help INFOMART tenants better respond to the attendee's needs. Each vendor's showroom is equipped with a badge scanner, which documents the attendees visit. This information is stored and used later to compile statistics which help focus marketing efforts of both tenants and INFOMART.

The Datapoint computers at INFOMART are interconnected by coaxial cable into an ARC(R) (Attached Resource Computer(R)) local area network. INFOMART officials selected the Datapoint system because of its favorable response time and resource sharing capability.

"We required a distributed network to place terminals wherever we needed them -- to add more or move them simply by plugging into the network wherever we might need to accelerate the badge-making process," said William M. Winsor, president of INFOMART. "Datapoint's automatic reconfiguration and the modular nature of the

7-9 | continued

SYSTEM HAS SOLVED THAT NEED. WE CAN PLUG AND UNPLUG TERMINALS
WITHOUT TAKING DOWN THE SYSTEM, AND IF ONE NODE FAILS, IT DOESN'T
AFFECT THE REST OF THE SYSTEM. WE WERE ALSO LOOKING FOR RESOURCE
SHARING CAPABILITIES AND DISTRIBUTIVE COMMUNICATIONS CAPABILITIES,
AND THE SYSTEM HAS ENABLED US TO SOLVE THOSE NEEDS," HE CONCLUDED.

PLANS CALL FOR THE REGISTRATION SYSTEM TO BE LINKED TO AN IBM(R)
MAINFRAME COMPUTER. INFOMART OFFICIALS ARE ALSO PLANNING TO
EXTEND THE SYSTEM OF REGISTRATION REMOTELY TO OTHER DALLAS MARKET
CENTER PROPERTIES LATER THIS YEAR.

DATAPOINT CORPORATION, A FORTUNE 500 INDUSTRIAL FIRM, MANUFACTURES,
MARKETS AND SERVICES LOCAL AREA NETWORKS, MULTI-FUNCTION WORK-
STATIONS AND DISPERSED COMPUTING AND OFFICE AUTOMATION SYSTEMS
WORLDWIDE.

-0-

INFOMART IS A REGISTERED TRADEMARK OF THE DALLAS MARKET CENTER COMPANY.
IBM IS A REGISTERED TRADEMARK OF INTERNATIONAL BUSINESS MACHINES
CORPORATION.

-30-

CONTACT: J.G. MILNE OR T.J. MOLDENHAUER, DATAPOINT, 512/699-4437.

⌐

7-10α

Exercise 3 Photos
Source: (a) Barbara C. Laing/*Dallas Times Herald*; (b) Vince Heptig.

7-10b

7-11

Exercise 4 Information

The Executive Shopping Plaza in Downtown Prosper has learned that Sachs Bros., an exclusive department store chain, will locate there. Two national chain department stores, Lomax, Inc. and Phillips, Inc., already are located there. They were the founding "anchors" when the shopping plaza opened five years ago. Sachs Bros. already has eight other locations in the state. More information will be given at a news conference at 11 a.m. Wednesday to be called jointly by the public relations department of the plaza (you) and a PR official for Sachs. The plaza is a 10-acre site adjacent to downtown just off of the interstate. Twenty specialty stores and six restaurants already are located in the plaza. The only quotes you have are from the president of Sachs Bros., a family owned chain, Allison Sachs: "Our business philosophy of being where the people are makes this site a perfect location for our newest store"; and from the managers of the two plaza anchor department stores: Lomax Manager C. A. Taylor, "Sachs Bros. has an excellent reputation, and we will welcome them as neighbors"; and Phillips Manager Ernestine Everetts, "Competition is healthy, and we welcome the news." Construction is scheduled to begin late this year.

6. You and the management of Ourbank are ready to launch a new communication program for Ourbank. Every sign, all printed matter, and all ads and promotional pieces from Ourbank will play up the idea behind *The Safe Place*. Write a release for the newspaper that explains the basis of the slogan and the campaign. It will be timed for Sunday release.

Notes

[1] E. W. Brody, "Antipathy Between PR, Journalism Exaggerated," *Public Relations Review*, vol. X, no. 4 (Winter 1984): 11–15.

[2] Philip Lesly, "Relations with Publicity Media," in *Lesly's Public Relations Handbook* (Englewood Cliffs, N.J.: Prentice-Hall, 1971), p. 348.

[3] Ivy Lee, *Publicity: Some Things It Is and Is Not* (New York: Industries Publishing, 1925).

[4] Edward L. Bernays, *Public Relations* (Norman, Okla.: University of Oklahoma Press, 1952), p. 47.

[5] Ibid.

[6] Rudolf Flesch, *The Art of Readable Writing*, 25th anniversary ed. (New York: Harper & Row, 1974), p. 25.

[7] Robert Gunning, *The Technique of Clear Writing* (New York: McGraw-Hill, 1968), p. 225.

[8] Otto Lerbinger, *Designs for Persuasive Communication* (Englewood Cliffs, N.J.: Prentice-Hall, 1972), p. 69.

[9] Christopher French, Eileen Alt Powell and Howard Angione, eds., *The Associated Press Stylebook and Libel Manual* (New York: Associated Press, 1980), p. 269. Used with permission of the Associated Press.

[10] For a description of publicity wire services, see D. Newsom and A. Scott, *This is PR*, 3rd ed. (Belmont, Calif.: Wadsworth, 1985), Chapter 10.

Selected Bibliography

Edward L. Bernays, *Public Relations* (Norman, Okla.: University of Oklahoma Press, 1952).

L. R. Cockran, "Beyond the Typewriter: How to Develop a News Release," *Associated Management* (May 1984): 97.

Rudolf Flesch, *The Art of Readable Writing*, 25th anniversary ed. (New York: Harper & Row, 1974).

Robert Gunning, *The Technique of Clear Writing*, rev. ed. (New York: McGraw-Hill, 1968).

Ivy Lee, *Publicity: Some Things It Is and Is Not* (New York: Industries Publishing, 1925).

Otto Lerbinger, *Designs for Persuasive Communication* (Englewood Cliffs, N.J.: Prentice-Hall, 1972).

Philip Lesly, ed., *Lesly's Public Relations Handbook*, 3rd ed. (Englewood Cliffs, N.J.: Prentice-Hall, 1983).

D. Newsom and A. Scott, *This Is PR*, 3rd ed. (Belmont, Calif.: Wadsworth, 1985).

G. R. Richard, "The Well-bred Op-ed: Increasing Your Institution's Exposure in the Press," *Case Currents* (January 1984): 32.

Richard Weiner, *Professional's Guide to Publicity*, 2nd rev. ed. (New York: Richard Weiner, 1982).

Martin Bradley Winston, *Getting Publicity* (New York: Wiley, 1982).

William Zinsser, *On Writing Well*, 2nd ed. (New York: Harper & Row, 1980).

8
Broadcast Writing:
News and Features

If it wiggles," the saying goes, "it's TV news." And the remark is only half facetious. With broadcast media, sight and sound are all that matter.

Radio stations, for example, are interested in the sounds of an event. The voice of the mayor reading a proclamation, the president of the electric company explaining a power outage, the hospital director telling about caring for tornado victims—any of these is far more likely to be used on TV than a news release telling what happened and what was said. For TV news, one 30-second film clip is worth a thousand news releases.

Facts, Sights and Sounds

Facts are the vital elements of any news story, whether for print or broadcast media. Sometimes a formal news release isn't really necessary—the PR writer can provide the media with a fact sheet and the reporters can write the story. But with the electronic media, facts alone are not enough. Whether you're planning a special event, holding a news conference or dealing with a crisis situation, you must also be aware of sights and sounds—or, to use the technical terms, visuals and audio.

Special Events

A special event is one of the most common activities PR people get involved with. Such events are held for various purposes—to raise money or just to draw media attention (the so-called media event). Whatever the purpose of the special event, the first thing to do when you're faced with one is to prepare a fact sheet. This act alone will help preserve your sanity.

The fact sheet should contain a description of all activities, plus the day, date, time and duration for each activity and the name of the person responsible for each. Give each person's title (in relation to the event) too. Once you have drafted the timetable, add all the background: where, when and at what time the event will be held; charges (if any); sponsors; and your name, plus all the places and phone numbers where you can be reached. Your fact sheet will then be essentially complete. See the fact sheets in Examples 8-1 and 8-2. 8-1 is a fact sheet for an *event* and 8-2 is a fact sheet for a situation—a news development.

On a separate page, you might want to add a brief history of the event, giving dates and milestones, as another basic element in your media kit (see 8-3). For example, to a fact sheet on this year's pro-am (professional-amateur) benefit, you might add a single sheet describing past benefits, naming participants and stating who won, what their scores were, how many dollars were raised, who benefited, who the sponsors were and where past benefits were held (if different from the current location). (See 8-4 for a media kit full of fact sheets developed for reporters to use as background in covering an event so that the goals of historic preservation could be advanced.)

For the wiggle that makes the announcement news for TV, you'll have to stage some activity to film or tape for an advance announcement of your special event. Thus, after the first of what is to be an annual event, you'll have video that was shot during the event (on videotape, 16 mm film or 35 mm slides) to use as visuals for next year. One word of caution: When you use last year's pictures as an advance story, be sure you label the pictures carefully. Sometimes editors get too busy to realize that you couldn't be sending a picture of something that hasn't yet happened—and will inadvertently label last year's pictures as this year's. Protect yourself by labeling the pictures clearly and appropriately.

On preparing for an advance story, you should document the event on videotape with sound (and an audio cassette for radio backup), 35 mm color slides, perhaps 16 mm film (if you intend to preserve the video), and, just for safety, black and white 8-×-10-inch photos with a matte finish (glossies glow in TV lighting). It is also a good idea to shoot some charts and graphs on 35 mm slides that show attendance figures and such from the previous year. You might also make a slide showing dates for the upcoming event.

When you stage an activity to photograph, don't *simulate* the event. You wouldn't want to perpetrate a hoax. Nor would you want to be wrongly accused of doing so. But feel free to shoot preparations for the event; they qualify as legitimate news. For audio you can use the people involved—dignitaries, if possible—

8-1a

Media Kit for a Meeting
Note the cover letter to editors (b), the facts sheet (c) and the
time-of-release control on each story (d). *Source:* Used with
permission of the American Heart Association.

WE'RE FIGHTING FOR YOUR LIFE

American Heart Association

NEWS RELEASE
PACKET 1984

THE AMERICAN
HEART ASSOCIATION'S
57th
SCIENTIFIC
SESSIONS

November 12-15, 1984
Miami Beach Convention Center
Miami Beach, Florida

8-1b

American Heart Association
National Center

Memorandum

October 26, 1984

TO: Editors

FROM: Howard L. Lewis, Chief, Science Information (214) 750-5340
         Al Salerno, Director, Division of Science
           and Public Information   (214) 750-5397
         John Weeks, Senior Science Writer   (214) 750-5330
         Ann Williams, Senior Science Writer (214) 750-5392
         Terese Arena, Radio/TV Reporter   (214) 750-5374
         Prabhu Ponkshe, Chief, Public Information (214) 750-5317

The American Heart Association's 57th Scientific Sessions will bring
an estimated 15,000 scientists, physicians, nurses and others involved
in health care to Miami Beach, Florida, for a week of news-making
events starting Monday morning, November 12. A press briefing for
guidance of reporters will be held at 8:00 a.m. Monday in Press
Headquarters, Room 154 at the Convention Center.

Scientific and medical participants will represent major institutions
in almost two dozen nations.

The accompanying press kit has stories for each day of the meeting.
We have set up several news conferences each day with experts in
various heart and blood vessel fields and with scientists reporting
the important research finds of 1984. Details of these conferences
will be available at the Press Headquarters.

In addition to the medical news there should be stories of interest to
feature writers on the various exhibits and the life support system
for handling medical emergencies. Food editors will be interested in
AHA-approved menus for all formal lunch and dinner events.

If you have any questions, you can reach us at the Dallas numbers
above until Wednesday, November 7. On Sunday afternoon, November 11,
we'll be at the Miami Beach Convention Center -- (305) 538-0011.

959D:SPID/HL/DS
10-OCT-84

8-1c

**American Heart
Association**

National Center

Memorandum

October 26, 1984

<u>TO:</u>

Medical and Science Writers
and City Editors.....................

Radio and Television News
and Program Directors................

Photo Editors.......................

<u>FROM:</u>

Howard L. Lewis, John Weeks,
Ann Williams, Al Salerno

Terese Arena

Prabhu Ponkshe and Cindy Whitcome

THE EVENT:

Significant advances in the research and treatment of heart and blood vessel diseases will be reported at the 57TH SCIENTIFIC SESSIONS OF THE AMERICAN HEART ASSOCIATION.

THE TIME:

Monday, November 12, 1984, through Noon, Thursday, November 15, 1984.

THE PLACE:

Miami Beach (Fla.) Convention Center

TELEPHONE NUMBERS:

Press Headquarters -- (305) 538-0011

PRESS HEADQUARTERS:

Room 154, Miami Beach Convention Center. The Press Room will be open 1-5 p.m. on Sunday, November 11, for early arrivals.

It will be open at 7:15 a.m. on Monday and at 8:00 a.m. on Tuesday, Wednesday and Thursday.

Typewriters and telecopiers will be available. We'll also have a quiet room adjoining for audio taping and for telephone interviews for radio stations anywhere in the U.S.

PRESS BRIEFING:

8:00 a.m., Monday, November 12 at the Press Headquarters by Dr. Bernadine Healy Bulkley, Program Chairman.

- more -

8-1c continued

57th Scientific Sessions - 2

NEWS CONFERENCES:

Nine or more news conferences are being scheduled where groups of reporters can interview panels of physicians and research scientitsts. A list of scheduled news conferences and names of participants will be available in Press Headquarters.

RELEASE TIMES:

All papers presented to the Scientific Sessions, as well as the news releases in this kit, are for release <u>when presented</u>.

News conferences have been designated for AMs or PMs release. We are defining these release times in wire service terms.

SPECIAL INTERVIEWS:

Many scientists have been invited to drop by the Press Headquarters <u>before</u> they deliver their papers. We will arrange interviews with others at your request.

REGISTRATION:

Correspondents should register at Press Headquarters where copies of papers, programs, press kits, abstracts and credentials will be available. We will limit accreditation to two people from any one publication, and three from any publication group.

Press badges will admit reporters to all of the scientific sessions, news conferences and the exhibit area.

Cardiovascular Conferences and "How-to" Sessions on Monday and Wednesday nights are small informal discussion groups and are <u>not</u> open to press coverage.

ADVANCE INFORMATION:

Copies of the special supplement of the October issue of <u>Circulation</u>, an AHA journal, are available upon request to (214) 750-5340 or (214) 750-5397. This journal contains abstracts of all the papers to be presented in Miami Beach.

960S:SPID/HL/DS
10-OCT-84

8-1d

News
Release

American Heart
Association

National Center
7320 Greenville Avenue
Dallas, Texas 75231

For Release:

Not to be used before
10:45 a.m. Monday
November 12, 1984

NR 84-3400 (Meltzer)
For more information, November 12-15
Room 154, Miami Beach Convention Center
Terese Arena or Howard L. Lewis
(305) 538-0011

TINY, EVEN-SIZED AIR BUBBLES HELP IMPROVE
IMAGES AND DIAGNOSIS OF HARD-TO-SEE HEART DEFECTS

News
Release

American Heart
Association

National Center
7320 Greenville Avenue
Dallas, Texas 75231

For Release:

Not to be used before
2:00 p.m. Monday
November 12, 1984

NR 84-3401 (Grossbard/Sobel)
For more information, November 12-15
Room 154, Miami Beach Convention Center
John Weeks or Howard L. Lewis
(305) 538-0011

CLOT-BUSTING PROTEIN PRODUCED BY
GENETIC ENGINEERS STOPS HEART ATTACKS

News
Release

American Heart
Association

National Center
7320 Greenville Avenue
Dallas, Texas 75231

For Release:

Not to be used before
9:00 a.m. Tuesday
November 13, 1984

NR 84-3404 (Zoll)
For more information, November 12-15
Room 154, Miami Beach Convention Center
John Weeks or Howard L. Lewis
(305) 538-0011

NEW EXTERNAL PACEMAKER PERFORMS
WELL IN FIRST CLINICAL TRIALS

News
Release

American Heart
Association

National Center
7320 Greenville Avenue
Dallas, Texas 75231

For Release:

Not to be used before
10:45 a.m., Tuesday
November 13, 1984

NR 84-3405 (Miller)
For more information, November 12-15
John Weeks or Howard L. Lewis
(305) 538-0011

SEXUAL PROBLEMS INCREASING AMONG
PATIENTS RECOVERING FROM HEART ATTACKS

8-1d continued

News Release

American Heart Association
National Center
7320 Greenville Avenue
Dallas, Texas 75231

For Release:

Not to be used before
1:00 p.m. Tuesday
November 13, 1984

NR 84-3410 (Addonizio)
For more information, November 12-15
Room 154, Miami Beach Convention Center
Howard L. Lewis or John Weeks
(305) 538-0011

'NUCLEAR STETHOSCOPE' MONITORS
CHILDREN AFTER HEART SURGERY

News Release

American Heart Association
National Center
7320 Greenville Avenue
Dallas, Texas 75231

For Release:

Not to be used before
9:00 a.m. Wednesday
November 14, 1984

NR 84-3412 (Rifkin/Uretsky)
For more information, November 12-15
Room 154, Miami Beach Convention Center
John Weeks or Howard L. Lewis
(305) 538-0011

FLUOROSCOPY MAY BE USEFUL IN
PREDICTING HEART ATTACK RISK

News Release

American Heart Association
National Center
7320 Greenville Avenue
Dallas, Texas 75231

For Release:

Not to be used before
2:00 p.m. Wednesday
November 14, 1984

NR 84-3417 (Summers)
For more information, November 12-15
Room 154, Miami Beach Convention Center
Howard L. Lewis or John Weeks
(305) 538-0011

BRUSH WITH DEATH HEIGHTENS PSYCHOLOGICAL
DISTRESS FOR SURVIVORS OF CARDIAC ARREST

News Release

American Heart Association
National Center
7320 Greenville Avenue
Dallas, Texas 75231

For Release:

Not to Be Used Before
9:00 a.m. Thursday
November 15, 1984

NR 84-3420 (Swensson/Sahn)
For more information, November 12-15
Room 154, Miami Beach Convention Center
John Weeks or Howard L. Lewis
(305) 538-0011

NEW ULTRASOUND TECHNOLOGY EASES
DETECTION OF HEART DEFECTS IN CHILDREN

8-2a

PR Story for All Media
The job is to get out an important public message, so all
media are used. Example 8-2a is the summary of the situation
and action to be taken; 8-2b is the cover letter and 8-2c is the
print-media announcement. Example 8-2d shows the television
copy and visuals for the news announcement; 8-2e is the radio
copy—two stories of different length. Because this issue is of
public interest, it merits public service time. Examples 8-2f
and 8-2g contain English and Spanish versions. The latter gets
the word out to residents whose first language is Spanish and
who might otherwise miss the notification. *Source:* Used with
permission of Michael Pellecchia.

Fact Sheet/Class Action   2.2.2.

Action Taken   Ms. Patricia Tenoso, senior counsel for
                                    the Western Center on Law and Poverty, a
                                    public interest law firm in Los Angeles,
                                    acted on behalf of Myrna Underwood, a
                                    Section 236 resident in Carson, California.

                                    (The Western Center on Law and Poverty, Inc
                                    (WCLP) is funded by the Legal Services
                                    Corporation. This corporation was created
                                    by Congress in 1974 to aid the 29 million
                                    poor across the nation. Groups similar
                                    to WCLP exist in all states.)

                                    Before filing the Underwood case, Ms. Tenos
                                    and other Center attorneys knew of approxi-
                                    mately 40 pending cases against HUD with up
                                    to 10 counts ruling in favor of tenants.

                                    It became clear that tenants nationwide had
                                    been deprived of subsidies that were legall
                                    theirs.

                                    In June, 1976, the Court certified that
                                    Underwood v. Hills (Carla Hills was Secreta
                                    of HUD. She was subsequently replaced by
                                    Patricia R. Harris.) was a nationwide clas
                                    and granted judgment for the tenants agains
                                    HUD.
                                    -

8-2a continued

How Current Section 236
Tenants Will Be Notified

It is estimated that some tenants involved
still live in Section 236 projects. Claim
forms will be made available through projec
managers.

Notices in English and Spanish will be plac
in highly visible spots throughout building;
to urge tenants to find out if they are liv:
in a Section 236 project, and to pick up
applications if they have lived in one durir
the time designated.

- -

How Other Eligible Claimants
May Be Reached

Among current Section 236 tenants are those
who will not see notices, and those who do r
realize that they are living in, or have li\
in, Section 236 housing. To reach those
tenants, as well as former tenants who have
relocated throughout the nation, news media
will be requested to urge their audiences t(
ask, "Do I live in a Section 236 project no\
Did I live in one during the specified time(
period?"

- - - - - - - - - - - . - - - - - - - - - - -

Fact Sheet/Class Action   3.3.3.

Monies to Be Used
for Refund

Refund monies do not involve public tax
dollars.

The source of funds is a special reserve
fund made up from a portion of the rent
paid by residents with higher incomes.
This fund was enacted by Congress and
designed for use on behalf of low income
tenants.

- - - - - - - - - - - - - - - - - - - -

Distribution
Controls

Settlement procedures have been as
elaborate as those of litigation.

Precautions taken to reduce the incidence
of fradulent claims include the following:

a. A five-level claim review procedure
involving manual checks and information
cross-checking.

b. Court approval required for final
distribution.

c. Unlike State welfare systems, this
one-time distribution will not be made
until all legitimate claims are thoroughly
checked to the satisfaction of the Committ(
of Counsel and the United States District
Court.

- -.

8-2b

September 25, 1979

BULLETIN TO EDITORS

It is impossible to estimate how many of your readers may be
tangibly affected by the information in the attached release.

The number of claimants who <u>no longer live in Section 236
apartment housing</u> may be as high as fifty percent.

Even those that do still live in such housing may not be aware
that they are claimants to the settlement and should take the
necessary steps to get their money.

There are more than 10,000 236 apartment units in New York City
alone. To find out the ones in your circulation area, a call
to the Dept. of HUD field office or a local municipal housing
services administration, or tenants group, may prove fruitful.

We will be glad to cooperate in providing any further information
you may need to better inform your readers.

###

8-2c

FOR RELEASE: September 25, 1979

FORMER TENANTS OF SUBSIDIZED HOUSING

TO CLAIM $60 MILLION

Tenants of U.S. Department of Housing and Urban Development (HUD)
Section 236 housing between 1975 and 1977 will soon lay claim to
$60 million cash, as a result of the largest class action settle-
ment on behalf of the poor in the nation's history.

The landmark suit against HUD was settled out-of-court last spring.
Now, owners and managers of Section 236 apartment housing nationwide will be notifying tenants that they may be eligible for
individual rent refunds of up to $500 or more from the HUD settle-
ment fund, according to Patricia Tenoso, a public interest attorney
who served as lead counsel on the case.

"We estimate that eligible claimants may number as many as 750,000
nationwide," Ms. Tenoso said. "Congressionally authorized rent
subsidies were witheld from some Section 236 tenants between
February 1, 1975 and September 30, 1977, and now HUD has agreed to
pay the tenants back the amounts they were effectively overcharged,"
she added.

8-2d

NORTH AMERICAN PRECIS SYNDICATE, INC.
201 East 42nd Street ● New York, N.Y. 10017 ● UN 7-9000

IS THERE A REFUND IN YOUR FUTURE?

1. Is there a refund in your future? There may be if you lived in a "HUD" federally subsidized apartment between February 1, 1975, and September 30, 1977.

2. Your residence must not have been just *any* government-subsidized apartment but one specifically designated as *Section 236 apartment housing project.* That's *very* important.

3. Ask your apartment manager for a claim form if you live, or have lived, in a Section 236 apartment. Or check your lease during that time. Either can give you the answer.

4. But get a claim form now. For more information, call toll-free, 1-800-824-7980. Who knows! There may be a refund in your future.

8-2e

RADIO ROUNDUP
a collection of features, oddities,
and helpful tips

NORTH AMERICAN
PRECIS SYNDICATE
201 east 42nd street
new york, n.y. 10017

(149 WORDS, 60 SECONDS)

IS THERE A REFUND IN YOUR FUTURE?

IS THERE A REFUND IN YOUR FUTURE? THERE MAY BE IF YOU LIVED IN A FEDERAL GOVERNMENT-SUBSIDIZED APARTMENT BETWEEN FEBRUARY 1, 1975, AND SEPTEMBER 30, 1977. IF, THAT IS, THE GOVERNMENT-SUBSIDIZED APARTMENT WAS DESIGNATED BY THE U. S. DEPT. OF HOUSING AND URBAN DEVELOPMENT AS A SECTION 236 APARTMENT. HOW CAN YOU FIND OUT IF YOU QUALIFY? ASK THE APARTMENT BUILDING'S OWNER OR MANAGER. IF YOU DO NOW, OR HAVE IN THE PAST, LIVED IN SUCH AN APARTMENT, YOU MAY BE ELIGIBLE FOR A REFUND—UP TO SEVERAL HUNDRED DOLLARS, IN FACT. YOU CAN GET OFFICIAL CLAIMS FORMS FROM YOUR BUILDING MANAGER, OR BY CALLING OR WRITING THE CLAIMS PROCESSING CENTER AT P. O. BOX 3613, LOS ANGELES, CALIFORNIA 90051. OR CALL, TOLL-FREE, 1-800-599-6719. ALL CLAIMS MUST BE POSTMARKED BY OCTOBER 30, 1979. IF YOU ACT NOW, THERE MAY BE A REFUND FOR YOU LATER.

\#   \#   \#

8-2e continued

RADIO ROUNDUP
a collection of features, oddities,
and helpful tips

NORTH AMERICAN PRECIS SYNDICATE
201 east 42nd street
new york, n.y. 10017

(163 words, 66 seconds)

A LOADED QUESTION—WITH CASH, THAT IS!

The right answer to this question may mean extra cash for you: Do you now, or did you between February 1, 1975, and September 30, 1977, live in an apartment subsidized by the Federal government? Not just ANY such apartment, mind you, but one designated by the U. S. Dept. of Housing and Urban Development as a SECTION 236 APARTMENT. That's important: SECTION 236 APARTMENT. If your answer to the question is "yes," you may be eligible for a rent refund up to several hundred dollars. You can get the answer by asking your apartment manager or owner, or by writing or calling the Claims Processing Center, P. O. Box 3613, Los Angeles, California 90051. Or call toll-free: 1-800-599-6719. Claim forms are available from your building manager or from the Claims Center. But remember: All claims MUST be postmarked by October 30, 1979. Get the answer to that question...and act quickly. It could be a question of more money for you.

\# \# \#

8-2f

J. WALTER THOMPSON COMPANY
NEWS
420 Lexington Avenue • New York, N.Y. 10017
(212) 867-1000

Contact: Michael Pellecchia
              John Higgins

Start Using: July 24, 1979

Stop Using: Sept. 16, 1979

WESTERN CENTER ON LAW AND POVERTY

Reading Time: 20 Seconds

VIDEO   AUDIO

Color Slide   If you lived in a HUD Section 236

(Rent Refund)   Housing project anytime between

                         February 1, 1975 and September 30, 1977

                         you may be eligible for a rent refund!

                         Get a claim form from your project

                         manager today. For more information

                         call collect 213 - 625-1244 -- call

                         collect 213 - 625-1244.

                    ###

8-2f | continued

J. WALTER THOMPSON COMPANY

NEWS

420 Lexington Avenue • New York, N.Y. 10017
(212) 867-1000

Contact:

Michael Pellecchia
John Higgins

Start Using: July 24, 1979

Stop Using: Sept. 16, 1979

WESTERN CENTER ON LAW AND POVERTY

Reading Time: 20 Seconds

VIDEO

Color Slide

(Rent Refund)

AUDIO

Si usted ha vivido in un apartamento
HUD Sección 236 por cualquier período
de tiempo entre Febrero 1 de 1975 y
Septiembre 30 de 1977, usted puede tene
derecho a una devolución de parte de
su renta. Pida hoy formulario de
reclamo al gerente del edificio. Para
obtener más informacion llame collect
al teléfono 213 - 625-1244. 213 -
625-1244.

###

8-2g

J. WALTER THOMPSON COMPANY

NEWS

420 Lexington Avenue • New York, N.Y. 10017
(212) 867-1000

Contact:

Michael Pellecchia
John Higgins

Start Date: July 24, 1979

Stop Date: Sept. 16, 1979

PUBLIC SERVICE ANNOUNCEMENT -

WESTERN CENTER ON LAW AND POVERTY

(Reading Time - 20 Seconds)

If you lived in a HUD Section 236 Housing project anytime
between February 1, 1975 and September 30, 1977, you may
be eligible for a rent refund! Get a claim form from
your project manager today. For more information call
collect 213 - 625-1244 -- call collect 213 - 625-1244.

###

J. WALTER THOMPSON COMPANY

NEWS

420 Lexington Avenue • New York, N.Y. 10017
(212) 867-1000

Contact:

Michael Pellecchia
John Higgins

Start Date: July 24, 1979

Stop Date: Sept. 16, 1979

PUBLIC SERVICE ANNOUNCEMENT –

WESTERN CENTER ON LAW AND POVERTY

(Reading Time – 20 Seconds)

Si usted ha vivido in un apartamento HUD Sección 236 por
cualquier período de tiempo entre Febrero 1 de 1975 y
Septiembre 30 de 1977, usted puede tener derecho a una
devolución de parte de su renta. Pida hoy formulario
de reclamo al gerente del edificio. Para obtener más
informacion llame collect al teléfono 213 – 625-1244.
213 – 625-1244.

###

8-3

Media Kit Contents
Source: Used with permission from Doug Newsom and Alan
Scott, *This Is PR*, 3rd ed. (Belmont, Calif.: Wadsworth, 1985),
pp. 264–265.

Media kits have to be tailored for each occasion, and if
mailed, they should also have a cover letter briefly explaining
the event. The contents are as follows:

1. *Basic facts sheet* detailing newsmaking event and explaining significance in strictly factual terms. Include important
   dates, times, participants and relationships (for example,
   company to holding company). Be sure name, address and
   phone numbers where you can be reached for additional
   information are on sheet.

2. *Historical facts sheet* giving background of event, individual or organization involved. Use simple date-event format.

3. *Program of event* or *schedule of activities*, including detailed time data. Give script, when possible, for broadcast
   media.

4. *Straight news story*, never more than a page and a half of
   double-spaced typescript for print media and one or two
   short paragraphs for broadcast media. Give both print and
   broadcast versions to broadcast newspeople. The print
   news media need only print version.

5. *Complete list of all participants*, explaining their connection with the event.

6. *Biographical background of principals*, updated with current information about them given priority, unless something in background is particularly related to the event.

7. *Visual material*, consisting of 8 × 10 (or 5 × 7 if head shots
   of a person) black and white glossy prints for newspapers
   and magazines and 35mm color slides (transparencies) for
   television and publications using color. Be sure all are
   good quality, have significance (tell a story or show an important participant) and have *attached* identification. (If
   media kits are being mailed, you may want to send slick
   proofs but certainly not to broadcast media.)

8. *A longer general news story*, tying in background information. May be as long as three double-spaced pages for print
   media, full page for broadcast media (about 60 seconds of
   copy).

8-3 | continued

9. Two or three *feature* stories of varying lengths for print media. There will be no broadcast versions, but the features should be included in broadcast news kits for background.

10. A *page of special isolated facts* that are interesting and that will stand alone. These often are picked up for incorporation into copy written by the newspeople or used as fillers.

11. Any *brochures* available about the event or organization or person, prepared either for the event or earlier (if the latter, be *sure to update* in pen).

Don't forget electronic networks that can help. Put your material on a PR wire service. Have releases and photos (still and slides) ready for the newswire people and actualities (voice quotes) on cassettes for the radio networks (many state and regional ones extra) as well as film clips and videotapes for television.

8-4a

Media Kit for a Special Event Tie-In
It is smart to piggyback on an event that is sure to draw
attention. Notice how the National Historic Trust has tied
in with the presidential inaugural parade (8-4a). When a
situation involves a need for interaction between an institution
and the news media, a news conference is needed. Materials
for the conference should be prepared so questions can be
asked. When possible, materials should be given or sent
in advance. Example 8-4b is a "stock" kit from Beverly
Enterprises—one prepared so other materials can be added.
The contents are: a fact sheet, a historical summary, a
statement of purpose, a *Fortune* reprint from publicity, a
corporate publication (one issue), an annual report, a brochure
(magazine size) and a folder (envelope size). *Source:* (8-4a)
Used with permission of the National Trust for Historic
Preservation; (8-4b) used with permission of Beverly
Enterprises.

National Trust for Historic Preservation

1785 MASSACHUSETTS AVENUE, N.W.   WASHINGTON, D.C. 20036   (202) 673-4000

January 10, 1985

```
Name
Title
Media Outlet
Street Address
City and State


Dear _____:

On January 21 a U.S. President will once again parade down Pennsylvania
Avenue, America's most famous main street, following the swearing-in ceremony
at the U.S. Capitol.  Observers of past Inaugurals will notice a major change
in President Reagan's 1985 Inaugural parade:  the parade route, Pennsylvania
Avenue, has had a facelift.  What had been a source of complaint by Presidents
since John F. Kennedy is now a focal point of pride in the nation's capital.
Historic buildings from the U.S. Capitol to the Mathew Brady photography
studio to the Old Post Office have been restored to their original dignity.
In a short time, the plan for rehabilitation of the Avenue will be complete,
and much of the credit goes to the National Trust for Historic Preservation.
```

8-4a | continued

The Trust has worked with the private sector, federal and local governments to bring America's main street back and the results are apparent to everyone who strolls or drives down the Avenue.

Do you plan to devote any of your 1985 Inaugural coverage to the impressive restoration of Pennsylvania Avenue, and to the contrast between the condition of the parade route in 1985 and past Inaugurals? If so, you will want to glance at the enclosed background material which describes the Trust, historic buildings on the Avenue and the federal tax incentives which have made the restoration possible.

Spokesmen from the Trust are available to talk with you about the success of Pennsylvania Avenue's preservation, from the historic significance of the buildings to the technical problems of restoration to the importance of retaining the federal tax incentives for historic preservation work.

I would like to call you in a few days to check on your interest in a Pennsylvania Avenue story.

Sincerely,

Beverly A. Reece
Public Affairs Officer

8-4α continued

FACTS

National Trust for Historic Preservation
A private, nonprofit membership organization
1785 Massachusetts Avenue, N.W. Washington, D.C. 20036

For additional information, contact: Office of Public Affairs (202) 673-4000

AMERICA'S MAIN STREET--PENNSYLVANIA AVENUE

On January 21 following his public swearing-in at the U.S. Capitol, President
Reagan will lead the Inaugural Parade down Pennsylvania Avenue--America's Main
Street. President Reagan and the nation will see a renewed and revitalized
Pennsylvania Avenue that day; a change due in large measure to the work of the
National Trust for Historic Preservation.

The historic West Front of the U.S. Capitol, site of the swearing-in ceremony,
was saved in 1983 from entombment in a 77-foot marble-covered extension
because of a campaign led by the National Trust. The Apex Building, now Sears
House, was rehabilitated using Trust-advocated federal tax credits for
historic rehabilitation. The Old Post Office was rescued from the wrecker's
ball by a local preservation group founded largely by National Trust staff.
Its shopping area, the Pavilion, was made possible by the same tax credits
used on the Apex Building. The National Trust paid for the first report
showing the economic feasibility of restoring the historic Willard Hotel; a
report that led directly to the current rehabilitation. These buildings have
witnessed over 125 years of Presidential Inaugurals. They stand today because
of the National Trust.

The History of the Inaugural Route

The route President Reagan will follow is the same one Thomas Jefferson took
180 years earlier when he rode on horseback from the Congress' House to the
President's House. Only 14 years before Jefferson unknowingly started the
tradition of an Inaugural Parade, Pennsylvania Avenue had been an idea in the
mind of Pierre L'Enfant, the man George Washington had hired to lay out the
plan for the new nation's capital in a 10-square-mile area ceded from the
states of Maryland and Virginia.

The nation's attention is given to Pennsylvania Avenue every four years at the
time of the presidential inauguration and on those infrequent occasions when
it is the site of parades honoring America's heroes or the stage for public
protests.

In 1791, when L'Enfant drew his plan for the city, he blended two common 18th
century plans; one that featured a series of axes, with avenues radiating from
there forming triangles, and a gridiron pattern with streets crossing at right
angles.

L'Enfant's principal triangle was to be formed by connecting the Congress'
House (the U.S. Capitol) with the President's House and a statue of George
Washington. The Washington statue was to be directly in line with the President's House. A second major triangle would be formed by linking the statue
and Capitol with a "Market Square" at 8th and Pennsylvania Avenue. Other
major squares would be at 6th and 12th Streets and Pennsylvania Avenue.

FACTS

National Trust for Historic Preservation
A private, nonprofit membership organization
1785 Massachusetts Avenue, N.W. Washington, D.C. 20036

For additional information, contact: | Office of Public Affairs (202) 673–4000

FEDERAL TAX INCENTIVES FOR HISTORIC REHABILITATION

Why are there federal tax incentives for rehabilitating old and historic buildings?

There are three basic reasons why Congress and three presidents--Gerald Ford, Jimmy Carter and Ronald Reagan--have supported federal tax incentives for historic rehabilitation.

1. In remarks to the first national videoconference on downtown revital-ization on September 18, 1984, President Reagan summarized the reasons for having federal tax incentives when he said, "Our tax credits have made the preservation of our older buildings not only a matter of respect for beauty and history, but of economic good sense."

2. Tax incentives are an effective way to encourage economic development and growth. In 1981, for example, Congress expanded the tax incen-tives for historic rehabilitation and added credits for older buildings to encourage investors to spend private dollars on projects in the northeast, midwest and mid-Atlantic states--areas hard hit by the recession and the flight of businesses to the Sun Belt. These areas also have the highest concentration of old and historic buildings. By encouraging their rehabilitation, Congress hoped to encourage the revitalization of deteriorating urban and rural com-munities, the retention of existing industries and the development of new businesses.

3. Tax incentives can be a more efficient way to achieve certain goals than direct expenditures by the federal government. Between 1966 and 1981 the federal government spent about $163 million for historic rehabilitation through a program of matching grants administered by state governments. Congress, however, recognized that more preser-vation work needed to be done and that private investment had to be attracted to old and historic buildings. The first tax incentives passed in 1976 were designed to attract such investment. To date, the federal tax credits have generated 43 times the dollar value in rehabilitation financed through the federal grants programs.

What are the federal tax incentives for historic rehabilitation?

The federal tax incentives are a three-tiered system of tax credits for investing in the rehabilitation of old and historic buildings.
1. 25 percent credit for the "certified" rehabilitaton of "certified historic structures."
2. 20 percent credit for buildings at least 40 years old.
3. 15 percent credit for buildings at least 30 years old.

FACTS

National Trust for Historic Preservation

A private, nonprofit membership organization
1785 Massachusetts Avenue, N.W. Washington, D.C. 20036

For additional information, contact: Office of Public Affairs (202) 673-4000

THE NATIONAL TRUST IS
PRESERVING MAIN STREETS ACROSS AMERICA

Pennsylvania Avenue. Broad Street. Market Square. Whatever its particular
name, the "Main Street" of a community is both the center of its commercial
life and a public, ceremonial place. It is where a city's business is done
and where individuals carry out the small transactions of their everyday
lives. It is also the place where people gather to celebrate the 4th of July,
to send their soldiers off to war and welcome them back again.

Pennsylvania Avenue is America's "Main Street." It is where Americans meet to
celebrate the inauguration of a President, to demonstrate for or against a
political cause, to salute their heroes.

Not too long ago Main Streets across America, including Pennsylvania Avenue,
were suffering from years of neglect and decay. Today that trend is being
reversed in many communities including Washington, D.C., as the preservation
and rehabilitation of old and historic buildings is made a central part of the
strategy for downtown revitalization.

The National Trust for Historic Preservation is leading and helping these
local efforts through its National Main Street Center, through financial
assistance in the form of grants and loans, with national recognition from its
awards program and through its support of federal tax incentives for historic
rehabilitation.

<u>National Main Street Center</u>

What: A human resource and technical assistance program to stimulate
             economic development within the context of historic preservation.

             The Center's Main Street Approach combines four elements—orga-
             nization, promotion, design and economic diversification—in a
             comprehensive strategy for downtown revitalizaton using Main
             Street's existing and historic assets.

How: The Center publishes technical information, produces audiovisual
             materials, conducts training courses and provides technical
             assistance to states and communities.

             Since 1980 the focus of the program has been a three-year pilot
             partnership among the Center, six states and 30 small cities. A
             list of the states and cities is attached.

             In September 1984, the National Trust held the first national
             videoconference on Main Street revitalization. More than 15,000
             people from 2,000 towns and cities gathered at 448 sites.
             Satellite communications technology linked the sites to the
             central location in Washington, D.C. This is the largest
             videoconference ever held. It was sponsored by the U.S. Depart-
             ment of Agriculture and the National Endowment for the Arts.

8-4a | continued

FACTS National Trust for Historic Preservation
A private, nonprofit membership organization
1785 Massachusetts Avenue, N.W. Washington, D.C. 20036

For additional information, contact: Office of Public Affairs (202) 673-4000

FACTS ABOUT THE USE OF THE
FEDERAL TAX INCENTIVES FOR HISTORIC REHABILITATION

<u>Both The Number And Dollar Value Of Projects Qualifying For The 25 Percent Tax
Credit Have Increased</u>

Fiscal Year	Projects Approved	Dollar Value of Rehabilitation
1977-78	512	$ 140.0 million
1979	635	300.0 million
1980	614	346.2 million
1981	1,375	738.3 million
1982	1,802	1,128.4 million
1983	2,572	2,164.9 million
1984	3,214	2,123.1 million
1985 Estimate	4,000	2,400.0 million

The Department of the Interior has said that <u>10,724</u> projects representing an
estimated <u>$6.94 billion</u> worth of rehabilitation have been approved since the
first tax incentives for historic rehabilitation were passed in 1976.

<u>Housing Is The Most Frequent Use For Preservation Credit Projects Between 1976
And 1983</u>

Multi-Family Housing	33%
Single-Family Housing	9%
Mixed Housing/Commercial (Stores, Offices)	13%
Commercial	40%
Other (Including Hotels)	5%

Source: National Trust, PRIME (Preservation and Rehabilitation Impact
Estimator)

<u>Cities Most Actively Involved In Historic Rehabilitation</u>

	Number of Projects
St. Louis, Missouri	350
Baltimore, Maryland	344
New Orleans, Louisiana	283
Savannah, Georgia	275
Washington, D.C.	263
Albany, New York	217
Philadelphia, Pennsylvania	214
Hartford, Connecticut	190
Louisville, Kentucky	178
Charleston, South Carolina	154

Source: National Park Service, Fiscal Year 1983 project applications

8-4a continued

FACTS National Trust for Historic Preservation
A private, nonprofit membership organization
1785 Massachusetts Avenue, N.W. Washington, D.C. 20036

For additional information, contact: Office of Public Affairs (202) 673-4000

NATIONAL TRUST FOR HISTORIC PRESERVATION

<u>What is the National Trust?</u> The National Trust is a private, nonprofit
membership organization. It was chartered by the U.S. Congress in 1949 and
has two basic purposes: to encourage the public to participate in the
preservation of America's history and culture and to own historic properties.

<u>Why is it called the Trust?</u> The historical model for private national
preservation organizations throughout the world is the National Trust for
Places of Historic Interest or Natural Beauty in England. It is also the
group from which the National Trust in the United States took its name. The
word "trust" is used to mean an organization that takes care of something
(America's architectural, cultural and maritime heritage) in the interest of
someone else (this and future generations of Americans).

<u>What does it do?</u> The National Trust operates in four general areas:
1. It gives technical advice and financial assistance to nonprofit
    organizations and public agencies to help them carry out preservation
    activities;
2. It offers educational programs for volunteers and professionals in
    preservation and for the general public;
3. It is an advocate for the country's heritage in the courts and with
    legislative and regulatory agencies; and
4. It operates special projects to show how a preservation approach can
    resolve particular problems.

<u>What else does the National Trust do?</u> The National Trust publishes a monthly
newspaper, <u>Preservation News</u>, a bimonthly magazine, <u>Historic Preservation</u>, and
a legal quarterly, <u>Preservation Law Reporter</u>. It also produces books,
newsletters and brochures on specific preservation topics.

To make the public aware of preservation, the National Trust sponsors
Preservation Week the second full week of May and does public service
advertising.

The National Trust sponsors educational seminars, technical workshops and an
annual national preservation conference each October.

<u>Does the National Trust own any historic properties or museums?</u> The National
Trust owns and administers eight historic house museums:

        Chesterwood in Stockbridge, Massachusetts
        Decatur House in Washington, D.C.
        Drayton Hall near Charleston, South Carolina
        Lyndhurst in Tarrytown, New York
        Montpelier, James Madison's home, near Charlottesville, Virginia
        The Shadows-on-the-Teche in New Iberia, Louisiana
        Woodlawn Plantation and the Pope-Leighey House in Mount Vernon,
          Virginia
        Woodrow Wilson House in Washington, D.C.

8-4a continued

National Trust for Historic Preservation

1785 MASSACHUSETTS AVENUE, N.W.   WASHINGTON, D.C. 20036   (202) 673-4000

J. Jackson Walter

President

J. Jackson Walter became president of the National Trust for Historic
Preservation on December 1, 1984.

A native of Swarthmore, Pennsylvania, Jack Walter most recently served as
president of the National Academy of Public Administration in Washington,
D.C. The Congressionally chartered nonprofit organization is a "who's who" of
practitioners and scholars of government management. The Academy provides
counsel on the practical aspects of public administration to federal, state
and local governments, and conducts and publishes studies on public
management. During his tenure, the Academy achieved both a new level of
prestige and influence and financial self-sufficiency.

In 1979, he became the first Director of the U.S. Office of Government Ethics,
an independent federal agency. Walter organized and put into operation a
highly effective program to enforce federal conflict of interest laws in the
executive branch. Initially appointed by President Carter, he was reappointed
by President Reagan and served until 1982.

Walter entered public service in 1976 when he became secretary of the Florida
Department of Business Regulation, the agency overseeing and licensing that
state's pari-mutuel betting, alcohol and tobacco sales, hotels and restaurants
and condominiums and land sales. Under his leadership, operating stability
and professional credibility were restored to an agency that had been the
focus of attacks by both the legislature and the press.

From 1966 to 1976, he practiced law in New England specializing in
environmental land use, historic preservation, municipal zoning and planning
law. His legal career included both private practice and serving as director
of planning and government relations for the region's largest rural land
marketing and development firm.

Born on November 6, 1940, Walter received his A.B., cum laude, in 1962 from
Amherst College and his law degree in 1966 from Yale Law School.

8-4a continued

8-4b

```
                        BEVERLY ENTERPRISES
                        FACT SHEET
```

The Company: Beverly Enterprises is the nation's
                             leader in long-term care with a ser-
                             vice network encompassing nursing
                             centers, facilities providing con-
                             gregate care, retirement living
                             apartments, home health units, durable
                             medical equipment outlets and pharmacy
                             services and operating in 44 states,
                             the District of Columbia and Canada.

The Operation: Headquartered in Pasadena, California,
                             Beverly operates under a decentralized
                             management structure, established on
                             the basis of the concept that the high-
                             est caliber of care can be provided by
                             local managers who are most cognizant
                             of community needs. Geographic divi-
                             sions oversee operations of nursing
                             centers and others provide specialized
                             long-term care services, alternative
                             lifestyles, or support systems for oper-
                             ating divisions and local components of
                             the company.

Divisions: Central: Fort Smith, Arkansas
                             Eastern: Virginia Beach, Virginia
                             Heritage: Rockville, Maryland
                             Information Services: Virginia
                             Beach, Virginia
                             Northern: Minneapolis, Minnesota
                             Retirement Living: Carmel, Indiana
                             Southern: Jackson, Mississippi
                             Support Services: Fort Smith,
                             Arkansas
                             Texas: Austin, Texas
                             Western: Fresno, California
                             Home Health Services: Torrance,
                             California
                             Bestview of Canada: Mississauga,
                             Ontario
```
```

8-4b | continued

Services:

As of 3/1/85, Beverly operated over 900 nursing centers with approximately 102,000 beds, 14 retirement living units with 1,856 apartments and more than 100 home health agencies. Other services include durable medical equipment units and pharmacy outlets specializing in medication systems for the elderly.

Employees:

Approximately 86,750

History:

Beverly was founded in 1963, beginning with three facilities in Southern California. Growth has occurred through aggressive acquisition policies and internal development.

Philosophy:

Beverly is a service company dedicated to meeting the needs of the elderly and other dependent persons by providing long-term and convalescent care consistent with the objective of helping them enjoy the best possible Quality of Life.

# # # #

8-4b continued

HISTORY OF BEVERLY ENTERPRISES

Over the past two decades, medical science has made many scientific, sociological and technological advances. Some of the most dramatic of these gains have occurred in the long-term care profession.

The leader in this progression of long-term care has been Beverly Enterprises, a diversified entrepreneural company established in 1963. The management of this company, recognizing the need to develop new approaches, formulated a viable, well-planned, solidly-structured operation that has set the standards which other health related organizations emulate.

The company, then known simply as Beverly, started with three convalescent hospitals in Southern California. From that modest beginning, Beverly soon operated twelve convalescent centers in six states and developed other commercial ventures. An underlying philosophical goal of giving the best in quality care in its nursing center began to emerge.

Beverly went public in 1966 and, soon after changing the company name to Beverly Enterprises, was listed on the American and Pacific Coast Stock Exchanges. In 1982, it was listed on the New York Stock Exchange.

In the early seventies, tight money, an erratic stock market and cutbacks in government spending caused Beverly to divest unrelated interests and concentrate on the delivery of long-term care.

Joining Beverly Enterprises in 1971 was the current chairman of the board, Robert Van Tuyle. Well known in the business and industry world, Van Tuyle further enhanced Beverly's philosophical goals while at the same time strengthening its financial and operating base by extending operations through acquisitions of additional nursing facilities. It was at this time that Beverly sold its interests in acute hospitals, plastics, printing and real estate, concentrating on long-term care.

The first major acquisition that began Beverly's predominance in the nursing home profession was in 1977 when the company purchased Leisure Lodges Inc., Fort Smith, Arkansas. This purchase not only doubled Beverly's size—making the company number two in the industry—but also heralded the company's serious intentions of assuming leadership in the long-term care field.

David Banks, the former chairman of Leisure Lodges, moved to California in 1979 where he then became president and chief operating officer of Beverly, the position he retains today. Under the operations structure for which he directed implementation, Beverly Enterprises is now recognized as a model of corporate structures—utilizing responsible management within decentralized divisional boundaries. The Pasadena headquarters offers support and guidance to these divisions through a strong corporate base of professional department heads.

In 1978, the Beverly Foundation, a nonprofit organization, was formed with the purpose of providing training, conducting research and supporting community-oriented projects that relate to the aged and the aging process. The Foundation's objective, to provide creative alternatives to aging, parallels Beverly's commitment to provide Quality of Life to its residents.

Beverly's entrance into alternative methods of health care delivery systems came in 1981 with entrance into the home health services field—delivering in-home health care services to individuals who do not require full-time nursing home services—and with expansion into retirement living.

Acquisition of major nursing center operators continued, including: The Medical Investments Corporation, 1979; The Progressive Medical Group, 1980 (this included acquisition of a computer system that provided the base for development of Beverly's Information Services Division); Consolidated Liberty, Inc., 1980; Provincial House, Inc., 1982; the Geri-Care Corporation, 1982, Mediplex, 1982, Beacon Hill, 1983; Southern Medical and Overcash-Goodman, 1984.

Throughout its growth and expansion into related services, Beverly has continued to implement, fund and develop new ideas. Its innovative internal quality assurance program signals the advent of a new springboard that will enable this progressive, caring company to continue its drive to improve the care of those who are dependent upon its services and for those who can so capably deliver those services.

8-4b continued

BEVERLY ENTERPRISES:
A SOCIALLY RESPONSIBLE CORPORATION

Beverly Enterprises, as described in the company's corporate charter, "is a service company dedicated to meeting the needs of the elderly and other dependent citizens by providing long-term and convalescent care consistent with the objective of helping them enjoy the best possible Quality of Life." By natural extension, this philosophy leads Beverly to support development and propagation of concepts, programs and innovations that yield benefits for all of society.

The practice is carried out within the company through the establishment of operating principles that charge all parts of the Beverly service network with responsibility for continually searching for innovative ways of enhancing Quality of Life. Since, in the Beverly interpretation, providing Quality of Life means meeting psycho-social as well as physical needs, the search for innovation is wide-ranging.

Individual nursing centers are encouraged to be both initiators of community services and agents for ensuring that residents receive these same services. This effort helps residents continue participation in community life.

With the active support and involvement of company personnel, residents of Beverly nursing homes and retirement living centers across the country sponsor, promote and participate in a variety of community projects and fund raising activities. These range from craft sales and quilt raffles at county fairs to bake sales and festivals within the facilities. Hundreds of thousands of dollars are raised annually for organizations such as the Arthritis Foundation, American Heart Association, Alzheimer's Disease and Related Disorders Association and American Diabetes Association.

Within local communities, residents and staff of nursing centers work together to support hospitals, chapters of the American Society for the Prevention of Cruelty to Animals, art groups, volunteer organizations and many other entities that provide both an important community service and a social outlet for residents. Facilities are the site for voting registration and polling places and community group meetings. They regularly sponsor health fairs at which community members can have their blood pressure checked and receive counseling on good nutrition, exercise programs and other health issues. They are active, vital parts of community life, contributing to community services and benefiting from them as well.

The staff associated with these almost 900 Beverly nursing centers and retirement living facilities also give generously of their own time to volunteer activities. Many come during off-duty times to visit with residents or participate in special activities. They serve as leaders of Cub Scout troops organized at facilities for developmentally disabled children. They buy birthday and Christmas cards and gifts. They use their free time to take residents on special trips.

These individual efforts by caring staff members are encouraged by the company. Beverly emphasizes the concept that residents should be viewed as a "family member," that the facility should be regarded as the residents' "home" and that everything possible should be done to make that perception a reality.

This is the essence of "Quality of Life" and Beverly does much to reinforce it through sponsorship of special programs. The company provides funding for a multitude of projects that have implications for the psycho-social and physical needs of those served. Support has been given to such programs as:

• Development of a film showcasing the importance of arts in the nursing home;
• A study on the importance of spiritual well-being for nursing home residents;
• Creation of a Girl Scout patch for participation on the Adopt-A-Grandparent program (a Beverly-developed program);
• A study on adaptive clothing for the disabled and nursing center residents;
• A conference on the care, treatment and prevention of decubitus ulcers organized by the Spinal Research Foundation of the Paralyzed Veterans Association;
• Senior and Special Olympics events;
• Plays and other programs designed to heighten public awareness of the special needs and concerns of the elderly;
• Research projects to study incontinency.

8-4b continued

All of these programs and many of the others sponsored by the company have ramifications for the Quality of Life for all dependent citizens. Beverly maintains that, as a leader in the long-term care profession, it has a responsibility to educate others, to expand awareness and understanding of the needs of elderly, ill and disabled persons and to encourage research of ways to better meet those needs.

Beverly fulfills much of this responsibility through major support of the independent Beverly Foundation. Founded in 1978 by the chairman of Beverly Enterprises, the Foundation was formed to promote improved systems and methods of care and self-help for older Americans through research, education and community development.

Beverly contributes to many projects through the Foundation, such as a multi-disciplinary conference on teaching nursing homes and research into contributing factors to advanced longevity. Beverly also works with the Foundation to disseminate information about some of the company's more innovative programs to the rest of the long-term care profession. For example, the Adopt-A-Grandparent program was created within the Beverly system and then expanded by the Foundation to encourage community involvement with other long-term care providers. Videotape training programs developed by Beverly to help upgrade quality of care in nursing centers also were turned over to the Foundation for distribution to others in the profession.

With significant support from Beverly, the Foundation develops manuals and other information materials to increase understanding about the needs and concerns of the elderly and enhance quality of care standards. Community forums are held to sensitize the public to the particular problems of senior citizens, to facilitate improved intergenerational relationships and to present self-help options to the older adult. These programs cover concepts such as shared housing, retirement preparations and coping skills.

Outside of the Foundation, Beverly works to share its knowledge, expertise, ideas and experience by devoting thousands of hours of staff time to cooperation with government agencies and other interested groups. Beverly personnel serve on state and federal task forces created to develop innovative ways of enhancing Quality of Life for dependent citizens at a reasonable cost to society. These task forces study all aspects of long-term care from improved regulatory systems to streamlined reporting mechanisms for reimbursement purposes; processes for measuring quality of care in nursing centers to the types of social services and activities programming necessary for meeting psycho-social needs.

Beverly also sponsors many training, research and education programs that are designed to increase understanding of the medical profession of the particular needs of the elderly and upgrade the quality of personnel interested in working with dependent citizens. Teaching nursing homes have been established in approximately 25 Beverly facilities and at least one program focuses on developing an interdisciplinary approach to treating the elderly. Annually, the company gives thousands of dollars to college scholarships for all disciplines represented in a nursing center. Currently, Beverly is working with the American Refugee Committee to design a program based in nursing centers that will train immigrants in all disciplines. Another training program involves an internship concept that will provide college students with many different types of course concentrations, practical experience in management, administration and service provision in a long-term care company.

The value of the contributions made by Beverly, its staff and those it serves is almost impossible to determine. It is impossible to document every local contribution or Beverly's involvement in every community activity. Many cannot even be measured in dollars. Also, the very nature of Beverly's business is such that a thorough attempt to do so could be considered self-serving. Beverly's business objective is helping people, particularly the aged, the sick and the disabled. Community service and involvement by and for those the company serves is a privilege Beverly takes very seriously. Needless to say, Beverly involves thousands of people in this effort, all of whom are committed to enhancing Quality of Life for dependent citizens.

8-4b continued

FORTUNE

WAY OUT FRONT IN NURSING HOMES

SERVICE 500/HEALTH/THOMAS MOORE

■ In *The Treasure of the Sierra Madre* a firecracker of an old prospector tells a hungry Humphrey Bogart about the wonders of finding gold. The faster he talks, the more Bogey's eyes light up. Robert Van Tuyle, the tireless 70-year-old chief executive of the largest U.S. nursing-home chain, Beverly Enterprises, talks just like that prospector. He sees so many shining opportunities in what most other people regard as a forbidding landscape that his mouth can hardly keep up with his ideas.

The nursing-home industry, three-quarters owned by profit-seeking corporations and proprietors, may seem an unpromising place to mine gold. But that's exactly what Van Tuyle, whose name rhymes with mile, has been doing. Since 1976 Beverly has increased its revenues 12 times over, largely through acquisitions. In 1982 alone sales rose a steep 68% to $816 million, making it the second-fastest-growing company in FORTUNE's ranking of the largest diversified service companies (see page 154). Net income climbed, too, by 62% to $26 million. This year Beverly estimates it will gross over $1.1 billion, most of it from 75,000 nursing-home beds in 643 homes. Costing patients $23 to $140 per day, they offer a wide range of accommodations, from spartan rooms shared by four and standard menus to comfortable single rooms and à la carte meals in chandeliered settings.

Beverly has taken off so fast that it now represents 7% of the investor-owned industry—more than twice as many beds as its nearest competitor, National Medical Enterprises' Hillhaven Corp. The stock is hot, its price zooming in the last nine months from $13 to a high of $36.75 a share, 18 times last year's earnings. Michael LeConey, a Merrill Lynch health care analyst who has been recommending Beverly stock for five years, remains bullish. He thinks the company could grab as much as one-third of the nursing-home business by 1990.

Unlike gold prospecting, Van Tuyle's industry has little to do with chance. More people are getting older no matter what happens to the economy, and government-backed Medicaid and Medicare programs pay about half the national nursing-home bill. Currently some 1.3 million Americans, 5% of those over 65, fill the country's 21,500 homes nearly to capacity. This year the industry's total revenues are expected to pass $30 billion, and the figure could more than double by 1990.

Growing at Beverly's breathtaking pace has not been easy. Nursing homes are capital intensive, labor intensive, and closely regulated by state governments and Washington—on the face of it a daunting combination. Beverly's after-tax profit margin was a thin 3.2% of revenues last year, and the company's debt-equity ratio—until recently 3 to 1—has raised eyebrows in the financial community. Like other nursing-home operators, Beverly is plagued by high turnover among the bulk of its work force, which draws the minimum wage or little more. Beverly also has a union battle on its hands. The AFL-CIO has made the company a top-priority target in its campaign to organize health care workers around the country.

NONE OF THIS dampens the enthusiasm of Van Tuyle, a tall, fidgety man with a cherubic face who came to Beverly as a director in 1971. The industry was going through its first big shakeout at the time. The advent of Medicare and Medicaid in the mid-Sixties had unlocked new sources of revenue. Medicare, which pays the first 100 days of convalescent care, currently accounts for only 1.7% of nursing-home revenues. The big spigot was Medicaid for the poor, with financing shared by the states and the federal government. Now supplying nearly 50% of nursing-home income, Medicaid pays for long-term "custodial" care of any oldster who is merely infirm—by far the majority served.

8-4b | continued

Leisure Hours

LETTER FROM THE PRESIDENT

SUCCESSFUL AGING

Dear Associates and Friends:

No matter how we try, no matter how many pills we take or how many creams we rub on our bodies, we cannot stop the process of aging, which remains a very real and natural part of living a full and meaningful life.

But rather than surrender to age and the physical limitations that often come with it, tens of thousands of senior citizens in and out of nursing homes are practicing "successful aging". These people are alert, active, interested, contributing members of society. In continuing to enjoy their lives, all these people share two obvious characteristics — a positive attitude about themselves and an acceptance of being where they are in life.

Because Beverly Enterprises believes strongly in constantly raising the quality of life for all senior citizens, not just those who require our diversified services, I am very proud that our company was able to make possible the publication of a beautiful new book titled "A Fine Age". This project, which is featured in this issue of **Leisure Hours**, focuses on remarkable people who have not stopped the aging process but have made it an ally in their lives. I sincerely hope "A Fine Age" will serve as a guide and example for both those who one day may or may not require our services.

One day all of us hopefully will be able to view the aging process for what it is and say, "The best is yet to come."

Sincerely,

Bobby W. Stephens
President
Central Division

8-4b continued

Financial Highlights

(Dollars in thousands
except per share amounts)

Years ended December 31	1984	1983	1982	1981	1980
Revenues	$1,420,073	$1,091,452	$ 805,796	$ 480,798	$ 291,882
Income:					
Before provision for taxes	$ 82,395	$ 61,447	$ 48,232	$ 29,575	$ 15,595
Provision for taxes	35,430	26,045	22,187	13,515	7,174
Net income	$ 46,965	$ 35,402	$ 26,045	$ 16,060	$ 8,421
Net income per share	$ 1.80	$ 1.45	$ 1.33	$ 1.08	$ .77
Weighted average shares used to compute net income per share	26,135,000	24,387,000	19,571,000	14,895,000	10,976,000
Cash dividends declared per share of common stock	$ .29	$ .28	$ .27	$ .23	$ .17
Total assets	$ 1,700,214	$1,397,571	$ 931,866	$ 448,910	$ 252,437
Long-term obligations	$ 990,484	$ 814,763	$ 549,129	$ 223,024	$ 131,856
Shareholders' equity	$ 434,522	$ 386,013	$ 252,515	$ 143,304	$ 62,363
Patient days	31,400,000	25,432,000	20,760,000	13,823,000	9,416,000
Average occupancy	90%	88%	89%	88%	88%
Number of beds	101,739	88,494	72,711	51,299	38,488
Number of employees	87,000	69,000	57,000	39,000	28,000

See Note 2 to Consolidated Financial Statements for a discussion of acquisitions and dispositions.

Beverly Enterprises (the ''company'') is the nation's leader in long-term care with a service network encompassing nursing homes, congregate care facilities, retirement living apartments, home health units, durable medical equipment outlets and pharmacy services. Headquartered in Pasadena, California, Beverly operates in 44 states, the District of Columbia and Canada under a decentralized management structure. This structure was established with the concept that the highest caliber of care can be provided by local managers who are most cognizant of community needs. Geographic divisions are supported by centralized purchasing and data processing services. A corporate-guided quality assurance network assists management at all levels.

8-4b | continued

T H I S   I S   B E V E R L Y

One of the major achievements of this century has been the gift of longer life. At the turn of the century, the elderly represented 2 percent of the total population in America. Today, their numbers have increased to 11 percent and by the year 2000, they will make up 15 percent of the population.

Aging — the process of growing old — begins at conception and ends at death. It is the one experience we all share. The changes that occur with the aging process vary tremendously from person to person. Understanding those changes and learning how to cope can make life better for both the aging and their families.

The transition to old age can be a rewarding experience — one that we can anticipate with enthusiasm and not with dread. Like every stage in life, it has its own challenges and potentials. At best, it offers rich possibilities for creativity and active participation. At least, it should be a dignified, satisfying period.

Beverly Enterprises is committed to making the transition into old age as smooth and rewarding as possible. We have developed a continuum of health care that ranges from retirement living centers to home health services to nursing homes.

As the nation's largest provider of nursing home and related health care services, we have been provided with a unique opportunity — that of helping aging Americans find their special niche as they move on to new roles in the community. We have been challenged to improve the quality of life for the elderly and are meeting that challenge in the following ways.

First, we provide a home. A home is far more than shelter, food and a bed. It represents security, a place to relax, to welcome family and friends, to explore new avenues of creativity. A home is sharing and caring about others, which includes accepting and assisting those members of the "family" who enjoy lesser degrees of health and mobility. It is an integrated unit, a living reality where employees, residents, families and volunteers work together to enrich the lives of those they touch.

Second, we recognize and ensure the individuality and privacy of each resident, thereby reinforcing their dignity. Clinical research has shown that the stereotypes of old age — senility, forgetfulness, inflexibility — are more myth than reality. For example, what is frequently thought of as senility may be anxiety or depression, both of which are treatable. We strive to meet the needs of each resident, structuring programs on an individual basis to help them enjoy their less physically active years.

Third, we help people adjust creatively to the changes that occur with aging. The capacity for growth, learning or simply taking pleasure in daily activities does not necessarily diminish with the aging process. Older people are very diverse with a lifetime of enriching experience to draw from. They are limited only by society's perception of "old age." Unless we begin to correct these stereotypes, we will fall victim to our prejudices on aging.

Beverly's staff is specially trained to be sensitive to the ever changing needs of the elderly — both physical and mental, spiritual and emotional, social and recreational. It is our privilege, as well as yours, to be actively involved in helping our elders understand and adjust.

We want to share with you what the men and women of Beverly are doing to provide quality care, making quality life a reality.

This is Beverly . . .

8-4b continued

We put
our heads
together
to define
Quality of
Life, and
created a
system to
measure it.

8-4b   continued

Why

Quality Assurance?

Beverly's goal is to create a total living environment where residents can satisfy personal needs, exercise freedom of choice and continue to realize their full potential.

Beyond quality care, our commitment is to Quality of Life. The means of fulfilling this trust is provided by our Quality Assurance program.

What

is Quality Assurance?

The Quality Assurance program is Beverly's pledge to the public that we accept the responsibilities entrusted to us as caregivers. It is a standardized, nationwide system of evaluating Beverly facilities.

But, to create this system, we found we first had to define quality care. A task force of residents, their families and Beverly employees met in focus groups across the country to contribute specific examples of what they considered to be essential elements of Quality of Life. Their answers became the focal points of our Quality Assurance program. We evaluate:

- *Maintenance of surroundings*
- *Respect and caring attitudes of staff*
- *Productivity and involvement of residents*
- *Quality of health care*
- *Family and community involvement*
- *Quality of leadership*

How

is Quality Assurance achieved?

Checklist & Manual
Once our group meetings defined our goals, we established checklists and a manual to define standards for each goal. These standards in many cases exceed federal and state requirements.

Toll-free Hotline
A toll-free hotline invites residents, families, and employees to express suggestions and concerns unresolved at the facility level.

Internal Reporting System
We have strengthened an internal reporting system which includes a review of State and Federal survey results in order to maintain a current picture of how facilities are achieving their goals.

Problem Resolution
Inservice training and consultation provide programs to upgrade services and care given.

to make the announcements. Have these announcements recorded by technically qualified people so they will be of broadcast quality. As the event gets closer, use interviews with some of the participants. Supply radio and television stations with your audios and videotapes.

So much for the advance. For actual coverage of your special event by the news media, find out at least three to six weeks in advance what mechanical equipment you will need to supply. You'll have to check out lighting and sound systems and prepare a list of what activities (of news value) will be available for coverage. When the news media arrive, you should be able to offer (again) all of your materials prepared in advance plus an update of what is happening that day and the next. Mention any changes or corrections in materials sent previously. (Supply these in writing when possible; for example, where the AHA menus are mentioned in Example 8-1, if a new AHA cookbook had unexpectedly been made available there would be a sheet describing this—an update, new information.) Also, give reporters a copy of a brief story in broadcast style. Attach this release to a copy of the longer story prepared for the print media. In reworking the story or in writing their own to fit the coverage, broadcasters will find the longer release helpful.

It's important at special events to have someone at a central location to answer the telephone and respond intelligently to queries from the news media. Give that person sets of all materials and a copy of your itinerary so he or she can find you. (During the event, check in every hour or so anyway.)

Remember that you will get only a few seconds, maybe a minute, of coverage. Use that time to direct competing media to different facets of the event. That way they will get better stories and you will get better coverage. Be absolutely sure of all your facts, because there will be no time for correction. The news media are not very forgiving of a PR source that causes them to broadcast an inaccuracy.

News Conferences

News conferences are called by public relations directors when a personality needs to interact with the news media. The person might be a celebrity, for example, whose time in the area is limited. In such a case, you might want to allow as many people as possible to ask questions. The opportunity to question is especially important if there is a controversy.

You may literally "call" a conference by using the telephone. But ordinarily you'll prepare an announcement, giving the reason for the conference, identifying the person (giving background if he or she is a celebrity) and detailing the time, date and place and who to contact (provide name, address and phone number) if there are any questions. If you are calling the conference to give information on a problem or to make an unexpected announcement, be sure you have prepared background materials to give to the media who attend. A package should contain a printed copy of the announcement, biographical material on the person (if appropriate) and background materials addressing the most significant questions. You should also have prepared a "shooting schedule" for pictures. Be sure to have a still photographer, an audio recorder and someone shooting both film and video-tape. You will need these records for your own reference and might also need to supply them to a medium that had mechanical problems.

(Remember, news conferences are not parties for the media. You might want to have coffee or soft drinks, but save the rest for a festive occasion that's not a working situation.) (See 8-4a for news conference materials.)

Crises

The crisis such as a plant fire or hostage situation is a disorganized combination of the special event and the news conference. The media will need information that even you as an insider will have difficulty getting. Nevertheless, getting and supplying that information is the most important service you can perform (see Chapter 16).

News Releases

As in the print media, news releases to the broadcast media are either advance stories of something about to occur or stories explaining what has occurred or what is going on. Although no news medium personnel will get excited about doing your promotion for you, most will use well-prepared advance stories if the event has enough general public interest. News releases on upcoming events should be extremely brief for the broadcast media—no more than two or three short paragraphs. However, you can send along your longer print-media version, a fact sheet, and, when appropriate, a brochure or printed program. If the event is likely to have regional interest, send a courtesy copy to the broadcast wire services, just to alert them to an event their reporters might be interested in. Be sure to identify the courtesy copy as such when you deliver the release (or in a cover letter if you mail it). (Refer to Example 8-1: a media kit with a) cover letter, b) list of activities and facts about them, c) the releases, each with a time for release.)

Hand deliver advance stories to the broadcast news media whenever possible. If this is not possible, telephone the medium to alert them that a release has been mailed to them. Most advance stories are given short shrift. Therefore, if you have any visuals from a previous event that will add interest, offer to make them available.

Timeliness is a problem for stories about events that have already happened. Nevertheless, most events of any significance—even past events—will be covered by the broadcast media. If you are supplying audio and visual materials, be sure you prepare them to meet media deadlines and mechanical requirements. Then call the news directors to let them know that the material is coming and hand deliver the package. Where the event was a speech, attach a complete copy to the brief release. You can file a courtesy copy with the wire service if the occurrence has regional interest, though, again, the wire services often provide their own coverage.

For television, you can offer graphs and charts that might help explain the event; for radio, offer broadcasters a telephone interview to flesh out their story and give it a sense of actuality. In the latter instance, be sure you have all the facts and figures within easy reach for the phone interview. Be aware that your interview will be edited. Still, if you are prepared, editors won't have to cut out dead air—gaps of silence—while you hunt down a fact. Refer to Example 8-2 for information cast in different styles for broadcast and print media. The fact sheet presents basic information. The bulletin to editors explains the significance of the information for media audiences. The September 25 news release is for print media. The TV Color Takes was sent out as a public service announcement (PSA) for television, and the Radio Roundup pieces as PSAs for radio. Note in the J. Walter Thompson PSA copy that the messages are in Spanish and English.

Talk Shows

Public relations practitioners frequently arrange for people to appear on radio or television talk shows. Occasionally, the PR person is the talk show guest. Shows of this nature are not as fluid as they appear. Generally, they are structured by the host in a brief period before the show is aired.

You'll need to prepare certain materials for such an event. The show's host needs to have a background sheet on the institution that the individual represents, the event or occasion for the attention and biographical information on the person being interviewed. All of this information must be very brief and in a form the show's host can take on the air—typed triple space on sheets of paper heavy enough so they won't rattle. The guest should have in mind all the information he or she is going to present. To prepare mentally, a briefing session the day before and again just before air time is usually required to keep facts and figures fresh. The guest needs to alert the host to information that should be presented for the benefit of the listening audience. If the talk show is on television, take some slides or materials that can be shown. Remember the wiggle.

Mini-Docs

The mini-documentary is a special type of news feature heard on radio stations. Mini-docs consist of a series of short features, generally on a significant issue needing public attention.

The mini-documentary developed out of the realization on the part of broadcasters that longer news features of 30 to 60 minutes were not holding audiences. The practice of breaking up a long story into serial form began in the print media, where it was discovered that such a format attracted a larger audience and sustained their interest in a topic longer than a single long feature.

Each broadcast mini-doc is about 3 minutes and 30 seconds long. Research for the entire series is done all at one time, and usually the whole series is written at once. Some writers prefer to write the whole script as though it were one unit and then break off segments, writing an appropriate introduction and conclusion to identify each one (see Example 8-5). Generally, the writer is asked to write promotional announcements that the station can use during the day to call attention to the series.

A public relations person can get involved in writing mini-docs in many ways. One is to work for a nonprofit organization at the national level, although local affiliates produce mini-docs too. These organizations are concerned with serious issues (mental health, heart disease, cancer and such)—that is usually why they exist. Another way is to prepare a series on an issue that is of vital concern to your commercial area. For example, a bank holding company did a series on how married women can get credit in their own names, and another on how unemployed college students can get credit. An insurance company did a series on estate planning. These projects may sound self-serving, and of course to a certain extent they are. But you can often approach stations about using a series that discusses the issue alone. Sometimes the source of a mini-doc is only identified by means of a single script credit line.

To be successful (that is, to be used by the broadcast media), mini-docs must follow the same rule as the well-written news release. They must be written as though they were prepared by the station—so neutral that no slant toward the source is perceptible. Because documentaries should not be slanted, sometimes the first selling job is the most difficult: convincing management that the time and effort is worth the slight direct tie to the source. Enlightened managements generally see the benefit.

Some national associations and government agencies produce mini-docs and make them available to stations across the country. If you attempt to produce a local mini-doc, you must first research the issue and prepare a proposal. Get management's endorsement of the written proposal, and contact the most logical station in your area about the project. Choose a radio station if the subject matter does not lend itself to visual representation. If you send the proposal to a television station, be sure that it also outlines the visuals—what could be demonstrated in the studio and what needs to be shot. You should approach the station as a resource person and writer. If the station is interested, make yourself available to provide all the information, write the scripts and submit them for editing by the station. Let the station provide the technical assistance and the talent. Stations at the local level are usually stretched for resources, but they are also looking for good public service projects. If they have what they consider quality control over the project, they are more likely to go along with what you propose.

8-5

Mini-Doc Outline
In developing a mini-doc, the writer needs to state the
problem clearly and concisely, then break it down into
components. The writer must make sure to cover all questions
about the problem.

Program One: Alcoholism is one of the nation's major health
problems. It is an illness affecting the entire
family. Help needs to be extended not only
to the alcoholic, but to the members of the
family as well.

Program Two: How do you know when someone is an
alcoholic? Identifying an alcoholic can be
as simple as answering twenty questions.
(Responses to twenty questions about
drinking and behavior.)

Program Three: Roles in the pattern of alcoholic behaviors:
the alcoholic, the enabler, the victim, the
provoker or adjuster.

Program Four: Alcoholism is a physical, emotional, and
spiritual disease. Patterns are the same,
regardless of age or sex.

Program Five: Avenues and agencies of help for the
alcoholic and the lives he or she affects.

Such an outline would be fleshed out by pulling out
the research data that appears in the proposal and placing
appropriate parts in each program content. The beginning of
each series needs a separate introduction to identify it as a
part of a whole. The conclusion should promote (promo) the
next portion of the series. The introduction and the conclusion
for each segment should be about 15 seconds each, for a total
of 30 seconds per segment.

Broadcast Writing Style

The basic difference between writing for broadcast media and writing for print media is that for the former copy must appeal to the ear. (In television and video, of
course, the visuals must capture the eye.) Copy must capture attention through
sound and word symbolism. The words must be clear enough to be understandable
the first time through. The listener will not have a chance to review what is said. In

radio, for the listener there's no looking back over a sentence to see what it meant, and no going back to the one preceding it to figure out a sequence of ideas. Each offering is a one-time-only presentation. To compensate for the lack of review opportunity, broadcast writers first tell listeners (and viewers) what they are going to tell them, alerting them to the content by calling up frames of reference. Then they present the content. Finally, in the summary, the writer again tells the listener what the message was. It takes a skillful writer to prepare material in this way so it doesn't sound redundant. While the writer follows this sequence, he or she must keep the time element in mind. Clarity and brevity are both important.

Because broadcast media are intimate, their style is conversational. Each listener or viewer experiences the broadcast media as an individual and responds to them personally. The relaxed style means that the leads, or first paragraphs, in broadcast stories, including news stories, are "soft." That is, the listener is introduced to the story before hearing it.

One type of lead like this is called a "throw-away": "Vacationers driving around the country this summer are likely to find lots of detours. The American Automobile Association says road repairs and construction are going on all over the nation." Another soft lead is the "angle" lead that hooks your attention: "Planning to drive your car on your vacation this year? Get ready for lots of detours. The American Automobile Association says road repairs and construction are going on all over the nation." If one news story is related to another, a soft lead may be used to introduce the two of them: "Vacationers planning to drive their cars this summer are likely to have some unexpected problems. Road repairs and construction have put detour signs up all over the nation. The longer routes may cause motorists to run out of gas because many small service stations in outlying areas have closed during the last year. A slow down in the economy is blamed on the closing of the gas stations, and winter ice storms are the cause of the road repairs." (The story goes on to say that the American Automobile Association will help car travelers plan trips to find out about detours in advance and the major oil companies are offering credit card holders lists of service stations open along both interstate, state and rural roads.)

We can make some other generalizations about broadcast writing. Because the tone is conversational, for instance, sentences are sometimes incomplete. We talk that way, so in broadcast journalism it's acceptable to write that way. Another way in which broadcast styles differ from print style has to do with sentence length. In broadcast writing, sentences are kept short in deference to the announcer, who has a limited amount of breath, and to the listener, whose attention span shouldn't be taxed. For the same reason, subjects and verbs are kept close together. Also, as a rule sentences should not begin with prepositional phrases; the basic information should be conveyed first. "According to a report from the Mason County Sheriff's office today, vacationers driving through are likely to find fewer service stations than last year." By the time you decide that fewer service stations might be important to you the "Mason County" is lost to all but those paying very careful attention.

Writers should avoid two peculiarities of newspaper style, sometimes called "journalese," in preparing broadcast copy. One is inverted sentence structure, where the statement precedes the attribution: "'Victims of the Mississippi tornado are all back in permanent housing,' said Scott Smith, director of emergency disaster relief." This sentence illustrates what *not* to do in writing broadcast copy. Since broadcast audiences may not be attending to the first part of the sentence, information should be presented the way it would probably be spoken in conversation: "The director of emergency disaster relief said that all victims of the Mississippi tornado are now back in permanent housing." The name of the director is not important to the story, so his title alone is used. If the story is a long one in which Smith is quoted, then his name would be used, but he would be identified in a separate sentence: "Scott Smith is the director of emergency relief."

The second newspaper-style characteristic to avoid in broadcast writing is the identification of subjects by age, job title and such. In newspapers this information usually follows the name and is set off by commas. But what is efficient in newspaper copy becomes cumbersome when read on the air. Again, the name of an individual is often not important at all—title identification is enough.

Here is a typical print story and the way it might be rewritten for broadcast:

> Vacationers traveling by car may be encountering an unusual number of detours this summer, according to James R. Ragland, manager of the Dixon American Automobile Association office.
>
> Winter storm damage all over the nation has resulted in more than the usual amount of road repair, and the severe winter also put a number of highway projects behind schedule, Ragland said. The result is detours in almost every state.
>
> AAA offices are trying to help motorists plan trips to at least be able to predict delays, Ragland said.
>
> The service is free to AAA members, and there's a nominal charge for nonmembers, according to Ragland. The Dixon AAA office is in the Chamber of Commerce Building at Fifth and Ledbetter.

Broadcast version (30 seconds):

> That severe winter the nation had is going to make summer vacations by car more difficult than usual, The American Automobile Association says. Triple A is offering travelers plans marked with all of the detours for road repairs and construction. Triple A's Dixon manager says the plans are free to members, but available to nonmembers for a nominal fee.

Physical Preparation

Like copy for print media, all broadcast copy is triple spaced and written on one side of the page. Some broadcast news departments prefer that copy be typed in all caps (capital letters), others prefer the standard combination of upper- and lowercase letters. Most public relations people supplying information to the broadcast news media use caps and lowercase. For radio, typewriter margins should be set for a 60-space line to give an average of 10 words per line. Most announcers read at a rate of about 15 lines per minute. So in radio news, one typed line takes about four seconds to read. A 30-second story is seven to eight lines long. (See the AAA story.)

The audio copy for a TV script goes on the right side of the page, opposite the video instructions. When you are writing for television and using only half the page (the audio side), set your margins at 35 and 70. With the margins set like this, you'll get about six words to the line, or about 21 lines a minute at an average reading speed, the equivalent of about two seconds per line. Thus, a 30-second TV story is about 15 lines long.

Much of the format for a broadcast release is similar to print copy. In the upper left-hand corner of the first page of each story is a slug line—the words identifying the story, the date, the name of the organization submitting the information, your name and phone numbers where you can be reached day or night. On the following pages, all you need is the page number, slug line (story identification) and your last name. The story's end is marked by the traditional "30," and "more" goes at the bottom of each page in the story. Remember never to break a paragraph at the bottom of a page. Also, be sure to leave plenty of margin space—at least 2 inches at the top and bottom and 1 inch on either side for editing. The editing is done by the station, not you. *Never* give a broadcaster copy with editing marks. If you need to make changes, retype the draft. And *never* mark up broadcast copy with newspaper editing or print media proofreading symbols such as "yeild" or "mayor Charlene Brooks Said Monday. *yesterday.*"

To facilitate reading by announcers, don't break words at the end of lines and don't split sentences between pages. If a word or name is difficult to pronounce, give the proper pronunciation in parentheses beside it *each* time it appears. The announcer should not have to go back and look for your previous instructions. Do not use diacritical markings you find in dictionaries to indicate the proper pronunciation. Use popular phonetics like the newsmagazines employ (SHEE-fur) for Schieffer, for example.

The AP broadcast stylebook offers the following suggestions for phonetic symbols:

> **The system used on the Associated Press broadcast wire is based on familiar principles of English usage with respect to the sound of vowels and consonants. For example:**
> Guantanamo (Gwahn-tah'-nah-moh).
> Juan Martinez (Wahn Mahr-tee'-ness).
> Feisal (Fy'-sal).
> Note that the apostrophe is used to indicate where the accent falls. It has been found from long experience that the following will cover virtually all contingencies:
> AH—is like the a in arm.
> A—is like the a in apple.

EH—is like the ai in air.
AY—is like the a in ace.
E—is like the e in bed.
EE—is like the ee in feel.
I—is like the i in tin.
Y—is like the i in time.
OH—is like the o in go.
OO—is like the oo in pool.
UH—is like the u in puff.
KH—is gutteral.
ZH—is like the g in rouge.
J—is like the g in George.

The symbol "ow" is subject to misunderstanding, since it can be pronounced as in "how" or as in "tow." Therefore it is necessary to handle some pronunciations like this: BLOUGH (rhymes with how).

It will be recognized, of course, that approximations are necessary in indicating the pronunciation of some foreign names. It is almost impossible, for instance, to indicate the nasals common to the French tongue. It is equally difficult to indicate the exact pronunciation of the umlauted "o" or "u."

Remember, the audience can't see punctuation marks. These just help the announcer interpret the copy. Don't use them unless they are essential for the announcer. And don't use colons, semicolons, percentage signs, dollar signs, fractions, ampersands and other exotica. Just use commas, periods, question marks, dots and dashes and quotation marks. Use quotation marks only when the use of the exact words is essential. It is better to rephrase a quote into indirect statements. If you feel that a quote is necessary, write in something like, "In his words," or "What she asked for was" or "the statement read" to precede it.

Use hyphens only when you want the letters to be spelled out individually, as in Y-W-C-A, as opposed to being read as a word, as in NASA. Don't use abbreviations unless you want them read on the air as abbreviations. Exceptions are such titles as *Dr.* and parts of names like *St.* Louis. If you don't know whether to write a word out or abbreviate it, write it out.

Numbers are difficult to follow if they're just heard and not seen, so avoid using them as much as possible. When you must, round numbers off and write them out—for example, "one thousand." Then there can be no risk of your having left off a digit. Broadcast stations use wire service stylebooks (and sometimes their own stylebooks) that give a consistent way of dealing with numbers. In writing the copy, it's best to spell out numbers. Broadcasters will change them if they want to. And to prevent errors, don't use A.M. or P.M. with times of the day; announcers wouldn't read the letters anyway. Write, for example, "this morning" or "tomorrow night." However, since your copy is going to the news media for handling, put dates in parentheses beside the weekday designation (Monday, May 1). When the copy is processed for reading on the air, that information will be omitted. But writing it in will prevent errors. Another expression to be avoided reading numbers is *per*, as in "miles per hour." Instead, use "miles an hour."

As for the treatment of names and titles, use the title before the name, and never begin sentences with a name, especially if it is unfamiliar. Where the title is long and cumbersome, break it up or shorten it. You generally do not use a person's middle initial in speech, so avoid using middle initials in broadcast copy unless they are important for clarification and identification or unless they are commonly used with the names in question. On second reference use the surname only, except when you are referring to the president of the United States or a member of the clergy. Clergy retain their titles on second reference—Rabbi Brown, for instance.

> *Print version:* Madison A. Clark, bishop coadjucator for the Episcopal Diocese of Dixon, today announced that $50,000 had been raised for the World Famine Relief project. The funds will be sent to the agencies designated to purchase and distribute food, Bishop Clark said. There are three such agencies: the American Red Cross, the National Council of Churches and CARE.

> *Rewritten:* Dixon's Episcopal Diocese has raised $50,000 (fifty thousand dollars) for the World Famine Relief project. The announcement came today from Bishop Madison Clark. Bishop Clark said the money will be sent to three agencies designated to purchase and distribute food in Africa.

Watch for and clarify obscurities. Be very careful about using pronouns. Listeners have trouble following the references. If you are dealing with specialized jargon, translate it. Use words and terms the audience will understand and relate to. If you are writing about little-known groups, explain who they are and what they do. Don't assume the audience will know or understand. And do use contractions, like *don't*, just as you do in speech. Use the active voice. It gives life and movement to your writing. When your audience's language is not English, provide a translated version of your information (see 8-6).

Much PR broadcast writing is done for 800 long-distance information numbers. Broadcasters can call these numbers each day to get a "new" story in the form of an actuality (a radio report from the scene or source—can be live, on tape or phone). PR sources do the writing, taping and promoting of this service (see Example 8-7).

Structural Considerations

The leads of broadcast stories differ from print leads, in which the who, what, when, where, why and how are often all crammed into the first paragraph. This burst of information can be confusing for the listener and difficult for the announcer to read. When you are preparing your broadcast story, first, alert listeners to what you are going to discuss, getting their attention with something they can

8-6a

Bilingual PR Writing
A large percentage of this nation's population is Spanish-speaking. You improve your chances of getting a message across to this audience if the public relations materials are written in Spanish. This is a comprehensive package from the American Heart Association that uses Castilian Spanish. The copy, which was reviewed by volunteers of Puerto Rican, Cuban and Mexican backgrounds, is sent on an audiotape cassette with the printed translation attached. A return card helps the American Heart Association see what is being used. *Source: Used with permission of the American Heart Association.*

1984

Contenido:
:30
1. Derrames Cerebrales
2. Derrames Cerebrales
3. Fumando
4. Ataque Al Corazón
5. Ataque Al Corazón
6. Alta Presión Arterial

American Heart
Association
WE'RE FIGHTING FOR YOUR LIFE

8-6b

```
AMERICAN HEART ASSOCIATION
SPANISH RADIO
"FUMANDO" (SMOKING)
84-S3
:30
```

FUMAR ES UNO DE LOS TRES FACTORES PRINCIPALES QUE CONTRIBUYEN A
UN ATAQUE AL CORAZÓN. LOS QUE FUMAN UNA CAJETILLA DIARIA SE
ARRIESGAN EL DOBLE DE LOS QUE NO FUMAN. EL PELIGRO DE UN ATAQUE
ES MAYOR CONFORME AUMENTA EL NÚMERO DE CIGARRILLOS FUMADOS. EL
FUMADOR QUE SUFRE UN ATAQUE AL CORAZÓN TIENE MENOS PROBABILIDADES
DE SOBREVIVIR QUE LA PERSONA QUE NO FUMA. ESTA CLARO PUES, QUE
SI FUMA, LAS PROBABILIDADES ESTÁN EN SU CONTRA. NO FUME MÁS.
INFÓRMESE LLAMANDO A LA ASOCIACIÓN AMERICANA DEL CORAZÓN.

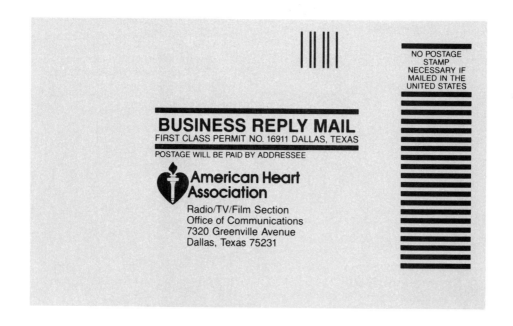

BUSINESS REPLY MAIL
FIRST CLASS PERMIT NO. 16911 DALLAS, TEXAS

POSTAGE WILL BE PAID BY ADDRESSEE

**American Heart
Association**

Radio/TV/Film Section
Office of Communications
7320 Greenville Avenue
Dallas, Texas 75231

NO POSTAGE
STAMP
NECESSARY IF
MAILED IN THE
UNITED STATES

8-7a

800 Lines Are Good PR Tools
The brochure explains the American Heart Association's use
of an 800 information line. They also provide these stick-on
labels so news directors and public service directors can call
for information and actualities. *Source:* Used with permission
of the American Heart Association.

american heart *radio*
news

. . . **November 17, 1983**   *The U.S. Surgeon
General releases the 1983 report, "The
Health Consequences of Smoking: Car-
diovascular Disease,"*. . .American Heart
Radio News reports the findings.

. . . **December 2, 1983**   *The first anniversary of the world's first permanent artificial
heart implant*. . .American Heart Radio
News talks to Mrs. Barney Clark about the
operation and her life during the past year.

. . . **January 12, 1984**   *Results of a major
study on diet and heart disease are released
by the federal government*. . .American
Heart Radio News interprets these findings
for the lay public.

. . . **February 16, 1984**   *The American
Heart Association leads two other health
agencies in publicly denouncing the advertising tactics of one of the country's largest
tobacco companies*. . .American Heart
Radio News unravels the issues.

American Heart Radio News covered all of
these significant events providing timely and
accurate reports and interviews with top experts in the field of heart and blood vessel
diseases.

1-800-527-4091
(In Texas call 1-800-442-3234)

**American Heart
Association**

213

8-7b

American Heart Radio News is a toll-free radio news service sponsored by the country's leading authority on cardiovascular health and science — the American Heart Association. It offers radio stations nationwide a source of news and information on America's number one health problem — diseases of the heart and blood vessels.

The stories are consumer-oriented, ready for broadcast and cover a variety of health tips and medical news involving every member of your audience. During the first four months of operation, more than 80 stories were reported by American Heart Radio News, including:

- the health consequences of fad diets
- the effect of noise on high blood pressure
- the therapeutic benefits of sex after heart attack
- children and cholesterol
- sleep's effect on high blood pressure
- the health consequences of secondary tobacco smoke

Three reports are available daily, each ranging from 35-45 seconds in length. They are professionally recorded to ensure high broadcast quality and most feature actualities with health experts.

To use the service, just dial 1-800-527-4091 any time of the day or night and tape the news stories over the phone. In Texas call 1-800-442-3234.

If you prefer the stories to have your own station's identification, we can record it over the phone upon request. We can also provide a promo tape for your news reports.

If you need additional information on a story, we'll help put you in touch with the experts.

For any of these additional services, just call us over our main toll-free number 1-800-527-6941.

American Heart Radio News is also an excellent source of story ideas for stations that produce their own medical reports. We can alert you to the latest science and medical developments in the prevention, diagnosis and treatment of heart attack, stroke and other cardiovascular diseases.

Either way, as a quick and accurate source of current news and information, or as a source for your own story ideas, American Heart Radio News can help you add a heart-health report to your next newscast.

Call us anytime
1-800-527-4091
(In Texas call 1-800-442-3234)

8-7c

Call us anytime
1-800-527-4091
(in Texas call 1-800-442-3234)

WE'RE FIGHTING FOR
YOUR LIFE

**American Heart
Association**

National Center
7320 Greenville Avenue • Dallas, Texas 75231
Printed by the American Heart Association's Office of Communications

americanheart radio news
1-800-527-4091
(In Texas call 1-800-442-3234)

americanheart radio news
1-800-527-4091
(In Texas call 1-800-442-3234)

americanheart radio news
1-800-527-4091
(In Texas call 1-800-442-3234)

americanheart radio news
1-800-527-4091
(In Texas call 1-800-442-3234)

relate to, something important to them. Using a summary statement is a good way to get into the story. Then you can give the essentials. Make your sentences simple; don't use long clauses at the beginning or end or between the subject and verb. As you develop the story, look for ways to connect paragraphs with transitions that make the story emerge and flow logically. Keep the listener and the announcer in mind, and think about how each will be able to handle the words you write. (The differences between material written to be spoken and that to be read silently are illustrated in Examples 8-8 through 8-12.)

Broadcast wire stories undergo much more reworking than newspaper wire stories, because the broadcast wire serves stations that use news directly from the wire on an hourly basis. One story, hour after hour, can get dull if the audience remains the same—and some offices have piped-in radio. Research can flesh out a breaking story both to give it depth and to keep the sparse facts from getting monotonous.

Supplying Tape (Audio and Video)

When you supply cassettes—audio, video, or video with sound—or reel-to-reel tape, you also need to furnish a script. Attach the script firmly to the cassette or the box for the reel tape. Identify the script with exactly the same title as that on the tape, and add your name, your institution's name and the address and phone numbers where you can be reached day and night. Broadcasters don't have time to play tapes to see what is on them. Of course, if they decide the story might be used, they will preview the tape, and they'll edit it if they schedule it to run. The station will also write a lead-in to the tape, so it's a good idea to supply additional information— for example, a copy of the news release covering the occasion for making the tape. Lead-ins identify speakers and action without detailing the content of the tape.

News conference materials from the American Heart Association's participation in the Coalition on Smoking Or Health were released when the Federal Trade Commission was asked to issue a cease and desist order to R. J. Reynolds Tobacco Company. In that news release, the person who did the research quoted in the Reynolds ad says their application is not valid. For broadcast you would want his voice on tape, and preferably you'd have a videotape from which you could use the audio only for your radio release.

A lead-in for either videotape or audio might read like this: "A coalition of health groups today asked the Federal Trade Commission to stop the R. J. Reynolds Tobacco Company from advertising with a scientific study to suggest there is no relationship between smoking and heart disease. A scientist who did the research quoted in the Reynolds ad says the study was not designed to show that cigarettes caused heart disease. Dr. Lewis Kuller is chairman of the Department of Epidemiology at the University of Pittsburgh and one of the principal investigators in the research the Reynolds ad quotes. Dr. Kuller says: (tape) 'Not only does R. J. Reynolds wish the public to believe that this study was designed to deal with the causation issue, but they also claim it was one of the most important studies undertaken to establish such causation between smoking and cardiovascular disease.'"

8-8

Original Release from Coca-Cola, Atlanta
When The Coca-Cola Company decided to bring back its
original formula as "Coca-Cola Classic," its news release
July 10, 1985, from corporate headquarters in Atlanta was
timed for maximum play on television network news that
evening. This was done to increase awareness for the
schedule of network spot announcements to be made by the
company president that evening and during the following
days. The release is actually a preannouncement that says
in positive ways that Coca-Cola is simply responding to
consumer demand and that a formal announcement will
be made at a news conference in Atlanta the next day. The
latter point is buried in the last paragraph. *Source:* Used with
permission of The Coca-Cola Company.

The Coca-Cola Company

news
release
FOR IMMEDIATE RELEASE.

Media Relations Department
P.O. Drawer 1734, Atlanta, Ga. 30301
Telephone (404) 676-2121

Contact: Carlton Curtis
           (404) 676-2678

COCA-COLA CLASSIC:

A NEW BRAND NAME FOR A FAMILIAR TASTE

ATLANTA, July 10, 1985 -- The Coca-Cola Company will
announce plans tomorrow to make available the original formula
for Coca-Cola under the name "Coca-Cola classic."

Coca-Cola classic will complement the Company's flagship
brand Coca-Cola as a new addition to Coca-Cola branded soft
drinks that include diet coke, cherry Coke and caffeine-free
products.

8-8 | continued

"Everyone wins," a Company spokesman said. "Over forty million consumers every day in the U.S. enjoy today's Coca-Cola, but thousands of dedicated Coca-Cola consumers have told us they still want the original taste as an option. We have listened and we are taking action to satisfy their request."

While it is a new brand name for the Company, Coca-Cola classic is the original formula - the original taste - for those consumers who have told the Company they want it as an option. The product will be available in some markets within several weeks.

Introduction of Coca-Cola classic will not affect plans for the flagship brand Coca-Cola as announced in April. The international roll-out of Coca-Cola with the new formula will continue this fall, and Coca-Cola classic also will be made available to bottlers internationally.

A news conference will be held at Company headquarters in Atlanta at 1:00 p.m., Thursday, July 11. The conference will be transmitted by satellite to New York news media at the Hotel Pierre.

# # #

8-9

AP Newswire Story, Takes and Write-Thru, for Newspapers
The news release from The Coca-Cola Company triggered a
series of leads and adds on The Associated Press Newswire
out of New York. The first information is advisory to editors
that an important story is in the making, flagged with
"urgent." Compare the first story to move at 3:40 p.m. to the
release from Coca-Cola. Then note the evolution of the story,
with the final lead and write-thru finished some two hours
later. *Source:* Used with permission of The Associated Press.

```
^AM-New Coke, 1st Ld, a3540,0009<
^URGENT<
^Eds: Coca-Cola says will bring back old Coke. Also moving
financial wires.<
    NEW YORK (AP) _ Coca-Cola Co. said it plans to bring back its
old formula for regular Coke within the next several weeks and will
call it Coca-Cola Classic.
    Tom Gray, a spokesman for Coca-Cola in Atlanta, said Coca-Cola
will continue to market its new formula, introduced in May.
    ^MORE<
    AP-NY-07-10-85 1540EDT<


^AM-New Coke, 1st Ld-1st Add,0208<
^URGENT<
^NEW YORK, new formula.<
    Since Coca-Cola announced in April that it was changing its
99-year-old formula for regular Coke, complaints from loyal fans of
the old formula have received considerable publicity. In addition,
Coca-Cola has said it has received 1,300 calls a day about the new
Coke, which was rolled out in May.
    Analysts have said sales of the new Coke have been spurred by
curiosity, heavy promotions and price discounts, but that
meaningful, independent sales figures for the new Coke won't be
available until the fall.
    But Hugh Zurkuhlen, an analyst with the investment firm Salomon
Brothers Inc., said Wednesday, ``My guess is that the June volume
was a little soft for new Coke.
    Coca-Cola said last month that its shipments of Coke concentrate
to bottlers in May were up 8 percent over a year ago, compared with
a 4 percent rate of gain for old Coke in recent months.
    PepsiCo Inc., meanwhile, has claimed that the reformulation of
Coke is benefiting sales of Pepsi-Cola. The Purchase, N.Y.-based
concern said case shipments of Pepsi rose 14 percent in May from a
year earlier, the biggest monthly gain in the company's 87-year
history.
```

8-9 | continued

```
^AM-New Coke, 1st Ld-2nd Add,ð229<
^NEW YORK, 87-year-history.<
    ``Everyone wins,'' said Gray, the Coca-Cola spokesman. ``Over 40
million consumers every day in the United States enjoy Coca-Cola
but thousands of dedicated Coca-Cola consumers have told us they
still want the original taste as an option. We have listened and we
are taking action to satisfy their request.''
    Coca-Cola said Coca-Cola Classic will complement the new Coke.
    And it said the return of the old Coke won't affect the rollout
of the new one.
    The international rollout of new Coke will continue this fall
and Coca-Cola Classic also will be made available to bottlers
internationally, the company said.
    Gray said Coca-Cola Classic will be available in ``some
markets'' within several weeks, but he declined to identify them.
    Coca-Cola said it would hold a news conference at 1 p.m EDT on
Thursday at its headquarters in Atlanta, and that reporters who
gather at the Pierre Hotel at the same time would be patched in.
    Coca-Cola's stock rose in heavy trading Wednesday amid rumors
earlier in the day that the company did have plans to bring back
its old formula.
    The stock, among the most actively traded issues on the New York
Stock Exchange, was up $1.25 a share at $71.25 in afternoon trading.

^By COTTEN TIMBERLAKE=
^AP Business Writer=
    AP-NY-ð7-1ð-85 1610EDT<
```

8-9 | continued

```
u a AM-NewCoke 2ndLd-Writethru a0693 07-10 0458
^AM-New Coke,(2nd Ld - Writethru,)a0693,0464<
 ^Eds: Combines previous and inserts reaction from group that backed
return to old formula. This provides 10-graf lead, picking up at
the 7th graf of original, beginning ``Analysts.´´ Verson also
moving on business wire.<
^By COTTEN TIMBERLAKE=
^AP Business Writer=
   NEW YORK (AP) _ Coca-Cola Co. said Wednesday it plans to bring
back its old formula for regular Coke within the next several weeks
and will call it Coca-Cola Classic.
   Tom Gray, a spokesman for Coca-Cola in Atlanta, said Coca-Cola
will continue to market its new formula, introduced in May.
   Coca-Cola's stock, among the most actively traded issues on the
New York Stock Exchange, was up $1.25 a share at $71.25 in
afternoon trading.
   Since Coca-Cola announced in April that it was changing its
99-year-old formula for regular Coke, complaints from loyal fans of
the old formula have received considerable publicity. In addition,
Coca-Cola has said it has received 1,500 calls a day about the new
Coke.
   ``Everyone wins,´´ said Gray. ``Over 40 million consumers every
day in the United States enjoy Coca-Cola but thousands of dedicated
Coca-Cola consumers have told us they still want the original taste
as an option. We have listened and we are taking action to satisfy
their request.´´
   Gray said Coca-Cola Classic will be available in ``some
markets´´ within several weeks, and both formulas will be available
to bottlers internationally.
   Gay Mullins of Seattle, who founded the Old Cola Drinkers of
America, a group dedicated to bringing back Coke's old formula,
called the news ``fantastic, it's great.´´
   Mullins said he thought his group, which has received national
publicity about its efforts, could claim at least part of the
responsibility for sparking Coca-Cola's decision to bring back the
old formula.
   ``I felt from the beginning that we would be successful,´´ he
said.
   ``We were given some bottles of the old Coke and we will raise
them on high and salute the company for its decision ... and I feel
anything we can do to help them we would be delighted to do,´´
Mullins said.
   Analysts have said sales of the new Coke have been spurred by
curiosity, heavy promotions and price discounts, but that
meaningful sales figures for the new Coke won't be available until
the fall.
   Coca-Cola said last month that its shipments of Coke concentrate
to bottlers in May were up 8 percent over a year ago, compared with
a 4 percent rate of gain for old Coke in recent months.
   PepsiCo Inc., meanwhile, has claimed that the reformulation of
Coke is benefiting sales of Pepsi-Cola. The Purchase, N.Y.-based
concern said case shipments of Pepsi rose 14 percent in May from a
year earlier, the biggest monthly gain in the company's 87-year
history.
   AP-NY-07-10-85 1624EDT<
```

8-9 | continued

u a A^-NewCoke 4thLd-Writethru a0742 07-10 0517
^AM-New Coke, 4th Ld - writethru, a0742,0556<
^Eds: Recasts lead to include consumer protests, adds 2 grafs from
royal Crown at end.<
^By CULLEN TIMBERLAKE=
^AP Business Writer=
    NEW YORK (AP) _ Coca-Cola Co., bowing to pressure from irate
consumers, said Wednesday it plans to bring back its old formula
for regular Coke within the next several weeks and will call it
Coca-Cola Classic.
    Tom Gray, a spokesman for Coca-Cola in Atlanta, said Coca-Cola
will continue to market its new formula, introduced in May.
    Coca-Cola's stock, among the most actively traded issues on the
New York Stock Exchange, was up $2.37½ a share to close at $72.37½.
PepsiCo's stock fell 75 cents a share to $57.
    Since Coca-Cola announced in April that it was changing its
99-year-old formula for regular Coke, complaints from loyal fans of
the old formula have received considerable publicity. In addition,
Coca-Cola has said it has received 1,500 calls a day about the new
Coke.
    ``Everyone wins,'' said Gray. ``Over 40 million consumers every
day in the United States enjoy Coca-Cola but thousands of dedicated
Coca-Cola consumers have told us they still want the original taste
as an option. We have listened and we are taking action to satisfy
their request.''
    Gray said Coca-Cola Classic will be available in ``some
markets'' within several weeks, and both formulas will be available
to bottlers internationally.
    Gay Mullins of Seattle, who founded the Old Cola Drinkers of
America, a group dedicated to bringing back Coke's old formula,
called the news ``fantastic, it's great.''
    Mullins said he thought his group, which has received national
publicity, could claim at least part of the responsibility for
sparking Coca-Cola's decision to bring back the old formula.
    However, in a six-cola taste test last month in Seattle, Mullins
consistently preferred anything but old Coke _ even choosing new
Coke in a head-to-head test against old Coke.
    Analysts have said sales of the new Coke have been spurred by
curiosity, heavy promotions and price discounts, but that
meaningful sales figures for the new Coke won't be available until
the fall.
    Coca-Cola said last month that its shipments of Coke concentrate
to bottlers in May were up 8 percent over a year ago, compared with
a 4 percent rate of gain for old Coke in recent months.
    PepsiCo Inc., meanwhile, has claimed that the reformulation of
Coke is benefiting sales of Pepsi-Cola. The Purchase, N.Y.-based
concern said case shipments of Pepsi rose 14 percent in May from a
year earlier, the biggest monthly gain in the company's 87-year
history.
    ``We're not surprised. Very obviously people across the country
do not like this (new) Coke,'' said Ken Ross, a spokesman for
Pepsi-Cola.
    ``We now have the opportunity to compete with one product that
lost to Pepsi in millions of taste tests and against one product
that the public hates,'' Ross said. ``That doesn't seem to be too
tough a challenge.''
    Royal Crown Cola Co. executive vice president James Harralson,
issued a statement in Chicago saying, ``The action will confuse and
frustrate consumers, who will be anxious to try a new brand
entirely.''
    He added that, ``Coke has hurt its credibility both with
consumers and its bottlers, who must be wondering if a third Coke
will be introduced when this plan also fails.''

8-10

AP Radio Wire
The first story to move on any wire was on The Associated
Press radio wire at 12:59 p.m. It is a story based on unusually
active trading in Coke stock; it was developed independent of
the news release later that day on "Coca-Cola Classic." Note
the terse but clear writing style. Note Coke's denial in the
story at 1:41 p.m. The final radio wire story is at 3:48 p.m.,
after the release from Coke, and contains confirmation of
what was denied only two hours earlier. *Source: Used with
permission of The Associated Press.*

AP-BUSINESSWATCH

    COCA-COLA

    (NEW YORK) -- STOCK IN COCA-COLA IS SHARPLY HIGHER TODAY -- AMID
MARKET RUMORS THAT THE OLD COKE MAY BE COMING BACK. TWO PROMINENT
INDUSTRY ANALYSTS SAY THEY EXPECT COCA-COLA TO REINTRODUCE ITS OLD
FORMULA -- AT LEAST IN THE SOUTHEAST AND TEXAS, WHERE THE NEW STUFF
HASN'T BEEN SELLING WELL.
    MARTIN ROMM, A BEVERAGE INDUSTRY-WATCHER FOR FIRST BOSTON
CORPORATION, THINKS THERE'S A BETTER THAN EVEN CHANCE COKE WILL BRING
BACK ITS OLD FORMULA. BUT, HE SAYS, THAT DOESN'T NECESSARILY MEAN
IT'LL GET RID OF THE NEW COKE. ROMM THINKS THE SOFT DRINK GIANT MAY
PUT TWO COCA-COLAS ON THE SHELVES -- IN ORDER TO GET A HEFTIER MARKET
SHARE.
    COCA-COLA STOCK HAS GAINED TWO DOLLARS A SHARE IN HEAVY TRADING ON
THE NEW YORK STOCK EXCHANGE TODAY.
    OFFICIALS OF THE ATLANTA-BASED SOFT DRINK FIRM HAVE BEEN
UNAVAILABLE FOR COMMENT.

AP-WX-07-10-85 1259EDT

At the end cue of ". . . causation between smoking and cardiovascular disease," you would want to give this closing copy for the announcer: "Despite the inconclusive results of the entire study, Kuller pointed out that men who
quit smoking had a coronary death rate almost 50 percent below those who kept

8-10 | continued

```
AP-BUSINESSWATCH

  COCA-COLA (TOPS)

  (ATLANTA) -- A SPOKESMAN FOR COCA-COLA HAS DENIED WALL STREET
RUMORS THAT THE SOFT DRINK COMPANY MAY RETURN TO ITS OLD FORMULA FOR
COKE.
  ACCORDING TO THE SPOKESMAN, COCA-COLA HAS NO PLANS TO CHANGE ITS
NEW FORMULA -- BUT, HE ADDED, ''AT THE SAME TIME, WE'RE KEEPING OUR
OPTIONS OPEN.''
  LEADING INDUSTRY ANALYSTS THINK THERE'S A GOOD CHANCE COKE WILL
BRING BACK ITS OLD FORMULA, AT LEAST IN THOSE MARKETS WHERE THE NEW
RECIPE HASN'T BEEN WELL RECEIVED.

AP-WX-07-10-85 1341EDT




AP-COKE (TOPS)

  (NEW YORK) -- THE COCA-COLA COMPANY HAS KNUCKED UNDER TO CONSUMER
DEMAND AND IS RETURNING ITS ORIGINAL FORMULA TO THE MARKET.
  OFFICIALS AT COCA-COLA COMPANY IN ATLANTA SAY THEY'LL BE BRINGING
BACK THE SOFT DRINK UNDER THE OLD FORMULA. AND THEY'LL BE MARKETING
IT UNDER THE NAME ''COCA-COLA CLASSIC.''
  IN ONE OF THE MOST HIGHLY-PUBLICIZED PRODUCT ADJUSTMENTS EVER, THE
MANUFACTURER ANNOUNCED IN APRIL THAT IT WAS RE-VAMPING THE TASTE OF
COKE. CONSUMER REACTION WAS MIXED, AND WHEN RUMORS OF A RETURN TO THE
OLD FORMULA SURFACED ON WALL STREET TODAY, COCA-COLA STOCK SHOT UP.
  COKE SAYS IT WILL KEEP THE NEW FORMULA ON THE MARKET, EVEN AS THE
OLD ONE COMES BACK.

AP-WX-07-10-85 1548EDT
```

smoking. The Health Coalition, which includes the American Heart Association, has asked the FTC to stop the Reynolds ad, and also is asking for Reynolds to buy corrective advertising."

8-11

What's News

*   *   *

Coca-Cola Co. reversed itself and said it will sell the old Coke alongside the reformulated version introduced in April. Coca-Cola bottlers had grown increasingly nervous over complaints by consumers about the switch.

Coca-Cola Co. To Bring Back Its Old Coke

Consumer Pressure Coaxes Concern to Sell 'Classic' Alongside New Version

By Scott Kilman

Staff Reporter of The Wall Street Journal

ATLANTA—Coca-Cola Co., worn down by die-hard opposition from fans of old Coke, reversed itself and said it will sell old Coke alongside the reformulated version introduced in April.

Old Coke will return in several weeks in some markets as "Coca-Cola classic," the soft drink concern said. Meanwhile, the reformulated version, which reached nationwide distribution last month, will continue to be sold as the flagship brand Coke. Old Coke all but disappeared from store shelves last month.

The move was lauded by industry observers as a fast response to market signals. But it represents a surprising turnaround for a company that prided itself as both a monitor and mirror of the American public.

In composite trading on the New York Stock Exchange yesterday, Coca-Cola closed at $73.375, up $2.375.

"We beat Coca-Cola," said Frank Olson of Old Coke Drinkers of America, a Seattle group that claims to have recruited 100,000 members in a drive to bring back old Coke. The group, which garnered heavy press coverage, had planned a protest march in Dallas later this month and was organizing a boycott in Australia.

Coca-Cola executives didn't return telephone calls to elaborate on the company statement. A company spokesman said Coca-Cola will release details of the Coke classic introduction today.

Coca-Cola bottlers, who had grown increasingly nervous about the grass-roots opposition to the April switch, said they favored the return of old Coke. "The results were showing that new Coke was testing out stronger than expected. That was the topside," said Crawford Johnson, a Birmingham, Ala., Coca-Cola bottler. "But some consumers were mad. It was almost a pyschological thing."

Coca-Cola had released figures showing that new Coke syrup shipments to bottlers were up a strong 8% in May. But Coca-Cola also had disclosed that it was getting 1,500 calls a day to its consumer hotline, compared with 400 daily before the April switch. Coca-Cola mailed coupons for a free six-pack of new Coke to those who complained.

Figures aren't available yet on how new Coke performed in June.

The decision to bring back old Coke and sell it alongside new Coke is a dramatic twist in the marketing strategy laid out by Roberto C. Goizueta, Coca-Cola chairman and chief executive officer. During the research on new Coke, Mr. Goizueta and Donald R. Keough, president and chief operating officer, mulled whether to introduce the new formula as a sister cola under the name "Coke 100" in commemoration of the company's centennial. But Mr. Goizueta torpedoed the idea for fear of confusing consumers and cannibalizing the flagship cola. "It was obvious the best tasting cola should be Coke," he explained in a May interview.

Industry analysts said Coca-Cola was forced to bring back old Coke to staunch the migration of customers to other soft drinks. "The further South it went the more disappointing the results," said Emanuel Goldman of Montgomery Securities.

Coca-Cola conducted extensive marketing surveys to convince itself that new Coke would be accepted by old Coke drinkers and even steal Pepsi drinkers. More than 200,000 drinkers secretly tasted variations of the new formula over a four-year period.

But Coca-Cola's research apparently didn't detect that many consumers would react emotionally to the departure of old Coke. "The company didn't fathom the depth of the emotional commitment to Coke," said Jesse Meyers, publisher of the Beverage Digest, a trade newsletter.

Coca-Cola introduced new Coke in hopes of blunting the popularity of PepsiCo Inc.'s Pepsi-Cola with younger drinkers.

8-12

USA Today Story
Although there is duplication between the readership of *USA Today* and *The Wall Street Journal*, *USA Today* is written for people on the move. That often means a provocative feature treatment. Note how *USA Today* treated the Coke story, compared to all the other examples. Coke subsequently dropped the "Coke Is It" slogan it had used for several years. Source: Copyright 1985 *USA Today*. Used with permission.

Two Cokes are it; 'Classic' is back

By Betsy Bauer   USA TODAY

Coke are it.

Pepsi meant that as a joke, but to millions it's the real thing, no laughing matter.

The Coca-Cola Co.'s announcement Wednesday that old Coke is coming out of retirement cheered fans of the 99-year-old original formula.

The comeback cola will be called "Coca-Cola Classic" and will share the shelf with new Coke, introduced in April and still the company's flagship.

Original formula Coke will be on shelves in selected markets in a few weeks, the company said. More details are to be announced today at a press conference in Atlanta.

Coca-Cola, which had been receiving 1,500 calls a day about new Coke, rushed in with ads on network TV heralding old Coke's return.

Some reactions:

■ "I want the first can of Classic Coke," said Gay Mullins, who founded Old Cola Drinkers of America, which fought for old Coke's return.

■ Sen. David Pryor, D-Ark., read news of old Coke's return into the Congressional Record, calling it "a historic moment" and proof that an "American institution" can't die.

■ Pepsico Inc. greeted the news with fighting words.

"What are they going to say?

Coke are it?" said spokesman Ken Ross. "We now have the opportunity to compete with one product that lost to Pepsi in millions of taste tests and against one product that the public hates. That doesn't seem to be too tough a challenge."

But can consumers really taste the difference in colas?

"Some can and some can't. The important thing is that people think they can," said analyst Emanuel Goldman of Montgomery Securities.

■ **Coke's about-face, 1B**

Conclusions

* The sights and sounds of events are important to broadcast news.

* Special events are the PR activities (other than crises) most likely to generate coverage by broadcast media, especially television.

* You'll need to prepare a fact sheet and a history of the event and videotape some activity.

* Broadcasters need material written in broadcast style, but because that means the copy will be brief, you should attach "FYI" ("For Your Information") to the longer print-media release.

* Be sure you are set up with facilities the broadcasters will need to cover your special events.

* Always post someone at a central location to respond to questions, and provide that person with all the facts you have given to the media plus all new, updated information.

* News conferences are called when someone needs to interact with the news media. In arranging news conferences, be sure you provide the news media with background materials.

* You should "cover" news conferences too—make audio- and videotapes for the record.

* Crises are disorganized combinations of special events and news conferences.

* News releases are either advance stories of something about to occur or stories telling what did occur or what is going on.

* For radio, you need actualities (voice) to give authenticity and to enliven your news.

* For TV you need audio and video—provided promptly so your story is timely and attention getting.

* Talk-show appearances are usually arranged by PR people, and you need to provide both interviewer and interviewee with appropriate information. The interviewee needs to be rehearsed, and the interviewer should be provided with biographical information and background materials well in advance.

* Mini-docs, or broadcast series, are short, related features that are usually first written as a unit and then broken up for programming.

* Some PR people produce and distribute mini-docs or series. Others may only assist newspeople by researching and perhaps writing.

* Broadcast writing style is conversational, and broadcast copywriters must remember that the listener has no opportunity to review or rehear a sentence or word once it has been spoken.

* When you write for broadcast you have two audiences to consider—the person who will read the copy (the announcer) and the listener or viewer.

* The physical preparation of broadcast copy is designed to help the announcer.
* The structure of broadcast stories is designed to help the listener.
* Broadcast leads are different from print leads in that they don't contain all of the news elements in the story.
* Broadcast news stories are rewritten regularly during the day to keep the material fresh, even when there are no new facts as in a breaking story.
* When you supply news as audio- or videotape, be sure you attach a script, carefully identified like the tape. Attaching a news release too will help the script writer fit the tape into a context.
* Most people in the United States get their information about what's going on in the world from watching television. A significant part of the population, especially those between 13 and 19, get theirs from radio.
* The two media are critical to communication. In times of crises or a breaking news story, they assume even greater importance.
* PR people must know how to provide information to the broadcast media that is appropriate for the media and interesting to their audiences.

Exercises

1. Rewrite the news release in Exercise 7-1 as a broadcast story.
2. Look at the position paper in Chapter 14, the one for which you wrote a print news release in Exercise 7-4.
   a. What audio actualities could you create using this paper? Indicate them by putting quotes around the first four words and the last four words you would use—for example, "When I saw that . . . we probably will not attempt to rebuild on that site."
   b. What video possibilities does this position paper offer?
3. Outline a radio series (a mini-doc) based on the position paper.
4. Rewrite the release announcing Ourbank's new communication program in Chapter 7 for both radio and television.

Selected Bibliography

Irving Fang, *Television News, Radio News* (St. Paul, Minn.: RADA Press, 1980).

Rolf Gompertz, *Promotion and Publicity Handbook for Broadcasters* (Blue Ridge Summit, Pa.: TAB Books, 1979).

Doug Newsom and Jim Wollert, *Media Writing* (Belmont, Calif.: Wadsworth, 1985).

Paul G. Smeyak, *Broadcast News Writing*, 2nd ed. (Columbus, Ohio: Grid, 1983).

For Pronunciation Guidance

Thomas Lee Crowell, Jr., *NBC Handbook of Pronunciation*, 3rd ed. (New York: Thomas Y. Crowell, 1964) or the British speech guide by Robert Burchfield, *The Spoken Word: A BBC Guide* (New York: Oxford University Press, 1981).

9
Writing
Advertising
Copy

Advertising, by definition, is time, space or position in a mass medium bought for the purpose of promoting a product, a service or idea. As a public relations writer, you will probably not write much advertising to persuade people to buy your product or to use your service. This kind of writing is ordinarily done by the firm's advertising agency. But you may write a lot of copy for "idea" ads. That's why idea ads are the focus of this chapter.

Ads that promote ideas run the gamut in terms of content. Some, like the Mobil Oil Company ad in Example 9-1, may address public policy issues. Sometimes ads like this are called *advertorials*. If they are presented through the broadcast or film media, they are often called *infomercials*. Other ads, like the one from United Technologies Corporation in Example 9-2, might simply present organizations as good corporate citizens. Such ads are often called *institutional*, *identity* or *corporate-image ads*.

Two special types of ads are also discussed in this chapter. They are public service and house ads. No money is exchanged in the placement of these pieces, but the two qualify in every other way as advertising.

Public service ads are ads that appear free in the print and broadcast media. United Way, Campfire Girls, the American Heart Association and a wide variety of similar organizations and causes benefit from such ads. See Example 9-3 from the Advertising Council.

9-1

Public Policy Ad
The Mobil Corporation has been especially active for several years in the use of paid advertising space and time to advocate its points of view regarding issues. It is an idea ad that in the print media is sometimes called an advertorial. The broadcast version of this same message is sometimes called an infomercial. *Source:* Used with permission of the Mobil Corporation.

Sorry, Mr. President, you've been misled

On Friday, March 28, you singled out Mobil Oil Corporation in a speech at the National Conference of State Legislatures, charging that our company had violated the Administration's price guidelines by $45 million. The White House said that Mobil was unwilling to refund this amount to consumers through a temporary reduction of 3 cents a gallon in the price of gasoline.

Our position, Mr. President, is very straightforward. We did not violate existing guidelines of the Council on Wage and Price Stability. And we were not asked by any government agency to reduce the price of gasoline by any particular amount per gallon. Further, we are most concerned that this charge—and your repetition of it last week—may represent a continuation of political maneuvering at the expense of our company, and our company alone, because of our policy of speaking out on energy issues, sometimes at variance with Administration policy.

Last year, you called for decontrol of domestic crude oil production subject to a so-called "windfall profits" tax. Shortly after Mobil disagreed publicly with the proposal—suggesting that controls might be continued on existing oil, providing newly discovered oil would be free from additional tax in order to encourage more exploration—it was reported that you called us the "most irresponsible company in America." We felt this allegation was unfair but decided not to answer because of the respect we have for the Office of the President of the United States. We felt at the time, however, that you had been poorly advised; and so, apparently, did the Congress, since its final version of the windfall measure favors new oil over old oil, accepting in substantial part the point we had made.

In this current situation, Mr. President, we are afraid that once again you have not been given the full facts; and, unlike the differing opinions we both have on the windfall profits tax, this time you have made the specific accusation that we overcharged our customers.

We present the facts here because we care about our reputation, not only as businessmen but also as honorable citizens trying to help solve America's energy problems:

1. At the time the COWPS guidelines were introduced in October, 1978, we were already (and still are) operating under Department of Energy mandatory price controls, in effect since 1971.

2. We found many of the new COWPS requirements in conflict with DOE requirements but struggled to live with both sets of controls.

3. Under the COWPS voluntary program, oil companies were permitted to recover increased costs in their prices for finished products, using either profit margin or gross margin standards. Each company was free to elect the standard suited to its circumstances; many opted for the profit margin standard while Mobil and a number of others elected gross margin. More than once, COWPS stated in writing that compliance under the gross margin test would be measured on an annual basis over the COWPS fiscal year ending each September 30.

4. When you and DOE urged the oil industry last June to build a large inventory of both gasoline and home heating oil simultaneously, Mobil bought supplies wherever we could, at higher-than-normal costs. We sold many of these products during the ensuing three months (COWPS' fiscal fourth quarter) at prices which helped us recover some of these extraordinary costs—exactly as the guidelines prescribed at that time.

5. Then, retroactively, in December 1979, COWPS changed these guidelines only for the companies using gross margin, requiring compliance on a quarterly basis for the fiscal year ended September 30, 1979. On the annual basis we had been working under, our prices were not only in compliance but well below COWPS guidelines. Under the retroactive rule change, COWPS announced on February 25 that Mobil was out of compliance and several other companies probably so. But COWPS named just Mobil.

6. Telegrams seeking clarification were sent by Mobil's president to COWPS and DOE but went unanswered. On February 27, Mobil's chairman wrote to you, Mr. President. On March 24, he received an answer from Alfred E. Kahn, your advisor on inflation, stating that he had asked R. Robert Russell, director of COWPS, "to give me an analysis of whether our standards, which set quarterly targets, unrealistically fail to take into account the normal flow into and out of inventories, and in so doing impose unreasonable burdens on petroleum refiners."

7. Midmorning on March 28, with White House encouragement, a Mobil director met with Mr. Russell, believing they would resolve the issue or at least get Mr. Russell's response to Mr. Kahn's request. Neither happened. It was really a non-meeting and we wonder why it was called.

8. Early that same afternoon, you leveled your attacks on our company, and the White House stated that Mobil had refused to reduce gasoline prices 3 cents a gallon for one quarter of 1980 to "repay" the alleged overcharges. The first time we were aware of such a figure was when we read it on the news wire that afternoon.

In summary, Mr. President, the rules of the game were changed retroactively. We were not out of compliance under the rules in effect when we were selling the products in question. Anybody can be thrown into violation when rules are made retroactively. We oppose retroactive rule changes which put companies into violation, particularly when they are applied selectively against companies that speak out.

© 1980 Mobil Corporation

9-2

Corporate Image Ad
United Technologies Corporation uses many methods to
promote its corporate identity. This ad attempts to relate
the corporation to the women's movement and, in doing so,
establish that UTC is socially responsible and aware. Such
messages are sometimes called institutional, corporate image
or identity ads. *Source:* Used with permission of United
Technologies Corporation.

Thanks To Sue

When her
family's possessions
were seized
to pay off her
father's
business debts,
she taught school
to help support
her family.
She worked for
abolition
and temperance.
She was arrested
and fined.
She found that
women's voices
were falling on
deaf ears.
She felt that those
ears would continue
to be deaf
until all women
could vote. And for
nearly 50 years she.
fought for that right.
It finally came
14 years after
her death.
And last week
more women voted in
a Presidential election
than ever before.
Susan B. Anthony
showed what you can
accomplish with
conviction and
determination.
Of course, it will
be a little easier now,
thanks to Susan.

9-3

Public Service Ad
Ads are routinely prepared free of charge by members of the
Advertising Council. Member agencies contribute the time
and talents of their employees. Copies of such ads are widely
distributed to the mass media who use them without cost on a
space- or time-available basis. *Source:* Used with permission
of The Advertising Council, Inc.

Picture your community without the Arts.

Imagine no theatre. No music. No sculpture or painting. Picture the arts gone and you picture a lot of beauty missing.

But the arts not only create beauty, they create jobs.

Because the arts attract tourists. And the dollars tourists spend in restaurants and hotels, on transportation and in stores.

The arts attract industry. Businesses prefer to locate in communities with a rich cultural life.

And the arts are an industry in themselves. Like any other industry they employ people, buy goods and services, and generate taxes.

Picture your community without the arts and you have to imagine industry and jobs gone, too. And after that, the people.

So it'd not only be pretty dull, it'd be pretty lonely.

Support The Arts
That's where the people are.

National Endowment for the Arts

 A Public Service of The Advertising Council

HOU 11/4

House ads are advertising messages that appear in a firm's own publications that, for instance, urge employees not to litter or to buy savings bonds or give blood. See Example 9-4 for an example of a house ad. In this example, the publishers of *Editor & Publisher* are promoting the magazine as an authoritative source of newspaper-related convention activities and information. Regardless of the sources or specific purposes, ads always try to persuade.

Advertising as a Persuasive Force

Many people believe that advertising has the power to make people buy things they neither need nor want. If this were true, then it would follow that advertising could be used by public relations professionals to make publics accept ideas they might otherwise reject. But advertisers will quickly tell you that advertising does not work that way.

Advertisers know that the power of advertising is limited to persuasion, not coercion. Used skillfully, advertising can stimulate in an audience a predisposition to buy a product, use a service or accept an idea. Advertising has proved itself to be economically efficient at persuasion, because it knows that you attract more bees with honey than with vinegar.

Appeal

The key element in the success of an ad is the relevance of the appeal—the honey—that it has for the receiver of the message. This appeal should be as direct as possible. In writing ads, don't leave the appeal to inference. Spell it out. An appeal can be emotional, rational or a combination of the two.

Emotional appeals tug at the heart. They suggest that the receiver can become happier, healthier, prettier, sexier, more successful, more patriotic or gain any number of other qualities if he or she behaves in a specific way. The number of emotional appeals open to the ad writer is apparently limitless. Rational appeals, on the other hand, appeal to the receiver's reason. Such appeals are likely to be based on economy, durability, profit, efficiency and performance among others.

Combination appeals use emotion first to get people to pay attention and then use rational appeals once the receivers are interested in the copy.

Positioning

A particular appeal works in concert with the marketing idea of "positioning the product." The writer expresses the appeal creatively in an attempt to carve out a unique niche for the advertiser in the minds of the public. For example, Hertz has been the dominant rental car firm for decades, with Avis in a distant second position. At some point, Avis decided to capitalize on its number two position and ap-

9-4

House Ad

All media sometimes have time or space available and they use the opportunity to run house ads promoting their own media. Some media actually budget with their sales promotion departments for house ads, although no actual money changes hands. In this case, *Editor & Publisher* used a house ad to promote the journal as an authoritative source of information about upcoming newspaper convention activities. *Source*: Used with permission of the Editor & Publisher Company.

FOR E&P READERS AND ADVERTISERS

More than half of the important events in the newspaper world—conferences, conventions and trade shows—take place during the first part of the year. With interests involving every segment of the industry, Editor & Publisher attends and follows up on every major gathering with special distribution, special coverage, or both. Here are some important E&P issue dates for you:

APRIL 6	American Society of Newspaper Editors, Washington, April 9-12.
MAY 4	American Newspaper Publishers Ass'n., Miami Beach, May 5-8.
	INCFO* meeting, Hot Springs, Virginia, May 6-May 8.
MAY 11	Newspaper in Education Conference, Toronto, May 15-17.
	ANPA Operations Management Conference Planning Issue.
	ANPA Publishers Post-Convention Issue. (The whole convention story.)
MAY 18	INPA† Conference, Boston, MA, May 19-22. (E&P Promotion Awards.)
MAY 25	Editor & Publisher Annual Advertising Linage Issue. (1984 linage.)
JUNE 8	ANPA Operations Management Conference, New Orleans, June 8-12.
	ICMA—Circulation Managers Conference, Columbus, OH, June 9-13.
JUNE 15	Operations Management Post-Conference Issue. (Complete report.)
JUNE 22	ANCAM—Classified Managers meeting, New Orleans, June 23-27.

Conventionally speaking, E&P covers the entire newspaper territory, so choose the meetings and issues valuable to you, and make your dates with us. We'll take you there in style. Call Don Parvin, Ad Manager, at 212-675-4380.

Editor & Publisher

11 WEST 19TH STREET, NEW YORK, N.Y. 10011

*INCFO, Now INFE—International Newspaper Financial Executives
†INPA—International Newspaper Promotion Association

peal to the public's inclination to root for the underdog. In this way, the "We Try Harder" idea was born.

Looking at the situation rationally, a Cutlass is a Cutlass, whether it has the Hertz or Avis logo on it. If there is no significant difference in the rental fees and services by the two companies, why should one rent a Cutlass from Avis rather than Hertz? There is no rational reason. Avis makes an emotional appeal to the prospective customer by positioning itself in the public's mind as number two. Everybody knows that number two has to try harder to be number one. Therefore, the suggestion is, you should rent the Cutlass from Avis, because Avis tries harder.

Behavior

Understanding what people think and do in different parts of society is critical to developing credible advertising. Good advertising writers are in touch with their publics. They understand that there may be a little snob (and maybe a lot) in all of us, because we like to relate to others and have others relate to us. Behaviorists spend a lot of time trying to understand our reference groups—organizations to which we belong or want to belong. We all want the comfort of belonging, of being accepted. It is for this reason that friends and family are important and that we seek their approval. We are also influenced by opinion leaders. Different segments of society have different opinion leaders, and moreover we each react to those leaders differently based on our own personality characteristics. For example, authoritarian types are particularly vulnerable to leaders who have status and authority.

If you are getting the idea that people don't respond rationally to a lot of advertising copy, you are correct. Most of the decisions we make are based on emotion, not reason. That is why good advertising copy is a complex blend of information (facts) and appeal (emotion). The best copywriters make unusual associations, see unique applications, and react to innovations with excitement and enthusiasm. Copy that promotes excitement and enthusiasm among consumers is the most likely to succeed.

Basic Guidelines for Writing Advertising Copy

Advertising copywriters are often believed to have a great deal more creative freedom than most other writers because they work under few artificial restraints. For example, you might consider writing a news release to be less creative than writing copy for an ad, because in the former you must conform to news writing style. But there are rules and restraints on ad copywriting too.

Purpose

To begin with, you must have a clear understanding of what you want to accomplish with the ad. Do you want your public to support the bond issue? Do you want your shareholders to vote for the recapitalization of the company? You must know the single (never multiple), specific purpose for the ad. And everything you put in the ad should contribute to that purpose. In editing the ad, you'll need to delete as excess baggage any word, phrase, sentence, paragraph or visual that does not specifically further the identified purpose. The receiver should not have to wrestle with trying to understand excess baggage in discerning the message you are trying to communicate.

Objective Facts

You'll be able to select a specific purpose for the ad only after carefully and thoroughly reviewing all the pertinent facts about the issue. You should review these facts not only from your "side's" point of view but also from that of your opposition. In fact, the latter review is just as important as the review of your own side. And both reviews have to be done with objectivity. Only then can you make an informed judgment about the strengths and weaknesses of your position as well as that of your competition. And only then should you attempt to derive a purpose calculated to capitalize on one of your strengths or to attack one of the opposition's weaknesses.

Objectivity is no less critical in rendering you able to prove what you say if you are challenged in a court of law.

The Publics

You should review the facts and select a purpose for the ad with a full awareness of the uniqueness of your public. You need to know their wants, needs and values. This is where demographic and psychographic information assumes great importance. If the members of your public are blue collar, averaging less than a median income, a ninth-grade education and a high rate of unemployment, you may have difficulty in persuading them to support a large bonding program to build a junior college in the community. This doesn't mean you won't be successful in gaining this support, but it does mean that you will have to write credible messages that clearly demonstrate the rewards such support will bring.

Media

Before you write the copy, you must know which medium or media you are writing for. One of the first concerns, of course, is meeting the technical requirements of the medium. An ad prepared for a newspaper may not meet the requirements of a magazine, and it certainly won't meet those of radio or television. If you are writing ads for media with which you are unfamiliar, first check the technical requirements in the most recent issue of *Standard Rate and Data Service* (*SRDS*). *SRDS* will also provide you with deadline information, rate scales, a list of key personnel and a wide variety of other data. *SRDS* is one of the bibles of the advertising business.

Beyond technical issues, you need to know a lot of other things about the medium you will use. How credible is it? How evocative is it? How do people react to it? What audience does it reach? What audience does it seek? What is its editorial slant? What have other advertisers experienced who have used it in similar situations? These are important questions, and you must know, not guess at, the answers. In some cases you may have to rely on word of mouth, but in other cases you will be able to gather a lot of information from the medium itself simply by writing or calling.

The Creative Approach

Never try to develop a creative approach or write a line of copy until you have first made the decisions specified above. These decision areas are parts of what advertising professionals call a copy platform. A copy platform is a succinct document that spells out pertinent information about the public and contains a simple statement of creative strategy. For example, a creative-strategy statement for a little-known candidate running for Senator against an incumbent might read like this:

> **To convince voters that Mr. X will represent the views of eastern Kentuckians better than Mr. Y.**

This statement clearly expresses your purpose. The question then becomes How will I do it? That's where creativity comes in.

Let's suppose that Mr. Y is noted for being absent from the Senate floor when important bills that may affect eastern Kentuckians are up for a vote. You could construct a series of ads in which Mr. X pledges to be in the Senate chamber during every important vote. The voters would probably want to hear this message, though they might simply consider the claim to be mere political rhetoric.

You could take the offensive and attack Mr. Y by showing his empty chair during a roll call. You could then support the point with a table, showing not only the bills on which Mr. Y did not cast votes but also the number and dates of his absences. In other words, you could provide a lot of solid, verifiable, convincing information that Mr. Y is not doing his job properly. Still another approach might be to show Mr. X, dressed in hunting garb and following some coon hounds on the scent. Mr. X would look up and explain that he and his "dawgs" were looking for Mr. Y. An obvious close would be a superimposed message like this:

> **Where *is* Mr. Y? Vote for Mr. X. You will always find him in the Senate.**

Of these three approaches, the first is mundane. It is low on persuasiveness because there is nothing unique about its claim. The ad neither excites the emotions nor challenges the reason. The second ad is more creative, and it contains lots of convincing and damning information about Mr. Y. It is more likely to be persuasive. But the third approach, which is obviously best executed for television, is not only more creative but it is also dramatically persuasive. How could a voter see that ad and remain free of resentment toward Mr. Y? And as resentment built, voters would be more easily persuaded to vote for Mr. X. Emotion is the essence of good creativity in advertising.

Visualization

As you read the discussion on creative approaches, it may have occurred to you that creative strategy in advertising includes visual as well as verbal thinking. If so, you caught on to an essential difference between writing news copy and writing advertising copy. A good advertising copywriter always thinks in visual as well as verbal terms. The reason that the hunting example above is so dramatic is that the visual element graphically characterizes the verbal message. In the best advertising copy, the verbal and visual content harmonize perfectly so that each complements and extends the message of the other.

Language

It is axiomatic that if you want to communicate with someone you must use language that the other person will understand. Language has certain rules, and if they are not generally observed, communication may be impossible or the result unwanted. Thus, the common rules of grammar and syntax are the standard in advertising, as they are in other forms of writing. You can break a grammar rule for a purpose—for example, to achieve a specific effect not possible with traditional rules—but doing so should be the exception, not the rule.

Always choose the simple over the complex word. Your public might be able to read and comprehend at the college-graduate level, but people generally prefer to read copy that is two to four grade levels below their ability. And if there is any doubt about the educational level of your audience, you should gear your writing to a level lower than you believe it to be. Obviously, if you are writing an idea ad for your company that will appear in a highly specialized professional journal, you should use language appropriate to that public. This may mean that you will use some professional jargon. If your ad is to appear in a general mass medium, however, simplify the language and avoid jargon.

Not only should you use simple words, but you should also use short phrases, sentences and paragraphs. Sentences should average no longer than twelve to fifteen words. Paragraphs should average about three to five sentences. Following these guidelines will help readability. If your message is easy to understand without being insulting to the intelligence, it will stand a better chance of being read than denser, more complex copy.

Repetition

Do you recall the outcome of Pavlov's experiment with his dogs? As the number of repetitions mounted, the dogs began to associate the meat powder with the sound of the tuning fork. When the repetitions were plotted on a graph, a learning curve took shape. Finally, the curve leveled—that is, after a while additional repetitions did not cause the learning curve to go higher. Thus, repetition is an essential principle of learning. You can apply this principle to your message in two basic ways.

The repetition principle applies first to the actual writing of copy.

The general rule is that you should repeat the essential point of your message at least three times in your ad. This does not mean that you have to repeat it verbatim, but only that you must repeat the idea. This is absolutely critical in broadcast messages because they are temporal.

The principle of repetition also applies to how frequently you will repeat the message to your public, over how long and in what time frame. Generally, if you are introducing a new program or idea, for example, you will need to plan to present your message fairly frequently during the early stages of your program. As your audience becomes familiar with what you are promoting, you can reduce the number of presentations and space them out while still maintaining a reasonable level of awareness.

When your program ends, the public will begin to forget at approximately the same rate at which it learned. Still, the public's awareness about what you said will never drop back to zero. Hence, it will take less effort in a subsequent program to raise public awareness to former levels. This is a good argument for sustained programming, of course, since it suggests that it is more efficient to sustain awareness than to build or rebuild it.

These general guidelines apply across all media and in all copywriting situations. Now let's review some guidelines for specific media.

Copywriting for Broadcast and Film Media

Brevity, clear style and sharp technique are the hallmarks of good broadcast and film copywriting. Specific time frames will vary among stations but you will usually write for periods lasting 10 seconds (25 words), 20 seconds (45 words), 30 seconds (65 words), or 60 seconds (125 words). The actual word limits may vary a little from radio to television to film, but in any case you can see that you have to tell a complete story in just a few well-chosen words. That is very seldom easy.

Because an audience's attention is easily diverted, your copy must be simple, direct and provocative. Avoid clichés and slang. Be careful to make smooth transitions from one point to the next. Personalize the message by emphasizing "you" at every opportunity. People respond personally to a message if they think it is directed to them. So try to write your copy as if it were a personal conversation between you and another person. Reward the audience for listening by sharing important information in an interesting way.

Keep the message credible by avoiding exaggerated claims; don't make any that you wouldn't make to your closest friend. Your persuasive appeal must be distinctive, so that your audience will remember it when they see or hear it again.

You must catch the attention of your audience in the first few seconds or you will lose it completely. Be sure to register the name of the firm or organization and let the audience know what you want it to do. A sense of urgency may help move the audience to action.

Radio, television and film have different technical capabilities, of course, but some styles of message presentation are common to all three media. One is the "slice of life," which is a mini-drama that presents a situation anyone might experience. It provides the context for the message.

Another is the jingle approach, in which music and words are combined to make the message memorable, identifiable and entertaining. A humorous approach is appropriate in any of these media. This may include anything from a cartoon (television or film) to a joke (usually radio only) to a mini sit-com (situation comedy). The difficulty with humor is in finding universal themes that will not go stale quickly.

Another technique is the interview. Here an announcer talks with representative members of your public. Still another approach is the testimonial. If you use a testimonial approach, however, be sure to establish the credibility of the people testifying. Otherwise, the audience will tune out your message.

You can use sound effects with any or all of these approaches. And you can combine the techniques themselves in some fashion.

Television and film have the additional benefit of permitting visual demonstration. This may be done through live action, with animation or with a combination of the two. In writing for television or film, consider the visual aspect carefully.

Your choice of a copy approach will depend above all on your resources—that is, money and facilities. Be prepared for the frustration that comes when you have to reject a creative idea because you can't afford to realize it. As you consider various techniques, you may want to review what others have done in similar situations. You won't want to copy from them but you should not hesitate to adapt ideas that have worked for others.

Copywriting for Television and Film

When writing copy for television or film, imagine how your ad will look as well as sound. This will help make the message stronger and more persuasive. Remember that you have to think visually as well as verbally.

Divide your paper down the middle so that you have two equal columns. Label the left column "description" and the right column "script." In the right column, begin to write the words and sounds you want your audience to hear. Concentrate on the single, basic idea of the message and remember to promise your audience some reward—a benefit that is both explained and supported.

Now go back and polish what you have written. Pare away unneeded words, phrases and sentences. Get the verbal message into what you believe to be a finished form. Then have someone read the script aloud to you. Make sure the reader doesn't study the message beforehand but reads it out "cold." Listening to your copy being read aloud by someone else will help you to spot parts that need to be corrected, eliminated or rearranged.

Now repeat the process, this time working down the left side and writing down the descriptions of the visuals that are to accompany the verbal message. But make certain that the visual images you call for match and interpret their verbal counterparts.

Remember that television and film are visual media and that one of their strengths is action. Avoid static scenes. If the image does not move, the audience will shift its attention to something more interesting. You must pay attention to the visual, but don't become so carried away that you forget the message you want to convey.

In television, it is common to carry the above process a step further and create a storyboard. Example 9-5 illustrates this idea. The storyboard depicts graphically what you have described down the left side of your script sheet. Although an artist is often assigned the job of making a storyboard, many copywriters find it is helpful in properly sequencing the visuals to make their own, using stick figures, and they may even write their copy under each frame so they can better judge its unity.

Copywriting for Radio

Approach copywriting for radio as you would approach that for television and film, by dividing your paper and labeling the columns to make a script sheet. That is simple enough, but writing really good radio copy is more difficult than writing for television or film. In television and film you have visual images to help you convey your message. In radio, you have only the visual theater of the mind. While this is a vast territory, it is one in which many copywriters get lost.

Begin to write your copy in the right-hand column. You'll have to search especially hard for just the right words to evoke the images you want to paint in the public's collective mind. That is, you'll have to imagine exactly what you want the public to see. Language can be your best ally or your worst enemy. It will be the latter if you use uncommon words, especially those that have regional or local usages. Be wary of these. Also, be cautious about using dialects.

Once you have written the message in the right-hand column, have someone read it "cold" so you can listen for semantic traps. Be sure that the mental images you evoke unfold in a logical, easy-to-follow sequence or you'll lose your listeners. You'll need to build excitement and drama, but be sure to drive home the message by repeating it at least three times in the script.

With the verbal content completed, work in the left-hand column and provide complete cues regarding music, volume changes, announcers, sound effects and similar production concerns. Check your descriptions against the verbal message in the right-hand column to make sure they match (see Example 9-6).

Although most commercials are prerecorded, some are read live. If you distribute your ad to stations in script form to be read live, be sure the words are

9-5

A Storyboard

After a television commercial's script is written, an effort is made to show what the commercial will look like to its audiences. That effort is called a storyboard. In its beginning stages, a storyboard has only artist sketches for the visual with copy lines below. This example is a presentation storyboard, showing pictures (photos) from the finished commercial. *Source:* Used with permission of General Electric Company.

9-6

Script Sheet
Jordan Associates, like agencies across the land, produces
local public service ads for local non-profit causes, as in
this case a 30-second public service announcement for the
Oklahoma City Conventions and Tourism Bureau of the
Chamber of Commerce. *Source:* Used with permission of
the Oklahoma City Conventions and Tourism Bureau.

Jordan Associates
Advertising/Communications

Nichols Hills Executive Center
P.O. Box 14005
Oklahoma City, OK 73113
(405) 840-3201 TWX-910-831-3339

RADIO/TV COPY

CLIENT_____ OKC CONVENTION & TOURISM _____

LENGTH_____ :30 _____ DATE_____ 10/15/84 _____

CODE___ OKC-84-10 _____ Job# 165-4-OKC _____

TITLE_____ EVENTS PROMO RADIO #2 _____ Final _____

MAN:	WHAT'S THAT, HONEY?
WOMAN:	IT'S OUR OKLAHOMA CITY WEEKEND bONUS bAG! LOOK INSIDE.

(SFX: Bag opens and voices become echoed)

(SFX: Cattle herd, mooing, gunshots)

(SFX: Indian war whoops, etc)

MAN:	WOW! THE COWBOY HALL OF FAME. . .STATE MUSEUM. . .ENTERPRISE SQUARE. . .THERE MUST BE DOZENS OR DIFFERENT ATTRACTIONS IN OKLAHOMA CITY!
WOMAN:	AND OKLAHOMA CITY IS SO EASY TO VISIT! NOW THROUGH MARCH, SPECIAL WEEKEND HOTEL PACKAGES AND DISCOUNT ATTRACTION COUPONS MAKE IT EASY FOR EVERYONE TO GET A HANDLE ON AN EXCITING OKLAHOMA CITY WEEKEND!
ANNOUNCER:	FOR MORE DETAILS, CALL THE OKLAHOMA CITY TOURISM BUREAU TOLL FREE, 1-800-6543-OKC.

simple to pronounce and smooth flowing, so that announcers will not foul things up by mispronouncing them. Placing the wrong inflection on a word or phrase can distort the message by giving copy elements the wrong emphasis. The safest step is to prerecord your spots. This applies to television and film as well.

Public Service Announcements

Public service ads or announcements (PSAs) for non-profit organizations can be elaborately produced videotapes, film with sound, some type of pictures with audio cassette or audio cassette only. Many of the organizations' national headquarters provide their own PSAs in these forms, and they usually leave room for a tagline to be added at the local level. More often, however, PSAs are produced locally for local agencies. Since the agency is begging for the time (and occasionally for the production time, too), most PSA scriptwriters try to keep things simple. See Example 9-6 for an example.

For television PSAs, local agencies may provide film or video footage to be edited as the visual for the PSA. A station announcer or a local personality may volunteer services to do the audio. Particularly if the volunteer is a local personality, you should write the script to match as closely as possible that personality's style of speaking.

It is more likely, however, that the visual part of the PSA will be a set of 35 mm slides supplied to the station with a script to be read by a station announcer. If the script has too many words to permit good delivery, it is likely to be thrown away. You should realize how little control you really have over whether your message will be broadcast. Your best assurance is to write an infallible script.

PSAs are more likely to be read live on radio than television. Scripts, without a cassette, are sent to the local station. If the script is no good, local announcers will often improvise, but if improvisation does not work, the script will be thrown out. To guard against this, listen to the announcers who might read your PSA, study their styles and write for their rate of delivery. If there is doubt, *under write*—that is, use fewer words.

Some people, of course, wonder about the value of PSAs, asking whether they really have any effect on audiences. It is unquestionable that PSAs can help in establishing and sustaining an organization's identity among a variety of types of audiences. However, their ability to affect behavior is quite limited. Mostly they affect only the behavior of individuals with higher than average socioeconomic statuses.

Copywriting for Print Media

There are some general guidelines that apply to ad copywriting for the print media. These guidelines turn on the concepts of attention, interest, desire, believability and action, sometimes referred to as AIDBA. Let's look at each of these concepts separately.

Attention

It is axiomatic that in order to communicate a message to a public, you must first command attention. Two elements of a print ad perform the attention-getting function. One is the headline and the other is the visual design. Although some argue the point, most of the really great copywriters of all time believe that the headline is the single most important element in an ad, period. The headline is the element most often responsible for stopping readers and luring them into the ad. A terrific visual may do this too, but it is the headline that makes the greatest and most lasting impact. Of course, the visual elements should be harmonious with the headline and its content. A good headline offers a promise to the reader. More often than not, it spells out a benefit to the reader as well. And it has to do this provocatively, so that the reader will pay attention.

The visual, in addition to gaining attention, helps to amplify the content of the head. Thus, the head and the visual express the same message but in different ways. Remember the principle of repetition mentioned earlier in this chapter. Showing the message is a way of repeating what the headline says. Whether in verbal or visual form, however, it is essential that the message convey—powerfully but simply—some benefit to the reader. Ads with the greatest attention-getting value are those that speak to the reader's self-interest.

The use of color can help gain attention. When you buy advertising space, however, remember that the use of color costs extra. This may affect your budget, so check the costs before you commit yourself to using color. Though color generally increases attention, it does not necessarily increase readership or retention of your message.

Interest

Remember that, by offering a benefit, the headline stops the reader. Thus, the next phase is to heighten the reader's interest. You can do this by making sure that the first sentence or paragraph of the copy flows naturally from the headline and expands on the headline's promise. For example, suppose your company is launching a re-capitalization program. The success of this program will depend on whether a majority of stockholders supports the program. Many stockholders, if not most, don't really understand recapitalization, so they are not necessarily apt to return a ballot. Your task is to make the program appealing enough so that they will want to find out more about the benefits to them of supporting the issue. An attention-getting headline in this case might be

**HOW TO INCREASE YOUR INVESTMENT
IN [NAME OF COMPANY] BY 36%**

That headline would attract the attention of any investor. The task now is to get the reader to understand the how-to. That becomes the function of your copy, especially the first sentence or first paragraph. These must tie in directly to the headline itself. Thus, the first paragraph of your copy might read,

> Each of your shares in [name of company] will increase from $50
> to $68 if you support the recapitalization program recommended
> by the board of directors.

If you owned stock in this company and you received this message, you would pay attention to it, because you would recognize how much money you could make by merely marking a "yes" on your ballot. The headline and first paragraph would speak your language. It would clearly be in your self-interest to pay attention to what the company was saying to you. That is the essence of "interest" in good advertising copy.

Desire

Once you have developed self-interest, the next step is to talk about why the idea is desirable. You can do this by filling in details of the plan in subsequent paragraphs: describe what the plan is, why it is needed, how it will benefit the company and its shareholders and when it will go into effect and supply other supporting bits of information. It is this part of the copy that promotes the idea that the suggested action is a desirable thing to do.

Credibility

Even if your message is provocative, your public may not believe it. The cardinal rule in this regard is to be as specific as you can. Note the specifics in the headline above. The line did not say "about 36%"; it said "36%" specifically. And the first paragraph of the copy did not equivocate on the dollar increase per share. It was very specific: "from $50 to $68." There is no room in this instance for misunderstanding the message. Never leave to inference what you want the reader to know. All your copy should reflect that same degree of specificity. If you hedge your claim, the reader will spot it immediately and begin to discount what you say. So be specific, concrete and direct. You will likely be believed, even if the reader decides against your point of view.

It also pays to remember that truth is sometimes stranger than fiction and more difficult to believe. This can be a major problem when you are asking readers to accept something that defies common experience even if it is entirely truthful.

Action

Action is the "bottom line" in advertising. You are paying for the space in which to present your message. Therefore, it makes sense for you to ask the reader to do something. Action is not as important in some idea ads as it is for product ads, especially ones that simply want to convey a positive image of the firm. But in some ads, such as the example above, you want shareholders to take an action—in this case, to support the recapitalization program. It would be at least a partial waste of the firm's money if you did not ask the reader to do something specific. For example, you might close the ad by saying that a ballot will be in the mail tomorrow and ask the reader to mark it and return it immediately in the postage-paid envelope. That kind of close to the ad would leave no doubt as to what course of action you want the reader to take.

Now that we have reviewed these points about copywriting for print media, let's look at each medium separately.

Copywriting for Newspapers

Newspaper advertising falls into two categories: display and classified. Display advertising is the advertising that does not appear in the classified portion of the paper.

For display advertising, words and visuals must provide a unified message, as audio and video do in television commercials. Newspapers are read hurriedly and have a fairly brief life. So it's a waste to use words and visuals just because they look or sound good. They have to have a purpose for being in the ad or they should be deleted. Readers won't read "fat" ads, because they don't have the time. While newspapers are known as a mass rather than a class (or selective) medium, they can saturate a specific geographic market more thoroughly than magazines, radio or television. And even though a newspaper is mass in appeal, there is typically some segmentation of audiences through features and special sections, such as the sports or business sections.

Display   Display advertising is especially good at promoting an immediate demand for products or services or achieving the acceptance of ideas (see Example 9-7). It works if you have a unified concept to convey along the lines of the AIDBA discussion above. The size of the space you buy will determine the proportion and sizes of the headline, copy, visuals, logos and other elements of the ad.

How much space to buy is a critical decision, for it determines how much competition for readers' attention there will be on the page where your ad appears. If you buy a full page, there will be no competing message on the page. If you buy a half page, there are likely two or three other competing messages—in addition to the editorial matter—all clamoring for the reader's attention. The smaller the space you buy, the greater is the competition for attention on the page.

Most newspaper ads are for local firms and addressed to local readers. A good copywriter takes advantage of the research information both about that medium and its market, and tries to tailor a message that will "fit" the market. Of course, national advertisers who use newspapers ordinarily can't tailor their ads to this degree. They might run the same ad simultaneously in newspapers all across the country. Remember, though: If you have the opportunity, write your ad with the local market in mind.

Classified   Most classified advertising sections offer some excellent illustrations of creativity in the use of a limited number of words. Ads in these sections are not for garage sales alone. Classified ads are used extensively by real estate firms and trans-

9-7

Display Ad
Creativity can make a product promotion exciting, as
illustrated by this ad—one in a series. The example appeared
in newspapers and magazines. Note the harmony between
the visual, the head and the copy. It was created by KCBN,
Inc. of Dallas. *Source:* Used with permission of Jim Haynes,
KCBN, Inc.

**At last,
a big fat juicy
guarantee
on big, fat, juicy
produce.**

If you aren't pleased with the produce you
buy at Tom Thumb-Page, we'll give you
double your money back. Because we
stand behind everything we sell and that's
a promise. Don't miss our special insert in
this newspaper for outstanding produce
values at Tom Thumb-Page.

TOM THUMB-PAGE
FOOD AND DRUG CENTERS

portation- and recreation-related firms. A professional copywriter for an agency is very likely to prepare hundreds of classified ads for clients. The technique employed here is simply to determine how many words you can get into a specific space. Deduct from this count the number of words that you *must* include—such as the firm's name, address and telephone number—and compose your message with the number of words left. Read the classified columns before you begin writing to help you appreciate the ingenuity of others and to learn the accepted abbreviations in that market. In the process, you'll also find out what your competitors are doing.

Copywriting for Magazines

Magazine audiences are highly specialized. Specific magazines appeal to particular types of people, regardless of where they live. Magazine advertising copy should exploit this specificity in magazine audiences. Both demographic and psychographic information are relevant here.

Although magazine readers do not necessarily devote immense amounts of time to reading magazines at a single sitting, they usually put them aside for rereading as their time and interests dictate. When writing for a particular magazine, you may want to get in touch with the sales promotion department for specialized information on the readership.

In writing your magazine ad, you should know its size and placement before you actually begin. Magazine space is ordinarily sold by the page or fraction or multiple of a page. It is possible to buy a special position for your ad, but you'll have to pay a premium for it, and that can run up the cost in a hurry. Also, know that most magazines allow, and even expect, a higher level of reproduction quality than newspapers exhibit, especially in the use of color and highly creative visual materials.

Look at several issues of the specific magazine your ad will appear in before you begin writing so you can get a feel for its character and the tone of its advertising content. You should look at the editorial bent of the magazine. Both of these checks may cue you to use or avoid a particular approach.

As with writing for newspapers, the verbal and visual elements should be complementary, not competitive.

Public Service Ads Both newspapers and magazines run public service ads for nonprofit organizations and causes (see Example 9-3, above). If you are preparing one of these ads for use by these media, observe all the rules that apply to ads you would buy. Remember, you are asking these media to give your message a free ride. If you want your ad run, play by the rules. Be as helpful as you can. You're not buying. You're asking—and hoping.

House Ads Newspapers and magazines run house ads on a space-available basis. Although no money exchanges hands, the promotion department of the medium is often given a budget for this purpose. It is then the department's responsibility to prepare a variety of house ads and to have them available to run on demand. Some house ads, however, are scheduled as if they were paid ads. They are usually ones that promote the magazine or newspaper as a good medium in which firms can reach a market or an audience (see Example 9-4, above). Or, particularly with newspapers, they promote subscriptions or the use of the classified ad section. Even though these are house ads, they are written and prepared in the same way other ads are.

Copywriting for Direct Response and Direct Advertising

The severest test of your ability as a copywriter is whether you can write effective direct response or direct advertising copy.

Copy that is designed to promote direct action by the audience is called direct response copy. It is the type of message that urges people to take immediate action such as mailing in a coupon, calling an 800-number, entering a sweepstakes or just generally getting people to figuratively raise their hands and say, "Hey, we're interested."

Direct response copy can appear in most any medium. The key is not the type of medium in which the message appears, but rather it is the type of message the medium conveys. If it urges the audience to do something now it is direct response copy. For example, a commercial on television from Publishers Clearing House touts its subscriptions and provides an incentive by offering fabulous sweepstake prizes. All you have to do is to call a toll-free number, but you have to call *now*.

Direct advertising copy appears in some written, printed, or processed form sent via a controlled method of circulation to individuals. There are three types of direct advertising.

Direct Mail   This includes all forms of mailed direct advertising, except mail order. It includes letters, postcards, booklets, broadsides, brochures, circulars, catalogs, and stuffers, among others.

Mail Order   Mail order copy is responsible for the entire "selling" job. It may appear in a variety of forms, from catalogs such as L. L. Bean to a letter urging the person to buy Christmas Seals.

Unmailed Direct Advertising   Unmailed direct advertising copy differs from direct mail and mail order only in its method of distribution. It includes promotional pieces that may be delivered to a person's home or it may be picked up in the store, showroom, fair, exhibit or at any other site where promotional efforts are employed.

All forms of direct advertising copy are especially difficult to write effectively because you have to create the medium as well as the message. You don't have the support of a preselected audience from the standard media.

Each message has to stand alone and produce results. In fact, success is carefully measured by the number of responses generated. These can be in any number of forms—for example, coupons, orders or queries—and the response rate measures precisely how much action you are able to generate with your writing. Once you have designed and written a successful ad that has proved itself, you are not likely to change it very much in the future.

Obviously, the overall design of coupons, order forms and related material has to be very good, so that people can respond easily.

Not all direct-response or direct-advertising copy are "single shot" messages. Some are developed to attract people before additional information is given to them. Hence, copywriters may be involved in a wide range of writing tasks related to subsequent messages in other forms. Whatever the form of the campaign, copywriters have a big job. They must write a large volume of words, and their firms depend heavily on them for their ability to move people to accept an idea.

Copywriting for Out-of-Home Media

The term "out-of-home" media refers to a variety of media—outdoor, transit, skywriting and the like. The key point to remember about these media is that readers go to them rather than the other way around. This characteristic imposes severe constraints on what you can say and how you say it in this context.

While each out-of-home medium is unique, the general guidelines for outdoor media apply to all the others.

Outdoor   There are two basic kinds of outdoor billboards. One is the poster panel, which is printed on large printing presses, and the other is the painted bulletin. Poster panels are a standard size: 12 feet 3 inches by 24 feet 6 inches. Three sizes of messages can fit onto these panels. A 24-sheet poster measures 8 feet 8 inches by 19 feet 6 inches; a 30-sheet poster measures 9 feet 7 inches by 21 feet 7 inches; and a 30-sheet bleed panel measures 10 feet 5 inches by 22 feet 8 inches. The 24-sheet poster panel has been the standard in the outdoor field for decades, but currently the 30-sheet panel is replacing it.

The "sheet" unit of measurement has its roots in the time when it took perhaps 24 or 30 sheets of paper to cover a panel. Printing presses are larger today, so most panels can be covered with from 10 to 15 sheets.

Many advertisers use poster panels routinely, changing their messages monthly or several times a year and advertising in many markets simultaneously. Once the cost of designing and producing the panel is absorbed, the costs become incrementally smaller as additional sites or markets are used.

The painted bulletin, as the name indicates, is painted by hand. It goes on a board measuring 14 feet by 48 feet. An advertiser will use "paints" only when cultivating a single or a few markets and when the message will not be changed within a year. Usually an advertiser will not use more than two or three painted bulletins, or paints, in a specific market, depending on the size of the market.

Outdoor advertising—called outdoor for short—is remarkably cost-effective when you need to saturate a market with an idea. The price of an outdoor campaign is based on what are called *showings*. A 100-show is one in which enough panels, including some illuminated for night viewing, will provide 100-percent coverage of the mobile market in a 30-day period. Studies show that it is not unusual for a 100-show to produce a high level of message repetitions, and to deliver up to an average of 25 or more per month. A 50-show, thus, would involve half the coverage and repetition of a 100-showing.

Copywriting is especially difficult for outdoor. Because the viewer may see your message for only a second or two, the message has to be especially simple and compelling in order to register on the mind. As a general rule, you can't use more than about eight words, including the firm's name, and expect the message to punch through (see Example 9-8). Also, there should be no more than three verbal and visual elements in the message. Hence, you must restrain yourself in both your verbal and visual thinking if you expect to write a good outdoor message.

Simplicity is the hallmark of good outdoor. If your message is complex, don't use outdoor. But if you can reduce your message to just eight words or less, and if you can employ bold, even garish, visuals, you will be able to do a lot with a little.

Although ads for subways, taxis and similar media have different size specifications, the same guidelines apply to them as for outdoor.

Copywriting for Sales Promotion

Point-of-purchase advertising, samples, contests, advertising specialties and cooperative advertising are sales-promotion pieces, as are coupons, booklets, brochures and mailers.

Point-of-purchase advertising is advertising displayed with a product, service or idea that is specifically designed to inspire the customer to buy on impulse. Most point-of-purchase advertising is strong on emotional impact, particularly symbolism, and ties in with other existing promotional materials to give additional recognition. Another promotional device is the sample, a free product sent out along with descriptive literature. The copy accompanying a sample often tries to inspire a sense of obligation in prospective customers by urging them to accept free samples.

Contests are designed to offer customers something extra and to keep awareness of the idea high through participation and anticipation. Advertising specialties can be anything with the corporate logo on it, but generally they are useful objects, like ice scrapers for windshields, or things with high visibility that will be remembered.

In cooperative advertising, the retail outlet appeals for direct sales while receiving support from the manufacturer. When the manufacturer's logo appears along with the retailer's in a local firm's advertising for a product or service, this is usually a tipoff that the ad is a cooperative one, with the retailer and manufacturer sharing in the cost of space, time or position.

9-8

Billboard Ad
Most billboard copy is extraordinarily brief, but the traffic
light at this intersection gives motorists plenty of time to read
this—even if they are slow readers. *Source:* Used with
permission of Philip Poole Associates.

This light takes forever, so why not read this billboard?

You'll be glad you did. And so will we. We'd like to help you see the light, so to speak.

Why not consider Bank of Fort Worth for all your banking needs? We have ample free parking, easy access, 12 drive-thru TV lanes (with extended daily and Saturday morning hours) individual attention, and the kind of people who make you glad you came by. So come by, if the light ever changes.

Bank of Fort Worth. We're just down the street at 600 Bailey. Member FDIC.

Conclusions

* Advertising uses persuasion. It cannot coerce.
* Successful persuasion is based on the right appeal, proper "positioning" and an understanding of how people will respond to the appeal.
* Basic requirements for advertising copywriting include an understanding of the ad's purpose, a careful review of the objective facts to be conveyed, an understanding of the public to be addressed, and a decision as to the media to be used. Internal requirements are a creative approach, visualization, precise language and repetition.
* Television and film media are dynamic, so movement must be integrated into messages for these media and the verbal and visual elements of the ad must be complementary.
* Copy for radio is written for the ear, not the eye. Words and sounds must be especially well chosen for radio ads so that the public can "see" the message.
* Although newspapers and magazines are static media, messages placed there must be dynamic and move people to act. Stages in developing these ads include attention, interest, desire, credibility and action. The headline is the most important element.
* Direct-mail messages are difficult to execute effectively because the message must also be the medium.
* Remember that the audience goes to out-of-home media, so simplicity is crucial in both words and visuals. The total message is limited to eight words and three elements.
* Writing copy for sales promotions often involves writing for a variety of media and methods. It is a good idea to review the discussion and illustrations in this chapter before writing any sales-promotion materials.

Exercises

1. Write five different headlines for ads to shareholders in the company explaining the recapitalization program discussed in this chapter.
2. Select one of the five headlines you wrote in the above exercise and write three different alternate lead sentences or paragraphs for the headline.
3. Write a radio script for the following situation: Your client is an industrial park. It has a lot of undeveloped land, plenty of water and power and the resources to build high-tech facilities for firms that may want to consider relocating to your area. In fact, state and local taxes will be waived in perpetuity for any firm locating in the state. That is, of course, a big incentive for firms to locate in the area. You are free to expand this information at your leisure.

4. Write a television commercial for the circumstances described in Exercise 3.

5. Write a newspaper ad that announces Ourbank's slogan, The Safe Place. First, determine the size and use of color. Then describe the visuals (if any) that go with the ad. Next, write the headline and then the copy. Remember that visuals, headline and copy should all tie together.

6. Write radio and television commercials that will air in the market the same day the ad (in number 5) appears in the newspaper.

Selected Bibliography

William H. Brannen, *Advertising and Sales Promotion: Cost-Effective Techniques for Your Small Business* (Englewood Cliffs, N.J.: Prentice-Hall, 1983).

Philip Ward Burton, *Advertising Copywriting*, 5th ed. (Columbus, Ohio: Grid Publishing, 1983).

Elizabeth J. Heighton and Don R. Cunningham, *Advertising in the Broadcast and Cable Media*, 2nd ed. (Belmont, Calif.: Wadsworth, 1984).

A. Jerome Jewler, *Creative Strategy in Advertising*, 2nd ed. (Belmont, Calif.: Wadsworth, 1985).

David L. Malickson and John W. Nason, *Advertising—How to Write the Kind That Works*, rev. ed. (New York: Scribner's, 1982).

Roy Paul Nelson, *The Design of Advertising*, 4th ed. (Dubuque, Iowa: Brown, 1983).

Kenneth R. Runyon, *Advertising*, 2nd ed. (Columbus, Ohio: Charles E. Merrill, 1984).

The First Medium (New York: Institute of Outdoor Advertising, undated).

Sherilyn K. Zeigler and J. Douglas Johnson, *Creative Strategy and Tactics in Advertising: A Managerial Approach to Copywriting and Production* (Columbus, Ohio: Grid Publishing, 1981).

10
Speeches
and Scripts

Delivering a speech is a hazardous undertaking. Ideas can never be conveyed intact. A speaker can only send messages, verbally and non-verbally, to an audience. It's the audience that gives those messages meaning.

For this reason, writing speeches and scripts demands more attention and care from the public relations writer than almost any other writing task. You can't simply write down your thoughts on a subject and expect them to be delivered successfully by any speaker. Audiences react emotionally to speakers based on their authority, trustworthiness, tolerance and friendliness, so the speech writer must consider these factors when writing. In essence, this means the speech must be personalized. The words must go with the person; the speaker must sound natural and not as though he or she were reading cue cards. A person who is comfortable with the words being spoken will be a more credible speaker.

Sometimes PR writers deliver speeches themselves, and in these cases it should be easy to write a natural-sounding speech. But there's more to consider than just the speaker. Whether writing for another person or for yourself, the speech writer must have an idea of what the audience will be like. What experiences do audience members bring with them? What do they expect from the speaker? What stereotypes do they hold—that is, what are the "pictures in their heads"? If you don't know these things, you won't be able to write an effective speech.

You need to know the language patterns of the audience, as well as of the speaker, because certain words used in particular ways can send thoughts down familiar paths. Remember that connotations of words are as important as denotations. And keep in mind that meanings change with time, and that the same words may mean different things in different contexts or in different parts of the country. This means you can't write like you talk, or like the speaker talks, without considering how the audience talks.

Words, important as they are, aren't the only thing to be considered. Non-verbal cues can help emphasize points or obscure them. Audiences are sensitive to body movements, gestures, facial expressions, physical appearance and displays of personality and emotion. Effective speakers use these non-verbal expressions to hold attention and to help get the message across. Most speakers videotape rehearsals to perfect the blend of words and non-verbal expressions.

Speeches

Many speech writers get stalled at the beginning because they don't ask some important questions: Why was the speaker invited to address this particular group? What do the group members expect to hear? What do you want to accomplish by having a speech given to that particular group? How can you choose a topic that will meet your needs and the group's expectations? You have to answer these questions before you start writing.

The next two questions have to be considered together: How long should the speech be? And what is the physical setting? A luncheon group won't tolerate as long an address as a dinner group, for example. People attending luncheons usually have other obligations; people who go to dinner are making an evening of it. Are there other speakers? Who are they and what are their topics? (These last questions are especially important if the speech is part of a seminar.)

Planning

After you've answered the above questions, make a list of proposed topics and begin your research. One of the best places to begin is the *Readers' Guide to Periodical Literature*, especially if the audience is a general one. You can look up the articles listed and find out what the audience might have been exposed to recently. If the audience is a specialized group, go to the publications that group members receive and find out what is being written. You'll learn their current concerns and get an idea of what the group is like.

Most speeches written for public relations purposes are informative speeches, so after you have determined what the audience has already been exposed to you will need to do research on the topic chosen. Although you may feel you know the material well enough to write a speech in your sleep, do some library research. All your knowledge of the topic is likely to be from an insider's point of view. You probably have seen some materials that come from competitors and critics, but you should look at what has appeared in the mass media as well. *The New York Times Index* is a good source. Most public libraries in metropolitan areas and in cities with a university have electronic research capabilities. Select your topic and have the literature searched for sources. Remember that in writing an informative speech, you are charged with offering the members of an audience new and valuable information, then helping them understand and retain it. When you are writing a speech for someone else to deliver, you need to meet with your speaker after this initial research to get an idea of what he or she thinks is most important and to determine the slant or approach for the presentation.

Paring

If you have done your research well, you will have many more ideas than you can or should introduce in a single speech. Begin paring. Cut away until you have no more than three items you want to communicate.

Select the three most important ideas you want people in the audience to carry away with them, and then present the ideas as something fresh and meaningful. (It helps if the ideas can be startling, but don't fake it.) Give the listeners some way to associate these ideas with others they hold. You'll have to repeat the ideas often to be sure they are retained, but don't be redundant. You don't want the audience thinking, "You just said that a few minutes ago." You also have to introduce the ideas in a logical sequence, using relationships that aid retention. It helps if you can break the pace of the presentation, adding some visuals when appropriate. Injecting humor helps people retain information, but there can be a problem with this if you are not delivering the speech. Humor is very personal. It's difficult to write humor for someone else unless you are both real professionals at your jobs. To be safe, use anecdotes, narratives that don't depend heavily on the style of delivery.

Persuading

As you convey these ideas, keep in mind what you want to accomplish with this message. Do you want to move the audience to take some action, to do something? If so, you had better let the listeners know what you want them to do, how they can do it and what their rewards will be. Perhaps you want to change their belief about something. Remember, a belief is acceptance of a truth, an acceptance based on experience, evidence and opinions. If you are going to try to persuade them to change a belief, you'll have to offer both logical proof and some emotional appeals.

Or you may only want to reinforce a belief. Many public relations speeches are of this nature. Give the audience reasons for retaining their belief and inform them of reference groups who also hold the belief. This will reassure your listeners that they are right in believing what they do.

The Mechanics of Organization

A speech has three parts: an introduction, a body and a conclusion. Contrary to what you've probably done all your life, don't write the introduction first. Just as you wouldn't write an introduction for a speaker until you knew who the speaker was, you shouldn't write an introduction for a speech until you know what will be in it.

Start with a title. The title should keep the main point of the speech in the forefront of your thinking. After you have a title, write down your purpose: to entertain, explain, convince or motivate. Then write the three ideas you want the audience to retain. Next, state precisely what you want the audience to do as a result of hearing the speech. You should then be able to write a conclusion.

Go back now to the three main ideas you want to convey and devise a theme to tie them together. You ought to be able to tie this theme in with the purpose of the speech. At this point, you should be ready to prepare an outline.

Begin the outline by listing the three main points on separate sheets of paper. Under each point, list the pertinent information you have gathered from your research along with what you already knew. Keep this list on the left side of the page. On the right side write a key word for an anecdote or illustration to go with each point. Now arrange all of the information under each point in a logical sequence, and you are ready to write.

Style

To be effective in stimulating images in the minds of the audience, you need to employ vivid words and expressive language. Be clear. Choose your words with precision. Be specific. Keep a thesaurus and a dictionary on hand to find the precise words you need. For emphasis and retention, use repetition, but use it effectively. Use transitions not just to connect the thoughts, but to remind and to underscore a point by reiterating it. Check that all of your words are appropriate to the purpose of the speech, the audience and the speaker. Involve the audience by using personal pronouns and asking questions that listeners must answer for themselves. Find some way to establish rapport—cite common experiences or use familiar situations and imagery, for example. Use quotations if they are not long and if they can be integrated into the ideas to give authority. Be direct. If you are ambiguous, an audience may leave wondering what you meant and come up with the wrong answer.

When you deliver the speech, support your points with a variety of timely, meaningful material. This can be audiovisual aids, statistics (not too many), detailed illustrations, and hypothetical or real situations. Comparison and contrast are effective too.

After you've completed the body of the speech, go back and write an introduction. The introduction is an integral part of the speech. It should lead smoothly, logically and directly into the body. It shouldn't look as though it had been pasted on as an afterthought. The introduction must create attention and build rapport. It should give the audience some sign of the direction the rest of the speech will take.

You can use various devices to create an effective introduction. For example, start with an anecdote or illustration to capture the audience's interest. Use a quotation or a bright one-liner, like a startling assertion or question. You might even use a suspense gimmick, which you can then refer to throughout the speech and finally tie into the conclusion. Some speakers begin with a compliment to help establish rapport, but there is some risk in this. You could come off as patronizing. You never want to apologize for yourself or the speech. You shouldn't have to!

When writing for someone else, keep in mind that person's favorite words, expressions and normal speaking pattern—long sentences or short, snappy ones. One speech writer records the speech-planning session and plays it during this part of the work. The basic speech is then personalized for the person who will be giving it.

After the speech, be prepared for response from the audience, either formal or informal. Think of questions the audience might ask and have your answers ready, in writing if necessary. Jot down some examples of the three points that you can develop extemporaneously—provided, of course, you are the one delivering the speech! For another speaker, develop some examples and write them down for review. Take a real example, if possible, from the speaker's own background, or use that background to create a story or metaphor the speaker might have thought of to illustrate the point. Summarize the three points so the speaker can reiterate them.

If you are delivering the speech, find out all you can about the physical location so you can think of appropriate gestures. If someone else is delivering the speech, you need to inform the speaker of the physical arrangements so appropriate delivery can be rehearsed and non-verbal expressions developed to reinforce the message. The physical situation is extremely important. For example, very subtle gestures are lost in a large auditorium. On the other hand, the slightest movement is magnified by television cameras.

Be sure you are comfortable with any visual aids or demonstrations. If you are not the one giving the speech, go over these carefully with the person who is. Mechanical failures can undermine both a speaker's authority and poise. Eye contact is important. Audiences don't like to be talked *at*. Find some people to look at and direct your message to them. Be sure they are scattered about the room so that attention doesn't seem to be focused in one spot. If you're facing a television camera, the audience is the red light.

Setting the Stage and Writing the Finale

In addition to writing the speech, the PR writer must provide a written introduction of the speaker. How the person with the message is presented is important to audience acceptance. Content has to be controlled. For example, it's common for the person inviting the speaker to ask for a resumé. The problem is that the resumé is often *read*. An introduction like that is lethal. Look at the following two summaries of resumés for the authors. Then, look at suggested general introductions for each.

10-1

Silly Speech
Source: Reprinted with permission of Johnny Hart and News
America Syndicate.

In public relations practice, you should offer to write the introduction for the person who will be presenting the speaker. There are problems in writing for a speaker you don't know. So, keep it short and simple and easy to read.

Douglas Ann Johnson Newsom is a professor of journalism and chairman of the department at Texas Christian University in Fort Worth. Earned degrees include Bachelor of Journalism, cum laude, 1954; Bachelor of Fine Arts, summa cum laude, 1955; Masters of Journalism, 1956; and Doctor of Philosophy, 1978. Wadsworth, Inc. is the publisher of three textbooks for which she is the senior co-author: *This Is PR*, 3rd ed., with Alan Scott; *Writing in Public Relations Practice*, 2nd ed., with Bob Carrell; and *Media Writing*, with Jim Wollert. She serves on the national steering committee for the William Randolph Hearst Foundation. In 1984–1985 she was president of the Association for Education in Journalism and Mass Communication, and she has chaired the national accrediting committee for the Accrediting Council for Education in Journalism/Mass Communication. She was on the executive committee of the Association of Schools of Journalism/Mass Communication and on AEJMC's Teaching Standards Committee. She also has been president of the PR Division of AEJMC. She served as secretary/treasurer of the Public Relations Foundation of Texas and was for eight years a trustee. She

was 1982 president of the Texas Public Relations Association,
1983 president of the North Texas Chapter of the Public Relations
Society of America, and 1981–1982 president of the Texas Journalism Education Council (now Southwest Education Council for
Journalism/Mass Communication).

PRSA named her Distinguished Educator of the Year in
1982, and she was named 1982 Outstanding University of Texas
Alumnus in Public Relations. Dr. Newsom is an accredited member of PRSA and in 1978 helped organize PRSA's Educators Section
which she headed in 1984. She is on the Board of the Foundation for
Public Relations Research and Education where she serves on the
education committee. She advises the TCU Public Relations Student Society of America and has been national faculty adviser to
PRSA. Memberships include Women in Communications, Inc.
Sigma Delta Chi, Society for Professional Journalists, International Communication Association, American Women in Radio and Television, National and Texas Press Women, Kappa Tau
Alpha, Phi Kappa Psi and Mortar Board. At TCU Dr. Newsom
chaired the Faculty Senate from 1983 to 1984 and served on the
Faculty Senate's Executive Committee from 1980 to 1985. She also
is a director of ONEOK, a diversified energy company and on the
advisory committee of the Gas Research Institute. She is on the
national education committee of Delta Delta Delta social sorority
of which she is an alumna.

Bob J. Carrell holds the Ph.D. in mass communication, with emphases in advertising and marketing, from the University of Illinois. His master and baccalaureate degrees are from East Texas
State University, with emphases in journalism, English and education. He did post-doctoral study in sociology and political science as a National Science Foundation fellow at Ohio University.

A native Texan, he has been in higher education 24 years,
including one year at ETSU, eight years at Texas Christian University (three as Chairman of the department) and 15 years at the
University of Oklahoma (12 as Director). He returned to TCU in
the fall 1981 semester as a distinguished visiting professor of advertising (on sabbatical leave from Oklahoma).

His primary teaching areas are advertising, mass communication theory, research methods and management.

He has eight years of newspapering, most of which is in
advertising, sales and management—all on Texas weeklies and
small dailies. Additionally, he has three years of professional experience in public relations.

He maintains an active research/consulting relationship
with a variety of organizations, media and corporations. Examples of the most recent are: (1) an advertising feasibility analysis for *Oklahoma Today*, a magazine of the Oklahoma Department of Tourism and Recreation, (2) defining legally what is/

is not advertising for the Attorney General of Oklahoma re ABC rules and regulations governing package stores, (3) consulting re advertising creative strategy for TG&Y, a discount retail chain of 900 stores across the country, but headquartered in Oklahoma City with an annual advertising budget of more than $65,000,000, and (4) marketing and communication plans for financial institutions, service firms, developers and retailers (hard and soft goods, full-line and specialty).

When you are writing the introduction for a speaker, your first consideration is establishing that person with the audience, in terms of acceptance— either as an authority or being like them or both. Sometimes the person is most important, and sometimes the topic is. But your introduction has to accommodate both. What you do is change the emphasis. Here are some introductions that might be used for the authors of this book, depending on where they are speaking and about what.

If Dr. Newsom is speaking to a PRSA chapter at your University, the introduction could be something like this:

> You've seen Dr. Newsom's name before, probably on one of your textbooks. She's the co-author of three: THIS IS PR, PUBLIC RELATIONS WRITING, and MEDIA WRITING. At Texas Christian University she is chairman of the journalism department and adviser to the PRSA chapter. She has been national faculty adviser to all PRSA chapters, and in 1982 was PRSA's Educator of the Year, the first woman to receive that award. In 1984 she chaired the Educator's section of PRSA, which she helped found in 1984. She also has been president of the North Texas Chapter of PRSA and president of the Texas Public Relations Association. Now she is on the board of the Foundation for Public Relations Research and Education, and she is also on a corporate board of directors— ONEOK, a diversified energy company. She is a member of many of the national professional organizations you know: Women In Communications, Inc., American Women in Radio and Television, Sigma Delta Chi—Society of Professional Journalists, International Communication Association, National and Texas Press Women, and three honoraries: Kappa Tau Alpha, Phi Kappa Psi and Mortar Board.

For a professional group, like the business and professional women's organization in the city, the introduction might be something like this:

> Our speaker today is a woman who knows what it is like to be "the first woman" or "the only woman." She is one of only a few women heads of journalism and mass communication programs in the nation, and she is the only woman on the board of directors of a diversified energy company. She was the first woman to receive the Outstanding Educator Award from the Public Relations

Society of America, and she was the second woman president in
the 75-year history of the Association for Education in Journalism
and Mass Communication. She is the author of three textbooks in
her field and holds four earned degrees.

These are general introductions that would work with the audiences
if you were not sure of the speaker's topic. What you have done is select information
from the speaker's background that would be important to these audiences. For the
students, stressing leadership in public relations organizations is important since the
speaker will be a role model. For the professionals, establishing the speaker as a female professional, like them, is important. If, on the other hand, the audience were
male, like the Optimists Club, for example, the speaker's authority would need to be
established as a leader in the field, with not as much emphasis, if any, on being a
woman in the field.

The speaker's topic is also important. If Newsom were addressing the
students about requirements for education in the field, information in the resumé
about her experience with the accrediting organization would be used. If she were
talking to the business and professional women about the complexity of handling a
career and family, information not in the resumé would have to be gained through a
phone call or correspondence.

Look at how the other author might be introduced. If Dr. Carrell
were talking to the ad club at your university, the introduction for him might look
something like this:

Dr. Carrell has been associated with the mass communication industries and education since his high school days in northeast
Texas. He is currently a professor in the School of Journalism and
Mass Communication at the University of Oklahoma, a school he
directed for 12 years.

His doctoral degree is from the University of Illinois in mass
communication, with supporting fields in advertising and marketing. His baccalaureate and master degrees from East Texas State
University emphasize journalism, English and education.

He has been active for many years in the Advertising
Clubs of Oklahoma City and Fort Worth and in the Business and
Professional Advertising Association, as well as the Association
for Education in Journalism and Mass Communication and its Advertising Division and in the American Academy of Advertising.

Dr. Carrell maintains an active consulting and research
practice along with his teaching and writing activities. His clients
include state and federal government agencies, advertising and
public relations firms, newspapers and magazines, financial institutions, manufacturers and national discount retail chain stores.

His professional experience includes eight years with
newspapers, mostly in advertising sales and management, and
three years in public relations. His experience in education in-

cludes 12 years as director of the School of Journalism at Oklahoma and three years as chairman at Texas Christian University.

Stressing his educational and professional experience in his field gives him credibility. Students also could see from his background and education a possible career path for themselves.

On the other hand, if the audience were the Oklahoma City Rotary Club, his current business and professional activities would be stressed, so he would be seen as an authority with current experience in the marketplace, not only in the classroom.

The introduction might be something like this, depending on his speech topic:

> Today's speaker is Dr. Bob Carrell, University of Oklahoma professor whom some of you probably met during his 12 years as director of the School of Journalism and Mass Communication. Dr. Carrell is the author and co-author of several books in the fields of advertising and public relations and a consultant to a number of Oklahoma companies. His research and consulting activities include state and federal government agencies, advertising and public relations firms, retail and banking institutions, national discount and manufacturing firms as well as newspapers and magazines. His topic today is "How the interrelationship of the marketing, advertising and public relations functions in business set the agenda for public opinion."

The other major writing job is preparing a news release about the speech. Since the audience for the speech may be limited, a news release gives the message broader circulation. For a major address, an institution usually includes publication of the speech in the promotion budget. The format is similar to a brochure, with the introduction of the speaker included, as well as a description of the occasion where the speech was presented. Copies are then mailed to lists of important publics for the message who were unlikely to have been present, usually with a cover memo (rarely a letter) or simply a business card. Specifications for reprint are also usually included. Reprinting the speech is usually permitted, although in some cases the speech is copyrighted. Where the latter is the case, it should be made clear so that those who want to use the speech or large portions of it will know that permission for use is required. (See Example 10-2 for a sample of a reprinted speech.)

Scripts

Speeches, as discussed here, are presentations that a person delivers before a live or an electronic audience. Scripts are formats for integrating visuals, such as slides or film or videotape, into a presentation.

10-2

PR Double Duty
Former RCA Corporation Chief Executive Officer Thornton F.
Bradshaw spoke at the 1984 Gerald Loeb Awards Banquet of
the UCLA Graduate Management School when he was just
finishing his tenure as both CEO and chairman of RCA. The
speech was well packaged as a brochure. *Source:* Reprinted
with permission of RCA.

Credibility in Business and Journalism

It is an honor to be chosen to speak
to this distinguished group of scriveners, reporters, evening stars, and dependents. I am a
dependent, a news maven, dependent on you
for my daily sustenance.

In my job, I get letters. Most of them—like the
following—do not fill my day with sunshine:

Dear Mr. Bradshaw:

*Does NBC want to profit from AIDS, V.D.,
drug abuse, mental illness, and suicide? You're
planning a new TV "comedy" series glamorizing
homosexuality. Everyone knows that lifestyle is
filled with disease and self-destructive behavior.
HOMOSEXUALITY KILLS! I'll keep boycotting
all NBC TV/radio shows, RCA products, and
Hertz car rentals until you stop making shows
that lead America's children into homosexuality.*

Sometimes I get nice letters, which I keep in
my pocket and touch occasionally, like prayer
beads. Here is one:

Dear Mr. Bradshaw:

*My name is Thornton and I am 9. I hate my
name because kids at school joke about it. It's
worse than mumps. You are the only other Thornton
I ever heard of. Where did you get your name
from? My teacher told me about you. I hope that*

is O.K. Will you be my friend? I sure need one with my dumb name.

> *Your friend,*
>
> *Thornton Reynard*

P.S. What do your friends call you? Did you ever get so mad you wanted to punch somebody.

I responded with the following letter:

Dear Thornton:

No one calls me Thornton so I have never had to punch anyone in the nose. Anyway, I was always afraid that I would get punched back. Everyone calls me Brad.

Why don't you ask people to call you Ray, which is the first part of your last name? You might spell it Rey, which in Spanish means king. If you do, don't tell anybody because kings are not very popular these days.

Thornton was my grandmother's family name, and she was very proud of it. I am proud of it, too, but as I said before everyone calls me Brad.

> *Best wishes,*
>
> *T. F. Bradshaw*

Now that's a good story, isn't it? A wonderful human-interest item for a slow news day. The trouble is that it's not true. Before releasing the letters to the press, we decided to get in touch with the boy and his parents to make sure we were not invading their privacy. We discovered that no one with the first name of Thornton lived at the return address on the letter. We also discovered that similar, fraudulent letters had been sent to other men with unusual first names. We had violated the first rule of journalism: never over-check a good story. We had asked one too many questions, and the story had evaporated on us. I had to take the letter out of my pocket.

Unfortunately, as the many good reporters in this room are aware, non-stories continue to get into print because too few questions have been asked. For instance, President Carter's widely reported difficulty in getting into a restaurant in Boston without his jacket and tie. Of course, the failing is not limited to the journalistic side of the line. Major corporations take out ads about the press and television that could not pass any reasonable test of fact and objectivity in the news columns. I am harangued at RCA's annual meeting with a mishmash of half-truths and conspiracy theories about NBC—how the Communists have taken over the newsroom. Now there's an idea for a Loeb Award entry—how a handful of ob-sessed publicity-seekers have stolen the annual meeting from America's shareholders. If only these grinches were polite!

And that leads me to what I want to talk about tonight—civility and reporting the news. Bill Paley once said, "Reporting the news objectively is not impossible; but it is very difficult." The difficult becomes closer to the impossible when each party involved is sure that the other party is moved by base motives. The news is seen as being tainted, biased. The readers are suspicious, precondi-tioned. The news makers are sure that what they do will not be fairly reported, so they try to in-fluence the press. The circle widens, getting further away from the core of objective reporting.

What is needed is more professionalism and more civility—in the sense of listening to and respecting the many voices of a vast, sprawling democracy and a diverse world. Civility also means keeping the noise level down.

My credentials are not particularly impressive—considering the kinds of people that have talked about the subject. I am not a professional. Put me at the scene of an accident and you won't get a very accurate report. But I have had some experience:

- as a media target—an oil man in the 1970s.

10-2 | continued

- as an advisor to government.
- as a chairman of a good newspaper.
- as an overseer of a television network.

Anyway, news reporting is everybody's business, so I shall tiptoe through the minefields.

First, political bias. There is a widespread feeling among businessmen that journalists are biased against them and that they let their bias creep into their stories. Perhaps the greatest source of this feeling was the widely misunderstood poll of 240 leading print and broadcast journalists conducted by Robert Lichter and Stanley Rothman in 1979 and 1980. The poll disclosed that more than 80 percent of the journalists had voted for the Democratic candidate in each of the presidential elections of 1964, 1968, 1972, and 1976.

What did not get much attention was the fine print in the poll—the journalists' responses to the detailed economic questions. Seventy percent of the journalists felt that private enterprise was fair to workers. Sixty-three percent thought that less regulation of business would be good for the country. Eighty-six percent agreed that persons with more ability should earn more money. And 88 percent opposed government ownership of big corporations. Hardly radicalism.

As to the journalists' 80-percent pro-Democratic voting record, I would judge that at least that proportion of my business colleagues voted for the Republican candidate in those elections. Does that mean that businessmen make business decisions to promote the Republican party? I doubt it. They make those decisions to increase the profits of their companies and their shareholders, to generate funds for investment and the creation of jobs, to advance their careers and enhance their bonuses, to expand their reputations and get favorable mention in the press.

Do journalists act differently? I doubt it. Journalists make news decisions on the basis of what is im-

portant and what is interesting; on what will get them on the front page or in the nightly news; on what will sell newspapers and improve the ratings; on what will enhance their reputations, their careers, and their salaries.

I do not mean to suggest that political bias—conscious or unconscious—never clouds news judgment. I do mean to suggest that a corrective process of compensation is often at work, sometimes to the disadvantage of Democrats. I think Jody Powell is correct when he observes that Jimmy Carter got rougher treatment from the press than has Ronald Reagan. Charm goes a long way, even with journalists, and it can work to the advantage of Democrats as well as Republicans, as my college classmate Jack Kennedy abundantly demonstrated.

If political bias is not a real issue, what then accounts for the growing public suspicions of the press and television? Arrogance may be a problem. News reporting is a profession, not a priesthood—although the matter may sometimes be confused.

I agree with what Larry Grossman, the new president of NBC News, recently told the network's affiliates:

. . . that there are too many occasions in which some of us in television news are guilty of arrogance, of showing off, and of intruding unnecessarily and offensively into private lives. On occasion, those of us in news have a tendency to act as if we are beyond honest criticism, and above the people we cover and the audiences we serve.

We must take care not to hold up the First Amendment as a shield for our own inadequacies. The news is a privileged profession, but it is not a priesthood. We need more self-examination, more self-criticism, more awareness of our weaknesses and our deficiencies. . . .

We must do everything we can to reestablish

10-2   continued

public trust not only for our own success . . . we must also reestablish public trust for the sake of the health and the vitality of our democratic society, whose very existence depends on a responsible and fair press.

Good words and a good start. But how do we stay on our side of the fence—the professional side—and not climb over to the beckoning green of the pundit? Not easily. As one of our best news people said, "When a reporter is assigned to a night court, he comes out with a sharpened sense of the inadequacies of our society and its institutions." And I would add, he wants to tell people what he has learned.

One thing we might all do is recognize that the world is now so complex that no individual has the experience, knowledge, and education to cover a reporter's waterfront. A bit of humility is in order. Even when we concentrate on an area such as business, there is no way an individual can become knowledgeable about the many facets of what is poured into the daily business pages. I readily admit that I cannot understand many of the diverse businesses that are grouped under the RCA sign—from semiconductors to network broadcasting to car rentals. But then again, I am getting fairly close to voluntary retirement and can afford to admit inadequacy.

What else? I would recommend that the press and television seize upon the rising appetite for hard news—as reflected strongly in recent polls—to reestablish public confidence in journalistic objectivity. Although investigative and interpretative reporting serve a purpose, sometimes an essential purpose, the pendulum may have swung too far, creating the impression that journalists are more advocates than observers. We would all be served by a return to stricter, more traditional standards of factual reporting.

What else? I think we can take practical action to defuse the popular notion that the press and

television are hostile to our major institutions, business, government, and perhaps the country itself. I am not arguing for a restraint on aggressive reporting of the ills of our society. I am arguing for looking more closely, more critically, at other societies—our political adversaries and our economic competitors. I recognize that it is difficult for American journalists to get at the facts in countries in which freedom of the press, as we know it, exists not at all or in attenuated form. But I do believe that we must broaden the scope of our reporting if the American people are to understand the challenges that confront them in an increasingly interrelated world and if they are to form a balanced judgment of the relative strengths of our own institutions. All politics is local politics, particularly in an election year; but all news is not local news.

Most of all, I believe the journalistic community should be more open and more candid in confessing its failings and in ventilating its difficulties. Too often, front-page whoppers are corrected on the inside, below the fold; evening news bloopers are amended in bland corrections dissolving into the commercial. We should be more direct with our readers and our viewers. Confession is good for the soul, and in the long run, I am convinced, it is good for circulation and good for ratings.

I am aware of the old newsroom axiom that readers are not interested in a reporter's problems. It was not a bad axiom for a simpler and more trusting time. But I don't think it works any longer. Journalists, particularly television journalists, have become celebrities, and they command large salaries, much larger than those of most readers and viewers—some larger than mine. In the news columns and on the air, these journalists come across as supremely self-confident and in total command of the facts. Not surprisingly, they tend to be taken at face value and are assumed, when in error, to be willfully so.

10-2 continued

If the press and television are to preserve their credibility, the public has to be educated to the immense difficulties of reporting the news—how complicated the issues have become, how hard it is for even the most expert reporters to get to the bottom of things, how demanding it is to put the facts together under the pressure of deadlines, how elusive and misleading are the special interests involved.

As a businessman with some firsthand knowledge of government, I can assure you that most non-journalists—even the most sophisticated—have only the slimmest understanding of a journalist's problems. Businessmen and government officials are accustomed to easy access to large quantities of information prepared by expert staffs. The information may not be relevant; it may not be needed; but they get it. It is hard for them to understand how difficult it is to be out there groping in the dark.

Some important businessmen have only the crudest of notions of how the system works. When I was chairman of *The Observer* in London at the time of the parliamentary elections in 1979, the editor informed me that the editorial board had decided to endorse the Labour Party for reelection. My personal view was that Labour had run its course and that Britain needed a change, specifically that it needed Mrs. Thatcher. I argued my case to the editor and reminded him that if *The Observer* went for Labour it would be alone among the serious papers in London. When he persevered, I told him to go ahead, he was the editor. In the American tradition, and certainly in the British tradition, I might have asserted my prerogative as the owner and publisher. But ARCO had bought the paper to save it, not to make it appear to be the tool of big oil.

Shortly after the endorsement was printed, I received a letter of protest from an important British businessman. He enclosed a bundle of clippings of the many ads his company had placed in *The Observer.* His letter was to the point: "Dear Brad—What the hell did you buy the paper for?"

The answer, though there was no sense in giving it to that particular advertiser, was: to preserve *The Observer*'s independence.

Shortly thereafter, I had the opportunity to demonstrate the point from the opposite end of the political spectrum. As the paper was being put to bed one Saturday night, the editor informed me that the craft unions had stopped the presses and were vowing not to continue unless we agreed to yank a story on labor violence in a bitter strike. I refused, and it looked for a while as if a great paper was on the verge of being killed by its own employees. Finally, the editor worked out a compromise under which the unions bought a small ad stating their position on the strike. The presses rolled, and *The Observer* survived.

My experience on *The Observer* and most recently my association with NBC have reinforced a long-standing feeling that businessmen are their own worst enemies in dealing with the press. For too long, their attitude was to shut the door and keep the press out. Tell them as little as possible and hope they'd go away.

In the early 1970s, I accepted an invitation to appear on "The Dick Cavett Show" for a whole hour to discuss the energy problem with Barry Commoner and Ralph Nader. What a wonderful opportunity to tell the story! At the end of the hour, I emerged battered, bloodied, and defeated. I asked the producer why I had been chosen. He said, "You weren't. You were the sixth oil-company president we asked."

This closed-door attitude has not had good results for the businessmen of this country. A stereotype has developed of the businessman as being solely dedicated to the bottom line, justifying anything—be it to shut down communities and throw people out of work or to foul rivers and streams—

10-2 | continued

in the mad pursuit of profit. Well, very little of that is true—at least in the businesses that I observe—but it is the presumed reality against which we must operate.

I ran into that reality in the early 1970s as part of the effort to persuade the American people that an oil crisis was upon us. We in the oil business lacked the credibility with the press to carry the argument.

I remember meeting with the chief of the Washington Bureau of a great newspaper in 1971. I poured out everything I knew about the impending oil crisis, told him why I thought it was a national issue, why I thought it would inhibit our foreign policy for years to come and eventually would create more havoc than the Fascist and Communist dictators. He said that he believed my story but that every solution I offered would enrich the oil companies. It would never sell.

It didn't sell for many years. One reason, aside from the suspicion of self-interest, was that there were virtually no reporters with the background to understand the problem. Eventually, the message got through—although it may have to be learned again when the current glut is no more. But much valuable time and momentum was lost. Business was principally to blame, but the press bore a share of the responsibility. There was a time, as you well know, when few self-respecting reporters wanted to cover business. Business reporting was the Siberia of journalism; political reporting and foreign correspondence were the Elysian Fields.

Like it or not, however, business is a dominant—perhaps the dominant—institution of our society. Our system cannot function well if business does not function well. And business cannot function well in an increasingly interdependent economic and political system unless the American people understand and support greater cooperation between business and government. And the people

will not understand unless there is a knowledgeable and responsible business press to educate them.

So it comes back to professionalism and civility—professionalism so that the raw material of our history can be known, civility so that people can hear it.

The Gerald Loeb Awards and the high quality of the recipients here tonight give me confidence that the press will be up to the task. Congratulations to all of you. I have been honored to be included among your company.

Differences and Similarities

A major difference between preparing a script and a speech is the audience consideration. A script is not tailored as specifically for a single audience, or a single event, as a speech. Approach script planning by first determining what you want to accomplish. Then think about the various publics who might be exposed to the presentation. After you have identified these publics, make a list of what each needs to know about the subject. Now you are ready to decide how to tell the story.

Planning

List the principal ideas you want to convey with the presentation. Arrange these logically so development is easy to follow. Use a narrative approach if you can. Make a master chart of the ideas, listing under each, as you do with a speech, the points you want to make. Beside each, describe in detail how you would present the point visually. Be sure each point has these elements: something to set the scene for the idea, something to carry the action of the line of thought forward and something to relate to a common experience that audiences can identify with.

Implementing

At this point PR paths diverge dramatically. Some PR people, because of budget pressures, shoot their own slides. Others have to scurry about to find a photographer who might be talked into donating time or talent. Or a large company with close associations might be talked into supplying the technical assistance. Large-budget operations just draw up a proposal for what is needed—slides or film, sometimes videotape—and send it to photographers or studios for bids.

The script writer has to work closely with the person preparing the visuals, because the visuals tell the story. The words are just there to help. There are two ways to go about this double-track operation: Select your visuals and write a script that fits them, or prepare the script and then give it to a photographer to "illustrate." When the visuals come from outside the organization, it is logical for the writer to first prepare the message that needs to be told.

Most photographers will function best with a series of conferences. The first would add details not in the proposal. The writer could share with the photographer chosen for the job the outline of points and a description of how these could be told with visuals. The photographer would then develop a shooting schedule, interpreting the intent of the script in terms of shots that need to be taken to tell the story.

After the first pictures are ready, another conference should be held to ensure that the photographer's conception of the story matches that of the writer. And when the shooting is complete, the writer and photographer need to see what is missing. At this point the strongest art should be selected; the most compelling pictures need to be arranged in the best way to tell the story. Also, the script may have to be revised at this stage. The importance of flexibility can't be overstated—

although it is sometimes difficult to be objective about finding the best way to tell the story when one's creativity is being judged.

After the art is chosen and the sequences planned, the script is ready for polishing, if it has been written. If it has not been written, you are ready to start.

Matching Words and Sights

Visuals have the power to set a mood, inject drama and explain in powerful ways. The words of the script should help the visuals do this. Most scripts are overwritten. Too many words interfere with the listener's ability to absorb the visuals. Allow time for the pictures to have an impact.

With slides, the question arises whether the script should carry the same information as that being seen, perhaps on charts or graphs. It's best to handle charts as they are handled in the print media. First the textual material prepares readers for the illustration by discussing it. Below the illustration there usually is a caption explaining the graph or chart. Readers then expect to see the relationship between the illustration and the point being made explained further in the textual matter. This same system works well in handling charts or graphs in a slide show. (See Example 10-3 for an excerpt from a slide show script.)

Writers with television-writing skills adjust easily to the slide presentation. Their experience with the medium transfers easily to writing the film or videotape script. Sometimes, though, they have difficulty with the time period. Television writers are accustomed to working with fragments of time. In a visual presentation, the time is usually about 30 minutes, but it can be twice that. In giving a long presentation, both unity and pace make the job quite different from that of writing an ordinary television script. (See Example 10-4 for an excerpt from a film script.)

Pace can be varied in both the script and visuals. And to keep audience interest it is essential to employ some of the techniques of the dramatist—suspense, dramatic foreshadowing and comic relief are a few. In a way, the script is half of a dialogue; the visuals form the other half, and both together tell the story.

Just as with speeches, promotion is involved in calling attention to the ideas presented in the script. A news release should be written and, if it is a long presentation that is going to a number of audiences, a promotional brochure should be developed.

Computer Advantages

Facts for the speech or script and various versions of the writing can all be stored on disc for reconsideration. Editing is simplified and printed copies of various versions can easily be produced. Computer graphic programs can produce excellent illustrations transferable to slides or overhead projections (see Example 10-5). For sophisticated slide presentations, computer-generated graphics can give simulated animation to visuals. The "Star Wars" of speech making offers challenges to the creative.

10-3

Slide Show
This six-minute script is typical of one prepared each
academic year by Texas Christian University's Department of
Journalism as a very low-budget recruiting tool to use when
students and their parents visit the facilities. The presentation
uses two slide projectors that are automatically controlled by
stimulus signals on the audiotape so that one view dissolves
into the next. The audio track has music and one-voice
narration. *Source: Courtesy Jack Raskopf.*

MULTI-IMAGE SCRIPT: TCU JOURNALISM--A HAND-TOOLED EDUCATION

TIME: 5'59"

WRITER, PRODUCER, DIRECTOR: JACK RASKOPF

FOR: TEXAS CHRISTIAN UNIVERSITY JOURNALISM DEPARTMENT

VIDEO	AUDIO
	INTRO MUSIC: SWIFT, FAST, ELECTRONIC BEAT TO GO WITH RAPID PACE OF MASS PRODUCTION, ASSEMBLY LINE SEQUENCES ON VIDEO.
	Modern mass production... with its speed...precision...technology... efficiency...and economy...has become the hallmark of progress as we move toward the opening years of the twenty-first century....

10-3 | continued

EXCEPT -- in education....
Here the TCU Journalism Department
stubbornly maintains its time-proven
concept of the "hand-tooled"
teaching-learning experience -- one of
individual concern...care...and
counseling....

Like the clasical philosophers of more
than two thousand years ago...TCU
continues to believe that students
must be grounded in the verities of
western civilization....those liberal

arts and sciences which form the
common core for all students at TCU
during their first two years --
regardless of their field of study....

The Journalism Department maintains
that the basics of producing
outstanding young professional
communicators is best achieved through
a close and understanding relationship
between teacher and
student...reflecting the nineteenth
century adage that "the only
ingredients necessary for a fine
education are to have a log--and a

teacher like Mark Hopkins at one end
and a serious student at the other
end..."

That "log" today has become quite
sophisticated, indeed....with an array
of modern mechanical and electronic
equipment to improve the speed and
quality of conveying information...and
to produce special effects that
enhance visual and audio
communication....

Through the Mod-dee Center for Visual
Arts and Communication, TCU is
determined to provide its students
with this modern "log" in order to
prepare our young people for careers
in...

news editorial journalism...

broadcast journalism...

photojournalism...

and in advertising...

and public relations....

However, the administration is firm in
its belief that it is still the

collective teaching body--the

faculty--sitting on one end of the log

10-3 | continued

who provide the basic -- and by far
the most important -- thrust of the
TCU Journalism edcuational
experience...as they share their
background...their expertise...and
their wisdom with students and convey
to them those intangibles of
professionalism...ethics...motivation..
..enthusiasm...and a sense of
obligation to society....

To be selected for the TCU Journalism
faculty an individual must have a
combination of significant
professional experience plus the
highest of academic
credentials....Five of the six
fulltime faculty members hold earned
doctorate degrees and the sixth is
currently working on her Ph.D.....

(VERY SLIGHT TRANSITIONAL PAUSE)

Besides classroom and laboratory
course work, students receive
invaluable hands-on experience by
working on TCU's award-winning
publications--

The Daily Skiff...

and

The Image Magaine...

10-3 continued

In addition, students participate in
off-campus internships...
Because of its excellent location in
the Fort Worth/Dallas Metroplex --
which has become a major communication
center in the Sun Belt -- TCU offers
students outstanding opportunities to
apply their classroom learning
experience for credit in the real
world of communication, commerce and
business....

Students are also encouraged to become
active in campus chapters of the
nation's major professional
communcation associations:
The American Advertising Federation...
The National Press Photographers
Association...
The Public Relations Student Society
of America...
The Society of Professional
Journalists--Sigma Delta Chi...
and Women in Communication....
(SLIGHT TRANSITIONAL PAUSE)
TCU Journalism education offers entree
into a career that can be
exhilarating...

10-3 | continued

exhausting...demanding...frustrating...

and fulfilling--all wrapped in one

appealing package....

For those serious students who want to

learn how to communicate accurately...

concisely...ethically...and with zest

through the mass media--

for those who have the motivation and

determination to work hard and to

study long hours--and who have the

mental and physical stamina to compete

on a fast track -- the TCU Journalism

Department faculty invites you to sit

on the "other end of that log" and to

share with them the TCU venture in a

"hand-tooled" -- NOT mass produced --

education in journalism.

                    END
              MUSIC UP AND OUT

10-4

Excerpt from Film Script
Source: Reprinted by permission of Michael O'Shea, Dallas, TX.

LAKE GRANBURY CHAMBER OF COMMERCE

PART I
CONVENTION AND TOURIST BUREAU

VISUAL	AUDIO
Fade in to the surface of Lake Granbury. Slowly, ghostly, a mellow-drama scene from the Opera House wafts, is heard, and then is gone.	
The surface continues to undulate gently. Pan of the Wagon Yard Antique shop interior is seen, as customers are heard inquiring about the ornate cash register ("Now, this was made in 18-- what?").	
Supered over the surface are now quickening scenes of the Courthouse, the jail, the Nutt House, the Opera exterior, the Chrysalis Conservatory, and the Daniel, Smith-Savage, Hanna Ford, and Carmichael houses. Quiet, intimate guitar music strums.	VOICE-OVER It's called a city--but, at its heart, it's really an enchanting world of its own:
A motor abruptly starts, the surface shimmers, a plane's wings are seen reflected in the ripples.	one tucked away in the central Texas hills, yet just a short jaunt from its metropolis neighbors, Fort Worth and Dallas, and only a tad further from Waco, Austin, and San Antonio.
The motor revs up, the plane bolts forward, headed toward the Riverboat Queen seen in the distance. Zoom forward to the Queen, with sound segues to its motors starting, then to the blast of its whistle. The Courthouse Square rises in the background, as the plane lifts off.	It's Granbury--cozy and close-by: a city of incredible charm.

Computer Graphics
This slide combines a picture with copy. Often slides may
have charts or graphics as well as copy. *Source: Courtesy Jack
Raskopf.*

Conclusions

* Writing speeches and scripts is a demanding task because of the combination of words and images and the performance element.

* Direct interaction with an audience, either in a speech or a slide presentation, brings out the best in most of us who really want to please others.

* Preparing material especially for audiences is the key to pleasing them.

* The person preparing the material must remember that although the audience is the ultimate receiver of the information, the person presenting it is most important. The speaker is both medium and message.

* Speech subjects need to be thoroughly researched but the points pared to three.

* The effect you want the speech to have on the audience should be the governing factor.

* You need to be sure you are using words and symbols that are meaningful to the audience.

* Words and symbols need to be appropriate for the speaker, too.

* Most PR people are in the business of preparing materials for others to use.

* Preparing material for presentation by others is a hazardous task, but a highly creative one.

* PR people must be skilled in preparing material for themselves or others to give.

* They must also be able to visualize the combination of pictures and words that will accommodate messages presented with slides or videotape.

* Speeches and scripts must have a sense of pace, a rhythm appropriate for both the material and the speaker.

* The script is a dialogue with visuals.

* Presentations are a PR function that demands rehearsal.

* Part of the PR function is to prepare the introduction for a presentation, releases about the presentation, and brochures, which, in the case of a speech, may be a reprint of the speech to be sent with a cover memo.

Exercises

1. Develop a slide script to recruit students to your school.

2. Write a PSA promoting your own school to potential students.

3. Check through recent issues of major newsmagazines and find an article that treats a major public issue. Using this article as a starting place, do further research and then write a 15-minute speech to be delivered at a civic club luncheon. Before you begin writing the speech, list the three major points you want the speaker to make. Assume that the speaker is president of a local company whose business is affected by the issue you have chosen.

4. Write a speech introduction for your professor in this course.

5. Attend a formal speech. Write an analysis of the content of the speech and critique the speaker's delivery.

6. The president of Ourbank will address the Rotary Club three weeks from today. His topic is the ailing banking industry. He wants to supplement the talk with some slides. Write the speech for him and develop a list of slides to illustrate his talk.

Selected Bibliography

David K. Berlo, *The Process of Communication: An Introduction to Theory and Practice* (New York: Holt, Rinehart and Winston, 1960).

Patrick Hartwell with Richard H. Bentley, *Open to Language* (New York: Oxford University Press, 1982).

J. T. Masterson, et al., *Speech Communication: Theory and Practice* (New York: Holt, Rinehart and Winston, 1983).

Anita Taylor and Teresa Rosegrant, *Communicating*, 3rd ed. (Englewood Cliffs, N.J.: Prentice-Hall, 1983).

Rudolph F. Verderber, *The Challenge of Effective Speaking*, 6th ed. (Belmont, Calif.: Wadsworth, 1985).

Part Four

Writing for Special Audiences

PR's special audiences are very particular readers who expect to be known, understood and addressed in specifically directed media.

11
Annual
Reports

William Zinsser, one of America's best writers of non-fiction, says annual report writing is "the art of obfuscation raised high."[1] The writing in annual reports has the reputation of being generally the worst of English prose.

Why is the writing in annual reports so bad? There is no single answer, but most authorities seem to agree that the problem stems, at least in part, from the inherent conflict between two issues: being truthful and "looking good."

Clarity Versus Accuracy

Publicly held companies must, by law, issue an annual report and it must be truthful. Truth is often equated with fact, and fact sometimes does not make a company look good. Because management has to have new capital to work with, and that means attracting new investors to the company's stock, writers of annual reports sometimes resort to obfuscation. That is, they gild the lily with writing that may be entirely truthful but is at the same time so murky that hardly anyone understands what it says.

On this point, a federal judge once remarked, "What has developed is a literary art form calculated to communicate as little of the essential information as possible while exuding an air of total candor."[2]

There are other reasons, of course, why annual report writing is so bad. Some company executives demand formality in writing because they believe this makes their divisions look more important. Some company presidents, for example, wouldn't think of writing a letter that just anybody could understand. Furthermore, some presidents who know nothing about writing insist on writing their own letters without the help (or subsequent editing) of a seasoned public relations writer. To do otherwise would make them look as if they did not know how to write.

Another reason the writing in annual reports is so bad is that it has to be cleared at many levels in the firm before it is finally approved. Everybody wants to add, delete or change words. "The legal department, the accounting department, and all the others tend to put in a few more terms or qualifications, just to show, if nothing else, that they are on the job," says Robert Gunning,[3] an expert on clear writing.

Once you are in an organization and have turned out an annual report or two, you'll probably begin to anticipate such changes and start writing gobbledygook to begin with. But this won't help, because the same people who made changes before will make them again. So it's best to resist the temptation to join the crowd, and instead to write simply, directly and clearly, as usual. Remember, the annual report is a public document, intended to communicate the status of the company to the public. Says Gunning, "Many writers fool themselves into believing they are writing for the public when they are actually writing to impress the boss."[4] He says that no accountant would fake the net income figure just to make the boss feel better. Yet writers often do the equivalent in annual reports.

The result is that annual reports end up containing long words, long sentences and long paragraphs, many of which are not needed at all. A National Investor Relations Institute study of executive letters in annual reports found that a good copy writer giving the letters a once-through chopped out 18 percent of the words without losing meaning.[5] That was with one editing pass. Could the writing have been shaved by 25 percent? It's likely. And it probably should have been.

Say It Right and Simply

But some executives will scream when you start shortening sentences and cutting out vague words. "You need those words to be accurate," they say. "It won't be correct if you say it any other way." You must recognize, too, that they may be right. Listen to them because they are experts in their fields, although they may not be expert writers. The point is not to say it right *or* to say it simply but to *say it right and simply*.

You will quickly find that it is not always easy to say it right and simply. You may have to spend an inordinate amount of time with a sentence or a paragraph to make it both right and simple. Usually the fog in annual report writing is not caused by the need for accuracy but by the inclusion of details and qualifications that don't bear on the main point of the sentence or paragraph. If a detail or qualification alters the point, include it. If it does not, delete it and make it another sentence or paragraph.

Some of these details and qualifications are better treated as footnotes so they don't get in the way of the message. On the other hand, footnotes are sometimes where the real truth of the situation is buried. This is a point often made by Jane Quinn, the author of *Everyone's Money Book*. She urges readers of annual reports to go first to the footnotes, because the footnotes best reflect the company and its profit picture.[6]

The key point to remember about this is stated clearly by U.S. Supreme Court Justice Benjamin Cardozo: "There is an accuracy that defeats itself by the overemphasis of details. . . . The sentence may be so overloaded with all its possible qualifications that it may tumble down of its own weight."[7]

Comprehension   Vague words are also known as glittering generalities. They are usually very abstract and impressive but they don't communicate much. As a professional writer, you must be dedicated not only to truth but also to making your copy understandable. Comprehension increases in direct proportion to your use of simple, concrete words. Remember, you are writing to communicate, not to obfuscate.

Annual reports that are not clearly written breed distrust. It is only human to be skeptical, even afraid, of the unknown. Lack of trust is a key issue. That was a key finding by Hill and Knowlton of New York when it surveyed 247 individual investors in seven cities. "Investors often distrust what they read in annual reports, and they believe that the reports frequently hide or fail to discuss bad news and problems," notes the *Public Relations Journal*.[8]

That's a pretty strong statement about the way people regard annual reports. Why this level of distrust? An illustration from the annual report of a major oil company explains:

> These various government initiatives increasing participation, royalty and tax rates, or any other similar changes in arrangements increasing government take, result in increases in cost to the Company liftings. As a result of such government actions, the cost of the major representative crudes lifted by the Company had increased by the end of the year by about $6.85 a barrel, or about 196%, over the cost of those crudes at the end of the year 1973.
>
> Costs are necessarily a major factor in pricing crude oil and products, and, accordingly, increases in costs resulting from government participation, higher posted prices, and higher tax rates have to be recovered through increased petroleum prices if, and to the extent that, competitive conditions and regulations permit. The materiality of the adverse effects on [the Company] of participation and unsettled Mid-East conditions cannot now be predicted.

That is horrendous writing. It scores about 22 on the Gunning fog index (see Appendix A), which means it is written at the level of a fourth-year doctoral student. While it may be intelligible to a professor of petroleum economics, even he or she would probably prefer something less dense. The second paragraph is especially bad because it contains no technical details to warrant its obscurity. It would have been much better to say

> When the cost of producing oil goes up, the company must charge higher prices. These price increases cannot, of course, exceed what competition or government regulations permit. [The Company] can't predict what effect Mid-East problems will have on business.

This is not flashy writing, but it is clear writing. Look at what the chief executive of the same firm said in his letter:

> The industry responded by pointing out that there are no "windfall" profits, that much of the reported profits are nonrecurring "inventory profits" and thus unavailable for capital investment, that dividend payments have not been excessive, and that higher cash generation is needed and is being used for reinvestment in projects to provide more petroleum and satisfy the environmental laws and regulations. We have some basis to believe that our messages are finally beginning to be heard.

Heard? Maybe. But probably not understood. The fog index on this paragraph is 23. The average sentence length is more than 36 words. That may be okay for a seventeenth-century novel but not for twentieth-century non-fiction. Most prose today directed to the general public has an average sentence length of 15 to 17 words. The clearest sentence in this piece is the last one, and it is at least eight words too long. Why not: "We think people are beginning to listen"?

Here is a typical paragraph from a company with problems:

> The drain on [The Company's] cash resources resulting from disproportionate capital contributions to [subsidiary] and working capital support for its deficits, coupled with generally higher working capital requirements of other subsidiaries resulting from higher prices, have made it necessary to restrict budgeted capital expenditures in 1975.

This paragraph has a fog index of 30. Here's what it means: The company is cutting back on spending because a subsidiary went bankrupt and (to add a qualifying detail) it is dragging down the whole operation with it.

Yet another example is from a firm that is having trouble selling some worthless land it owns in the West. But thanks to a deal made with another firm, it may be able to dump its real estate soon. How did this relatively simple fact get reported in the annual report? Read:

> We were less successful than we had hoped last year in achieving our goal of disposing of the properties of our land division, located principally in the western part of the United States. While conditions in real estate were difficult, we did conclude an important joint venture with [name of other company], which we expect will facilitate the disposal of our real estate assets.

Do you still wonder why many people laugh about the writing in annual reports? The situation may change, however slowly, because government regulators are getting serious not only about telling the truth in annual reports but also about telling it plainly. As one observer notes, "Companies are finding out that the report must *communicate* with shareholders instead of giving them only what management wants them to see."[9]

It is easier to point out what is wrong with the writing in annual reports than to tell how to do it right. The first step, however, is to follow the principles of good writing. But even this is not enough; for your annual report writing to be successful you must do it with a purpose. This means that you must proceed from a carefully drawn plan. One does not write an annual report on whimsy; rather, one approaches it as an important undertaking. The annual report is "the most expensive, time-consuming, sensitive and important document that a corporate public relations . . . officer will be called upon to execute in the course of any given year."[10] It only makes sense that such an important task be done right.

Planning the Annual Report

Although our main concern here is writing, in writing an annual report you should never forget that the report is a publication—much like a magazine, in fact. It takes careful planning to produce a unified product. Art, design and writing must all mesh if communication is to be effective. Before you decide on format, choose type or begin to write, you must establish the report's purpose.

Purpose

The fundamental purpose of most annual reports is to provide investors with financial data and a description of the company's operations. But annual reports can do much more than this, and good ones do. Not only can the report tell the company story to investors, it can also be used to present the company's views to many other audiences—the media, community leaders and employees, for example. No law says that annual reports must be sent only to stockholders and to the Securities and Exchange Commission.

Thus, the first step in annual report planning is answering these questions: What should the report accomplish? Do you want to comfort investors, sell stock or paint a glowing picture of the company in order to attract new customers or employees? Is the purpose merely to maintain good employee or investor relations? Will the report be used to convey the company's point of view on key issues to community or industry leaders and to the media?

Obviously, the purpose is closely related to the audience. Whatever you want to say, you must know who will be reading the report so you can tailor your message to them. Stage two of annual report planning, then, is to define your audience.

Audience

Annual reports are written primarily for stockholders, but stockholders are rarely the only audience and they may not be the most important audience. Some companies—for example, those owned by holding companies—don't sell stock directly to the public. Annual reports for these firms might be directed to an entirely different audience—perhaps to employees or legislators.

As with any piece of writing, then, it is important that you first define your audience or audiences. If there are two or more significant audiences, you must also establish their relative importance. That means you must set some priorities. For example, if you are writing the annual report for a firm in a heavily regulated industry, logically you will be concerned with both stockholders and those who regulate. But these are only two of what might be a fairly lengthy list, as follows:

Stockholders

Potential stockholders

Stockbrokers

Financial analysts

Employees

Customers

Potential customers

Suppliers

Legislators

Regulators

Reporters and business editors

Editorial writers

Community leaders

Consumer advocates

Educators

The list could be extended by several additional publics. However, you get the point that your annual report might be directed to several audiences. And, given the type of firm and its industrial field, the list may include some of the above or a completely different list of audiences. It all depends on the purpose behind the report.

Don't start writing until you first list all your possible audiences. Then establish some priorities—not all of the audiences will be important. If you have difficulty establishing priorities, enlist the help of company management. Construct a short questionnaire that lists the options and a scale of importance for each. Company executives, who know the relative importance of these audiences, will be of great help. Once you have clearly identified your major audience it will be relatively simple to direct your report to them.

Even if you identify and direct your report to only one audience, remember that others may also read it. If you are writing for stockholders, for example, remember that some stockholders may also be employees. In such a case it would not help employee relations to stress how well your firm is holding the line on costs by paying low wages.

Writing the Report

Once the purpose is set and audiences are identified, you can begin compiling information to be used in the report. The first concern at this stage is content: What should the report say?

Determining Content

Determining content is probably the biggest problem in writing annual reports. In probably no other writing task is determining content so difficult. An individual writer, composing a piece on a single topic, merely gathers information, decides what to say, and then says it. As an annual report writer, however, you will have to please many people before the report is ever distributed to its intended audience, and you will therefore run into some difficulty in writing material that is truthful, clear and acceptable to all.

Fortunately, there are some guidelines regarding content. For instance, government rules specify certain items that must be included (see Appendix B). Some of the essentials, either required by law or generally demanded by the investment community, are these:

Financial summary

Letter from the chief executive

Corporate description

Narrative section describing operations

Balance sheet and income statement

Statement of sources and use of funds

Notes to financial statement

Auditor's statement

Ten-year statistical summary

Most of these essentials are simply tables of numbers, and they won't be of immediate concern to you as the writer, but their content may provide important clues to points to be emphasized in the narrative portion of the report. The key point to remember here is that accountants supply the numbers; writers supply the words. Providing the words usually means writing the chief executive's letter and the narrative section of the report.

Executive's Letter   When preparing the executive's letter, you must first meet with the chief executive to find out how he or she wants the letter written. Sometimes the executive will write a letter and turn it over to you for editing or rewriting. Sometimes it works the other way around. And sometimes the writer interviews the executive and then prepares a letter based on the executive's responses. Above all, the letter should "sound" like the chief executive. Any of these procedures is acceptable as long as a good letter is the result.

But what makes a good letter? There's no agreement on this—or even on what the letter should contain. Some simply summarize the year's financial results. Others may ignore money matters and talk about social problems facing the company and its industry. Still others may combine financial material and social commentary into a lengthy treatise designed to convince everybody that things are really better than they seem. Different letters are appropriate in different circumstances.

Annual reports usually rated highest by financial analysts, however, contain letters that adhere to a few basic principles. First, the best letters don't delve deeply into financial matters. Letters crowded with statistics are difficult to read. Except for brief mention of key financial results, the numbers are best left for the tables and charts in the body of the report. Second, an incisive, concise letter is preferable to a lengthy dissertation that attempts to cover the minute areas of operation. Third, analysts expect the executive's letter to be devoted primarily to results of the previous year and expectations for the coming year or two. And the letter should include a discussion of future problems as well as anticipated successes.

Whatever the focus of the letter, it sets the stage for the narrative of the report, where the company's operations are described in detail. (See Example 11-1.)

Narrative   The body of the annual report is where you tell the company's story. This section contains a general description of the company or institution; its location, purposes, products or services; and its related activities. The narrative reports the results of the previous year and the plans for the future, even if these are mentioned in the executive's letter. The narrative needs to disclose and discuss events, management decisions, sales, mergers and conditions that have had significant effects on the company's operation.

At the same time, the narrative must also achieve the communication objectives set for it during the planning process. If the report's purpose is to get people to buy stock, then the narrative must give reasons why the company's stock is a good deal. You can do this best not by talking dollars and cents but by describing the company's position in the industry, its management philosophy, and its foresight and record of success.

The narrative of most annual reports also covers such topics as plans for expansion, research and development programs, and the nature of the firm's customers or markets. But merely presenting such basics isn't enough. Financial analysts want information on the problems facing the company and its industry, and a

11-1

Annual Report Executive Letter
Diamond Shamrock is noted for producing clear, understandable annual reports. In this example, the executive
letter is actually three, one each from the chief executive
officer, the chief operating officer and the vice chairman.
Diamond Shamrock's quarterly reports—mini-versions of
the annual report—are equally clear and understandable.
Source: Reprinted with permission of the Diamond Shamrock
Corporation.

To Our Shareholders:

The past year has been one of the most active and exciting in the history of Diamond Shamrock.

We merged with Natomas Company, bringing us well over 50,000 barrels a day of net oil production, more than a five-fold increase, and adding geothermal energy to our business mix.

We acquired Sigmor Corporation, one of America's largest independent gasoline and convenience store retail chains. Sigmor also brought us a second refinery, enabling us to increase total crude oil throughput capacity 65% to nearly 117,000 barrels per day by the beginning of 1984.

We joined with some of the nation's leading oil companies in drilling an unusually promising high-stakes exploratory well off the North Slope of Alaska, indicating that we have achieved the size and financial strength to pursue opportunities of that magnitude.

Those were the milestones – the events by which we will remember 1983.

Write-offs result in loss for year.
The Alaskan exploratory venture demonstrated the risk and the potential of frontier exploration: The well encountered a vast reservoir which once held possibly billions of barrels of oil. However, the reservoir lacked an essential geologic feature – a trapping mechanism to seal the oil in place – allowing the oil to leak out long ago. It was a dry hole.

Because we wrote off that total investment of $194.3 million, pre-tax, and charged against earnings an additional $91.4 million in pre-tax adjustments and write-downs at year-end, we are reporting a loss from operations of $60.2 million, or $0.76 per share, for 1983. This compares to $149.5 million, or $2.37 per share, of income from operations in 1982.

Financial strength maintained.
The past year brought other developments which, though less dramatic, are most significant in indicating the fundamental strength of our businesses and in signaling our future direction.

As we had anticipated, demand for energy lagged behind the rate of economic expansion, resulting in increasing pressure on refined products profit margins, continuing curtailments of natural gas purchases, a downward drift in oil prices, and severely restricted demand in spot coal markets.

Despite these conditions, we achieved near-record cash flow from operations of $477 million. Debt as a percentage of capitalization increased modestly to 37.8% at year end, well within our 35% to 40% target range. The dividend held steady at $1.76 per share, reflecting our strong cash flow. Sales reached a record $4.0 billion, up from $3.2 billion in the previous year.

11-1 | continued

Increase in oil production tops operating achievements.

Our Exploration Company set a new record for crude oil output, increasing oil production 6% from properties owned prior to the merger with Natomas.

Combined with four months of oil production contributed by Natomas, our total crude oil output rose 207% to 31,963 barrels per day averaged over the entire year. Oil production will increase dramatically again in 1984 as we benefit from a full 12 months of output from Natomas properties.

We increased our exposure to potentially significant new oil and gas reserves by acquiring additional exploratory prospects in the Gulf of Mexico, in Colombia, offshore Tunisia, and in the China Sea and the Dutch North Sea.

We continued to increase our natural gas production capacity, building total deliverability to 400 million cubic feet per day. The location and cost-effectiveness of our production and our contract mix could allow us to substantially increase gas volumes and profitability in the next two years, given a sustained, even modest, increase in demand.

We further upgraded our refineries, increased refining capacity, added a near-record number of branded fuel outlets, and sold a record number of gallons of refined products in 1983.

We began aggressively seeking long-term contract customers for a one-billion-ton Alaskan coal resource, in which we are operator and 50% interest owner. Several years of study has confirmed that we could become the lowest-cost supplier of energy to rapidly expanding Pacific Rim economies.

These developments represent opportunities to find, produce, and deliver substantial new supplies of oil, gas, and coal in 1984 and beyond.

Solid performance expected in 1984 as investments continue to pay off.

As an investor, what can you expect from Diamond Shamrock in 1984? Good performance.

In exploration and production, we will continue the same kind of highly focused drilling program that gave us record U.S. production in 1983: We will develop our most promising acreage while seeking outstanding exploratory prospects.

New domestic oil tracts already on stream will, we believe, result in a solid increase in crude oil volumes during 1984, while our Indonesian operations should increase the high production levels achieved in 1983. Our domestic natural gas production capability has increased substantially, although we expect only a modest increase in delivered volumes for the year due to continuing excess deliverability nationwide.

11-1 | continued

We will increase capital spending for exploration and development to $500 million worldwide. Given the lower cost of drilling and our rifle-shot approach to exploration, that investment bodes well for future production.

In refining and marketing, the competitive environment will keep pressure on profit margins. We will enhance profitability by enlarging our market share through an expanded number of company-owned and jobber outlets. Since we operated our refineries near 100% of capacity, as sales rise we also plan to increase refining capacity through incremental expansions.

We expect a repetition of last year's excellent performance in coal, based on our long-term sales contracts and efficient mining operations.

Our chemical businesses will show substantial improvement as the industrial economy expands, and will continue to provide attractive cash flow to the company.

Finally, our geothermal operations should show increased earnings as prices and capacity utilization rise.

The strong cash flow from these operations and from other sources, such as redeployment of assets, should reach an all-time high of over $1 billion – more than adequate to fund record capital spending and investments of more than $700 million, support our dividend, and pay down debt.

In short, we anticipate net positive results from all our businesses. Diamond Shamrock's earnings should rise substantially above the level reached in 1983 before write-offs and adjustments.

As we look to the year ahead, we believe you can expect solid performance from Diamond Shamrock.

William H. Bricker
Chairman and Chief Executive Officer

J. L. Jackson
President and Chief Operating Officer

J. Avery Rush, Jr.
Vice Chairman

February 16, 1984

discussion of current economic conditions and their impact. This was clearly indicated in a survey of analysts by Opinion Research Corporation:

> Analysts, in fact, are critical of companies that do not make some attempt to put their own strategy and plans into some industry perspective and historical context. . . . Analysts indicate a strong interest in how companies deal with general social and economic problems affecting their company or industry, as well as the impact of government regulation of their industry, another major theme in top-rated reports.[11]

Analysts make names for themselves by being able to read financial statements. You can't make your company look financially healthy if the numbers show that it isn't. So don't try to pull the wool over analysts' eyes by writing a glowing narrative when the situation does not warrant it. What you must do is treat problems candidly but emphasize what the company plans to do to solve them. If the plans are sound, your candor may sell lots of stock. Even if it does not, you'll certainly earn credibility for your company in the financial community.

Also, discuss the status of the natural resources (if any) your company depends on, including the possibility of shortages and how the company will cope with them. Describe the marketing, advertising and public relations strategies that have been designed to communicate your firm's goals and objectives. Tell how the firm is responding to demands for greater corporate responsibility. All of these are just as relevant to annual reports as the bottom-line figures of the income statement.

It is inevitable, of course, that even if you are determined to include all of these things, you will have to fight the space battle. Something may have to be left out. How do you determine what can be deleted? First, check with the corporate attorney to identify items that must be included by law. As examples, the firm may be involved in significant legal action or in some major financial transactions. Next, identify the items that most stockholders and analysts expect to see in any annual report. These include financing, capital expenditures, consolidations, research, marketing and energy supply, to name just a few.

Selecting specific events to include in these categories is more difficult, however. One approach is to ask the executives in charge of company divisions which events and actions of the past year were the most important. This personal-interview technique is quite common. In fact, some annual reports simply use verbatim interviews with division heads—in a question-answer format. If you do this well, this format can provide the necessary information. But there is some resistance to this format among stockholders. In fact, a survey by Northern States Power Company found reaction to such interviews to be overwhelmingly negative.[12] Don't let this keep you from doing interviews. Just keep in mind that the purpose of most interviews is to provide raw information.

Another approach to gathering information from company executives is to use a written questionnaire. A simple survey can often help you get the information you need to gauge the relative importance of different topics—and thereby help you decide what to leave out. The simplest questionnaire merely asks executives to rate the importance of a few key areas. Such a form might look like Table 11-2. To meet the needs of any given situation, you could add or leave out categories. In addition, you might give space for comments or observations about the problems or successes designated most important. A more extensive questionnaire might be called for if you want more detailed information. A series of short-answer questions, for example, such as those in Table 11-3, could bring more useful responses.

Responses to questionnaires like these will help you choose topics to include in the annual report. But you should never rely solely on such surveys. If your own research shows that something else is important and should be in the annual report, don't leave it out because it didn't appear on the survey forms. Put it in and be prepared to explain why you included it.

Theme

Once you have settled on the content, the next step is putting it together in a cohesive way. You want the firm to appear to be well-managed, well-organized and unified. The annual report should mirror these qualities from cover to cover.

The most common way to ensure cohesiveness is to find a theme. A theme is an organizing principle that provides a creative peg on which you can hang content. It helps you position content so that it flows naturally. Although each element should be sufficiently strong to stand alone, when all elements are taken together they have superadditive qualities, totaling a sum much greater than the individual parts.

For example, you might build an effective theme out of a significant event in the life of the company that occurred during the past year or that is on the horizon. Or you might find a theme in some major event or development that affects the industry, not just your company. A new product or service could supply a theme, especially if it meant that the company was moving in a new direction.

A good theme is one that provides context for content; it should never overpower content. And it should never call attention to itself. Most important, some analysts are wary of reports that are heavy on theme and light on facts. They sometimes suspect that the theme is a mask to hide behind.[13] The point is that you should use a theme but use it with good judgment.

Style

With purpose, content and theme defined, you can begin to write. That means dealing with the question of the style of writing in the report. Formality is often the first question of style.

Many annual report writers and most corporate executives might object to the informal style advocated by readability experts like Flesch and Gunning.

11-2

A Simple, Structured Questionnaire

In Column A, rank the areas in which the company has
achieved the greatest successes during the past year (1 =
greatest success). In Column B, rank the areas in which the
company has experienced the greatest problems in the past
year (1 = greatest problem).

A		B
_____	Marketing and sales	_____
_____	New product development	_____
_____	Employee relations	_____
_____	Community relations	_____
_____	Stockholder relations	_____
_____	Government relations	_____
_____	Energy supply	_____
_____	Public information	_____
_____	Customer service	_____
_____	Other: _____	_____

Such objections are often based on the belief that an annual report is a very serious
document and that informality is therefore inappropriate. It is true that style should
be appropriate to the document and to the audience. However, neither the document nor the audience should be the sole determinants of style.

Style is part of what you say. If your company wants to portray itself
as a friendly, informal, neighborhood firm eager to do business with just plain folk,
then a stuffy style is as inappropriate for the annual report as it would be for a commercial on television. But a firm that wants to be viewed as formal and sophisticated
could be expected to use a formal writing style in its annual report in which contractions and humor are kept at a minimum—or prohibited altogether.

Even if the style is formal, that is no excuse for foggy writing. The
annual report must be readable and comprehensible, whatever the style. No company wants to be viewed as complex and confusing. And no company wants to give
the impression that the person representing the firm in print is incapable of thinking
clearly enough to write understandable prose. Many astute observers note that in
one way or another fuzzy writing is usually a sign of fuzzy thinking. You should

11-3

Annual Report Questionnaire for Executives
Source: Reprinted by permission of World Industries, Inc.,
Lancaster, PA.

1. Inside the company, what do you think was the most significant event of the past year?

2. Outside the company, what event of the past year do you think had the most significant impact on the company?

3. What event of the past year had the most significant impact on our company's industry?

4. What was the most important event or development in your division of the company during the past year?

5. What do you believe was the most significant accomplishment of your division of the company during the past year?

6. What do you believe was the most significant accomplishment of the company as a whole during the past year?

7. What do you believe to be the most important problem facing your division of the company?

8. What do you believe to be the most significant problem facing the company as a whole?

9. What do you believe to be the most important problem facing this company's industry?

10. What are the most significant things the company is doing to deal with these problems?

keep that point in mind—and it would probably help if you passed that word to the legal staff, too.

The fact is that the final wording of the annual report is frequently the result of a clash between writer and lawyer. Attorneys should have the last word in matters of law, but too often attorneys are given the last word, period—even regarding writing style. And that can be bad news for simple writing. "If a man draws a document that only he can interpret," Gunning writes, "he has built himself a degree of security. He must be retained to interpret it." [14]

Attorneys would not all lose their jobs if their writing became more understandable. And most lawyers don't intentionally confuse things. But most lawyers are simply not good writers. They are not trained as writers. So when it comes to issues of style, the professional writer must have the last word. One critic of annual reports commented on this situation:

> I don't know whether it would be better for PR men to redraft what the lawyers have written, or for the lawyers to review the work product of the communication expert, but I do know that we must do a better job of telling the company's story—good or bad—if the purpose of the securities laws are to be fulfilled.[15]

Timing

Clearly, an annual report is a major project for any firm, and it is critical that the report be issued on time. That means setting and meeting deadlines over a long period. It is not unusual for the production of an annual report, from its inception at the planning stage until its delivery to the audience, to take six or seven months. One reason it takes so long to produce a good annual report is that the writer has to await the final version of the financial data at the close of the fiscal year before wrapping up the final details. Then the final report has to be approved at many levels in the organization.

There is no foolproof method of scheduling and producing an annual report. However, you should review the approximate schedule of a typical annual report of a company whose regulatory agencies require copies no later than March 31 of each year, as shown in Table 11-4. This timetable will not work for every company or institution, but it will serve as a rough guideline for most situations.

Conclusions

* The prose in annual reports is often very bad.
* There is often a conflict between telling the truth and looking good.
* Annual reports must, by law, tell the truth, but they often mask the truth with foggy writing.
* Writing in annual reports should be clear and simple.
* Preparation of good annual reports includes careful planning, definition of purpose and identification of important audiences.
* Some major divisions of content of annual reports are the chief executive's letter, which sets the stage for the entire report; the narrative description of the company's operations for the last year; expectations for the future; and financial summaries.
* Writing style may range from informal to formal, but purpose behind the report can also influence style.
* Production of an annual report is usually spread over several months. This is due, at least in part, to the fact that content has to clear through so many levels in the organization.

11-4

Annual Report Timetable
Source: Reprinted by permission of World Industries, Inc., Lancaster, PA.

This is a sample production timetable for the annual report of a company whose regulatory agencies require a copy of the report by March 31.

September: Begin preliminary planning.

October: Send questionnaires to company executives. Compile research from company publications and other sources on events of the year.

November: Interview executives. Decide on theme and approach. Begin cover design. Collect photographs and assign additional needed photographs to the photographer. Begin production of charts and graphs and other artwork.

December: Begin writing preliminary draft of chief executive's letter and narrative. Complete photographs and artwork, except for financial charts.

January: Circulate draft of narrative for review by various company departments. Begin layout and design. Revise draft of chief executive's letter and narrative as required.

February: Circulate final draft of letter and narrative for approval by executives, lawyers, auditors and other company departments. Make final corrections. Complete layout and design. Have type set on narrative, letter and financial tables (if available). Deliver camera-ready copy to printer by end of the month.

March: Review proofs provided by printer. Make final corrections.

Exercises

1. Get a copy of an annual report from a publicly held company and another from a foundation. Do a written comparative analysis of:
   a. Purpose
   b. Audiences

c. Content

d. Style

2. Review the executive's letter in the publicly held annual report. Rewrite at least two paragraphs from it that you consider foggy. Turn in your version as well as a copy of the original.

3. The president of Ourbank asks you to prepare the executive's letter that will appear in Ourbank's next annual report. Submit a draft.

Notes

[1] William Zinsser, *On Writing Well* (New York: Harper & Row, 1976), p. 139.

[2] Darrell Luery, "Keeping a Finger on the Public Pulse and the Corporate Thumb off the Scale," *Public Relations Journal* 28 (February 1972): 15.

[3] Robert Gunning, *The Technique of Clear Writing* (New York: McGraw-Hill, 1968), p. 227.

[4] Ibid., p. 227.

[5] Robert Mayall, "Sensitizing Your Management to the Needs of the Annual Report," *Public Relations Journal* 33 (September 1977): 16.

[6] Jane Bryant Quinn, *Everyone's Money Book* (New York: Dell, 1979).

[7] Rudolph Flesch, *The Art of Readable Writing*, 25th anniversary ed. (New York: Harper & Row, 1974), p. 135.

[8] "Annual Report Credibility," *Public Relations Journal* 40 (November 1984): 31.

[9] Peg Dardeene, "Emerging Trends in Annual Reports," *Public Relations Journal* 33 (September 1977): 8.

[10] Mayall, p. 13.

[11] Opinion Research Corporation, "Guidelines for Communicating Effectively with the Investment World," October 1975, p. 6.

[12] Leo Northart, "Editor's Notebook," *Public Relations Journal* 33 (September 1977): 6.

[13] "Making Sense of Annual Reports," *Money* 14 (March 1985): 201–202.

[14] Gunning, p. 244.

[15] Luery, p. 16.

Selected Bibliography

"Annual Report Credibility," *Public Relations Journal* 40 (November 1984): 31–34.

Peg Dardenne, "Emerging Trends in Annual Reports," *Public Relations Journal* 33 (September 1977): 8, 48.

Joseph J. Graves, "Critical Questions and Honest Answers: Spice for Effective Annual Reports," *Public Relations Journal* 33 (September 1977): 17–18.

Robert Gunning, *The Technique of Clear Writing*, rev. ed. (New York: McGraw-Hill, 1968).

Darrell Luery, "Keeping a Finger on the Public Pulse and the Corporate Thumb off the Scale," *Public Relations Journal* 28 (February 1972): 14–16, 45–46.

"Making Sense of Annual Reports," *Money* 14 (March 1985): 201–204.

Robert Mayall, "Sensitizing Your Management to the Needs of the Annual Report," *Public Relations Journal* 33 (September 1977): 12–16.

Leo J. Northart, "Editor's Notebook," *Public Relations Journal* 33 (September 1977): 6.

Opinion Research Corporation, "Guidelines for Communicating Effectively with the Investment World," October 1975.

Jane Bryant Quinn, *Everyone's Money Book* (New York: Dell, 1979).

S. D. Warren Company, "Ins & Outs," 1981.

12
Magazines and Employee Relations

Magazines can be a powerful public relations tool. They allow a greater depth of treatment than most other media, permit more vivid and attractive display and enable writers to compose messages for specific target audiences.

Sometimes that audience is internal—when a magazine is published for the employees of an institution, for example. Sometimes it is external, as with magazines like *EXXON USA*, which go to the media and to community leaders. By one estimate, more than 10,000 public relations magazines are published in the United States.

The success of such publications is determined in part by format, illustrations and design, editing and proper distribution. But the most important element of any magazine is the writing—its quality, its relevance and its appropriateness for the target audience. The most beautifully designed, illustrated and printed magazine in the world cannot sustain success without well-written articles, because it won't communicate much.

Topics

It may seem trite, but it is nevertheless true that if you expect to succeed as a magazine writer, you must give priority to developing good topics for articles. Sometimes, your topics will be assigned to you by your superiors, but more than likely you will be left to your own devices most of the time. While a good writer can usually make a mundane topic interesting, success can be assured only with a consistent inventory of good article ideas.

Finding Topics

If you know your readers well, certain topics will virtually suggest themselves. Your own flashes of insight may not be sufficient, however, to fill every issue of the magazine you work on. Fortunately, they won't have to. There are other sources for article ideas.

First, however, let's talk more about knowing your readers. As a writer, you need to move about your organization and get to know people from all areas of operation. You can't know everyone personally, of course, but you should get to know at least a few people in every area. Personnel can be good sources of ideas, and they also can be foils against which you can gauge the value of an idea.

It is becoming common for firms or organizations to perform what is called a communication audit. This is a systematic form of evaluation of the effectiveness of the organization's communication programs, including the magazine, if one is issued. These audits zero in on strengths and weaknesses in the organization's communication program. Some of these findings become fodder for good magazine articles. (See Example 12-1.)

Managements will sometimes conduct organization-wide employee surveys. These may include readers of the magazine who are customers or who have more than a passing interest in what goes on there. Such surveys may be treasure troves for article ideas.

Public opinion surveys, like those done by George Gallup and others, are a common source of ideas. They regularly take the pulse of the American public. You should make it a practice to read, study, clip and save these polls for future reference. Even if the topic of the poll report seems unrelated to your firm or industry, analysis later on may show otherwise.

Additionally, you must regularly consult both local and national newspapers and a variety of consumer magazines. Clip (or copy) items that strike your interest, even if a specific article idea does not leap at you. Watch both network and local television news, public affairs and special events programs. Listen to a broad spectrum of local radio stations, and tune in some of the news and commentary programs on public radio.

It should be obvious, of course, that you must read the appropriate professional, trade, industrial and scholarly journals. And you should go to meetings of all types. These can range from local service club meetings to national professional conventions. The point is that you must go.

Any one or all of these may be the source of an idea. And an article idea may come when you least expect it. The idea you want won't come looking for you. You have to be on the alert all the time. If you're not tuned in, you may not recognize it. The clue may be a word or a phrase, even out of context, or a major event. You have to pay attention to what goes on around you.

12-1

Magazine-Audience Audit
The Eagle is published by Anheuser-Busch Companies, Inc.
for employees and retirees. This report on the results of a
communications audit is but one of many similar features
about the company and its personnel. *Source:* Courtesy of
Anheuser-Busch Companies, Inc.

The Anheuser-Busch Eagle

We asked and you told us...
COMMUNICATION AUDIT

The results of the Employee Communication Audit conducted in the Fall of 1984 show that A-B employees give the company high marks for the effectiveness of its corporate communication efforts.

The best measure of an organization's communication effectiveness is what employees believe about the organization and about how it treats them. The audit indicated that employees have very positive beliefs about A-B and how it communicates with them.

That's not to say there is no room for improvement. Some methods of communication are seen as more effective than others. Also some audiences believe the company communicates better than do others. The most variation in responses was between hourly and salaried employees.

The audit questionnaire was send to a random sample of more than 2,500 Anheuser-Busch Companies employees last September. Approximately 36% of the surveys were returned, an excellent rate—and one that gives a high level of confidence in the results. Many employees also took the time to write in comments with thoughtful suggestions for improvements.

In its report, the independent consultants who conducted the audit said that by "using innovative and high quality communication vehicles—from publications to direct mail to meetings to contests—Anheuser-Busch corporate communications have helped create a sense of family and strong loyalty to the company. A-B employees firmly believe in the company's drive to stay number one, in its devotion to quality and its commitment to growth.

"The fact is that Anheuser-Busch communicates with its employees better than most organizations. And it can be rightly pleased with the results of this study. Yes, there are areas where improvements can be made. But those improvements will only make a great company greater."

The Employee Communication Audit was conducted by Savlin/Williams Associates, Inc., a communication consulting firm in Evanston, Ill. The Corporate Communications Department coordinated the audit with the consultant.

The research techniques used included focus groups of employees to elicit broad-based information about the communication atmosphere at Anheuser-Busch Companies; open ended interviews with management members; and a confidential questionnaire, which was sent to a random sample of Anheuser-Busch Companies employees.

A valid statistical methodology was used and a conservative approach was taken in handling the statistics. The sample was established with the goal being to have a 95 percent level of confidence in the answers. For example, many of the questions were rated on a scale of 1 to 10. If the mean on any response was 8.0 and the standard error .05, then we can be 95 percent confident that the "real" answer falls between 7.95 and 8.05.

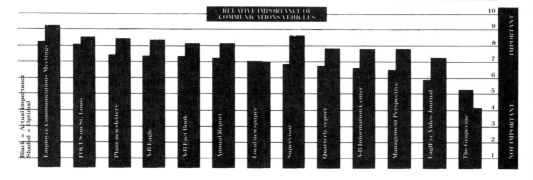

RELATIVE IMPORTANCE OF COMMUNICATIONS VEHICLES

Purpose of audit

The audit was conducted to evaluate the effectiveness of current corporate communications and to determine what information employees want and need. Management's communication needs were also evaluated. The audit is part of A-B's ongoing effort to produce quality communication programs and strive for excellence in all endeavors.

What's next

The information gleaned from the audit will be used to develop a long-term communication plan and to improve the effectiveness of current communication programs.

Short-term, based on the audit's results, the following activities are already under way:

1) A communication plan is being developed to tie closely to the company's strategic goals.

2) The A-B Golf Classic Drawing program will be eliminated. This contest was rated low in importance by most employees.

3) Specific comments and results about all of the individual communication vehicles are being closely studied and each vehicle analyzed. For example, comments about the **A-B Eagle** regarding length of articles and coverage of plants and breweries will be considered in light of employees' communication needs.

4) The Corporate Communications Department is looking at its efforts in assisting plant newsletter editors with local communication, because of the importance employees placed on plant newsletters and their need for more local information.

5) The need for various home mailings is being closely studied. Most employees like to receive information at home, but some felt that they received too much mail from the company. The volume was perceived as inconsistent with the objective of cutting costs—a message most employees have heard loud and clear.

Already a system is being tested in St. Louis to deliver certain information, formerly mailed to the home, to employees through the Department Head mailing system. In December, the Photo Contest Calendar was distributed through Information Centers instead of being mailed.

In the future, more changes are probable, as current programs are revised or replaced with new ones. We'll keep you informed on changes as they're made.

Following are some highlights of the audit's results:

Beliefs about the company

The audit showed that employees overall strongly agree with certain messages that the company communicates. They believe an objective is to produce quality products, (mean: 9.506 out of 10.00) and another to grow and diversify (mean: 9.374). Many agreed strongly that an A-B objective is to stay number one (mean: 8.549). The only statement about A-B that received lukewarm agreement was that ''job security is adequately explained'' (mean: 6.029). This is another area we will study.

Communication vehicles

Employees generally believe that existing communication vehicles are important.

They were rated as follows: 1)Employee Communications Meetings; 2)FOCUS on St. Louis; 3)Plant newsletters; 4)A-B Eagle; 5)Fact Book; 6)Annual Report; 7)Local newspaper; 8)Supervisor; 9)Quarterly Report; 10)Information Centers; 10)Management Perspective; 11)EaglEye Video Journal; and 12)the grapevine. The ratings ran from a low of 5.340 (the grapevine) to a high of 8.319 (the communications meetings). The scale was 1.0 (lowest) to 10.0 (highest).

In general employees believe that most vehicles should be even more important, especially the supervisor.

Employees generally give communication from headquarters high marks; however, they are hungry for information about their own work location or subsidiary. Many commented they wanted to hear news that affected them from headquarters, and in a timely fashion. This will be studied.

Regarding the **A-B Eagle**, most employees (77.5%) read most or all of it.

Thank you

A special thanks to all who responded to this audit. In the future, you will hear and read more about changes and improvements in our corporate communications programs, and we will refer to the appropriate audit results at that time.

Evaluating Topics

Really, finding good ideas for articles is not that difficult. The hard part is recognizing which ones are good and which are bad. Once you get an idea for an article, you must evaluate it by considering two criteria: reader interest and reader consequences.

Reader Interest   The first question to ask about a topic is, Will the audience be interested in it? To answer that question you have to know your audience—their interests, predispositions, likes and dislikes.

Are you writing for business leaders who are intensely interested in the state of the economy? Are you writing for a blue-collar group with less than a high school education? Are your readers professional people who are interested in job performance and growth? Is your magazine aimed at consumer advocates, government regulators, university professors? Unless you know your audience, you might as well evaluate your articles by consulting fortune cookies. And if you publish articles that do not address the interests of your audience, you're wasting a lot of time, money and trees.

Consequence   The value of an article idea is also gauged by its consequences to the reader. That is, the article must be important to the reader as well as interesting. It has to have "consequence" for the reader. Even where good intuition helps you evaluate interest you may trip over consequence. The reason is that some ideas that don't bubble with interest do have consequence. They are important to readers. Good writers or editors will tell you that they try to make their magazines mixtures of articles they think people want to read with articles readers ought to read.

The real problem comes when lack of interest gets in the way of reading something that is important to your readers. As a writer, this is a terrific challenge. You will have to work doubly hard to make the story so good readers can't pass it up. Even if you can't make the story interesting you should make it clear why the story is important. This may inspire more people to read it.

Angle

Making the importance of a story clear is not always easy. Readers may not recognize immediately, for example, that an article has consequence for them. You have to grab the readers' attention and draw them into the story by informing them at the outset that there is some point to the article. That is, you must tell the story with a specific approach, called an *angle* or *slant*. The angle must hook readers, get them interested, and lead them naturally into the main topic or point of the article.

It is very difficult to write a good article without a good angle. Magazine articles can't simply be "about" something. An article that is merely "about" federal regulations does not sound interesting and it probably isn't. If it is clear that it is about federal safety regulations, however, and your readers are primarily people who work in the oil patch, they may have unusually high interest in the article because they recognize the consequence of poor safety.

On the other hand, if the story is "about" federal regulations in general and this is perceived as uninteresting, you can overcome the lack of interest with good writing. For example, a lead that begins with a sentence that says, "Federal regulations costs you $3.86 each working day," may spark interest, hitting as it does a central point of concern for almost everyone—the pocketbook.

An angle does not always leap to the front, either. For example, a writer was preparing an article for a university magazine about research in the biology department. At the time, several professors in the department were collaborating on a research project on Asian clams. That's hardly a fascinating topic in itself, but the idea of doing an article on clams was better, and more specific, than doing one on research in the biology department. But the angle was still missing. Further interviews uncovered the information that this species of clams reproduced at a rapid rate and was becoming so populous that the clams threatened to block some waterways, such as irrigation canals and industrial water supply lines. Here was the angle—at last. Small clams the size of a half-dollar were threatening to disrupt the water supply of giant industries. Again, notice that the writer did not come up with the angle immediately. First came the general topic. The specific angle was the result of alert research.

Research

Once you choose a general topic for an article, you have to research it. Research is a major component in magazine-article writing at several stages.

You have to do some general research on the background of the article idea so you'll know where to begin. At this stage, you may have a general idea of what you want to say or even the kind of conclusion subsequent research may support. If a conclusion comes early in your research, be wary of it, for you will be limited in your perspective on the information by selective perception. This may blind you to other points of view, making your article less effective than it otherwise might be.

This is not to say that your article should not make a point, or that it shouldn't come down on one side of an issue or another. In fact, most PR magazine articles do, and should, take a position on a particular issue. But you still want your research on the topic to be objective so that the weight of the evidence will support the side you take. If you reach a conclusion too early in your thinking, you might ignore information that may render your conclusion invalid. An article as full of holes as Swiss cheese is usually neither credible nor persuasive.

Research techniques for writing magazine articles are similar to the general techniques of PR research discussed in Chapter 3. But it is helpful to follow a few basic steps in article research.

Background Research

First, you should do general background research on the topic. You may already know a great deal about your topic. If you don't, however, find out how your topic fits into the overall scheme of things. An article about inflation, for example, requires some general knowledge of economics.

Next, become more specific—narrow your research down to the topic of your article. You should check the *Readers' Guide to Periodical Literature* (or other appropriate bibliographies) to find out what has been written and who has spoken on the topic recently.

Reviewing these articles and speeches will give you helpful background on the topic, and will tell you what your audience has been reading—assuming that you know (and you should) which magazines your audience reads. For example, if your audience includes university science professors, you know they probably read *Science*. Ministers probably read *The Christian Century*. You need to know what your audience reads so you can avoid duplicating what is now old news. Offer them something they haven't read before, or at least a new perspective on an old idea.

After reviewing what your audience are likely to have read, go to what they probably haven't read—technical and trade journals, limited circulation newsletters or government documents, for example. Compile from these sources the facts and figures you will need to build your article.

Pay special attention to figures. The right statistics here and there can help make an article measurably better, and if you don't write them down when you come across them you'll have trouble finding them later. It's hard to know ahead of time which statistics you'll need, so note all the facts and figures you can find that are possibly relevant.

At this stage you are probably ready to form some possible approaches to the article. Try to find angles that haven't been explored in publications to date. Once you have arrived at some tentative angles and have focused your research on specific material that will help you decide on the best angle, you're ready for step two of the research process: interviewing.

Interviewing

Some of the best material for your article will come from personal interviews with experts on the topic. Interviews not only provide additional information and insight, but they can also give you the direct quotations and anecdotes you need to bring a dull article to life.

In most settings, there will be an ample number of experts within your organization on whom you can call for help and information. However, you may occasionally need to call an outside expert, like a university professor. Or if you're writing about federal regulations, you might want to call one of the regulators.

There are a few basic interviewing protocols you should follow whether you're talking with people inside or outside your organization.

Let the person to be interviewed know ahead of time what it is you want to talk about. Give him or her a chance to prepare, especially if you will be asking specific questions that may require some research before your interview. Remember that this is not a *news* situation in the usual sense of the term. And let the interviewee know ahead of time that you want him or her to read the story before it is published to verify its accuracy.

Prepare a list of questions in advance. Design the questions in such a way that they will encourage the person you are interviewing to open up and extend the discussion into relevant areas you had not anticipated.

Don't ask leading questions at the outset. Be as neutral as you can with your questions, at least early in the interview. As the session progresses, it may be appropriate to ask specific leading questions to clarify points of view.

Use a tape recorder, but first ask the interviewee for permission to turn it on. Then make the recorder as inconspicuous as possible. For example, turn it on and leave it on. Then it usually is ignored. Even though you may use a recorder, always take notes. Do this for three reasons: (1) Writing down salient information will help you get into the flow of the conversation and understand points more clearly. Remember that writing demands thought. (2) The person being interviewed is generally pleased to see you making notes of what he or she has said. Note-taking confers importance to what is being said. (3) Machines don't always work.

Writing

Once you've researched the subject and determined the angle, you're ready to write. And the best place to start is at the beginning—with the lead.

The Lead

William Zinsser says, "The most important sentence in any article is the first one."[1] It is axiomatic that if readers don't finish the first sentence, they aren't likely to go to the second. And they'll never read the third sentence or anything else you have to say.

So the lead must do two things. It must grab the readers' attention and it must tell the readers what the article is about.

A bland, dull lead that says nothing a reader does not already know isn't likely to induce anyone to read on. To attract attention leads should be concrete and visual. They should offer something that readers can relate to and understand. If the lead is about unfamiliar things, the reader is likely to think the article won't be interesting. You must link unfamiliar material in the lead to something that is familiar.

The lead must state the central point of the piece. Let the reader know at the outset what the article is about and what the point is. You can't expect a reader to read through several sentences or paragraphs to find out what the topic is.

The lead can be the first sentence, the first few sentences or, in some cases, the first few paragraphs. It can be a simple, direct statement; it can be a quotation; it can even be an anecdote that illustrates the main point of the article. Any device can be used, as long as it gets the readers' attention and informs them of the point of the article.

For example, here is a simple lead that makes an article about Easter eggs seem interesting:

> In the southwestern corner of the Soviet Union, decorating Easter eggs is not child's play. In fact, children there are often forbidden to touch the Easter eggs, much less hide them and play with them.[2]

This first paragraph creates interest, and the next paragraph immediately discloses the subject of the article:

> The reason for this "adults only" egg is because Ukrainian Easter eggs are unlike any other decorated eggs you have ever seen. These gaily colored, intricately designed eggs are, indeed, works of art that often remain on display for decades. Called *pysanky*, the Ukrainian eggs are carefully, and even secretly, designed and dyed each year as part of a religious tradition that dates to 988 A.D., when the Ukraine accepted Christianity.*

This lead succeeds because the writer did not simply write that "Easter Eggs are something special in the Ukraine." Instead, he found an interesting angle—Easter Eggs that children aren't allowed to hide or play with. And he didn't let the angle he selected get in the way of telling readers exactly what the article was about. In other words, the lead flowed naturally into the body of the story.

Once the flow of the lead to the body gets the reader going, the flow must continue to keep the reader interested all the way through the article. To accomplish this, the article must be properly developed.

Development

The purpose of the body of the article is to support and develop the point made in the lead. The point must be amplified and extended to clarify its implications and importance. The story must flow smoothly and logically, with each paragraph leading naturally to the next and each paragraph adding something to the story.

As the article develops, you should answer the questions that will naturally come into the readers' minds. Make sure these answers are linked closely with what comes before and what follows, so that the reader will be able to see how each bit of information fits into the picture. This requires close attention to the transitions between sentences and between paragraphs.

---

* Proper editing would have changed "988 A.D." to "A.D. 988." B.C. follows dates; A.D. precedes them; and "because" in the first sentence becomes "that."

Besides amplifying the point made in the lead, the body of the article must also verify and illustrate it. It is one thing to make a bold statement in an interesting way to grab the readers' attention. It is something else to convince them that your point of view has merit.

Verification and Illustration

You can't communicate effectively by assuming that readers will accept and absorb your statements as given to them. Generalizations must be supported with specific examples. Statements of fact that are not general knowledge should be attributed to an appropriate source. Contentions should be backed up with solid evidence.

Frequently you can support your position simply by stating the relevant facts. Just remember that "facts" are not opinions. They are indisputable, observable or recorded pieces of information that can be readily verified.

Some facts can be used without any specific attribution or further verification because they are so well known—"George Washington was the first President of the United States," for example. Feel free to use similar facts that can be found in any standard reference work, like "Columbus is the capital of Ohio" or "Alaska is the largest state in the Union."

Other facts—like statistics and survey results, for example—are also useful, but in most instances these should be attributed to their source. If you use the results of a public opinion poll, include important information like who took the poll and when it was taken. Furthermore, when using survey results or statistics take care that the figures you cite are really applicable to the situation at hand.

For less well-known facts you should also give a source, whether a document or an expert in the field. A quote from an authority can be used to verify statements of opinion as well. But be sure the person you quote has the expertise necessary for forming an intelligent opinion on the topic.

Sometimes straight facts won't make your case, especially if they are unfamiliar to readers. So you must illustrate your point with specific examples. If you are writing about marine geology and want to make the point that vast mountain ranges are found beneath the ocean surface, it might not be enough to say just that. Give an example—the Mid-Atlantic Ridge, say, which winds down the Atlantic and even pierces the surface of Iceland.

Another device that might help you illustrate your case is the analogy—an example of a parallel relationship between your subject and an unrelated but easier-to-grasp idea. For example, if you are trying to explain how utility rates are set, you might draw an analogy with the charges for renting a car, something that most people will more readily understand. Remember, though, that analogies don't prove anything. They merely illustrate and clarify points of information.

A good lead, logical development and adequate verification are the skeleton of an article. Good articles must then be fleshed out; the story must be brought to life. Readers must be given pictures to help them visualize what you are telling them.

Good writers use devices that involve the readers in the article. Some of the methods for doing this are anecdotes, direct quotations, humanization, dramatization and description.

Anecdotes

One of the best devices for involving the reader in a piece of writing is the anecdote. As Stanford Professor Bill Rivers says, "No other element of an article is more important."[3] Anecdotes break monotony, illustrate points and give readers something to visualize. If they deal with familiar things, anecdotes can help people relate to the subject of the article. Anecdotes "show" readers something rather than merely telling about it.

Quotations

Another way to break monotony and make writing more natural is to use direct quotations. Quotations help make the writing more personal, more like conversation, and therefore more readable.

Be careful about using too many quotations, however. They can add to interest, but often a direct quote doesn't make the point in the clearest possible way. It is best to make a point in your own words and then use a quotation to amplify or illustrate it.

As for style, the writing is usually more effective when the quote begins the sentence and the source is identified in the middle (if it's a long quote) or at the end.

Humanization

Whenever you write, you are writing for people. And people are more interested in people than in other things. As a general guide, people are interested first in themselves and then in others. Always look for the aspects of a subject that touch the lives of people. Use personal words and phrases where you can, and address the reader directly if it fits the situation.

One of the best places to find examples of humanizing is the *Wall Street Journal*. The *Journal's* front-page feature stories invariably begin not with economic facts and figures, but with an example of a specific person in a specific city. That person's problems (or business or economic situation) introduce a subject more general in scope. The facts and figures follow to verify and illustrate the point of the article. But the story is introduced and told in human terms.

When a *Journal* writer did a piece on a trend toward the four-day workweek, for example, she had at her disposal such statistics as 1.2 million Americans (2 percent of the full-time labor force) already work four-day weeks. The lead, though, began like this:

> South Padre Island, a Texas resort area, was nearly deserted when Terry and Vicki Shea and their two sons arrived for a winter weekend late last year. They had driven 300 miles to the national

seashore from their San Antonio home on Thursday night. They had the whole place to themselves the next day, but by noon Saturday hordes of sunseekers were swarming over the beach. . . . Ralph and Cindee Hurlburt also have their Fridays off. . . . What Mr. Shea and the Hurlburts have in common is that their Fridays are free regularly, and so are their Saturdays and Sundays. They are among an estimated 1.2 million Americans for whom the four-day workweek, with all its attendant problems and pleasures, has become a reality. . . .

Dramatization

The humanization of writing is best accomplished by placing the topic in some dramatic context. A discussion of a new medicine, for example, could be limited to a dry description of the chemical composition of the medicine and its biochemical action inside the body. Or the story could be told in the context of a doctor treating patients. Often such dramatization can keep a reader, who would otherwise not read it, involved with an article.

Description

Good description can be hard to write, but it can also be an important factor in conveying a complete picture to your readers. Readers will understand and retain more information if you can place a picture in their heads. That's what description is all about: painting pictures in the mind.

One way to illustrate or describe something unfamiliar is to compare it with familiar things. It's not very helpful to say that a new machine is "big." But if you say it is "as big as a typical house," the words create a visual image in the mind's eye. The reader can relate to an average house and, while he or she may never see the machine, an idea of its size is communicated clearly. Skillful use of simile and metaphor can make your message clearer, livelier and more interesting to read.

All these devices for involving readers apply to magazine articles for just about any audience. But for certain specific audiences, there is more to consider. The employees make up an audience of special concern to most organizations.

Employee Publications

Most companies or institutions have an employee publication of some sort. Refer to Example 12-1 for an example. Often the employee publication is a full-fledged magazine; sometimes it looks more like a newspaper or newsletter. But whatever the format, the writing in employee publications should follow most closely the style of magazine articles.

Why? Because even if an employee publication looks like a newspaper or a newsletter, it rarely functions as a medium for hard news. Unless it comes

317

out daily (and few, if any, do), an employee publication cannot compete with other information sources available to employees. Informal communication networks among supervisors and secretaries can spread news faster in the organization than can the AP wire. And when important events occur or major decisions are made, they are generally announced at once rather than held for publication in the next month's employee magazine.

Furthermore, employee publications can be an extremely potent tool of internal public relations, and they should be used to accomplish more than telling of the shop foreman's new baby or the vice president's successful fishing trip. (This is known as the dead-fish-and-live-babies syndrome.) As experienced employee publication editor Don Fabun points out, employee publications today must appeal not only to the switchboard operator, but "to an atomic physicist, a systems engineer, a market analyst, and an operations analyst. These latter are not likely to be interested in, or motivated by, bowling scores and a detailed account of the company picnic."[4]

Employee publications can help generate support among employees for corporate goals and objectives. Articles can build employee morale and enhance job satisfaction, thus boosting productivity. Publications can create a broader understanding among employees of the problems a company faces.

How can these goals be accomplished? Mainly by keeping such objectives in mind when you're writing articles for employees, and by following the principles of magazine writing outlined earlier in this chapter. Specifically, you must orient the writing to the reader. Explain the significance of events from the point of view of the employee—not from the point of view of the board of directors. In other words, don't relate verbatim a new company policy as handed down from on high. *Explain* the policy and tell what it means to the reader. But explain it in an interesting way—find a good angle, write a good lead and make the article as human and dramatic as possible.

If you take this approach, your firm's employee publication can be a valuable asset to any organization. Articles about a company's achievements in research can generate pride among the employees, giving them a good feeling about being part of the company. Articles about the need to save energy or improve safety records can motivate employees to improve their performance in those areas. Articles about the relationship between your company and the well-being of the community can give employees a sense of involvement in a socially useful occupation. Articles emphasizing the accomplishments of individuals can be an incentive to other workers.

If you write articles on such subjects skillfully, so that employees will read them, you can accomplish much more than you would with a publication written strictly for entertainment or for relating social fluff. This does *not* mean that an employee publication should be a propaganda piece for the view of management. Rather, such a publication can be mutually beneficial to both the individual employees and the organization as a whole. See Table 12-2 for a checklist for magazine-article writing.

12-2

Checklist for Magazine-Article Writing

1. Is the lead interesting and specific? Does it approach the story from a slant or angle designed to catch the reader's interest?

2. Is the idea in the lead developed and supported by the rest of the article?

3. Are statements verified or properly attributed? Are general statements supported with specific examples?

4. Are anecdotes used throughout the article, both as illustrations and as devices to increase reader interest?

5. Has sufficient use been made of direct quotations?

6. Is the writing dramatic? Has the story been told in human terms?

7. Is description adequate to give the reader an accurate picture of the subject?

Conclusions

* Magazine articles offer vast public relations opportunities to writers.

* Finding topics for magazine articles is not terribly difficult but evaluating them may be.

* Reader interest is one criterion for gauging the value of an article idea. Reader consequence—or importance—is another. Even if an idea is low in interest, it may be important enough to write anyway.

* One of the keys to effective magazine article writing is to identify a clear angle or slant and use it. A good angle is sometimes hidden and can't be discovered without extensive research.

* Backgrounding the article is critical and the use of interviews is common.

* The actual writing should first give priority to constructing a lead that attracts readers and holds their interest. The body of the piece has to develop, verify and illustrate the central point of the article.

* Anecdotes, quotations, human interest, dramatization, and description are techniques that involve readers with your writing. Use them.

* Employee publications should use the magazine-article-writing style rather than the hard-news style.

* Employee publications done well can contribute a lot to the success of the organization.

Exercises

1. Select a feature story from the *Wall Street Journal* and do a written analysis of its writing style. Analyze the lead and the body. Identify the elements of human interest, anecdotes, quotations, dramatization and description, and then explain how these helped make the story interesting.

2. Assume you are a writer on the staff of an electric utility firm and you have been assigned to do a feature on emerging trends in power generation. Develop an angle and write a lead for the story. Provide a full, written explanation that justifies your use of the angle and the lead.

3. Write a comparison of the feature-writing styles in your local newspaper with those you see in a consumer magazine of your choice.

4. You are a systems analyst with the phone company. Write a feature story about your hobby that will appear in the monthly employee publication.

5. As part of the overall promotional plan for Ourbank, you write a feature story to appear in the state's banking magazine. It will emphasize Ourbank's communication program. Also, provide a description of visuals that will accompany the article.

Notes

[1] William Zinsser, *On Writing Well* (New York: Harper & Row, 1980), p. 59.

[2] B. R. Hughes, "Ukrainian Easter Eggs," *Fort Worth*, April 1976, p. 35.

[3] William L. Rivers, *Free-Lancer and Staff Writer*, 4th ed. (Belmont, Calif.: Wadsworth, 1986, p. 306.

[4] Don Fabun, "Company Publications," in *Lesly's Public Relations Handbook*, ed. Philip Lesly (Englewood Cliffs, N.J.: Prentice-Hall, 1971), p. 135.

Selected Bibliography

Don Fabun, "Company Publications," in *Lesly's Public Relations Handbook*, ed. Philip Lesly (Englewood Cliffs, N.J.: Prentice-Hall, 1971), pp. 134–143.

William L. Rivers, *Free-Lancer and Staff Writer*, 4th ed. (Belmont, Calif.: Wadsworth, 1986).

13
Newsletters
and Brochures

Among the media often used by PR professionals to reach their publics are newsletters and brochures.

The term *newsletter* refers to a variety of publications sent regularly to members of organizations or special interest groups. A newsletter combines some of the characteristics of both a newspaper and a letter.

Brochure is a term that, used in the strict sense, signifies printed pieces of six or more pages, published only once and distributed to special publics for a single purpose. Used loosely, the term may also refer to pamphlets, booklets, flyers, circulars, leaflets and tracts.

Pamphlets are generally smaller than brochures and have less color and fewer illustration. *Booklets* range from pamphlet-like publications of a few pages up to publications the size of a small monograph. *Flyers* and *circulars* are usually single sheets that may be mailed, often in bulk, or distributed directly (like those you may find stuck on your windshield in a parking lot). *Leaflets* are similar but they are usually folded, although not stapled or trimmed. *Tracts* are pamphlets or booklets whose content promotes a political or religious point of view.

Newsletters

The main purpose of newsletters is to communicate regularly with members of a group. Sharing of information with members is a principal way the organization sustains itself. This is as true for a firm and its relations to employees as for members of a group bound together only by a special interest.

Employee Newsletters

Good managers know that the success of the firm or institution rests on the cooperation and support of employees as much as on their own managerial skills. As the organization grows and it becomes increasingly difficult to communicate policy on a personal basis, a newsletter is usually developed for this purpose.

Internal Communication   Newsletters thus become a principal channel of internal communication. (See Example 13-1.) Their content is carefully selected, written and presented to convey to employees as much about the organization as possible, especially information that helps them do their jobs better.

Employee newsletters are heavy on information and light on persuasion. This is true for corporations as well as for institutions. Since the corporation or institution is the employer, there is always at least implied persuasion. Both use newsletters to give employees a common experience and a feeling of belonging, and to promote identity and unity.

Personal Touch   Newsletters are often expected to help humanize what may otherwise be viewed as an impersonal relationship. Because of this, a common thread of content runs among newsletters: a focus on employee accomplishments.

Often these are work-related accomplishments. For example, an employee may be given special recognition in the firm's newsletter for having developed a new materials handling system that saves the firm thousands of dollars annually. The firm is obviously better because of the employee's contribution, which is acknowledged among his or her peers in the newsletter. Such recognition also implies that others can get the same kind of treatment if they contribute beyond the normal call of duty.

Employees are often recognized, too, as people worth knowing because of their dedication, skill or accomplishments in areas not related to their jobs. For example, Rose McKenna devotes many hours of volunteer service weekly to the Big Sisters program. Her drive and enthusiasm for the cause is a principal reason why the program has achieved such outstanding success over the last few years. Rose McKenna is someone you should know, not because she is one of three quality-control supervisors at the plant but because she is what she is. Firms and institutions routinely encourage employees to take an active interest in community affairs. When the Rose McKennas of the world do this they create good will toward the firm or institution, even if that is not their primary purpose.

13-1

Internal Newsletter
This newsletter from Liberty in Oklahoma City circulates to
employees as a means of keeping them briefed on what is
happening in the economy. This newsletter also circulates to
some non-employees, such as boards of directors and officers
of key clients of the bank. *Source*: Reprinted with permission
of Liberty National Bank and Trust Company.

LIBERTY
THE BANK OF MID-AMERICA

ECONOMIC REALITIES

MARCH 1985

Several times this week I sat down to write a cogent and coherent piece on the
recent happenings in Washington. It didn't work. What is happening in Washington today does not lend itself to cogent and coherent writing. A true reflection of
today in Washington must be amorphous and muddied. A kind of random walk
through The World's Largest Theme Park.

As we have been saying for several weeks now, it is increasingly unlikely that
Senate Majority Leader Robert Dole (R., Kans.) will be able to formulate and
clear through the Senate an ambitious deficit reduction package... ....So how
does it all come out? The answer is that things will have to get worse before they
get better. March will be devoted almost entirely to foreign policy issues - MX
missile, Nicaragua and arms talks. The latter conclude just in time for Congress
to go home for the April 5-14 Easter recess. This means May is the earliest
possible date for Senate action, and the House has no intention of doing
anything until the Senate acts.

Mark L. Melcher
Prudential-Bache Securites
Washington

The major reason that no concensus seems to be able to come out of Washington is that no one
really believes that there is a problem of major proportions with the current level of Federal spending.
Unless there is a "crisis" there is little concern about anything. The "if it ain't broke don't fix it"
mentality also seems to be the standard operating procedure on the Potomac. The problem is that
continued budget deficits of the $200 billion class are to be treated as almost commonplace. Such
unheard of deficits have been run for several years now and the "wheel has not fallen off yet" so there
must not be a lot to worry about. Employment is up and inflation is down and while some sectors have
been hurt by declines in commodity prices, the overall economy appears in reasonably good
condition. Underlying the continuing flow of basically good news is a growing number of concerns
that if not corrected will dominate the long run and possibly prove destructive.

13-1 | continued

The graph portrays the rise over the past 40 years of Federal Government outlays as a percentage of Gross National Product. The long term meaning of this chart is that Federal spending in relation of the entire economy is greater now than at any time in the post WW II experience with the exception of the

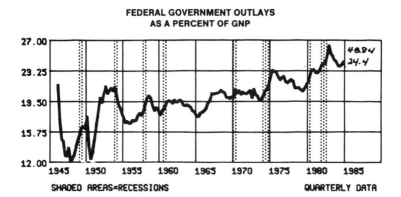

**FEDERAL GOVERNMENT OUTLAYS
AS A PERCENT OF GNP**

1982 recession and its aftermath. Two years into the current recovery, Federal spending continues to expand at a faster rate than the overall economy. The year to year change for the fourth quarter of 1984 was 9.8% for Federal spending compared to a 9.5% rise for the overall economy. With the large current backlog of appropriated but unspent funds on the part of the Defense Department and the gradual slowing in the private sector, no reversal in the Federal/private spending growth is to be expected.

For the most recent reported period, the expansion of Federal debt continues to outpace that of the private sector. The year-to-year expansion of Federal debt through December was 16.6% and for the private sector it was 12.8%. As can be seen with the help of the first two graphs, the expansion rate of

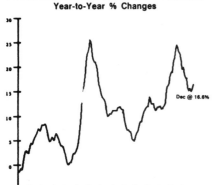

DOMESTIC NONFINANCIAL DEBT — FEDERAL
Year-to-Year % Changes

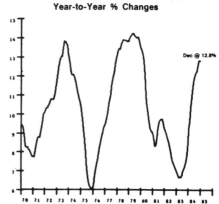

DOMESTIC NONFINANCIAL DEBT — OTHER
Year-to-Year % Changes

13-1 continued

Federal debt has slowed while the expansion rate has increased for the private economy as the economic recovery has matured. The combination of the two rates of increase is portrayed in the third graph. Since Federal debt has historically been a small part of overall debt, the total chart is more reflective of actions in the private sector. Continuations of the current deficit levels off into the future will gradually change this. Whatever the source, the increasing and slowing rates of debt expansion have basically mirrored the strengthening and weakening of the economy. An obvious concern from the last chart is that the U.S. seems to be headed toward another peaking in the rate of debt expansion which usually is related to a slowing that results in recession. The peaking of the economy and of demand for new debt does not coincide but they are related. The unfortunate part seems to be that the higher the peak in borrowing, the greater the decline on the other side and the longer it has taken for the system to reliquify and prepare for another round of growth. A related concern is that each recovery over the past fifteen years has required more rapid debt expansion in order to get the economy really roaring. The final outcome in the two previous expansions has been surging inflation and new peaks in interest rates.

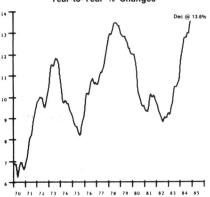

DOMESTIC NONFINANCIAL DEBT — TOTAL
Year-to-Year % Changes

This time around the rate of inflation has been very modest and continually below the levels that economists have predicted. This has been accomplished by a valuation on the dollar that has almost consistantly improved relative to the value of foreign currencies. The strength of the dollar and the need for foreigners to export resulted in a rising flow of low cost foreign goods or high priced status symbols that have tended to limit the demand for domestically produced goods. The U.S. consumer has enjoyed an improving standard of living. The U.S. industrial producer has had difficulty maintaining profit margins because of an inability to raise prices and has been losing market share to foreign product. Only because of the cut in effective tax rates since 1981 have many businesses been able to improve their cash flow. As can be seen from the next graph, along with the fall of the dollar during the late 1970's, a tremendous surge in net exports took place, partially as a result of massive dollar denominated loans to foreigners. The reverse of

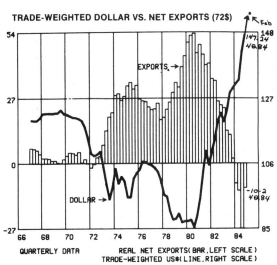

TRADE-WEIGHTED DOLLAR VS. NET EXPORTS (72$)

QUARTERLY DATA   REAL NET EXPORTS(BAR,LEFT SCALE)
                   TRADE-WEIGHTED US$(LINE,RIGHT SCALE)

13-1   continued

that has been seen since 1981 as the rush to collect those loans has developed, the discovery was made that many could not be serviced and the dollar strengthened almost without let up. The scramble to acquire dollars and the run up in the value of the U.S. dollar in conjunction with stimulative fiscal and monetary policy have meant that U.S. net exports have turned negative for the first time. Net exports during each quarter of 1984 were negative. In terms of 1972 (inflation adjusted) dollars the deficit in net exports was over $14 billion. In terms of current dollars the deficit was more than $60 billion. Because of the continued strength of the dollar this year and the rising realization that there are more values abroad, spending this year is likely to be even heavier than last. Running foreign trade deficits of this size means that foreigners are acquiring more and more U.S. dollar denominated financial assets. In other words, foreigners are financing no small portion of the current economic expansion. Some observers believe the U.S. is becoming a debtor nation for the first time since before WW I. The problem will be when it comes time to pay them off. If the dollar is weaker at that time then it will be all the more expensive to pay off the debts currently being built up. There are then two worrisome factors that are keeping the current expansion alive. These include rapid expansion of Federal and foreign held debt.

Another factor that will generally support an expansion is increased employment. From September 1984 to January 1985 U.S. employment rose by a monthly average of almost 300,000. In February the net increase was barely over 100,000. Production jobs declined by over 100,000 while service sector jobs increased by over 200,000. The drop in the former may have been the result of weather conditions. The determination of that will have to wait until the March data is out. In the meantime weekly figures for new unemployment claims have been rising modestly. This has been a traditional early indicator for weakness or strength in employment. Over this entire recovery there has been a much more rapid expansion on non-production jobs than industrial production jobs. The U.S. Labor Department has noted that employment in "business services" - such as personnel and data processing companies - has increased by over 30% over the past two years. One in every eight jobs created has been in this segment of employment. The long-term implication of the shift to a service economy is that production of goods will come to be done abroad while distribution and servicing will be handled domestically. The longer term implication is that if the dollar remains as relatively strong as currently then the U.S. may cease to be a major world industrial country. The parallel with Great Britain toward the end and following its colonial era is worrisome. British manufacturing could not compete with the flood of low priced goods from the colonies but a balance of trade was maintained by Britain exporting heavy industrial goods that the colonies were not allowed to start up. The British economy has not recovered from the breakdown of this mercantilist system after WW II.

In the post WW II era the U.S. through various international and domestic agencies has actively promoted the development abroad of many very complex industrial plants ranging from steel plants in the 1950's to oil refining and chemical plants during the 1970's. These plants were built as symbols of national pride in many cases rather than as a result of economic need. The pre-construction justification was as thinly veiled in economic feasability terms as many "pork-barrel" projects in the U.S. Once finished, they do provide "jobs" even if the product has nowhere to go. The result in many cases is that production must be continued with the excess beyond domestic needs dumped on the world market if for no other reason than to service the U.S. dollar denominated debt that built the plant. The excesses of the 1970's have come to haunt the rest of the world. The strong dollar and the expansion of debt has insulated the U.S. from having to face these problems.

13-1   continued

Capital goods spending is a segment that usually sustains the economy toward the end of an economic expansion. The sequence is as follows: (1) after rebuilding liquidity the consumer starts spending, (2) business sees inventories falling to less than comfortable levels, (3) business expands production and eventually hires more workers, (4) the newly employed start spending, everyone feels good and start borrowing to buy deferred items such as cars and houses, (5) capacity starts to run short and cash flow is up so business starts spending on new equipment and later on new plants, (6) the capital spending boom and finally borrowing to sustain it keep things rolling, (7) the consumer reaches a debt saturation level and slows spending, (8) business realizes that demand has fallen and cancels or stops capital spending, (9) recession follows. The next two charts show how rapidly consumer installment debt has expanded and how a new peak has been set relative to income. Of all the various indices available, this explosion in installment debt is the scariest in terms of the sustainability of the economic expansion. At levels well below the current highs the Carter Administration was placing on credit controls during early 1980. At the time it almost became unpatriotic to borrow. The result (along with other things) was a recession that basically did not end for two and three/quarter years (Feb. 1980 — Nov. 1982). Because of changes in the tax laws the capital goods spending recovery came on very early during this recovery. The availability of new computer products and the ability to rapidly depreciate them set off a spending boom. Much of that demand has now been satisfied and few feel that the year-to-year change from this point will be large. Capital spending in other segments (such as machines and plants) has been dynamic but less than might be expected considering the strength and duration of the recovery. The major reason is that operating rates (usage compared with plant production capacity) have not gone through the roof. The surge of imported products has limited the need to add to domestic capacity. As can be seen by the next chart, nondefense capital goods orders have fallen rapidly in recent months. This decline may not relate to an expectation that the economy has slowed as much as to concerns that

CONSUMER INSTALLMENT DEBT
Year-to-Year % Changes

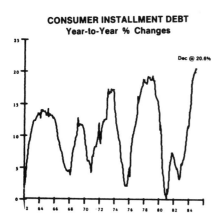

Dec @ 20.6%

CONSUMER INSTALLMENT DEBT
As a Percent of
WAGE & SALARY DISBURSEMENTS

Dec @ 25.2%

13-1 | continued

ORDERS CAPITAL GOODS NONDEFENSE

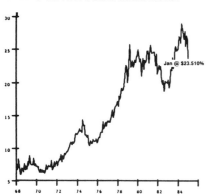

Jan @ $23.510%

the tax laws may again be changed. As mentioned, some capital spending may have been speeded because of law changes that made it more attractive. Such speedups ultimately make the downside drop that much worse. In the current instance, however, business may be taking a wait and see attitude about what, if anything, is actually passed. As the perception becomes stronger that the Congress and the Administration are not really going to do anything, spending may well again pickup. If that turns out to be the case then a revival of capital spending should show up by the end of the second quarter.

The recovery can be sustained in the face of a strong dollar and rising imports so long as debt continues to expand rapidly. The way it appears right now is that no one is concerned enough about the long-term effects of how this is all happening to do anything about it. If anyone describes a problem the solution continues to revolve around papering it over with more debt. The unfortunate part about this is that if enough debt fuel is dumped on the flames of prosperity, the flame can be suffocated. In the meantime, both monetary and fiscal policy seem to be motivated by concerns to keep growth alive for hopefully the next four years so that the U.S. can grow its way out of the deficit problem. The road may be bumpy but for now the expansion appears sustainable at real rates of expansion approaching 4%.

Charles B. Johnson
Trust Department

BOND POLICY

Interest rates rose during the first half of 1984 because of concerns about rising inflation and rapid economic expansion. Rates fell during the second half and until January 1985 as inflationary expectations fell, the dollar remained strong, the rate of economic growth slowed and the Federal Reserve loosened money growth. During January many bond buyers were almost in a panic to buy in the hope that rates would continue downward. Fed funds (interbank overnight loans) started rising in February and after a poorly placed 10 year and 30 year U.S. Treasury auction the market went briefly into free fall for lack of buyers. The dealers appear to have been particularly unprepared for a market decline. After the Federal Reserve and other central banks came in and sold dollars in a one day attempt to stop the dollar's rise, the market really collapsed, stabilized and then recovered as the perception developed that the intervention was not to be sustained and the early expansion numbers for 1985 may not be as large as originally perceived. From the bottom to the top, rates on long-term U.S. Treasury securities have risen by 1 percentage point so far this year. The single biggest jump took place when concerns developed about the continued strength of the dollar. The feeling is that if the dollar is perceived to be fundamentally weakening a rush out of it will mean that large blocks of funds will be pulled out of the U.S. financial markets. If that happens a major source of debt funding will be withdrawn and therefore, rates will rise rapidly assuming that debt generation continues as it has. If the dollar stays strong then the markets will have to find other things to discount.

13-1   continued

One of those things is that the reserves the Federal Reserve provided to the banking system at the
end of last year and during early 1985 will fuel a large volume of loans as this year moves on which

NONBORROWED RESERVES + EXTENDED CREDIT

Feb 27 @ $39.841

will mean that the expansion will not likely deteriorate over the next six months. The reserves that have been infused into the banking system provide the base upon which rapid loan expansion can be accomplished. The interest rate may not be at a level that appears cheap but the funding is available and so far there appears to be no unwillingness to borrow on the part of individuals, business or government. (Recent proposed borrowings in the tax exempt bond markets were as high as ever recorded). Funds are available for housing and autos and both sectors will likely be strong this year. Now that the Fed is no longer loosening, borrowing pressures from all segments of the economy can continue to push rates upward. Many segments of the economy will reach overextended levels during the next year but no one wants to consider the effects of that now

since there will be another election in 19 months. It is recommended that cash balances be
maintained and that purchases be made on market price dips of only the highest quality issuers.
Should the dollar suffer a major drop, rates could rise sharply.

STOCK POLICY

The stock market's upward momentum was brought to a halt in February. The major market indices
were virtually unchanged for the month. The principal factor that brought the stock market advance to
a standstill was the turnaround in the bond market. Increasing interest rates create a more competitive alternative investment vs. stocks. More recently the earnings outlook has also been downgraded
and led to the early March decline in stock prices.

With a competitive lid on price to earnings ratios due to the increase in interest rates, earnings
progress will become critical for further stock price advances. The earnings outlook for the overall
market has continued to come under pressure from the increasing value of the U.S. Dollar. The value
of overseas earnings translated into our currency has been producing negative comparisons, but the
first half of 1985 will likely be under even greater pressure than 1984 comparisons. Domestic pricing
flexibility is also under increasing pressure from foreign imports. Fortunately, the U.S. Dollar has
stabilized over the last two weeks. Unfortunately, the year to year comparisons on translation rates
are worse today than in 1984. If the U.S. Dollar begins to decline, investors may be willing to look
through the results of the next couple quarters and see better comparisons late in 1985.

13-1 | continued

We would begin to look at securities that have been able to bring good results to the bottom line despite significant currency translation penalty. These securities stand to be major beneficiaries of an eventual reversal of the U.S. Dollars strength and have less near term risk than investments in U.S. firms significantly affected by import competition. To accommodate additional exposure in this area we would continue to sell cyclical stocks and be willing to slightly increase equity exposure especially if the market continues to weaken. Initial reaction to a weakening U.S. Dollar could put added pressure on interest rates as foreigners sell U.S. securities. This could easily further weaken the stock market and create the opportunity to acquire desirable securities at favorable levels. Therefore, we would walk and not run into increased exposure for stocks.

TRUST DEPARTMENT
March 12, 1985

In their efforts to humanize the firm or institution, newsletter writers sometimes use humor. Humor is, of course, a good method of conveying some information. However, unless you have a special gift at writing humor, avoid it, because poor humor can come across as trite. And it can be inadvertently offensive as well. If you use humor now and then, remember that you should never poke fun at anyone other than yourself or the firm or institution.

Special Interest Newsletters

The term *special interest* describes group relationships bound by a common interest other than employer-employee. These interests range the gamut of life-styles, economic theories, political beliefs, religions, social organizations and professions. These interests are most visible through involvement in groups, clubs, associations or causes. One of the most common means of communicating with people is through newsletters devoted to their special interests.

Life-Styles   If you enjoy flying a Cessna 120/140, you probably receive a newsletter regularly from Cessna. Among its content is an emphasis on "fly ins," a common point at which 120/140 pilots can gather to exchange tidbits about the joys of flying these aircraft. But because of speed and fuel limitations, not all 120/140 pilots will be at these meetings, even those designated as the "annual" meeting. While a newsletter from Cessna is not a substitute for the pleasure of flying, it can be an effective means of keeping people informed. Most life-style-related enterprises—whether linked to fishing, scuba diving (see Example 13-2), art collecting or gardening—have similar means of communicating with members (see Example 13-3).

The purpose of these newsletters is to communicate information about the special interest that binds the group. Information in these newsletters is highly targeted and seldom presents anything not directly related to the interest of the group.

Writing style is often informal and, depending on the field of interest, may involve jargon. For example, a newsletter for personal computer hackers may be filled with computerese. If you are really interested in communicating fully, you'll minimize the jargon and stay with simple English. But there is no defense for using the language badly.

For example, after a recent change in ownership, a new manager was appointed at a 200-unit apartment complex. One of the first things the new manager did was produce and distribute a newsletter to all the residents. Here is a verbatim copy of the first paragraph:

> INTRODUCTION
> HI! I am [personal name] your NEW manager at [name of complex]. I would also like to introduce [personal name] your maintenance man. You all know [personal name] whom is still here to assist you. I would like to have a resident-staff get to gather as soon as possible, so we can all meet and get to know each other. I will let you know when.

13-2

External Newsletter
This is the front page of the first issue of *Dive Notes*, a newsletter published by Frank's Underwater Sports Shop in Oklahoma City. It grew out of the increased popularity of scuba diving. The newsletter is filled with information on forthcoming dives, classes, safety training seminars, new equipment and other items of keen interest to those who like diving. *Source:* Reprinted with permission of Frank Best Thompson.

DIVE NOTES

| Vol. 1, No. 1 | Oklahoma City, OK | March 1985 |

Carribbean trips offer fun

COZUMEL—Rich, azure waters roar against white beaches in greeting to travelers here. The unique friendliness of Mexican hospitality makes the visitor at home in this Carribbean island, but the adventure has yet to begin.

"Diving the reefs of Cozumel is a class adventure", according to Frank Best Thompson of Frank's Underwater Sports Shop, 1415 N. May. "We have divers sign up for this trip time and time again, there is a lot to see—it's one of the top rated dive spots in the world."

Palancar Reef stretches upward more than a hundred feet from the ocean floor. Most divers will plan their dives for 80 feet or so. Caves are numerous; the reef is a myriad of moving color. Species of fish you'll see in few other places move about, some as curious about divers as you are them. Moray eels undulate from ambush spots, looking for a passing dinner. Large groupers move gracefully about the reef.

But Palancar is only one of many reefs that make Cozumel a diver's showplace.

And Cozumel is only one of many exotic places Frank Best Thompson takes his divers.

Bonaire, May 5-12, a week of South American diving for $1095."

The trip prices include airfare, lodging and equipment rental.

Check 'em out. Start out this summer right!

Bonaire, off the coast of Peru; the Grand Caymans, and many other trips are planned.

"If you haven't been in the ocean before, you're missing out on lifetime adventure", Thompson said. "We have a Cozumel trip coming up April 11-14—four days of beautiful reef diving for about $550—and

SCUBAFEST '85
"FILM FEST"

Frank's Underwater Sports is proud to announce SCUBAFEST '85! This thrilling program will be held Saturday April 20th, 7 p.m. at DOC SEVERINSEN'S restaurant and club, address, 201 N. Meridian. The program will feature the latest fashions for diving and swimming during the style show. This years feature program will be given by Internationally Acclaimed Underwater Photographer/Journalist RICK FREHSEE. Rick will have a series of slides and movies from around the world, to entertain us, including one of the finest fresh-water diving, multi-slide presentations ever made called "The Bonne Terre Mire".

SCUBAFEST '85 is a must for anyone interested in diving and the underwater world. DOC'S will offer drinks at reasonable rates for those of age. This family event will be considered a private party for all ages so bring a friend.

13-3

Informal External Newsletter
Serious gardeners, especially rosarians, remain alert to new
information that will make their thumbs greener. *Bev Dobson's
Rose Letter* is one of the most authoritative newsletters on
hybrid roses. *Source:* Reprinted with permission of Beverly R.
Dobson.

Bev Dobson's Rose Letter

215 Harriman Road, Irvington, NY 10533   1-914-591-6736

Number 7   May/June 1984

LETTERS AND PHONE CALLS

In response to many inquiries about
'Taxi' and 'Dolly Parton' I searched back
through several years' worth of ARS magazines, but failed to turn up any registration or code name for either. Keep watching for these two to pop up in the near
future, we hope, and
in the meantime, do
put them on the show
table anyway.

Many have asked
what non-registered
but code name record-
ed varieties are
most likely to turn
up on the show
tables this season.
Well, anything could
turn up for imports.
From Canada, here
are the European roses
most likely to turn
up:
American Independence
  (Meifinaro) Min mp
Angelique (Ankori)
  HT o-r
Austra Gold or Austro-
  gold (McKung) HT my
Ave Maria (Korav) HT c/s
Canary (Tancary) HT dy
Dolce Vita (Deldal) HT c/s
Fortuna (Kortuna) HT c/s
Julie Delbard (Deljuli) F ab? dp?
Lancôme (Delbolp) HT dp
Night Light (Poullight) LCl o-r
Parador (Meikinosi) HT my
Rosanna (Korinter) LCl c/s
San Valentin (Dotcris) Min mp
Sensass Delbard (Delmoun) LCl mr
Spectra (Meizalitaf) LCl rb? yb?

Many thanks to Fred Welford of Mansfield,
Ohio, for the photocopy of his letter from
Seizo Suzuki. This verifies that 'Blue
Sky' is the alternate name for 'Aozora,'
under which name it must be shown.

A good letter from Janet Henson of
Kodak, Tennessee, brings up several
points to share with all. To help revise
our book dealers' lists: Barbara Cole no
longer deals in garden books but has
changed to horses. Question mark on
Barbara Cyrus as she has not replied in
several months to an inquiry with a SASE.
Richards Flowerbooks
now out of business due
to age and failing eye-
sight. Second Life
Books has moved to
Quarry Road, P. O. Box
242, Lanesborough, MA
01237. Edward F.
Smiley, R.F.D. 5, 45
Liberty Road, Bedford,
NH 03102 does not send
out a list, but will
try to find scarce
books. He came up with
ARS annuals for Janet
at reasonable prices.
Janet is very pleased
with Trevor Griffiths'
book, My World of Old
Roses, "a really beau-
tiful book," and I
agree and recommend it
also. More about
Trevor Griffiths later.

This question came from several recently: How important is it for the casual
or small scale exhibitor to belong to the
rose organizations such as FIRE and ARS?

The answer is, this type of exhibitor
will not feel the need for membership in
the various rose organizations. When he
or she reaches the point of feeling this
need, they have turned the corner and
become serious exhibitors. Some rose
shows are open only to members of the
local club, but many are open to all, with
the exception that certain prizes and
awards are reserved for local members and/
or ARS members.

In the first six paragraphs (about 330 words), there were no fewer than 60 mistakes in spelling, grammar and syntax. The new manager's idea was good, but it was so poorly executed that his credibility among residents became a joke.

Economics   People are concerned with their money: how to make or save it and how to make it grow. Newsletters represent a lifeline to important information for people concerned with such issues. Banks, savings and loans, thrifts, brokers and investment firms all use newsletters extensively. And if you belong to an investment club whose members help each other learn the ins and outs of investing, a newsletter is likely to be issued, calling attention to the date and subject of the next meeting.

Some commercial newsletters also deal with economic issues. These are efforts designed to sell knowledge for a profit. For example, the Standard & Poor's Corporation of New York issues a monthly newsletter, entitled *Emerging & Special Situations*, designed to help subscribing investors keep up with what's going on in the stock market.

Politics   Political groups and parties of all types use newsletters extensively. Although these letters are usually designed to meet the needs of members, they are also used to recruit new members and to impart information to "unbelievers."

Political candidates use newsletters to share information among workers in the campaign. Once elected, politicians often use newsletters as a means of communicating regularly with constituents. Such newsletters are especially important to incumbents, who are in complete control of the content. Newsletters are also used by incumbents to float trial balloons on issues and to seek input via questionnaires, although the questions are often loaded.

If you join a local political action group in support of a cause, you are likely to receive a newsletter at regular intervals. Such newsletters are important documents that reassure members and assert the "party line" to those outside the group.

Religion   Religious organizations and church bodies use newsletters regularly. Many local churches send members a newsletter every week, not only about what is planned for the next worship service but also covering special concerns like a pending building program or the collection of food for the needy. Denominations also use newsletters extensively. Such newsletters often circulate on the regional or national levels and are likely to focus on broad social or doctrinal issues. The writing style is often formal and doctrinaire in tone.

Social   The term *social* embraces a wide range of human activities and special interests. It may be used to describe a broad range of newsletters. For example, if you are a member of a fraternity or sorority, you probably receive a newsletter regularly about the group's activities. When you leave the campus, an alumni newsletter (or perhaps a magazine) will follow you for the rest of your life. On the other hand you may be an avid bridge player in a group that meets for weekly bridge sessions. A newsletter may be a regular feature of this activity.

When you enter professional life, you'll take part in a variety of community activities. Among these may be membership in a fraternal organization such as Rotary or Business and Professional Women. Each of these organizations has a local newsletter, as well as national publications designed to keep you posted on what's going on.

Professional   One of the most important newsletters to you in your career in public relations is the professional newsletter. For example, *pr reporter*, *PR News*, *O'Dwyer's Newsletter* and others are designed to help you do your job better. They keep you posted on the latest developments, issues, techniques and ideas in public relations. Similar newsletters are published for a variety of other professional fields, such as advertising, accounting, law and medicine, among others.

Technical Considerations   There is no one way to prepare a newsletter. The writing style may range from informal to formal, but it is always keenly focused on the interest of the group at hand. Some newsletters are simply typed and photocopied, folded and mailed. Others are elaborately designed, typeset and printed on fine quality paper. Budget, of course, is a key factor in determining the appearance and method of reproduction. The important point to remember is that the content of the newsletter, not the appearance, counts most. If the content is perceived as important by readers, you have accomplished your purpose.

Brochures

Many brochures are developed to sell a product, service or idea. Real estate agents use brochures to show property and to describe the advantages of owning it. Sometimes realtors use a brochure to sell the services of the company, rather than specific properties offered by the firm. Most professional PR people receive at least one brochure a week describing some seminar that has been designed to help them improve their skills. PR professional groups publish brochures offering members as speakers to interested groups. Selling talent is selling a service from which others can benefit. Others may promote membership, affiliation or participation. (See Example 13-4.)

Some brochures sell intangibles by describing the worth of an idea— for example those designed to get support (usually financial) for foundations. One mental health foundation sends out brochures "selling" its publications and audiovisual materials at prices that barely cover mailing costs. The foundation "sells" ideas for sound mental health but offers the materials to justify its existence, its reason for being.

Brochures can be informational in the strict sense, too. For example, Tel-Med is an organization that provides medical information by telephone in some communities. If you are concerned about an ailment, you can simply dial the Tel-Med number and get a recorded description of various illnesses, suggested treatment

335

13-4

Brochure
As with many organizations, this brochure from American
Women in Radio and Television, Inc. promotes membership. The brochure explains the rewards members get from
affiliation with A.W.R.T. *Source:* Reprinted with permission
of A.W.R.T.

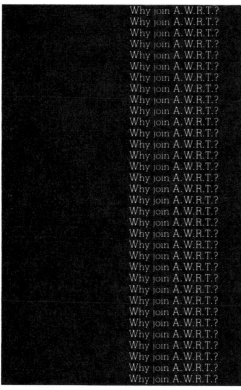

A Membership in

offers you . . .

CREDIBILITY—For over 30 years, A.W.R.T. has
been an articulate voice commanding increased
attention by the broadcast industry. In the past
year, for instance, A.W.R.T. was:

- asked by Congressional committees to testify on key industry related issues affecting
  women.
- instrumental in arranging an annual tele-
  communications conference with the FCC.
- contacted by presidents of networks and
  broadcast groups for assistance.
- queried regularly by the press for A.W.R.T.'s
  position on issues affecting women in the
  broadcast industry.
- called upon by three government agencies
  to help with special nationwide projects.
- used as a source for recommending women
  for positions on the boards of industry related
  organizations.

"A.W.R.T. means being recognized by my
peers and co-workers as someone who cares
about the industry."

Jeanette Greer, Vice President
KFDM TV, Beaumont, TX

"My involvement in A.W.R.T. has paid off in
achieving my career goals and in attaining
recognition and credibility in the broadcast
industry."

Audrey Hunt, Past National President
A.W.R.T.

"—more and more a recognized credential in
the business world."

Leslie Todd, Vice President
Hood, Hope & Associates, Tulsa, OK

13-4   continued

PROFESSIONAL GROWTH—Local chapter meetings, area conferences each fall, special workshops, seminars and an annual National Convention expose A.W.R.T. members to the expertise of such interesting and influential people as FCC commissioners, news correspondents, network presidents and owners of successful businesses.

"A.W.R.T. provides the opportunity to develop and improve skills of time management, delegation, negotiation and public speaking."

**Marlene Belles, Controller
KTVU TV, Oakland, CA**

"From the day I joined A.W.R.T. my world expanded. The growth of that world and of my personal and professional life has never stopped."

**Charlotte Tharp, Community Relations Dir.
WHAS, Inc., Louisville, KY**

"I would not have achieved the position of president of a national public relations firm were it not for A.W.R.T. The role models and the outstanding men and women who have addressed A.W.R.T. over the years shaped my style and directed my career."

**Jean Anwyll, President
McKinney/Public Relations
Philadelphia, PA**

"My having an opportunity to purchase a radio station was a direct result of my A.W.R.T. involvement."

**Jeri Warrick-Crisman
President/Gen. Manager/Owner
WNJR Radio, Union, NJ**

OPPORTUNITY TO MAKE A CONTRIBUTION—Members of A.W.R.T. who have "made it" in their area of expertise, have the opportunity to share the secrets of their success with other A.W.R.T. members who welcome their advice and guidance.

"—afforded me an opportunity to repay some of the knowledge and experience I have gained by passing it on to others."

**Sadie Adwon, Past National President
A.W.R.T.**

"—and the satisfaction that comes from helping other women move up the ladder."

**Muriel Fox, Executive VP
Carl Byoir & Associates, New York, NY**

"I remain a member of A.W.R.T. as a way of saying "thank you" to those women who have helped me and because my media education must continue. A.W.R.T. is my classroom now."

**Nancy Hughes, VP Comm/PR
Denver Chamber of Commerce
Denver, Colorado**

FRIENDS—PEER CONTACT—As you become involved in A.W.R.T. you develop lasting relationships with other men and women in the communications field. The national "network" of colleagues is a major benefit of membership.

"—no matter where I travel, there is always an A.W.R.T. member to meet and enjoy."

**Esther Van Wagoner Tufty
President/Bureau Chief
Tufty News Service, Wash., DC**

"—association with other industry leaders"

**Elizabeth Bain, Former National President
A.W.R.T.**

"Active membership has afforded me a unique opportunity to make professional contacts of the finest quality."

**Mr. C. B. "Rik" Rogers, VP/GM
WPLO/WVEE Radio, Atlanta, GA**

DON'T MISS OUT! If you are career-minded, goal-oriented and a woman on the move, A.W.R.T. is for you! You cannot afford *not* to be a part of the network. Use the return post-card for more information and an application to join the chapter nearest you.

A.W.R.T., 1321 Connecticut Ave., NW
Washington, D.C. 20036 (202) 296-0008

13-4 | continued

WHY JOIN A.W.R.T.?

. . . read what our members are saying . . .

A professional opportunity . . .

American Women in Radio and Television, Inc., is a national non-profit membership organization of qualified professionals in the electronic media and allied fields. Founded in 1951, American Women in Radio and Television is the nation's oldest continuing professional broadcast organization. The objectives of A.W.R.T. are:

- to **work worldwide** to improve the quality of radio and television
- to **promote** the **entry, development** and **advancement** of women in the electronic media and allied fields
- to **serve** as a medium of communication and idea exchange
- to **become** involved in community concerns

Over three thousand members of American Women in Radio and Television are engaged in over ninety job categories, encompassing the widest spectrum of professional occupations. On-air broadcasters; owners; executives; managers; creative personnel; administrators; attorneys and corporate planners are only some of the positions held by A.W.R.T. members in a network of sixty local chapters and members-at-large, throughout the world.

and expected outcomes. Information about the service, the telephone number to call and the hours during which volunteers can cue the right tapes are contained in an informational brochure.

Informational brochures about subjects like the suicide prevention hotline, accidents and crime deterrence are often produced as a community service. A druggist may dispense, along with prescriptions, a brochure on how to prevent poisoning accidents and what to do if an accident occurs. Such informational brochures perform a service and generate good will for those who distribute them.

Concept   The primary consideration in the development of a brochure is the concept behind it. Art and words have to work together to convey an idea, to sell the message. If there is not a clear, sharply focused concept behind the brochure, it may be ineffective. For example, if you are producing a brochure for a new apartment or office complex, you will probably want to emphasize what is *new and different* about the complex. You'll want to compare the new complex with others, since the others will be the frame of reference of your readers. You should emphasize what is new and different about your complex, however. If the complex already exists, the brochure must consider the desired image you want to project for the complex, but if you are presenting a notion that diverges from the commonly held view, you will have a problem with believability and acceptance.

However, presenting a known product in a new way often succeeds. Approach the task with insight and imagination. Try to think of symbols in words and art that will evoke the image you want to convey. Keep that image in the forefront of your thinking as you select words, art, color and design for the brochure.

Validity   Even if you naturally want to put your best foot forward, you must always be concerned with the accuracy of your presentation. You must be careful in collecting information about the subject of the brochure. Make certain, for example, that each office in the building being promoted does indeed have a thermostat control before you include that information in the brochure. If a firm rents space and installs computer components that need special temperature control—and there is no thermostat—you can be challenged for misrepresentation in the brochure you produced.

Brochures about investment opportunities are particularly hazardous. You need to spell out carefully all the financial considerations, and review the copy with both an accountant and an attorney before going into production. The underlying reason for this is the same as for the office or apartment complex—people should be assured of getting their money's worth. A professional organization's foundation offered a brochure detailing for potential contributors the benefits of membership in the foundation. The group's attorney was adamant that the mechanism for providing these benefits be in place before the publication went to press. Colleges and universities, for example, are taking hard looks at their catalogs and brochures after being informed by counsel of cases in which institutions were taken to court for promising more than they could deliver.

Informational brochures are easier to prepare than "image" brochures. Image is often nebulous. Information is concrete. Accuracy is critical. Completeness is necessary.

Write First   Once the concept is settled, you should write all of the copy for the brochure. Write everything you want to tell. Next, determine what you can show. Perhaps you can delete some copy. Perhaps you can substitute a sentence for a whole paragraph. The key point here is to settle on the verbal content first. This step is necessary because it will give you important clues as to how you can make what you want to say easy to read. And it helps to design tables, graphs, charts and other visual matter that may aid understanding. Finally, look at the whole piece, including the graphics, to determine the size and form of your brochure. After you make a decision on this, you can cut and polish your copy before you get to the tough jobs of designing the brochure and fitting your copy to the space allotted.

Fitting Copy and Design

Designing newsletters and brochures to display information attractively is important in gaining attention for your message.

Newsletters have a great deal of room for copy since they do not use many, if any, illustrations. The danger is crowding the piece with too much copy. Headlines, indentations and generous paragraphing help break up the copy in a word-heavy piece. If your story is better told with graphics and design, then a brochure is the format you should use.

Audiences for newsletters are likely to be fairly cohesive groups. Those receiving a particular newsletter are members of an audience because they already belong to a club or are employees of a firm, or they are philosophically aligned or at least inclined toward a group. Brochures are more likely to go to those who are somewhat unreceptive.

Brochures also have a longer life than newsletters. As their name implies, newsletters have much in common with newspapers and are often read for their content and then discarded. Brochures, like magazines, are more likely to be kept around and referred to more than once. Sometimes they are even passed along to other people.

Use   The purpose of the publication, then, is closely aligned with its use. When you are deciding how to communicate with an audience, you have to determine what you want to accomplish and then go about achieving that goal in the way most likely to succeed. If you have a diving shop in the Virgin Islands, for example, you can excite the imagination and probably stimulate business better with a brochure that presents more pictures than words. On the other hand, if you want to keep in touch with all the Corvette owners in your state, you're better off with a newsletter full of copy about rallies and parts.

How you are planning to distribute the piece has a great deal to do with its design, too. If you intend the newsletter or brochure to be a self-mailer, one side will have to carry your return address, the postage and the mailing label. Furthermore, the whole piece will have to meet the specifications of the U.S. Postal Service. Always check with the postmaster in the community where the piece will be mailed. Postal regulations seem to be pretty clear but they are often open to interpretation. It is better to check first than to be sorry later.

If the newsletter or brochure will be used as an enclosure, stop and think about this before you design it. How are you most likely to send it? With what? When? To whom? All of these questions will probably dictate a design that deserves its own matching envelope.

What the receiver will do with the piece also has a bearing on the design. Will the brochure wind up on a bulletin board, for example? Some newsletters and brochures are designed with that purpose in mind. A copy is sent to the president of a group, who then posts it for others to read. Others may be designed for display in a rack or countertop display unit. In both cases, the display unit has to be designed to call attention to the piece, and the piece has to be designed to call attention to itself. For example, a brochure for a microwave oven may be designed for display adjacent to the oven itself. The intent would be to provide information at the point of sale. Or the brochure may be designed to be picked up and taken home, where it will be studied and then used in decision making. Selling brochures like this have to be designed to carry information that is persuasive.

Some brochures are designed for one person to give to another. Many health information pieces are like this. For example, a physician may give an expectant mother a brochure on prenatal care, or a counselor may give a high school student a brochure on how to select a college. Such brochures are designed to stand alone, but they are usually supplemented and complemented by advice from the person giving them out.

Writing To Fit   When you are writing the copy, you have to prepare the message to say what you think needs to be said in an appropriate way. Then you have to decide how you are going to convey the information in the available space. Some professionals are experienced enough to be able to "write to fit," but most prepare the message and then spend a lot of time trimming it to fit, substituting illustrations for words, if appropriate, and generally tailoring the message to the medium. A newsletter is somewhat more flexible because pages can be added, but that usually costs money. A better solution is to first determine your information hole and then write the message to fit it.

Fitting Copy   You will want to review the copyfitting methods in the Appendix C. This is mandatory. If you have not done much copyfitting, you will quickly discover that it is the bane of most brochure writers and designers. If you learn to do it well, it will save you lots of heartaches. If you don't, it will become a chore that you dread, a constant source of frustration and, done badly, a financial drain on your budget.

As a basic set of guidelines, you need to keep the following in mind: Set your typewriter so that it will produce a 60-character line. Four lines of 60 characters of typewritten copy will generally produce about 2 square inches of 8-point type. Ten-point type is .25 larger than 8-point type, so 10-point type will produce approximately 2.5 square inches of type. Twelve point type, it is .5 larger than 8 point, so with 12-point type the amount of type will be about 3 square inches.

The most precise method of fitting copy is to do a unit or character count of your copy. Then determine the average character count in the size and face of type you want in a specific line length. You can establish this count for a specific typeface and size by taking a sample of at least 2 square inches (12 picas or 2 inches wide by 6 picas or 1 inch deep) and establishing the average number of characters per 12-pica line. If you determine that a particular face and size has an average of 26 characters per 12-pica line and you want to use an 18-pica line, just multiply 26 by 0.5 and you get an average count of 39 characters.

Remember when fitting copy to allow for additional spacing between lines and paragraphs. Also, you'll want additional space above and below headlines. This space has to be figured into the overall design.

The same typeface comes in a variety of styles. The most common are condensed, regular and extended. Condensed type lets you crowd more characters into an inch. Extended type allows for fewer characters in an inch. As a general rule, stay with the regular face and cut out words rather than trying to crowd them with condensed faces or smaller point sizes. Remember that even if your message is glowing, it will not be read if it is not inviting to the eye.

Make words count for you. Select words that tell the story best, words that stir the imagination and excite interest. Emphasize the most significant elements in the information you want to convey by both word choice and graphics. Active verbs will convey emphasis. You can, of course, use typographic treatments for emphasis, too, such as italics, all capital letters, colored ink or paper, and other design elements. A brochure to call attention to the danger of common household items that are poisonous has only the word "Poison" in bright red letters across the front of a detergent box. The single word and the graphic combine to make a powerful statement about common items in the home that we don't normally think of as poisonous. Internally, in the copy, words can be used just as significantly and graphically.

The key point to remember is that writing to fit has two essential meanings: First, it means writing words and using graphics that fit the space. Second, it means writing to fit the message to render it powerful, understandable and effective.

Conclusions

* Newsletters combine some aspects of newspapers and letters and are issued regularly.

* Employee newsletters are used as a means of internal communication.

* The content of special interest newsletters ranges the gamut of life-styles, economic theories, political beliefs, religions, social organizations and professions.

* The term *brochure* encompasses pamphlets, booklets, flyers, circulars, leaflets and tracts.
* A brochure combines some of the features of a magazine with limited purpose and is issued just once.
* A clear concept of content and dedication to accuracy are requisites to writing and designing good brochures.
* Fitting copy and designing good newsletters and brochures are demanding tasks for the professional in public relations.

Exercises

1. Find a newsletter that deals with a life-style and one that goes to a professional group. Do a written analysis of their purposes, content, writing styles and formats.
2. Find an employee newsletter from two firms, each from a different industry segment. Write an analysis of their purposes, content, writing styles and formats.
3. Get a copy of a brochure promoting your department or school, then write an analysis of its purpose, content, writing style and format.
4. Select a brochure your household has received in the last few weeks and analyze the writing. Then rewrite at least six paragraphs of the copy. Turn in your written analysis, the brochure and your six rewritten paragraphs.
5. You have been promoted from public relations writer to vice president for communications at Ourbank. Write a story for Ourbank's newsletter announcing that fact. Explain management's devotion to an expanded communication emphasis at Ourbank and what this means to all employees.
6. Design and write a brochure that will fit inside a standard business envelope. It will be sent only to Ourbank's commercial clients. Its emphasis will be on the convenience and safety of night depository services at Ourbank.

Selected Bibliography

Robert S. Cole, *The Practical Handbook of Public Relations* (Englewood Cliffs, N.J.: Prentice-Hall, 1982).

Philip Lesley, ed., *Lesley's Public Relations Handbook*, 3rd ed. (Englewood Cliffs, N.J.: Prentice-Hall, 1983).

Carol Reuss and Donna Silvis, eds., *Inside Organizational Communications*, 2nd ed. (New York: Longmans, 1985).

14
Backgrounders and Position Papers

For some companies, it happens several times weekly. For others, every month or so, maybe once a year or even less often. Frequency aside, your firm will get a call from a reporter.

The reporter may ask questions like: "What's your position on [name of act] now before the Congress in Washington?" "What's your firm's stand on the cause of the pollution in [name of river or area]?" "What does your company believe will be the impact of the new EPA rules?" "I'm doing a story on declining innovation in your industry. Can you give me some information?"

Your company executives must be able to respond quickly and knowledgeably to such questions. A "No comment" response is not acceptable. And if an executive promises to call the reporter back, this must be done faithfully. If such queries are not handled with skill and dispatch, the firm loses credibility in a hurry. The firm's credibility is tenuous, nebulous and capricious. A thoughtless response can do unlimited damage.

The role of the public relations writer in such instances is to provide either in-depth information on the topic in the form of a backgrounder or a clear, definitive company point of view in the form of a position paper. In this sense, as the PR writer you are the eyes and ears of company spokespersons. You have to arm them with facts, solidly researched and documented, organized in logical fashion, clearly written and easily understandable.

This sort of writing is somewhat different from the usual tasks of writing news releases or copy for ads and brochures. It usually requires a lot more in-depth research and the preparation of a report called a *backgrounder* or a *position paper*.

The really good PR department does not wait, however, until a reporter calls to begin developing basic information for backgrounders and position papers. PR staffers routinely comb through popular and specialized media and documents, searching for salient bits of information affecting their firm or industry. These bits of information are accumulated and filed for reference. When the task of writing a backgrounder or position paper is before them, they already have a head-start on its research.

Sometimes backgrounders and position papers are done and simply filed away for later use. The hope is that they will not be needed, but when they are PR personnel can respond quickly and appropriately to queries from any source.

Preparation of backgrounders and position papers is often the first stage in the planning of a new public relations program. For example, assume that an electric utility is considering a new way of charging for the use of its electricity. It calls for higher rates during the day but very low rates at night and on weekends. The PR department should prepare a backgrounder that describes the history of this time-of-day pricing structure, where such methods have been tried and with what success, the availability and cost of "time" meters, and related points. Of course, the back-grounder should also compare this method to the one in use and to other methods.

At some point, company management will decide to stay with the present system or go with the time-of-day system. The backgrounder will help management make this decision. If the decision is to adopt the time-of-day system, the backgrounder is then used as the basis for developing and writing a company position on the new system. Both the backgrounder and the position paper will contain the information necessary to write news releases, ads, brochures, speeches and articles for the company magazine or newsletter.

Backgrounders tend to be heavy on facts and light on opinion. Position papers are heavy on opinion or interpretation, supported with only a few facts. Both can deal with broad or specific questions or issues. However, backgrounders tend to deal with general topics while position papers tend to treat a specific issue.

For example, a backgrounder might deal with the broad topic of the transportation of coal, reviewing technological, economic and environmental questions and related issues. A position paper, however, would focus on a specific proposed law that would, if passed, regulate coal slurry pipelines. It would take a pro or con position and present facts to support the position.

Backgrounders

Backgrounders have many purposes. They serve as an information base for both company executives and employees. They provide source materials to copywriters preparing ads, news releases, brochures, speeches or articles for the company magazine. They may also be used as documents to hand out to reporters or to members of the public who may inquire about a certain topic. And company executives on the speaker's circuit can use them to bone up on a subject so they can field questions from the audience. Rarely does a backgrounder meet only one of these uses; keep all of them in mind.

The hallmark of good backgrounders is accuracy and comprehensiveness. This means that the topic must be thoroughly researched.

Research

Doing research for a backgrounder will often use all of the research skills, techniques and sources discussed in Chapter 3. Read that chapter again and review each point as it might apply to researching a backgrounder.

The key point is that you are not professionally responsible if you leave one bit of salient information unread or ignored in your evaluation. It just might contain the germ of an idea or the fact that makes all of your other material inconsequential or misleading. This can be fatal to the firm because company spokespersons have to rely on you for the information they will convey to members of the media or to the public.

Research is a never-ending process. Once a backgrounder is completed, it becomes less useful with each passing day because of new information. You should establish the practice of accumulating pertinent information, filing it and updating the backgrounder at regular intervals. Backgrounders that do not include the very latest important information are worthless.

Writing

The writing of a backgrounder begins first with a simple statement of the issue and why it is important. Including such a statement may appear trite, but it is necessary as a guideline to your research on and writing about the topic. It keeps you on the right track. This opening statement should be both precise and concise. While it helps you in the writing, it also tells the reader what to expect in the document.

Once your opening statement is honed to perfection, write the body of the backgrounder. Be sure to provide an adequate, clear history of the issue, a thorough discussion of the current situation and implications for the future.

Background   As the name implies, backgrounders give the background on a topic or issue. It should provide a fairly complete historical overview so a reader unfamiliar with the topic can understand how the current situation has evolved. You have to answer the question: Why are things the way they are today? You can't answer this question without giving details about how things were, and how and why they have changed.

The typical backgrounder on an issue includes details like significant historical events, enactment of legislation, changes in government and company policy, and applicable social conditions. It specifies names, books, documents, articles and reports that played an important part in the development of the issue. In sum, this section of the backgrounder should describe the evolution of the current situation.

Current Situation   Having built a foundation on the past, you should now examine the current situation, including a review of current public and company policies. Perhaps these points could be extended to include a discussion of alternative policies now being considered.

The purpose of a backgrounder is to assemble and convey information, not to judge it. Any discussions of policy or alternatives should be from an objective, neutral position. Stick to facts. Describe policy options, discuss their good and bad points, but don't make value judgments about them.

For example, if the issue is the high cost of home heating and its effects on poor people, one policy to consider might be the use of energy stamps to help people pay their utility bills. This idea has its good and bad points. One writer might say:

> Using energy stamps is a poor way to solve the problem because stamps require a massive, wasteful bureaucracy and excessive government funding.

Another writer might say:

> Using energy stamps is an excellent solution to the problem because stamps could be easily administered by existing government organizations.

Both writers may be justified in their points of view, but this is a backgrounder, not a position paper. Instead of taking a position, write to inform by saying:

> Use of energy stamps is one solution to this problem. An energy stamp program would require government funding and a system for administering these funds. Such a program might be administered by existing organizations.

Implications   To this point, we have considered the historical background and the current situation. The next step in writing the backgrounder is to examine the consequences of selecting one policy over another. If the backgrounder does not address such future implications directly, it should at least highlight points that must be considered.

A backgrounder on national energy policy, for example, might discuss gas and electricity production from coal as a substitute for declining oil reserves. Such a discussion would surely include a supply-demand analysis, an evaluation of current technology, and an analysis of economic and environmental effects. It would also include an assessment of this method's ability to meet the country's demand for more energy.

These are obvious points, but less obvious are the following complex implications: Even if this method can efficiently meet the energy needs of transportation, the use of great quantities of coal for this purpose will diminish its supply for the generation of electricity. And while production of energy for transportation is possible, energy generated from coal puts more carbon dioxide in the air than some alternate methods and eventually can create climatic changes.

Identifying the implications of a certain policy includes anticipation of developments. In this sense, the PR writer has to be aware of the flux of ideas about the issue and which of these may gain or lose support over time. Perhaps a public policy change is being debated now in Washington, or perhaps an extensive government study is underway, the results of which won't be released for a year. Perhaps the topic will be the focus of a convention this year. In all of these cases, the issue and its implications are likely to be in the news now and in the future. As a PR writer, you must follow these developments.

Documentation

You must present full documentation of the information you use in the backgrounder. Before you try to write the backgrounder, get a reliable style manual, such as Kate L. Turabian's A *Manual for Writers of Term Papers, Theses and Dissertations*, and study it carefully.

While a backgrounder does not require the same rigorous scholarship and style common to reports and proposals discussed in the next chapter, this manual, or one like it, can help you properly cite the material you use in the backgrounder. You should use a footnote or endnote system of citation and include a complete bibliography at the end.

It is important to carefully cite your sources because people using the backgrounder, whether from inside or outside your firm, may want to pursue a specific point more fully. Or if they find a discrepancy between the facts in the backgrounder and those in some other source, they'll want to check out the publications you have cited.

Position Papers

As the name signifies, a position paper is designed to state a firm's position on an issue. (See Example 14-1.) The issue may be local, regional, national or international in scope. For example, suppose your firm opposes a national health insurance plan under consideration in Congress. The position paper tells why. Your firm may also take a positive position regarding a substitute proposal authored by a senator from the local district. The position paper should explain why it supports the substitute plan.

Like the backgrounder, the position paper requires extensive research. Much of the information you need will be found in the backgrounder, so

14-1

Position Paper on the Licensing of Lay Midwives
The paper begins by giving statistics to establish the
significance of the issue—the growing use of midwives in
parts of Texas and rising interest in the need for midwife
regulation. The position taken—that midwife regulation
should not be adopted—is stated with five supporting reasons.
The five points are then discussed in more detail throughout
the paper. Note that the paper does not simply give figures
and arguments against midwife licensing. The writer also
discusses evidence that seems to favor licensing and analyzes
that evidence to show its shortcomings. Source: Courtesy
Chris B. Siegfried.

THE CASE AGAINST LICENSING LAY MIDWIVES

In 1975 midwives delivered 5,050 babies in Texas. This figure was only
2.3 percent of all the live births in the State that year, but it represented
an increase of 90 percent over the number of midwife deliveries in 1970. Since
1975 the rate has continued to increase. Reasons for this increase are unclear, but two general trends are apparent. First, more and more babies are
being delivered by midwives in counties along the Mexican border. And second,
many young urban couples are choosing to have their babies delivered at home
by midwives.

Many persons believe the first of these trends is caused by alien
mothers crossing the border to have their babies. Babies born in Texas have
the benefit of U.S. citizenship or, if taken back to Mexico, have dual citizenship until age 18. This practice may or may not be the reason for the
large number of deliveries in the valley. At any rate, the statistics point
to the fact that large numbers of Mexican-American babies are delivered by
midwives.

The second trend can be attributed to a number of things--the women's
movement, rising hospital and doctor fees, the growing disaffection from the
medical profession in general, the return by many young couples to a pioneer,
do-it-yourself lifestyle. For whatever reasons, the number of home births
among young urban women is increasing, and the number of midwives along with
it.

This growth in the number of midwives has raised questions about
regulating the practice of midwifery by some type of licensing. The chief
argument given for regulation has been the need to safeguard the public from
unskilled or incompetent practitioners. There are flaws in this argument,
however, and in fact the weight of the evidence indicates that licensing of
lay midwives is not desirable. The arguments against regulation include:
(1) restriction of practice, (2) problems of enforcement, (3) problems associated with midwifery being a cultural practice, (4) side effects such as
rising fees and maldistribution of personnel, and (5) the new negative sentiment in the state towards professional licensing.

Each of these arguments is discussed below.

The Need to Safeguard the Public

Safeguarding the public has been a common rationale for professional
licensing legislation. In the case of midwives, however, safety figures are
too sketchy and conflicting to build a strong case for regulation.

14-1 continued

Critics of lay midwifery, for example, talk of the dangers involved in unsupervised deliveries made by lay persons of unknown training and skills. Figures collected by Texas Department of Health for 1974 do not substantiate these fears. Out of 4,421 midwife deliveries, only 36 or 0.81 percent resulted in fetal deaths. This figure compares to 2,473 fetal deaths or 1.2 percent for nonmidwife deliveries. Not only do these figures fail to build a case for regulation of lay midwives, but they appear to suggest that midwife deliveries are safer than others. (Along these lines, one study published recently in *International Childbirth News* compared home births to an equal number of hospital births and found home births to have fewer cases of infant distress, maternal high blood pressure, postpartum hemorrhage and birth injuries.[1] Furthermore, some countries that use midwives extensively, like The Netherlands, have lower infant mortality rates than the U.S.)

Critics of lay midwifery point out that lay midwives do not have the skills to recognize or cope with birth complications. These critics fail to mention that prenatal screening can identify those births most likely to need specialized care and that 90 percent of all births occur without any major complications.[2] In addition, many urban midwives deliver babies only if they have easy access to a hospital.

The American College of Obstetricians and Gynecologists (ACOG) recently sent out a news release saying that "out-of-hospital births pose a two to five times greater risk to a baby's life than hospital births."[3] This assertion is based on data from only eleven state health departments, however. And of this eleven "only four . . . identified stillbirths occurring at home." This sparsity of data finally leads the ACOG to conclude that it cannot make an accurate comparison.

Two other points need to be made about figures like those put out by the ACOG. First, no attempt is made to correlate the number of fetal deaths with economic status of the mother or with data about the availability of prenatal care. Good prenatal care will greatly improve the life chances of mother and baby. And second, it cannot be assumed that all "out of hospital births" occur in private homes or that all are attended by lay midwives. The statistics simply are not broken down to a degree that allows meaningful comparisons to be made.

One final point to be made about the safety argument is found in Patrick O'Donoghue's book *Evidence about the Effect of Health Care Regulations: An Evaluation and Synopsis of Policy Relevant Research*. O'Donoghue points out that "licensure stops at least one step short of actually assuring on a continuing basis the quality of health care delivered by a practitioner."[4] This is because it does little to ensure safe practice over the professional lifetime of the health care practitioner. Most licensing laws operate to ensure certain entering qualifications, but few can assure the continued competence of the practitioner. There are no mechanisms to protect the public from the licensed practitioner who is no longer competent to practice.

Restriction of Practice

Any legislation aimed at regulating lay midwives may ultimately restrict their practice. Among certain population groups and in areas where obstetrical services are scarce, this may prove to be a great disservice.

The two groups of women making the greatest use of lay midwives are Mexican Americans and young feminists. Mexican Americans use midwives partly out of cultural tradition but also because other health personnel are unavailable to them. Last year the *Corpus Christi Caller* reported that "20 percent of all the children born in the Lower Rio Grande Valley were delivered by *parteras* outside hospital facilities."[5] (*Parteras* is the Spanish word for mid-wife.) The *Caller* went on to point out that parteras are used because other types of professional health care are "too often financially and geographically inaccessible. Most *parteras* charge what the family can afford."

Until more health professionals agree to serve in underserved rural areas and barrios, poor Mexican Americans will continue to rely heavily on the services of lay midwives. Regulation of midwives may help to further cut off this group from needed health services.

For young feminists, the regulation issue involves rights and individual freedoms. Feminists say that women should have more control over the birthing process and that the medical profession is largely responsible for taking childbirth out of the warm, home environment and placing it in the cold confines of a hospital delivery room. Moreover, many young women believe it is important to the psychological strengthening of the family unit to have the entire family present at the birth of a new family member. Few hospitals allow this practice.

Of course, regulation would not have to mean an end to the practice of lay midwifery. (Though in other states this has often been the case.) But, depending on how legislation is drawn, it can severely limit how and when and under what conditions midwives practice. For example, Connecticut prohibits midwives from attending any women in labor who are not at least seven months pregnant. Many states have laws that prohibit midwives from attending any except cases of normal childbirth. Still other states prohibit midwives from practicing without sponsorship or medical backup from a physician. Not only do regulations like these restrict practice of midwives, but they make criminals of midwives who deliver babies due to the unavailability of other medical personnel.

The groups supporting regulation are a clue to the function regulation would serve. Frequently, the group to be regulated promotes regulation because it has the most to gain from controlling entrance into the profession. In this case, however, it is not lay midwives but the dominant health professionals--doctors, nurses, and nurse midwives--who are supporting regulation. Needless to say, the beliefs of most of these health professionals about home births and midwifery are antithetical to those of lay midwives.

Doctors and nurses also have a financial motive for promoting regulation. According to *Time* magazine, "Obstetrics is one of the largest and most lucrative specialties in U.S. medicine."[6] Midwives present a threat to the income of those who practice obstetrics. Obviously doctors hope to keep their stranglehold on this specialty by making it more difficult for midwives to practice.

Problem of Enforcement

There are at least two reasons why any mechanism to regulate the practice of lay midwives will not be easy to enforce. First, the Texas Department of Health will be the enforcing body, and it is not funded or structured adequately to permit enforcement. Some rural counties in South Texas, for example, have only a single health officer to oversee all public health functions for the county.

The second thing that will make enforcement difficult is the nature of the practice of midwifery. Midwives seldom advertise their practice or solicit business. Many midwives have practiced in the same community for years, and customers learn about them chiefly by word of mouth. Though Texas law requires all midwives to register with the local registrar, very few of them do so now. These facts taken together seem to suggest that any attempts to enforce regulation would run into difficulties.

14-1 | continued

One other point about enforcement should be made. Because of the nature of midwifery and the limited resources the state would probably commit to enforcement, any regulation is bound to be differentially enforced. The Department of Health will have to depend largely upon complaints to inform it of unsafe practices of a midwife. And those people who have chosen to use the services of an unlicensed midwife will not be likely to file a complaint. In fact, even those who use the licensed midwives will not be likely to complain if they are young, poor, or Spanish-speaking.

On top of this, licensed midwives would be reporting on unlicensed ones. This would clearly work against the elderly, Spanish-speaking parteras who have practiced for years, because they are the persons least likely to comply with new regulations.

In short, the enforcement problems accompanying regulation of the midwife practice are monumental. And the wisdom of passing regulating legislation that has a poor chance of operating effectively is questionable.

Midwifery as a Cultural Practice

Still another argument against licensing can be made on the grounds that midwives are an intricate part of the Mexican-American culture. For years, lower-class Mexicans and Mexican Americans have used neighborhood parteras to deliver their babies. Part of the reason for this is financial. The partera, however, is a well-established and widely accepted part of the community support system. She may be preferred even by those who can afford other medical personnel because she is known by the mother and the family, operates in a familiar setting, speaks Spanish, and because she is female. Childbirth can be a frightening experience, especially for young mothers. The partera has the ability to transmit warmth and comfort to young females that they cannot receive from Anglo male doctors in a hospital setting.

Regulating midwives, then, may amount to regulating a long-held cultural practice.

Side Effects of Regulating Health Personnel

O'Donoghue mentions a number of side effects that result from licensing health personnel. Most of these side effects are detrimental to the consumers of health services.

First of all, personnel licensing almost always serves to reduce the supply of health practitioners, and the resulting manpower shortage almost always brings about rising fees. Second, as a general rule, licensed practitioners prefer to practice in urban areas where they can make more money. This means that after they are licensed, health personnel often leave the rural areas where they are needed most. Still a third drawback to licensing health personnel is the reluctance of states to accept licenses issued by other states. This reluctance limits interstate mobility of health personnel and also exacerbates the maldistribution problem.

It is not clear how many of these side effects will result from the licensing of lay midwives. Undoubtedly, those midwives who have practiced for years in the same community will want to remain there. But with the growth of the practice, some of those events mentioned above would be likely to occur. So, once again, licensing may be an ultimate disservice to the public.

14-1 | continued

Negative Sentiment about Licensing

One final argument against regulations is the growing sentiment among many legislators to curtail professional licensing. Although more and more professions are petitioning the state legislature for licensing ordinances, recent activities of the Sunset Commission have cast a shadow of doubt over their chances for getting bills passed. The pattern in the past has been for the legislature to create an independent licensing board to oversee all functions related to testing, issuing, and revoking professional licenses. Recent investigations by members of the Sunset Commission, however, have revealed that many independent licensing boards do very little to regulate their professions. The commission is recommending combining some boards, abolishing others, and putting still others under the auspices of state agencies.

The midwife licensing bill (H.B. 1314) introduced last session placed the responsibility for granting licenses directly under the Department of Health. Placing the licensing responsibility within a state agency rather than with a board probably made the bill more palatable to House members. But at the same time, this approach gave control of the licensing process to a profession whose beliefs and practices are antithetical to those of lay midwives. Any future attempt to set up a licensing mechanism for midwives should avoid giving complete control of the licensing process to the medical profession. (One way this might be done is to set up a board of lay midwives under the Health Department and to give this board direct regulatory responsibility. After all, lay midwives operate with principles that are different from those of other health practitioners who render obstetrical care, and they are in the best position to judge the practices of other lay midwives.)

Recommendations

For the reasons given above and others, regulation of lay midwives is not advisable. Lay midwifery exists and will continue to be used by certain population groups despite efforts to regulate or do away with it. If physicians and others are truly concerned about public safety they should give their assistance to lay midwives in the form of training or medical backup. In addition, the Texas Department of Health should set as its priority not introducing measures to regulate midwives but providing good prenatal care clinics so that every woman in Texas has a greater chance to have a safe pregnancy and delivery. Measures taken to help update and improve the practice of midwifery and measures taken to upgrade prenatal care services will be a far greater service to the people of Texas than regulation will be.

NOTES

[1]"Home Births Might Be Better," Fort Worth Morning *Star-Telegram*, December 13, 1977, p. 19A.

[2]"Rebirth for Midwifery," *Time*, August 29, 1977, p. 66.

[3]American College of Obstetricians and Gynecologists, "Health Department Data Shows Danger of Home Births," January 4, 1978 (news release).

[4]Patrick O'Donoghue, *Evidence about the Effect of Health Care Regulation: An Evaluation and Synopsis of Policy Relevant Research* (Denver, Colo.: Spectrum Research, Inc., 1974), p. 91.

[5]Hilary Hilton, "Working toward a Better Beginning," *Corpus Christi Caller*, June 26, 1977, p. 8a.

[6]"Rebirth for Midwifery," p. 66.

new research should be minimal. However, at this stage you will need to solicit the impact of management, which must look at salient information very carefully, sort out the pros and cons of alternate positions. and then make a policy decision.

Once that decision has been made, it is then possible to write a thorough position paper on the company's point of view. If PR professionals in the firm are held in high esteem, management may ask that a proposed position be written and used as a basis for discussion. A draft position paper is written with the expectation that it will be approved in principle, modified or rejected. After modifications are completed and approved, a final version is prepared for distribution to management and other publics.

Whenever a new issue surfaces, the PR department should alert management to the need for a position paper. In effect, recognizing and stating an issue is the first step in writing a position paper.

Stating the Issue

No position paper can have much value unless it states the issue clearly. Your job as the writer demands that you describe the issue fairly and honestly. *Don't* distort the issue to suit your purposes or to make it easier to form—or defend—an opinion. The purpose of a position paper is to address an issue squarely, not skirt it.

If your firm is an oil company and you must write a paper on its position regarding excess profits, you would not be addressing the issue directly if the major thrust of your paper is a claim that profits are necessary to attract capital and to reinvest. The issue is not whether profits are needed, but whether profits are excessive and, specifically, whether your firm is making an unfair profit. Don't dance around the issue; meet it squarely near the beginning of the paper. One of the most obvious ways of doing this is by providing relevant background.

Background

If you want your position paper to be comprehensible, you must provide pertinent background information. But remember a position paper is not a historical analysis; leave that to the backgrounder. Give just enough background to provide a context for your position and to help your readers understand why the subject under discussion has become an issue. The nature of the issue usually makes the need for extensive background information unnecessary, but be sure to give enough on which to base and defend your position.

Position

Don't keep your readers in suspense. Come to the point immediately. Don't try to build suspense by including things like elaborate recitation of facts and flashy figures, then culminating with an eloquent conclusion.

State your position first so readers know where you stand. Then support it with facts and figures, logically organized and clearly written. Use examples or metaphors that readers can understand. Use statistics sparingly but include enough to support and reinforce your points.

Long lists of numbers might be appropriate in a backgrounder, but in a position paper they will only clutter up your argument and cloud understanding by the reader. Make your point in clear, plain language, then select just the right statistic to support it. If you feel a lot of statistics should be included as support material, put them in an appendix so they don't overpower the paper. Always provide the sources of your statistics. Readers who spend time with such information place a lot of weight on the authority behind the numbers.

Consider Both Sides   Although a position paper should come down strongly on your side of an issue, don't ignore opposing sides. You are expected to amass as much information as you can in support of your point of view, but don't stack the cards.

"Card-stacking" is a propaganda device whereby all the supporting arguments are given but no opposing data is mentioned. This gives the impression the favorable evidence is more overwhelming than it really is. The position paper may seem impressive at first glance, but when readers discover other points of view they will distrust not only this message but others you send them later.

It is far better to state opposing points of view and refutations of them than to ignore them. This is especially important when the opposition has some good points. Acknowledge the cons, but show why you think these points are outweighed by objective evidence. You may not win many converts with this tactic, but you will gain respect, even among your foes.

Consider the Audience   Although most position papers are written for internal use by management, some are written for distribution to other publics. Even when writing a position paper you believe will be used internally only, you must keep in mind other potential publics.

For example, a position paper may be written for presentation to the board of directors by management in an attempt to explain company policies to stockholders. But Wall Street analysts may ask to see the company's position. And how about the media's business editors? They may ask for and should be given copies.

This can pose a serious problem to you as a writer because information that makes sense to your management may not make sense to the general public or to stockholders. It would be ideal, of course, to write one version of the position paper for use by all possible audiences, but the nature of the issue may make this impractical. You may have to write more than one version of the same paper. You should not tell a different story in each version; you should tell the same story differently and appropriately. Remember, too, that different publics may be more concerned with some questions than with others, so alter the emphasis of each version of your position paper accordingly.

Recommendations

It is generally perceived as bad form to be against something without offering a solution. Taking a position means you are both against one thing and for something else. If you omit your inevitable proposals from your position paper, you will inevitably be asked what you recommend as a suitable substitute to something you oppose.

For example, if Congress is considering a national health insurance plan that your firm opposes because it means higher taxes, that is a suitable topic for a position paper. But if that's all you say, you really haven't faced the issue, which includes coming up with an alternate solution. If the issue is significant enough to command company attention, the company has an obligation to help with its resolution.

Format

When the writing is completed, its format and method of distribution must be determined. A backgrounder or position paper intended for internal use is usually typed on plain or letterhead paper, copied, assembled and stapled, then delivered. Those distributed outside the firm may be produced the same way or they may be elaborately produced as a printed booklet or monograph, embellished with art, color, good design and typography, then printed on expensive paper.

Some firms prepare backgrounders for public consumption on special forms. These forms contain a printed company heading with the word "backgrounder" prominent. Other companies, particularly those in heavily regulated industries that require a large number of backgrounders or position papers annually, produce punched versions suitable for inclusion in a loose-leaf notebook. When new versions of positions are called for by management, the old ones can be removed and the new ones inserted. Sometimes long and exhaustive backgrounders and position papers are distributed spiral-bound, even if they have been simply typed and copied.

Backgrounders, and sometimes position papers, often include charts and illustrations to help explain the topic. Preparing these for reproduction is usually the job of an artist, but you should be fully aware of their content, how they look and where they will appear in the finished report. The location of these visuals close to appropriate verbal segments makes the information easier to understand.

Conclusions

* Any firm can count on receiving inquiries about background information and positions on issues. Every firm should prepare for these by producing backgrounders and position papers in advance.

* Backgrounders serve as sources of information for company executives, public relations writers, media personnel, financial analysts, the general public and a variety of other publics.

* Backgrounders should always provide an historical context, a description of the current situation and a discussion of the implications of the matter under study. This information should be free of opinion.

* Position papers state a position on a topic. They are basically opinions supported with a few facts. They should treat opposition points of view as well.

* When the firm takes a position against something, it should also suggest alternate solutions.

* Backgrounders and position papers, especially backgrounders, should fully acknowledge sources of information used in their preparation.

* Clear writing is a must.

Exercises

1. Imagine you are the PR writer for a medical organization that *favors* licensing of lay midwives. Prepare the opening paragraphs of a position paper to support your organization's opinion. In outline form, indicate what you might include in the rest of the document.

2. Review the background research information you put into draft form in Chapter 3. Now, write a backgrounder for Ourbank on why so many banks have failed recently.

3. Management at Ourbank is troubled that the state legislature is considering the abolition of branch banking. Ourbank is soon to open its first branch on the northwest side of Serendipity. Management asks you to write a position paper that favors branch banking. This position paper and, possibly, the backgrounder in Exercise 2 will be used as documents in support of Ourbank's lobbying efforts with legislators.

Selected Bibliography

William L. Rivers, *Writing Craft and Art* (Englewood Cliffs, N.J.: Prentice-Hall, 1975).

Heil Sheehan, Hendrick Smith, E. W. Kenworthy and Fox Butterfield, *The Pentagon Papers* (Chicago: Quadrangle Books, 1971). Besides being of historical interest, this book is amply illustrated with backgrounders and position papers.

Kate L. Turabian, A *Manual for Writers of Term Papers, Theses and Dissertations*, 4th ed. (Chicago, Ill.: The University of Chicago Press, 1973).

15
Memos
and Letters,
Reports
and Proposals

Public relations professionals write lots of memos, letters, reports and proposals in their everyday routine office work. They may also write lots of such pieces for key officers in the organization, because these forms of writing frequently function to persuade in some way. The purpose of this chapter is to give you some basic guidelines to follow when you must write any or all of these forms.

Memos

The word *memo* is the short form of *memorandum,* meaning an informal reminder of something important that has or will occur.

Internal Communication Memos are restricted to communication within the firm. They should never be used to communicate with people outside the organization. Letters serve the latter purpose.

A good memo disseminates information simply and begins with a guide to its contents, as in the following example:

September 7, 1985

To: John Gill, comptroller

From: Susan McConnell, director, external relations

Subject: Planning conference for 1986 annual report, September 14, 2 p.m. in the board room

Because people in the firm have the same mail addresses, it is usually unnecessary to use anything more than a departmental designation. When the writer and receiver know each other, the memo style may be even less formal, containing only first names and no titles. This is especially common when the memo is to someone in the same office or immediate area of operations.

The body of a memo ordinarily differs little from the body of a letter. Memos are usually shorter, however, and there are often more visual cues, such as lists of numbered items. It is designed to communicate salient information quickly and efficiently.

Memos can range in tone from formal to informal. Memos directed up the chain of command tend to be more formal while those directed down the chain tend to be less formal. The most informal of all are memos moving between persons at the same level in the organization. The exception to these guidelines turns on personal relationships. For example, an account executive in a PR firm would probably write a fairly formal memo to the president of the agency, unless the president happened to be a fishing partner.

Memos ordinarily have a limited audience. They are usually addressed to just one person or to a small group. At times, however, they may be directed to a large audience. For example, the president of the company may distribute a memo to all 600 employees simultaneously stating that the firm had just recorded its highest annual profits ever. This information, of course, would also be appropriate in the company newsletter and in releases to the media, but the memo is often used to share important information quickly with all employees.

Visual Cues In addition to the style of salutation noted, the memo usually has a number of visual cues imbedded in it that help communicate important information quickly.

The most important of these stylistic characteristics is the use of common words, short sentences and brief paragraphs. The latter is especially important, because a memo is typed single space with double spaces between paragraphs. A paragraph, of course, is supposed to represent a new, but related, thought. In effect, each paragraph is a subsequent "take" in the thought processes that organize information related to the content and purpose of the memo.

Other visual cues, often not found in letters, are indented paragraphs (for emphasis), numbered items to further indicate important matter, fragmented sentences (for emphasis, but be cautious about using these often), and lists of items, often in vertical format rather than serially in a paragraph.

Context   There is a tendency among memo writers to assume that because the person addressed in the memo is a member of the team, he or she knows all the pertinent background information related to the topic at hand. This is often a mistake. If you want to be understood, provide clarifying information that makes what you say comprehensible and that leaves little room for misinterpretation. Do not, of course, provide superfluous information.

Providing a context for your message is especially important if the memo is directed to persons with whom you do not work regularly. When in doubt, always provide appropriate background materials. These may not be needed, but it is better to be safe than sorry.

Classifications of Memos

The tone and tempo of a memo depends on its purpose, style and audience. There are six general categories of memos: bulletin, essay, informative, action, summary and file.

Bulletin Memo   The bulletin memo usually has a sense of urgency about it. It is generally brief and may be somewhat terse in style. It is the telegram of the memo world. It always conveys a sense of immediacy. The bulletin memo gets its name from the bulletins that appear on the wire services notifying editors that something important has happened or is about to happen. Given the nature of its content, such a memo may wind up being posted on a bulletin board, even if it is addressed to just one person.

Essay Memo   An essay memo is usually a lot more descriptive than a bulletin memo. It is used for "let's talk it over" material or situations. Its content may range from management philosophy to questions of how to get employees to clean up the coffee room after using it. The style is often conversational and flowing.

Informative Memo   The informative memo is usually a detailed descriptive piece of writing. An example might be a memo from the account executive, with informational copies going to the account group and client. This memo might document actions taken and their results. Or it might recommend programs for the future and describe projected outcomes. The style and tone of these memos is usually fairly formal.

Action Memo   The action memo describes action taken or planned (see Example 15-1). Such memos, especially those dealing with future actions, often contain places for responses by recipients. For example, there might be a space for the receiver's initials on a section to indicate that he or she accepts responsibility for the

15-1

An Action Memo: PR Planning Memo
One of the most important kinds of memos PR people write is
the memo outlining a major PR program. This mock memo is
prepared as though a single PR consultant was in charge of
planning the public relations for the American Revolution.
Note that the first step is to give a clear statement of the
campaign objectives; this is followed by a synopsis of the
research findings. Target audiences are designated next,
followed by a discussion of "vehicles" of communication (we'd
call them media today). Finally, the strategy for implementing
the program is discussed.

MEMORANDUM

To: S. Adams

Re: Independence and Necessary Public Relations Programs

                         OBJECTIVES

     To begin with, we must formulate objectives more specific than "inde-
pendence." Saying what we want is easy; saying what we have to do to get it
is a little more difficult. As with the PR campaign against the Stamp Act,
we must specify the objective in terms that tell us what we must do. With
the Stamp Act, we wanted repeal. But our specific objective was to prevent
the act's enforcement.

     If we rephrase "independence" to describe what we really want, we
might say "to establish home rule and prevent the interference of the British
in the internal afairs of the colonies." In a sense, we had "home rule"
before 1763. But our research on British attitudes shows that return to the
pre-1763 days is impossible. Hence, complete separation is the only way to
achieve home rule.

     But what will this require? Above all, it will require unification
of the colonies and belief in a common purpose: independence from Britain.
No plan for separation will succeed unless all the colonies join together.
Thus our primary objective is:

     To effect a unification of the colonies.

     Achieving this objective will require a massive, well-coordinated PR
campaign throughout the colonies. The objective of such a campaign should
be:

     1. To generate common attitudes among the inhabitants of the various
         colonies.

     2. To sustain and organize popular sentiment.

     3. To change the attitude of the people toward Great Britain from one
         of allegiance to one of repudiation.

15-1 **continued**

RESEARCH

A thorough examination of English common law, colonial charters,
newspapers of the last decade and British and colonial history formed the
major portion of the research effort for this project. In addition, during
my recent tour of the colonies I interviewed a number of key political
figures to gather their insights into the current situation. To this has
been added the report from Benjamin Franklin on opinions in Britain and
France. I list below the major research findings.

Legal Basis for Independence

There can be no doubt that taxation of an Englishman without his
consent (through representation in the taxing body) is a violation of his
rights. This is the clear message of the Glorious Revolution (1689), and
it is reaffirmed in various ways by the colonial charters. Furthermore,
during the reign of Queen Anne, the crown agreed to recall the provincial
governor after the New York assembly complained that he had taxed the subjects without the consent of the assembly. This action seems to have established royal consent to the doctrine that taxation without representation
is unconstitutional.

No responsible person, in the colonies or England, argues that
direct representation of the colonies in Parliament is feasible (see the
resolutions of the Stamp Act Congress). Thus if Parliament persists in
taxing us, we have no administrative remedies, as our lawyer friends would
say. It thus becomes a clear case of Parliament's violating our rights
through unconstitutional action; they are the lawbreakers. We are thus
legally--and morally--justified in breaking our ties to the empire.

Current State of Opinion in the Colonies

Despite the anti-British feelings displayed at the time of the
Stamp Act, ties to Britain remain strong. We are, for the most part,
Englishmen who just happen to live on the other side of the Atlantic.
The physical distance is trifling compared to the closeness of language,
history and culture.

In fact, it is not an exaggeration to say that the colonies feel
closer to England than they do to each other. At first glance, barriers
to achieving unification would seem almost insurmountable.

But research has turned up some encouraging signs. Since the
beginning of this century the colonies have joined in several wars, most
recently the seven years' battle against the French. Fighting on the
same side brings peoples together, and joining in battle again would not
be a completely novel affair. Furthermore, the colonists have in common
their "rights as Englishmen," along with the heritage of fighting for
these rights, which have been passed down from 17th-century England. Most
of us share a common language, and we hold a common allegiance to the
crown. Upon these common beliefs and traits we should be able to build
a movement for unity.

True, these common features have not led the way to unity so far.
In essence, this is because the tie to Britain has been strong; each
colony needed Britain more than it needed any other colony. But this
need was largely due to the threatening presence of the French on our
western borders. With France gone, the tie to England can be weakened.

One further point should be made about weakening ties to Britain.
A great many of our people came to America because they didn't like

15-1 continued

things in Britain. Thus we have a ready-made broad base of support for
any anti-British movements we undertake.

Support will also come from certain specific groups. Printers and
lawyers, with the memory of the oppressive Stamp Act fresh in their minds,
will back efforts for home rule. An extremely important group that will
favor self-rule is the clergy. The faith of Protestant Christianity is one
of the most central characteristics of colonial culture. It sets us apart
from the English, and is perhaps the best spot through which to drive a
wedge between the colonies and the crown. After all, the church is a most
powerful social institution. The colonies have at least 3,000 churches
serving a dozen and a half denominations. And most church leaders fear
above all else the establishment of an Anglican episcopate on the North
American continent. By promoting such fears we can increase the clergy's
hostility toward Britain.

Opinion in England

Opinion toward the colonies in England has changed dramatically
since the French and Indian War. English officials view the colonists as
spoiled children, and they are determined to crack down on the colonists
and bring them "into line." Parliament may have repealed the Stamp Act,
but further measures are sure to follow.

The person in England whose opinion is most important, of course,
is the king. Most colonists see the king as wise and just; it's Parliament that is to blame for the tyrannical taxation. Our research indicates
that this view is rather naive.

King George is certainly a courageous and resolute ruler. He does
not lack intelligence. But, without being too unkind, we must report that
the king suffers from moral obtuseness and is also stubborn and vain. Most
colonists don't know that George favors suppression of the colonies by
whatever means might be needed. He has absolutely no sympathy for our appeals in the name of "liberty."

The king's views are shared by many in Parliament. But also in
Parliament are those who support the American cause and understand our
arguments. Such procolonial voices can be quite important; their protests
will no doubt inhibit the ministry from pressing an all-out war against the
colonies, at least at first.

Feasibility of Achieving Independence

Research shows that independence is possible. It will not be granted
by the king without a fight. But a war for independence can be won. The
English army is not in top shape; George will probably have to hire mercenaries to invade the colonies, and mercenaries do not make the best fighters.
We have an exceptional military weapon in the backwoods riflemen, who, as
marksmen, far surpass anything the British can put in the field.

AUDIENCES

My research findings indicate that certain obvious key audiences
should be the primary targets of our PR efforts. These include:
1. Printers
2. Clergy
3. Colonial leaders
4. Certain Members of Parliament
5. The French government

15-1   continued

Printers are obviously among the most influential people in the colonies. By controlling the press, they control the flow of information to the public. They constitute our highest priority target audience.

Clergymen, as noted above, can also be of great value in swaying public opinion. They are generally experienced orators and have captive audiences every Sunday.

If we are to achieve unification of the colonies, it is imperative that political leaders in each province be subjected to our communication efforts. Those who already agree must be provided information to support their view; those who are undecided must be persuaded to join the cause.

Members of Parliament who are inclined to support the colonies should be kept informed of our problems. They may be helpful in moderating any possible punitive acts by Parliament. Eventually, of course, war will break out despite the help of our friends in Parliament. At that point we must hope to receive aid from France. Thus, the French government must also be persuaded of the merits of our case.

We must also be aware of certain groups making up the colonial public. Some communications must be designed for the intellectuals, those who make up the colonial assemblies and the like. The lower classes, the backwoods farmers, and the illiterate and poorly educated are other groups we must consider. Special interest groups like mechanics and merchants must also be persuaded, and we must obtain the support--or at least the neutrality--of blacks, Indians, and French Canadians.

VEHICLES

To be effective, our PR program must use the proper vehicles of communication to reach each of our target audiences. Such vehicles can be of three types: written, verbal, and visual.

Written Vehicles of Communication

Beyond any doubt, newspapers will be our most important and most effective method of communicating to large audiences. More than 20 newspapers are published now, and that number is growing; more than 40 should be in operation ten years from now. It is essential that we develop good working relations with the press, for without its cooperation we can never hope to unify opinion across the colonies. We must use this medium in all ways possible.

Primarily, we will use newspapers as an outlet for political essays designed to promote unity among the colonies and animosity toward Great Britain. Newspapers will also be valuable as a medium for reprinting letters and documents helpful to our cause. We may, for example, want to print the Magna Carta, the Bill of Rights, and perhaps parts of some colonial charters. Resolutions passed by colonial assemblies can be reprinted across all the colonies.

15-1 continued

Newspapers do have serious limitations, however. Space restrictions force essays to be briefer than we would sometimes like. Developing our arguments in sufficient depth to convince the intellectual classes will require a different medium--the pamphlet. Pamphlets give writers the space they need to build a thorough and complete case for their propositions. Most colonial (and British) leaders are avid pamphlet readers, and propagating our ideas in this form will help develop unified thinking among the key citizens in each colony. Pamphlets will serve to present the overall, complete statement of the American position while newspaper essays can attack more specific points.

While pamphlets are an excellent device for reaching the upper classes, they usually are not read by the majority of the people. In addition to the newspapers, then, we must have a vehicle designed specifically to reach the lower classes. The broadside, or handbill, is perfect for this purpose. It's ideal for rallying crowds and inciting the emotions, since it can be distributed quickly or posted in gathering places. Broadsides rarely identify any source or author, so they can be as inflammatory as we like without fear of reprisal. Broadsides can reach many more people than newspapers can, and they are more effective in gaining attention to a specific issue. They are also easily distributed by clandestine methods, making censorship impossible.

Broadsides and newspapers both reach many townspeople. But seldom do they fall into the hands of our rural citizens. The country people have no regular means of communication with the city, yet it is important that they get our message also. The best possibility with them is the almanac. It is not a timely medium; people get new almanacs no more than once a year. But the only printed matter many rural citizens own is an almanac and a Bible. Indeed, nearly every household has an almanac. While newspaper circulation commonly numbers in the hundreds, Ames of Boston sells 60,000 copies of his almanac each year. Almanacs can't present news, but they can place our general arguments before the country people.

Verbal Vehicles

While written material will be the most important device for disseminating information, we must realize that only about half the men in the colonies can read (and only about a fourth of the women are literate). Furthermore, not everyone who *can* read actually *does* read. So we must devise means for reaching the nonreaders.

The most obvious way is through speeches. Public addresses can gather large crowds. Sermons can also get our message across; here we must enlist the aid of the sympathetic clergy. The best of the speeches and sermons can be reprinted in the newspapers or in pamphlet form.

We must remember that the great majority of the public is not interested in the philosophical and constitutional issues. In fact, most of them can't grasp such complexities. But we must communicate some flavor of the substance of these issues, and verbal communication can help accomplish this. One device especially well-suited to this goal is the slogan--the short, simple but expressive phrase that condenses volumes of elaborate reasoning into a quick, emotional, potent statement of feeling and fact. "No taxation without representation!" is an example. It coveys a substantial amount of the essence of an important issue, but nobody needs to be able to read to understand and remember it.

15-1 | continued

Taking the brevity of the slogan one step further, we can instruct our speakers to use certain key words again and again, some evoking the positive aspects of our position and others calling forth images of British unfairness. Words standing alone can be just as powerful as slogans. "Tyranny" or "Oppression" or "Slavery" can be the words that characterize the practices of the British; "Liberty" or "Freedom" or "Independence" can be the watchwords of the revolution.

One other verbal device we might try is the song. People who can't read a word can remember uncountable verses of song lyrics. If we can introduce songs that carry our message, and if the songs become popular, we can reach a far greater audience than we can with newspapers, pamphlets and speeches.

Visual Vehicles

Complementing the verbal approach toward those who don't read should be devices aimed at the eyes rather than the ears. Illustrations can be used on broadsides to depict the British in an unfavorable light. Almanac covers are convenient spots for cartoonlike drawings either to idolize the heroes of our side or lampoon the British. One of our most successful illustrative devices during the Stamp Act campaign was the snake cut in pieces. Used with the slogan "Join or Die," this can be a most persuasive cartoon.

Other visual symbols can be created and ingrained in the public consciousness. Liberty trees and liberty poles can be the rallying points for demonstrations, serving as focal points for public attention to the issues.

Other Vehicles

Several miscellaneous devices can add to the overall effect of our communications program. Town meetings, for example, can be forums for publicizing our views. We can coordinate town meetings throughout New England so the same message is received by many audiences at once.

Other less formal methods can be used for communicating ideas and information. Certain taverns can be designated information centers where those in support of our cause can gather to discuss the latest news.

STRATEGY

Our research shows that popular sentiment favoring independence will come about only after war breaks out with Britain. The first phase of our PR strategy, then, must be geared to preparing the people for war by building up ill feelings toward Britain and by promoting a sense of intercolonial unity. A second phase of PR strategy will be used after war breaks out, with a third phase to be put into effect after independence is actually declared.

Strategy before War

Our most important objective is to effect a sense of unity among the colonies. This will, of course, be difficult. The diversity of the colonies is well known. However, we have noted two major common threads running through the colonies (aside from the fact that almost everyone speaks English). They are: (1) Every colonial charter guarantees its citizens the rights of Englishmen; and (2) colonists from north to south share a common allegiance to the crown.

We must use these common threads to create a new consciousness, a new spirit of American nationalism among the colonists. Distinctions between New Englanders, New Yorkers, Georgians and Virginians must be made to appear trivial.

15-1 | continued

Our heritage as Englishmen is a common bond that must be used to turn
the colonies against England. We must champion our rights as Englishmen.
The early years of our communication efforts must arouse opposition to all
those acts of Parliament that ignore our rights. We must heavily emphasize
that parliamentary acts denying our rights are unconstitutional, and that
if we are to be true to our common heritage, we must oppose them.

This is, of course, an appeal to principle. Some people are motivated by high principle, others by self-interest. Interests differ, but
principle is universal and unifying, so appeal to principle must be our
primary thrust. We must also, however, provide arguments for those susceptible to self-interest appeals. If one group in particular is taxed or
oppressed, we must stress to others that they may be the next to be stung
by the ministry's punitive measures. By creating a common bond of sub-
ordination to an unjust Parliament, we can create another unifying element--
the sharing of a common enemy--and further our objectives.

In pursuing this strategy, we can enhance feelings of unity while
encouraging derisive attitudes toward Britain. In generating these ill
feelings we must be careful not to break one of our common bonds--alle-
giance to the crown. King George must not become the object of our attacks
during this phase of the campaign. Though we know better, we must appear
to believe that the king is good and wise, merely out of touch with the
situation in America, and kept in the dark by the ministry. All our wrath
should be directed at Parliament. In this way we will avoid severing too
soon one of the strongest ties among the colonies.

With these considerations in mind, we can outline the following
elements of our PR strategy in the prewar years:

1. Prepare pamphlets aimed at political leaders that detail the legal
   and moral arguments opposing parliamentary acts of taxation or
   oppression.

2. Prepare a continuous flow of newspaper essays designed for the
   general public, stressing the *principle* that Parliament has no
   right to tax, and emphasizing possible future taxes that might
   damage each group's particular interests.

3. Stress in all messages our common heritage as Englishmen and our
   determination to stand on the rights of Englishmen, as loyal subjects of the king.

4. Direct all expressions of outrage at Parliament, the ministry,
   or colonial governors, but not the king.

Finally, as soon as general sentiment warrants, a conference similar to the Stamp Act Congress should be convened. As soon as armed conflict breaks out, such a congress should become permanent in order to
coordinate colonial opposition to the British forces.

Wartime Strategy, before Independence

Until war begins, public statements favoring independence will be
useless; in fact, they would damage our cause by appearing too radical. Once
war begins, however, the idea of independence might be mentioned. But it
will take at least a year of fighting before colonial leaders will be willing
to vote for independence. Thus, our strategy for the early part of the war
should follow this outline:

15-1 | continued

1. During the first six months, mention the possibility of independence in newspaper essays but do not promote an immediate vote at this time.

2. During this time allow a small amount of criticism of the king to appear.

3. Six to eight months after the war starts, prepare a pamphlet setting forth the case for independence in strong terms. Distribute the pamphlet widely and have large portions of it reprinted in the newspapers.

4. Use newspapers during the following months to support the ideas of the pamphlet and generate vocal public support for independence.

Our pamphlet calling for independence must address the question of loyalty to the king. This will be the time to sever all ties to the crown. Attacking George personally might prove difficult; instead, we should attack the very notion of kingship, saying, in effect, that no matter how nice a guy George is, all kings are bad because the very idea of "king" is bad.

Postindependence Strategy

After the colonies vote for independence, it will still be necessary to win the war to keep it. In large measure, strategy during this period will be typical war strategy: engender hatred for the enemy, boost national morale, induce desertions of enemy soldiers. Of special importance during this period will be communications abroad. We must persuade other countries, especially France, that we are worthy of diplomatic recognition and military aid.

The above has been a bare outline of what we must do to achieve our objectives. I will proceed at once with the planning details. If all goes well, we should have independence in ten years.

initialed action. Or, in the case of a supervisor, the initials might indicate approval or disapproval of the planned action.

Action memos sometimes convey a sense of coercion. This may be the case, for instance, when the author of the memo does not assign or suggest responsibility but seeks volunteers to assume responsibility. Coercion is implied when the impact of the information says, "If you don't select an area of responsibility, one will be assigned to you." If you're alert to this inference, you'll quickly "volunteer" for the area of action that you will do best and enjoy most. Why sit back and wait for an assignment you will neither handle well nor enjoy doing?

Summary Memo   A summary memo is basically a detailed descriptive memo in essay or outline form. Discussions and actions are collected under appropriate topical headings to facilitate progress during a meeting. The summary memo is often used, too, in evaluating the progress of a program. In this case, the summary memo reflects an accumulation of information over time. The summary memo often explains actions taken or planned.

File Memo   As the name implies a file memo is written for the file only. It is not addressed to another person, but simply records information as it occurs and is stored in the file for reference. Memos of this type are used extensively when the program being planned is complex, when many people are involved in some ongoing action or program, or when sharp divisions in points of view arise as to how or if something should be done. As for style and tone, it may be terse, almost cryptic. The purpose, remember, is merely to "record" information for internal use.

In a sense, a file memo is something like a diary. It records names, dates, places and points of information. If there is serious debate over how or if something should be done, the file memo should always identify persons with their respective points of view, even including verbatim accounts as necessary.

Facts Affecting Use of Memos

Memos should be personalized as much as possible. Involve the recipient with your memo by emphasizing "you." This is not only a pleasant way to write, it is also effective.

The way your memo is distributed may have an effect on the attention it receives. One of the common ways to disseminate a memo, rather than making several copies of it, is to route it among people who should read its content. A routing slip is attached and the memo is passed from one person to the next. Each person initials the slip to indicate it has been read, then passes the memo on to the person whose name appears next on the list. While routing is a common practice, it can be a problem if the content of the memo is timely. People are prone to assign a lower priority to a message attached to a routing form than to a message addressed to them personally. Therefore, even if you save some paper and copying costs by routing memos, you may wind up paying a high price in lost opportunities.

Posting memos on a bulletin board is a common practice, but it can be even less effective than routing them. The company bulletin board is often filled with messages unread by many people in the organization. If you intend your memo for posting, design it like a poster. Add graphics to gain attention and treat the content like a bulletin to encourage easy, quick reading.

If your memo is to be distributed to a large number of people in the organization, you have a number of options. The best way, of course, is to send the memo to each person by name, title and address. An alternative is to provide supervisors with a stack of copies and rely on them to pass a copy along to each employee. While many supervisors will be careful to distribute the information, others will not, and a communication breakdown will result.

Some memos are best suited for special methods of distribution. For example, an announcement about changes in employee insurance coverage may best be stuffed into payroll envelopes. You can count on employees opening their pay envelopes and seeing your memo. On the other hand, a memo about the company picnic might be better mailed to employees' homes, since you'll want spouses to know about the event, too.

The setting in which the memo is received may also influence its effectiveness. Obviously, the company picnic is a social event that involves the employee and spouse. Therefore, it is appropriate to send the memo announcing it to employees' home addresses. On the other hand, a memo calling a meeting of department heads should be sent to the recipients' respective offices, not to their homes. In general, if the memo is social, send it to the employee's home; if it is business, send it to the employee's work address.

Letters

The memo form is used inside the organization, but the letter form of communication is used outside the firm. Still, on formal occasions a letter might be used inside the firm, too—for example, to inform recipients that they have been promoted or that their salaries have been raised.

The typical business letter has six parts—heading, salutation, body, close, signature and reference matter. These parts are treated in turn below.

Heading   The heading has two parts. The first is the identity of the sending firm, its mailing address and, often, its phone number. This material is usually printed on the letterhead of the firm. The second part is the date, plus the name, title and address of the recipient. The heading should always contain these elements, even when you know the person you are writing to quite well. Always document the sender and receiver completely and accurately.

Salutation   In the salutation you address the person to whom you are writing. This might appear to be a simple proposition, but it can cause some problems if you are insensitive to your receiver.

Suppose you are writing a letter from your CEO to Doug Newsom, one of the co-authors of this text, seeking names of persons who might be used as PR consultants. You might address Doug variously as "Dear Mr. Newsom," "Dear Professor Newsom," "Dear Dr. Newsom" or "Dear Doug." The first salutation would be incorrect because Doug's name is Douglas *Ann* Newsom, but she goes by Doug. The second form would be acceptable, because she is a professor. The third form would be correct, too, because she does have an earned doctorate. The last form would be correct only if your CEO knows her personally. Two points are illustrated here: Avoid using a gender-specific title if you don't know the gender. And do not use a title if you don't know that it is correct.

If you are writing a promotional letter to be sent to hundreds of clients, and it will not be personalized by name, use salutations like "Dear Customer," "Dear Client" or "Dear Colleague" (see Example 15-2). Even if these salutations are impersonal, they are better than ones that might be genuinely offensive.

Body   Generally the body of a letter will follow the same general styles outlined in our discussion of memos, except there is no such thing as a "file" letter, only a "file" memo.

The level of formality in the tone depends on the relationship between the writer and the recipient of the letter. If there is a personal relationship, the letter may have a casual salutation and a conversational tone. In general, the tone of the body will be more formal if the letter is going to a person whose status is higher than that of the writer; it will be more informal if the writer's status is higher than the recipient's.

Close   The close of a business letter contains two elements. One is an urge to action, if that is the purpose of the letter, or an offer of further help. The other is a complimentary statement that appears above the signature. Most business letters close with a simple "Sincerely" above the signature block. Business letters between friends outside the firm sometime close with "Best regards," "Cordially yours" or simply "Cordially." Letters between strangers are more likely to have a more formal close, such as "Respectfully yours" or "Respectfully." Whatever the form used, note that only the first letter of the close is capitalized.

Signature   The name of the writer should always be typed; the written signature will appear over it. The signer's title should also be typed immediately below the signature line if the title is not printed on the letterhead.

When the recipient is a friend, the signer might inscribe only his or her first name. If little or no personal relationship exists between the writer and the receiver, however, the full signature is required.

15-2

Thank-You Letter
Source: Reprinted with permission of Barry Harper.

BARRY HARPER   **C.B. HARPER**

Harper's Blue Bonnet Bakery and Catering Service
3905 Camp Bowie Blvd.   731-4233
Fort Worth, Texas 76107

March 26, 1985

Dear Customer;

The entire staff of Harper's Blue Bonnet Bakery would like to say "THANKS" for shopping with us through the recent Camp Bowie construction project. The crew laid the last brick in the first phase of the repaving project on March 22, 1985. The second phase is not scheduled to begin until June 1985.

There is a beautiful new brick street where all that mess was on your recent visit to the Bakery. You are invited to come by and admire it with us. We are certainly proud to have the historic old bricks without the car wrecking bumps.

Thanks again for making the effort to shop with us during the construction. As an added thanks to our "Construction Veterans" we will give you two dollars off on your next purchase with this letter.

Thank you,

Barry & Vicky

Barry and Vicky Harper

Reference Matter   All business letters typed by a person other than the sender should contain symbols below the signature block that look like this: BC:rlb. The capitalized letters are the initials of the writer and the small letters are the initials of the person typing the letter.

The next element in the reference material is a notation about enclosures, if any, that go with the letter. This notation reads like this: Enc.: [name of enclosure]. This note serves both as a form of documentation by the sender of the message and a flag to the receiver that material is enclosed.

The third element in the reference material designates whom, if any others, are to receive copies of the letter. This designation reads like this: cc: [name of persons who also received copies]. The "cc" comes from pre-photocopy days when copies were made via carbons and its stands for "carbon copy." A variation is "bcc." This goes on the copy you retain in your office but not on the copy sent to the addressee or to those listed under "cc." The "bcc" stands for blind copy. It is used when you want to share information with another without letting those who received official copies know about it. Remember that "bcc" is typed on your own copy only and that it reminds you that another person got a copy other than those formally listed on the letter.

Promotional Uses of the Letter in PR

Although a letter may be used for a variety of business purposes, it is an important tool in many PR situations, especially those involving promotional efforts. In this sense, the business letter is used in much the same way as an ad or a brochure. Just because the letter is promotional in nature does not give you license to wax eloquent and mire the reader in a semantic bog.

A promotional letter has to be just as crisp and to the point as a standard business letter. (Refer to Example 15-2.) It also may be, and often is, longer than a typical business letter. In longer promotional letters, the form and style of presentation are critical. There should be a definite logic to your message, with each paragraph building on the previous one. And the letter should conclude with a specific urge to action. As for form, you'll find readers are more receptive if you use devices like subheadings, italics, boldface, underlining and indents. These help the reader spot the important things in your message.

The cardinal rule to remember in promotional letters is to reward readers with clarity and simplicity. The more you are asking of the reader, such as money or time or support for a cause, the clearer you must be. Don't leave anything to guesswork.

The best way to test the clarity of your letter is to read it from the point of view of the receiver. If you are not good at role playing, have a friend who has not seen the letter read it aloud to you. It is amazing how many bugs can be spotted this way.

Reports and Proposals

The requirements for organizing and writing reports and proposals are similar enough for both to be considered together. The terms *report* and *proposal* as used here refer to extensive documents that are researched, written and presented much like a traditional scholarly research paper or the manuscript for a monograph or book.

In fact, if you must write a report or proposal of this type, the first thing you should do is get a copy of one of the popular style manuals like Kate L. Turabian's *A Manual for Writers of Term Papers, Theses and Dissertations*. Such a source will save you innumerable hours of research time, because it will show you as you begin to research the project what information you need to gather and how to credit it.

Organization of Reports and Proposals

After research on the topic is completed, you are ready to begin to organize and write your report or proposal. This requires special skills and attention to details, because there are often as many as seven major sections of a finished project: letter, front matter, synopsis, body, references, bibliography and appendix.

Letter   A letter of documentation and sometimes one of transmittal should always accompany a report or a proposal.

A letter of documentation, sometimes called a cover letter, addresses the person or persons who will consider the report or proposal. It usually describes both the content and the people who did the research, planning, writing and illustrating. The letter may also end with a brief summary of findings or recommendations, and call attention to any conditions that may affect adoption or rejection. Finally, it should indicate where the person who signed the letter can be located. A letter of documentation is sometimes made a part of the report, in which case it should be inserted immediately following the front matter discussed in the next section.

A letter of transmittal is needed when a person or group has been authorized to do a report or proposal. It should seek to establish the credibility of the report or proposal. The letter should note who gave the authorization and when, as well as a summary of results or recommendations. It may sometimes include a list of acknowledgments of special help or meritorious work by individuals who contributed to the project. Such a letter, too, allows you to include information that may not belong in the body of the document but that provides additional insights into what is there.

Skillful use of letters of documentation and transmittal gives you the opportunity to prepare readers of the document for what follows.

Front Matter   Front matter in a report or proposal follows the same general principles as the front matter of this book. It consists of a cover page, a table of contents, and a list of tables, figures and illustrations. These pages are numbered serially with small Roman numerals (for example, iii, iv, v and so on). Although the cover page is counted in this series of numbers, no number appears on the cover page.

Synopsis   If a synopsis is used, it appears at the end of the front matter and before the body of the report or proposal. Usually no more than a page or two in length, it is a digest of the content of the document. It should be so concisely written that reading it gives the reader a clear picture of what is in the document. A synopsis is also known as an abstract or an executive summary. In the business world, executive summary is the term most often used. Remember that point because you'll be expected to use it when your employer asks you to do a report or proposal.

Body   The body of the report or proposal follows the executive summary. You have already written several term papers in your college career, so you need only a brief reminder about basic organization: introduction, body and conclusions.

The introduction should review for the reader the background of the problem being studied, the scope of the effort in the study, and how you will go about conducting the study. You will also need to explain to the reader why the study is important, as well as any special problems encountered in the conduct of your research and how these were resolved. The latter point is especially important because it prepares the reader for any limitations of the study.

The body of the paper should be built around a single, simple statement. Called a thesis statement or hypothesis, it provides a sense of unity for the entire paper. It is the organizing principle that helps you to address the issue point by logical point. Develop each point and support it with pertinent facts. Use headings and subheadings to guide the reader through the body of the paper.

Conclusions should derive naturally from any summary findings in the report or proposal. Sometimes, recommendations will stem from your conclusions. Conclusions and recommendations should be stated clearly. This sometimes takes courage because you may conclude or recommend something that your readers may prefer to ignore. Also, clarity is necessary because a report or proposal that is subject to many interpretations is not very useful to anyone.

References   In a report or proposal of this type, it is necessary that you properly cite the source of every piece of information that is not common knowledge to your audience. This means that you must use footnotes or endnotes, with complete bibliographic citations, so anyone can locate and read the original materials. In this sense, proposals and reports are exactly like scholarly research papers.

In addition to footnotes or endnotes, it is necessary to include a full bibliography. The bibliography, of course, includes all of the basic sources cited in the footnotes or endnotes but it also includes sources you reviewed but did not specifically cite in the body of the paper. The purpose of the bibliography is to show the reader what you chose to use from a broader spectrum than was actually cited.

Appendix An appendix contains any charts, tables, illustrations, maps, copies of questionnaires and other exhibits that could not be woven into the body of the paper. As a general rule, the only items of this type to appear in the body are simple tables and charts that illustrate specific points. More complex material goes in the appendices. Be certain, however, that you interpret the complex materials sufficiently so the reader will understand their importance. Each appendix should be labeled separately—as Appendix A, B and so on.

Readability and Applicability

A reader of your report or proposal should conclude something from what you have written. Two factors will influence the outcome: readability and applicability.

Readability If your report or proposal is in a specialized field, your reader expects to see jargon common to that field used in your document. But this is not a license to use jargon without restraint. On the contrary, you should write in plain, simple English with just enough jargon to establish your credibility with the reader.

Jargon invariably makes your writing more difficult to understand. Review the readability formulas in Appendix A. Try out Gunning's fog index on some samples of writing in your report. Then go back and do some severe editing to make it clearer and easier to understand.

Unless you are an extraordinarily gifted and lucky writer, you will not be able to write a good report or proposal in the first draft. You will probably have to write the whole report at least twice. You may have to rewrite several times. In this sense, the art of good report and proposal writing is rewriting.

If time allows, you are sure to improve the readability of your report if you can write a draft and then put it aside for a week or more. When you pick up the document and read it cold, trouble spots will jump out at you. Fix them immediately and do the reorganizing and rewriting necessary to clarify the draft.

And don't forget that headings, subheadings, indented segments, underlining and other visuals may help to improve readability.

All these points apply to both reports and proposals but one consideration applies to proposals alone. In a sense, proposals resemble ad copy. They are meant to persuade, to sell ideas. So showmanship with words counts more in proposals than in reports.

Applicability

When you do a report, you will want your readers to accept the document as meaningful and significant enough to prompt a course of action. You'll want your readers to say, "This is important. We should do something." As for your proposal, you'll be trying to evoke this response: "This is a really good idea. Let's go with it."

You will elicit such judgments only if the reader perceives what you have written to be clear, reliable and justified. Additionally, what you present should be singularly relevant to the situation. And any action you call for must be made to appear easy to accomplish.

Conclusions

* Memos are used for communication inside the organization, not between organizations.
* There are six types of memos: bulletin, essay, informative, action, summary and file.
* Memos are most effective when addressed to persons as individuals. Effectiveness declines when they are distributed *en masse* or are posted.
* Business letters are used for communication outside the organization.
* There are six principal parts of a letter: heading, salutation, body, close, signature and reference matter.
* Letters are often used as promotional tools by people in public relations.
* Reports and proposals are done much like scholarly research papers.
* Reports and proposals can have as many as seven parts: letter, front matter, synopsis, body, references, bibliography and appendix.
* Jargon is expected by readers in specialized fields, but it should be used with restraint.
* Style and visual elements should be used in reports and proposals to improve readability, understanding and acceptance.

Exercises

1. You are a PR writer for a hotel in a major resort community. Some extensive remodeling will begin next week on the west wing of the ninth floor. West-wing rooms will be closed, and guests in the east wing will have to put up with some noise and unsightly construction equipment. Prepare a letter for people who have reservations for next week in the east wing on the ninth floor. Explain that the inconvenience will be kept to a minimum.
2. Draft a memo to establish a company-wide employee newsletter.
3. Draft a second memo defining the purposes and content of the newsletter.
4. You head the writing staff of a company's PR department. One of the jobs coming up is preparation of an annual report. Write a memo to your staff calling a meeting for Monday, 2 p.m., to plan next year's annual report.

5. You have just completed evaluating the writers under your supervision. One is not doing well. He writes well enough, but he misses deadlines too often. You've decided on a month's probation, after which you will review with him his status. Write a letter informing him of his probationary status and what he has to do to retain his job.

6. Write a report to the president of Ourbank. It should outline all of the publics with which Ourbank should be concerned. It identifies which of these publics are most important, it explains why they are most important and it identifies communication programs you are considering for these special publics.

7. Write a memo to all of the loan officers at Ourbank. Describe in it how you plan to promote the lending services of Ourbank to which publics. Ask the officers for their appraisal of these ideas and inform them that you want to schedule a personal conference with each of them about this topic.

Selected Bibliography

Glenn Leggett et al., *Handbook for Writers*, 8th ed. (Englewood Cliffs, N.J.: Prentice-Hall, 1982).

Kate L. Turabian, *A Manual for Writers of Term Papers, Theses and Dissertations*, 4th ed. (Chicago, Ill.: The University of Chicago Press, 1973).

16
Crisis
Communication

The term *crisis communication* embraces issues management, since it is good public relations to intervene in a developing situation before it becomes a crisis. And issues management, in turn, is primarily a research function, the purpose of which is to identify and track trends and events likely to affect the institution and any of its publics. However, beyond issues management, which involves all of the communication tools and planning previously discussed, there is the critical event, serious unforeseen development. For the purposes of this chapter, we will use the term *crisis* exclusively to refer to the critical event.

Planning

No one likes to think about calamities, but public relations people are trained to consider and plan for "worst case" possibilities. If you work for a refinery, you need to assume that there will be a fire sometime, somewhere. If you work for a chemical company, there will be a "hazardous substance" case, sometime, in some form, somewhere. But you don't have to be involved in "dangerous businesses" to encounter a crisis. For instance, your CEO might be kidnapped and held for ransom, or one of your products might be abused by consumers or contaminated by a sociopath or terrorists, causing death. Anything that *can* happen, *will*. You need to be prepared for it.

Public relations crisis planning has grown more sophisticated since the 1960s years of coping with the social turmoils of that decade. An example is the 1984 campaign launched by the A. H. Robins Co. to warn women who still might be wearing the Dalkon Shield to get rid of it. This was, in effect, a product recall 10 years after the product was first associated with the death of some wearers who had miscarriages that were termed "infected spontaneous abortions." The campaign was suggested to Robins by outside counsel Burson-Marsteller because some women might still be wearing the Shield. The campaign said Robins would pay to have the Shield removed. A year after the print and broadcast advertising was paralleled with a program to reach physicians, Robins had received 18,000 calls and removed 3,730 Shields at a cost of $700,000. The recall campaign was timed to be completed before the announcement of settlement claims of 198 lawsuits against the manufacturer. The manufacturer denied the timing was critical, but it certainly helped blunt the adverse publicity of the lawsuit settlements.[1]

Corporate Information

Part of being prepared is routine. It means having current corporate fact sheets containing all necessary basic information in the files at all times. Such information comprises:

1. Addresses of the home office and all branches or subsidiaries, if any, and all telephone numbers, including the numbers of security people and night numbers that override the main control and put you through to the person on duty.

2. Descriptions of all of the facilities, in detail, giving layouts and square footage and number of people in each area (very important facts in case of fire or cave ins).

3. Biographical information on all employees, and long, in-depth pieces on the principals. Often called "current biographical summaries," these are useful for speeches and introductions, but here they might become "standing obits," material ready to use with only the addition of cause of death.

4. Photos of all facilities and all principals (recent photographs, not the architects' rendering of the ten-year-old building or the CEO's favorite photo from several years past).

5. Statistics on the facilities and the institution: number of people employed now; cost of buildings and equipment; annual net (or gross); descriptions of products or services, or both if that is the nature of the institution; major contracts with unions and suppliers; details of lawsuits pending or charges against the institution; information on regulatory or accrediting agencies with some sort of oversight covering the institution, its products, and its services (for instance, Food and Drug Administration

over products in that area or hospital accreditation over health
care institutions).

6. A history of the institution, including the major milestones and
prepared like a fact sheet.

Simply keeping all these materials up to date is a major undertaking,
but it is vitally important. Most institutions handle this kind of thing piecemeal,
updating employee biographies annually, and photos less frequently, and gathering
new and relevant facts once the base is established. A periodic review of these materials is very important. Make a checklist and use it, marking down the date of the
last currency check next to it.

Corporate Plan

When one of a company's coal mines caught on fire—and not for the first time—
corporate executives were actually in a meeting with the PR director and outside
counsel to develop a crisis plan. News coverage of the fire, which trapped the
miners, was devastating. There is never a good time to plan for a crisis, but *now* is
important. And it is critical not only to have a plan but also to make sure that everyone understands the plan. One chemical company anticipated disaster with an
elaborate plan, but unfortunately treated it as top secret, never even sharing it with
the managers in the field. So when the crisis actually occurred, the manager had to
"wing it" until people in the corporate offices could locate and activate the plan.

A recent study by Hill and Knowlton's Strategic Information Research
subsidiary was reported by *PR News* to have found 66 percent of the 94 Fortune 500
industrial companies as either having a crisis plan or developing one. Additionally,
PR News said 47 percent of those companies are conducting crisis-management
training programs for their employees.[2] The chemical industry has launched its own
public awareness campaign through the Chemical Manufacturer's Association.
CMA's Board Chairman Edwin C. Holmer was reported by *PR News* as saying the
industry was going to increase public access to hazard information about chemicals.[3]

The whole chemical industry shared with Union Carbide the unfortunate publicity involved in coverage of the gas leak at a plant in Bhopal, India,
December 3, 1984. The leak caused the death of more than 2,000 people. In 1983
the whole town of Times Beach, Missouri, had to be abandoned because of high
dioxin levels, and the year before, a train wreck released hazardous chemicals in
Livingston, Louisiana. The Media Institute analyzed coverage of these events, and
has said of the Bhopal coverage that it was much more of a neutral tone. The research study also said that a major difference in the Bhopal stories was the reliance
on information from the company involved, Union Carbide.[4]

In a crisis, the first response is often to contact the creators of the
institution's PR image. But before the situation arises it's important to develop a good
plan and be sure everyone likely to be involved knows what to do. Having the plan
in writing helps, but some institutions find that such plans are put aside until it's too
late. Seminars involving role play can help those who might be responsible in time

of a crisis to understand the plan. It's important for you, as the writer of the plan, to know who will play specific roles as well.

The crisis planning by institutions goes beyond the communication aspect. Most institutions where crises are especially likely, such as industry, hospitals, prisons and banks, have employees who are crisis trained. The way a situation is handled as it is occurring can make the public relations job easier or more difficult. For example, writing about hostage-taking, which is a fairly common experience in hospitals, clinical psychologist James Turner says that staffs need to be trained in handling the hostage-takers in the first few minutes, before police officers and negotiators arrive.[5]

Designated Spokesperson   The most important point in crisis communication is to have one person only communicating with the news media and other external audiences. Someone else needs to handle the internal audiences, and the two have to coordinate their communications so both internal and external audiences receive the same message. Where the messages fail to match a severe credibility problem develops. The best precaution against this is to develop a communication procedure.

A Communication Plan   Your first step is to identify people likely to be the principal participants in the communication plan. Also, you should decide on which media will be used in a crisis: memos, closed circuit television, computer terminals, telephones—whatever is likely to work in a given crisis situation. The internal and external spokespeople should create a system for checking message statements. Usually, the internal message is developed first and the external one is composed from that.

When time is critical and people are not where they are usually found, a telephone operation becomes particularly important. You or the person in charge of communications needs to be highly skilled in getting facts, taking questions and dispensing information accurately. You will have to act like a reporter first, finding out as much as you can about the situation. Anticipate questions from the news media. Have your own photographers and interviewers out gathering the story. If you don't take these steps, you won't have enough documentation later, and you will not know what the reporters are getting or how accurate their information is.

Your first job will be to get a statement on the severity of the disaster or crisis from someone in authority. You'll need to have the statement both typed and audiotaped. Then you'll need to develop a fact sheet telling what is known. Review this information with the attorney to assess the legal ramifications of the information you will be releasing. All information given on the telephone should be drawn from these prepared and checked sheets. Never designate more than two people as spokespersons; otherwise you will lose control of the situation. Conflicting information is highly likely at a time when no one is certain of events, and that jeopardizes your credibility. Your role is not censorship, but coordination.

Crisis Teams   The institution (corporate or nonprofit) involved will create crisis communication teams from staff and outside counsel (if any is regularly used) to create the necessary level of expertise. These teams should be able to deal with the crisis so that the institution can go on about its regular activities as normally as possible. Nothing contributes more to the atmosphere of uncertainty than involving all the institution's decision makers in the crisis and thus allowing the day-to-day business to come to a halt. When this happens observers can conclude that there is not much depth to management and that the firm needs everyone it can get to handle a problem.

Handling the Crisis

When a crisis first occurs, the announcement results in some sort of consultation. Ordinarily this is a face-to-face meeting, but it could be an electronic one—for instance, a telephone conference call or a satellite teleconference. Of primary importance at this meeting is that a record be kept—a fairly detailed one of the points discussed and the responsibilities assigned. In fact, it may be your specific responsibility to get a memo from the meeting.

Almost immediately, and sometimes before such a meeting takes place, you will need to make a response release, addressing the situation, and in doing so you will need to check attributed quotes with the institution's attorney if the release contains any mention of responsibility or damages.

For the broadcast media, you will want to have an actuality of the statement from the spokesperson. And you will need your own photographer's pictures from the crisis scene—black-and-white and color stills, and videotape or film (maybe both). Some companies maintain ENG (electronic news gathering) equipment so that they can receive pictures of the disaster immediately at corporate headquarters.

You may need to call a news conference so that news media representatives can pose questions. If you do, you should be prepared with a list of the points you want to make. For this conference you should also anticipate the reporters' needs and questions.

As news develops you will be issuing bulletins to keep internal and external publics informed. Some of these bulletins may be put on an electronic system such as teletext or videotex. Additionally, you will be preparing letters to various related publics to keep them aware of your control of the situation. For example, a university experiencing a number of fires sent letters to parents, and a company that found a problem with a certain lot of its product sent letters to the consumers it could identify through warranty cards. In some cases, you may need to plan special advertising. One utility that had gotten a bad safety review of its nuclear plant and several days of bad publicity, for instance, felt it necessary to buy space for its own message.

Constraints Sometimes a company cannot communicate as freely as it would want to in a crisis. A good example is the corporate takeover. T. Boone Pickens's attempt to take over Phillips Petroleum in 1984–1985 (the battle began December 4, 1984) is a good illustration. Phillips Petroleum is the major employer in its corporate headquarters, Bartlesville, Oklahoma, and it hoped the townspeople would be on their side and express themselves. They weren't disappointed. Townspeople built a huge bonfire, wore T-shirts supporting the company, and perhaps more importantly, talked to the 200 plus newspeople who came to the town of 40,000 to cover the story. Charles M. Kittrell, Executive Vice President of Phillips Petroleum Company, said "The media seemed to be pulling for us." This was important because the company couldn't do much about telling its own story. There are legal restraints on a company in such a situation. The company did hire outside counsel to help PR staff director Bill Adams, and Adams attributes most of the media support to long years of "cultivation" of media.

The Pickens siege was followed by another launched by Carl Icahn. Community support was stimulated again and media events were developed by the townspeople that couldn't be ignored. For example, one night in freezing rain, the stockholders in the town lit a bonfire with Phillips motor oil to burn Icahn's proxy cards. The coverage brought support from all over the nation, according to Kittrell. The company also learned something, he said. "We learned that not everyone will support you when the chips are down. . . . We learned where our public relations efforts need beefing up. . . . We learned we need to better understand what motivates people to buy and hold our stock."[6]

Continuing Problems   Sometimes a situation is one that has been around for a while, but suddenly surfaces as the result of either an accident or investigative reporting. Such a situation, mast-bumping problems with helicopters that cause crashes, won a Pulitzer Prize for the *Fort Worth Star-Telegram*'s Washington correspondent, Mark Thompson. Bell Helicopter Textron was the focus of a series of articles on the problem to which its officers and public relations people attempted to respond. The series ran in 1984. In 1985 the company lost a lawsuit brought by families who had lost someone in a mast-bumping accident. The families were awarded $3.6 million. The reporter was complimented by many for having the courage to attack a "hometown" corporation. (Bell Helicopter is in the Dallas/Ft. Worth metroplex.)[7]

If the situation has raised the possibility of a continuing problem, such as pollution, you may need to prepare a position paper. This paper should contain graphs and charts explaining the problem, the background, the current crisis and some views of the possible outcome. But its content should be strictly factual, not speculative. As the coverage of the crisis from the internal PR staff continues, you may put together a slide presentation or even two—one for internal use to help educate employees on dealing with the crisis and one for external publics to let them know how the institution is responding. If the crisis has caused substantial damage, either in lives or property, it will have some impact on a profit-making institution's stock price. That means you might have to prepare information about the crisis for the annual report somewhere down the road.

There are both short-term and long-term projects in crisis communication, and the key in both is maintaining credibility. It is difficult to maintain openness in communication from day to day when a crisis is ongoing, but the institution that attempts to close up during that time is asking for trouble.

The news media themselves are not impervious to crisis, and some plan for it. Like the mail service, the delivery of the news is taken for granted. A Hart-Hanks publication for its chain used as its cover story for the June 1985 edition how one of its papers, the *Greenville Herald Banner*, responded to a storm that damaged the paper's printing plant. The only electricity available that day was in emergency areas, but the managing editor's home was on the same line as the hospital, so her house became the office and stories were sent by telephone to a neighboring town's paper (*Denison Herald*), which printed the edition for the Greenville paper. Crisis stories live beyond the event, as you can see from the speaking engagements of people involved and post-crisis publications. This is something that cannot be ignored in considering the handling of emergencies. The aftermath is either a good story or a bad one.[8]

Also, during the crisis is no time to get slack about details in communication, since every fact will be seized upon with particular zest by the media. Candor, care and accuracy are always important in PR, but they are critical in a crisis.

Other texts have referred to the public relations problems marketing can create, and the best example for 1985, and maybe since Ford's Edsel, is the New Coke story. Ford claims that the Edsel was a learning experience that taught them what people really wanted in cars and put them years ahead of the other car makers. Coke only learned what perhaps should have been obvious for a soft drink that has its own fan clubs: Public opinion won't tolerate a change of a 99-year-old formula, regardless of the Pepsi challenge.

The case study of the market introduction appeared in ADS, June 1985. The story of the secret planning meetings held by McCann-Erickson to reposition Coke mentioned $70 million worth of advertising in 1985.[9] Add to that some more bucks to bring back the original and call it Classic Coke. The public opinion crisis, *pr reporter* says, illustrates some important public relations points:

1. Even the most successful media coverage only opens a subject for discussion.

2. Opening a subject for redecision fosters cognitive dissonance.

3. People don't care about facts.

4. Psychology surrounding a product is as important as the product.

5. Behavioral science could help anticipate possible issues (rule of abuse for change in relationships since the product is personal, and the rule of participation where people have a part in change).

6. Marketing statistics are still only guesstimates.

A portion of the headline on the *pr reporter* piece says, "How Number-Crunching Overlooks Human Nature."[10] The problem is that numbers have to be interpreted. In this case, Coke had to regroup and even faced some credibility problems with a few people speculating that this was all a marketing gimmick to begin with. For a company that is so closely tied with the nation's value system, that's a crisis.

As soon as possible after the crisis is over, the public relations department should evaluate its activities during the crisis, with a view toward making improvements.

The Significance of Planning

One reason for discussing crisis plans in advance is to get input from top management on how to handle the news media, employees and their families, suppliers and government representatives. Some top managers firmly believe in letting out as little information as possible. Some believe that it is possible to say one thing to one public and something else to another without any ill effects. As a public relations person, you will need to know just where management stands on basic issues such as this *before* a crisis occurs. A good method is to hold discussions of crisis plans and disaster preparation, exposing top managers to hypothetical situations in order to test their reactions. Simultaneously, they can modify their positions.

In any crisis, the PR person's role is as difficult as it is critical. As the go-betweens, PR people can find themselves on slippery turf. You need to command the facts and keep control over all the communication aspects of the situation. Remember to simplify and clarify, humanize and localize, and employ candor and honesty as your best defense.

The term *crisis communication* may soon be passé, according to Ronald E. Rhody, Bank of America's senior vice president of corporate communications. The reason he offers is that crises will become a part of normal operations. That's probably a valid assessment from someone whose company had 26 "negative newsbreaks," as he calls them, between September of 1984 and May of 1985. His staff, he said, had "crisis withdrawal pains" in the one "dry" month of April because they had become "crisis junkies." Despite his humor, the news coverage was national in all events and in some of the most prestigious and widely circulated publications in the United States, such as the *Wall Street Journal, The Los Angeles Times, The New York Times, Time, Business Week, Fortune, Newsweek, The Economist* and *The Financial Times of London,* not to mention the wire services and syndicates. Crises, as Rhody sees it, are a byproduct of the times of socioeconomic change. In addition to handling the crisis communication, his staff moved 177 releases, did 117 major interviews and staged 35 major news conferences, one of which was the bank's first video conference linking the bank's people with reporters in New York and San Francisco by satellite.[11]

In any times, crisis or otherwise, Rhody acknowledges the two types of media relations: the "take charge" school and the "sit on it" school. The latter he dismisses as "arrogant" and, as he puts it, only serves to "delay the day of reckoning." If more than three people know something, he says, it will leak, and news media organizations now have the resources to pursue a story until they get it. In the "take charge" mode, Rhody says, you have more control over how the story is first presented. He does advise caution in two areas: (1) having the courage to say "I know but I can't tell you" in areas involving disclosure, competitive situations or sensitive negotiations, and (2) not being "blackmailed" into participating in a story when it appears that a writer's mind is already made up about how the story will be cast.

The communication strategy Bank of America uses, Rhody says, is this:

* Limit liability.
* Cushion the investors.
* Determine if similar situations existed elsewhere in the bank and impose safeguards to prevent other occurrences.
* Protect the privacy of employees under investigation.
* Maximize possibility for recovery.

Conclusions

* Crisis communication entails issue management, since the best PR is preventive.
* The critical event is the crisis.
* You need to plan for crises, and always anticipate the "worst case."
* Routine corporate communication becomes critical in a crisis and must always be up to date.
* A corporate crisis plan must be developed and placed in the hands of people who will need it.
* Crisis plans can often be "taught" by role playing.
* There should be no more than one or two designated spokespeople in a crisis.
* These spokespeople should be trained in handling media and individuals who are under stress.
* The spokespeople handling internal and external communication must coordinate messages to avoid discrepancies that reduce credibility.
* Crisis teams should take over the crisis situation and permit the others in the institution to go on about their daily work to inspire continued confidence in the institution's ability to cope with the problem.
* Almost all the communications writing tools discussed in this book might be used in a crisis.

Exercises

1. You are the public relations director for a university and you learn that a student has shot and killed a faculty member in a dispute over a grade. What do you do? Detail your plan.

2. Your university has an honor code whereby those who observe academic dishonesty are responsible for reporting it. A work study student in the computer center says that hackers have been able to get into the university's registration system and, over a period of two years have been changing grades for a fee for scholarship students who must maintain a certain average. All of the hackers have been associated with the university at one time or another as students. One has graduated and left the campus; the other is now a teaching assistant in computer science. As PR director what do you do?

3. It's homecoming at your university, and many activities are planned for the alumni and parents who are on the campus. As the PR director, you get a call from one of the vice presidents. He tells you that the doctor in the health center just reported that five students have been admitted with some mysterious, apparently contagious disease in the past twelve hours and a number of other calls from students to the center suggest that an epidemic is afoot. What do you do?

4. Your university has been named as one of the "diploma mills" in a wire service news story that is getting wide publicity. Two networks and two wire services are calling you about it and the local news media representatives are camped in your outer office. The university has an extension unit, but you don't know anything about this particular situation. Develop a plan, explaining what you would do first.

5. Develop a crisis plan for your university. Then check with your school's public relations department to see what their plan recommends, if the school will release it. (For security reasons, many schools will not.)

6. Write a communication plan for Ourbank. This plan will include detailed plans for public relations, advertising and marketing issues. It will also include a crisis communication plan. Review all of the information about Ourbank in Part Five of the text, your backgrounder on bank failures and what should go into a communication plan, then write it.

Notes

[1] Christopher Policano, "Case Study, A. H. Robins and the Dalkon Shield," *Public Relations Journal*, Vol. 45, No. 3 (March 1985): 16–21.

[2] *PR News*, Vol. XLI, No. 23 (June 10, 1985): 1.

[3] *Ibid.*

[4] The Media Institute, *Chemical Risks: Fears, Facts and the Media*, "Forward," p. v, "Special Section, Bhopal Tragedy: First Look at Media Coverage," pp. 57–58.

[5] Jack C. Horn, "The Hostage Ward," *Psychology Today*, Vol. 21, No. 7 (July 1985): 9.

[6] Charles M. Kittrell, "Hostile Takeovers: Pressure on Public Relations," 4th annual Arthur W. Page Lecture, The University of Texas at Austin, April 25, 1985.

[7] *Bell Helicopter Series Sweeps National Honors for Texas Paper*, publication of the *Fort Worth Star-Telegram*.

[8] Melva Geyer, "Storm Tests Diaster Reaction," *Editorial Focus*, June 1985.

[9] Sam Meredith, "Brainstorming at 'The Bunker': Secret Summit Reveals Coke's New Formula Best Marketed with Established Campaign," *ADS*, Vol. 3, No. 20 (June 1985): 5.

[10] "Coke's Difficulty with Acceptance of New Formula Illustrates Important Public Relations Theories, Shows How Number-Crunching Overlooks Human Nature," *pr reporter*, Vol. 28, No. 27 (July 15, 1985): 1, 2.

[11] Ronald E. Rhody, "Nobody Told Me It'd Be Like This," speech at the Public Relations Roundtable, San Francisco, Calif., May 28, 1985, reprinted by Bank of America, pp. 2–4.

Selected Bibliography

Charles M. Kittrell, "Hostile Takeovers: Pressure on Public Relations" (Austin, Texas: The University of Texas Arthur W. Page Lecture and Awards Program, 1985).

Geri Diane Lee, "The Effects of Organizational Structure on Crisis Communication in the Chemical Industry" (thesis, 1983, The University of Georgia).

The Media Institute, "Chemical Risks: Fears, Facts, and the Media" (Washington, D.C.: The Media Institute, 1985).

Doug Newsom and Alan Scott, *This Is PR*, 3rd ed. (Belmont, Calif.: Wadsworth, 1985).

Walter D. St. John, *A Guide to Effective Communication*. Copies available from author, Department of Education, Keene State College, Keene, NH 03431.

Mark Thompson, et al., "Pulitzer Prize: Bell Helicopter Series Sweeps National Honors for Texas Paper" (Ft. Worth, Texas: Ft. Worth Star-Telegram, Capital Cities, 1985).

James Turner, "Violence in the Medical Care Setting: A Survival Guide" (Aspen Corp., 1984).

Part Five

Writing for PR—
A Project

Familiarity builds confidence, so this
exercise attempts to give practice in all the
aspects of PR writing treated in this text.

I

Introduction

Ourbank is one of the old-line banks in Serendipity, a community of 120,000 in the Midwest. It was one of three banks in the town for several decades. Then, in 1968, growth in the market saw the introduction of two competitors. Another bank was chartered in 1979, and another late in 1984. Still another competitor is chartered to begin operation in 1986. Since branch banking is now possible, Ourbank is constructing a branch on the northwest side of town, an area of affluent families mostly involved in business and the professions.

Changes in state banking laws stemming from about the time of federal deregulation have changed the market dramatically. Not only do new banks represent more direct competition, but so do savings and loans, thrifts and credit unions, all of which offer many services that formerly were available only at banks.

Ourbank has never had a marketing or public relations plan. But management now sees the need to correct this situation as quickly as possible.

Since you are the vice president for Ourbank's communication program, it is your responsibility to develop a communication plan. One of your first steps is to analyze the situation, based on information available in the bank records. The following section shows what you found.

Historical Analysis

You discover that the bank calls—statements of financial condition—required by law to be published at the close of each quarter are very useful in giving you a sense of what has happened in Serendipity. For example, when you look at the total time deposits (see Table P1-1), you discover that in 1963 Ourbank was in second position among three banks with 32% of all time deposits but that our share dropped to only 19% by the end of 1984.

This could be rationalized easily by looking at the fact that Ourbank's time deposits had grown by 2,999% in the 22-year period. But a check of the last column shows that time deposits in all banks increased by 4,034%. It may be that competition can be blamed, but a look at TB2 shows it dropped only 3% of share in the same period. That may mean only that TB2 was doing an aggressive job of promoting itself and that Ourbank was pretty passive.

A look at demand deposits (see Table P1-2) (those which can be withdrawn on demand without penalty) shows much the same thing, but the combined growth is not nearly as dramatic. Ourbank had lost 8% of its share by 1984 but TB2 had gained a full point. Who was the big loser? Apparently TB1 felt the impact of new competition more than all the other banks, because it lost 19% of its former share. The bank most active in gaining demand deposits was TB3, which moved from 13 to 21%.

When time and demand deposits are added together, they produce a profile of the total deposits in all banks in Serendipity. Ourbank lost 10% of its share

Table P1-1 Total Time Deposits of Serendipity Banks * (000) (Periods ending December 31)

YEAR	OB	%T	TB1	%T	TB2	%T	TB3	%T	TB4	%T	TB5	%T	TOTAL	%G	CUM %G
1963	$ 4,364	32	$ 4,165	30	$ 5,172	38	$ —	—	$ —	—	$ —	—	$ 13,683	—	—
1968	7,482	25	7,166	24	10,044	33	3,838	13	1,593	5	—	—	30,123	120	120
1973	21,377	25	14,172	16	28,317	33	12,508	14	10,549	12	—	—	86,923	189	535
1978	34,522	21	26,279	16	58,450	36	32,907	20	10,065	6	—	—	162,223	87	1,173
1979	43,818	20	31,373	14	88,938	41	42,300	19	10,813	5	1,233	1	218,475	35	1,497
1980	47,815	16	57,055	20	107,566	37	56,481	19	13,468	5	7,447	2	289,832	33	2,018
1981	63,877	16	67,080	17	148,343	38	79,461	20	17,225	5	15,382	4	391,368	35	2,760
1982	78,588	16	65,921	14	182,124	38	97,877	13	25,101	5	30,993	6	480,604	23	3,412
1983	96,154	18	99,907	18	192,301	34	108,691	19	31,930	6	36,839	7	565,822	18	4,035
1984	104,729	19	108,625	20	194,303	35	105,932	19	38,432	7	**	—	552,021	(2)	4,034

* Derived from bank calls.
** Time deposits do not show in last call; hence, share, growth and cumulative growth are distorted for each bank in 1984.

Note: QB = Ourbank; TB1, TB2, TB3, TB4 and TB5 = the five competitive banks (Theirbanks).

Table P1-2 Total Demand Deposits of Serendipity Banks * (000) (Periods ending December 31)

YEAR	OB	%T	TB1	%T	TB2	%T	TB3	%T	TB4	%T	TB5	%T	TOTAL	%G	CUM %G
1963	$ 3,898	24	$ 5,796	36	$ 6,593	40	$ —	—	$ —	—	$ —	—	$ 16,287	—	—
1968	5,212	22	5,798	24	8,422	35	3,094	13	1,341	6	—	—	23,867	65	65
1973	9,199	20	10,058	21	16,129	32	7,125	15	4,305	9	—	—	46,816	96	187
1978	15,934	16	13,223	16	30,207	37	17,158	21	5,361	7	—	—	81,883	75	403
1979	18,322	19	13,454	14	38,497	39	20,272	21	6,239	7	1,247	1	98,031	20	502
1980	21,482	19	19,260	17	41,295	36	23,070	20	6,149	5	4,362	4	115,618	18	610
1981	15,643	13	16,674	14	50,891	42	26,722	22	6,281	5	6,396	5	122,607	6	653
1982	15,539	15	15,079	15	36,808	36	21,694	21	6,924	7	7,287	7	103,331	(2)	534
1983	16,760	15	15,868	14	37,598	34	20,084	18	5,903	5	15,162	14	111,375	10	584
1984	14,358	16	15,503	17	37,357	41	19,137	21	5,397	6	**	—	91,752	(7)	563

* Derived from bank calls.
** Demand deposits do not show in last call; hence share, growth and cumulative growth are distorted for each bank in 1984.

of the market in the period, although that's somewhat better than TB1, which lost 15%. TB2 was able to cut its total loss of share to only 7% in the same period. TB3 now has 18% and TB4, still a relative newcomer, has moved steadily to claim 9%. (See Table P1-3.)

When TB3 and TB4 entered the market, in the first year they gained 22.7% of the market, a big chunk of which came from TB1's share, as seen in Table P1-4 which compares total assets of all the banks by year. Ourbank and TB2 also lost, but TB2 regained and protected its share pretty well throughout subsequent years. In 1981, however, Ourbank seems to have started to make some of the right moves, because share has increased a little each year since.

You are aware that indexes are sometimes helpful in putting large numbers into perspective. That's why you constructed Table P1-5. Because TB5 did not enter the market until 1979, you have to select a base year that is more recent than you like, but you can't do anything about that, so you select 1982 as base. This index seems to suggest clearly that Ourbank is indeed on the move, especially compared with TB1, TB2 and TB3. The index number for TB4 is impressive, but closer examination of previous tables shows that TB4 has been vegetating for years. Any small growth in total assets is magnified by an index. And since TB5 has been a competitor for such a short time, its showing in the index is best ignored.

You have been around Ourbank long enough to know clearly that it is very conservative regarding loans. And you know that banks make money by lending money and charging interest on it. If the loan is not sound and can't be collected at all or only for a few cents on the dollar, then the bank loses money. Hence, if bad loans are common, not only are a bank's profits endangered but the safety of depositors' money is threatened. That's why it is always useful to look carefully at the level of loan activity. See Table P1-6 for a profile of Ourbank and its competitors.

Ourbank was tied with TB1 for market loan share at 30% in 1963. TB2 was 10% ahead. Because of economic changes in the late 1970s and early 1980s, Ourbank became even more conservative—to the extent that its share of loans by Serendipity banks dropped to 10% in 1981, from a high of 30% in 1963, and Ourbank closed out 1984 at 14%. TB1 seems to have followed much the same pattern. However, TB2 continued to loan at a high level, closing 1984 just 3 points off its high of 40%. The other banks seem not to have been affected much during this same period. However, the conservative loan practices of Ourbank are clearly seen in this table.

You know, of course, that a review of loan activities is not adequate in itself; you must also look at the capital of each bank. That will tell you the strength of the bank and how easily it can absorb some bad loans without endangering the safety of its depositors' money. Study Table P1-7. You can see that Ourbank has increased its capital over the years, as have the other banks, but as a percentage share of the total capital in Serendipity Ourbank controls 24%, a larger proportion than each of the other banks has except TB2, which has lost relative capital by 9% over the years. This clearly suggests that Ourbank is in a relatively strong capital position. But how strong?

One of the best ways to answer that question is to look at the capital-

Table P1-3 Total Deposits of Serendipity Banks * (000) (Periods ending December 31)

YEAR	OB	%T	TB1	%T	TB2	%T	TB3	%T	TB4	%T	TB5	%T	TOTAL	%G	CUM %G
1963	$ 8,244	27	$ 9,961	33	$ 11,765	40	$ —	—	$ —	—	$ —	—	$ 28,970	—	—
1968	12,694	24	12,964	25	18,466	34	6,932	13	2,934	5	—	—	53,990	86	86
1973	30,576	23	24,230	18	44,446	33	19,634	15	14,853	11	—	—	133,739	148	362
1978	50,456	21	39,502	16	88,657	36	50,065	21	15,426	6	—	—	244,106	83	742
1979	62,140	20	44,827	14	127,435	40	62,572	20	17,052	5	2,480	1	316,506	30	993
1980	69,297	17	70,015	18	148,861	37	79,551	20	19,617	5	11,809	3	399,150	26	1,278
1981	79,520	15	83,754	16	199,234	39	106,183	21	23,506	5	21,778	4	513,975	29	1,674
1982	94,127	16	81,000	16	219,722	38	119,571	20	32,025	5	38,280	7	584,725	14	1,918
1983	112,914	17	115,775	17	229,899	34	128,775	19	37,833	6	52,001	8	677,197	16	2,238
1984	119,113	17	124,128	18	231,660	33	125,069	18	43,830	6	61,882	9	705,682	4	2,336

* Derived from bank calls.

Table P1-4 Total Assets of Serendipity Banks * (000) (Periods ending December 31)

YEAR	OB	% OF TOT.	TB1	% OF TOT.	TB2	% OF TOT.	TB3	% OF TOT.	TB4	% OF TOT.	TB5	% OF TOT.	TOTALS	% OF GROW.	CUM. % OF GR.
1963	$ 13,124	28.7	$ 15,473	33.8	$ 17,139	37.5	$ —	—	$ —	—	$ —	—	45,736	—	—
1968	19,684	24.3	17,117	21.2	25,708	31.8	10,708	13.3	7,630	9.4	—	—	80,899	76.9	76.9
1973	34,535	22.9	27,380	18.2	48,909	32.5	22,202	14.8	17,460	11.6	—	—	150,487	86.0	229.0
1978	56,665	20.2	51,277	18.3	100,071	35.8	54,545	18.5	17,303	6.2	—	—	279,861	85.9	511.9
1979	69,550	19.3	60,005	16.7	138,977	38.6	68,053	18.9	18,984	5.3	4,081	1.1	359,650	28.5	686.4
1980	77,989	17.7	77,540	17.6	163,464	37.0	86,412	19.6	22,239	5.0	13,684	3.1	441,328	22.7	864.9
1981	90,189	15.6	97,524	16.9	218,861	37.4	117,402	20.3	27,483	4.6	26,393	4.6	577,852	30.9	1,163.5
1982	106,423	15.7	114,419	16.9	249,862	36.8	131,113	19.3	35,696	3.8	41,778	6.2	679,291	17.6	1,385.2
1983	125,474	16.7	129,312	17.2	255,515	34.0	140,669	18.7	41,787	5.6	58,040	7.7	750,797	10.5	1,540.6
1984	133,451	17.3	134,118	17.4	252,911	32.8	137,106	17.8	47,713	6.2	66,503	8.6	771,802	10.3	1,587.5

* Derived from bank calls.

Table P1-5 Index of Total Assets of Serendipity Banks *
(Periods ending December 31)

YEAR	OB	TB1	TB2	TB3	TB4	TB5	COMBINED
1963	12	14	7	—	—	—	7
1968	18	15	10	8	21	—	12
1973	32	30	20	17	49	—	22
1978	53	49	40	42	48	—	41
1979	65	52	57	52	53	10	53
1980	73	68	65	66	62	33	65
1981	85	85	86	90	77	63	85
1982**	100	100	100	100	100	100	100
1983	119	113	102	107	117	138	111
1984	125	117	101	105	134	159	114

* Calculated from bank calls.
** Base year is 100% of total assets of each bank.

to-loan ratios (sometimes called debt-equity ratios) of banks in Serendipity. These ratios are shown in Table P1-8.

In order to stay in the good graces of bank examiners, the Federal Reserve recommends that a bank maintain a ratio of one dollar of equity for each six to eight dollars it lends. This general guideline is deemed by banking experts to be an acceptable level for accomplishing two essential purposes:

1. A bank that uses ordinary prudence in evaluating loans can make loans in this ratio without endangering the safety of depositors' money.

2. Loans made in this general ratio allow sufficient safety without cutting off local sources of financing for growth and development in the community. At the same time, this guideline is used to warn banks that if they chronically lend at ratios of less than 1:6 they are unlikely to make enough money to pay savers competitive interest rates.

Table P1-8 shows that Ourbank has the best record of staying within the guidelines. Because of a rash of bad loans, TB1, TB2, TB4 and TB5 are operating well beyond the recommended safety bounds. TB3 was in that position but it has brought its ratio almost back to the upper limits of the recommended ratios.

Along with this information, you construct one final summary table, based on 1984 only. This is Table P1-9. Even if it contains some of the same information as in preceding tables, it also shows three additional ratios. These are capital-to-deposits, equity-to-assets and loans-to-deposits. In all three cases, Ourbank has better ratios than any of the other banks.

After reviewing the results of this analysis, several conclusions can be drawn. Ourbank is rocksolid and conservative. It has a demonstrable record of prudent management of its resources and protecting the safety of its depositors' money. It has been relatively passive regarding promotion and marketing of its services.

Table P1-6 Total Loans of Serendipity Banks* (000) (Periods ending December 31)

YEAR	OB	%T	TB1	%T	TB2	%T	TB3	%T	TB4	%T	TB5	%T	TOTAL	%G	CUM %G
1963	$ 5,636	30	$ 5,713	30	$ 7,816	40	$ —	—	$ —	—	$ —	—	$ 19,165	—	—
1968	8,914	23	9,590	24	13,365	34	5,085	13	2,405	6	—	—	39,359	105	105
1973	17,749	22	14,468	18	27,828	34	11,860	15	8,848	11	—	—	80,753	105	321
1978	29,235	19	24,320	16	58,508	36	32,907	21	10,986	7	—	—	155,956	75	713
1979	34,402	17	31,661	16	77,416	39	41,362	21	12,265	6	451	1	197,557	21	931
1980	41,462	16	44,077	17	97,707	38	50,445	19	14,742	6	8,041	6	256,391	30	1,238
1981	48,806	10	58,580	12	130,725	27	76,126	16	19,950	4	15,263	3	489,760	23	2,455
1982	63,282	14	67,229	15	167,748	38	84,251	19	26,718	6	29,815	7	439,043	(1)	2,191
1983	68,215	15	69,238	15	167,443	36	90,728	19	31,991	7	38,630	8	466,245	6	2,332
1984	70,421	14	76,994	16	183,106	37	85,057	17	34,432	7	43,374	9	493,384	6	2,474

* Derived from bank calls.

Table P1-7 Total Capital of Serendipity Banks* (000) (Periods ending December 31)

YEAR	OB	%T	TB1	%T	TB2	%T	TB3	%T	TB4	%T	TB5	%T	TOTAL	%G	CUM %G
1963	$ 1,090	31	$1,011	29	$ 1,379	40	$ —	—	$ —	—	$ —	—	$ 3,480	—	—
1968	1,349	22	1,334	22	1,887	31	960	16	590	9	—	—	6,120	76	76
1973	2,818	24	2,231	19	3,646	36	1,837	16	1,040	9	—	—	11,572	89	233
1978	5,382	27	3,447	17	6,597	33	3,064	15	1,463	7	—	—	19,953	72	473
1979	6,104	24	4,186	17	8,196	32	3,773	15	1,443	6	1,548	6	25,250	27	626
1980	6,977	23	6,147	20	9,965	32	4,610	15	1,550	5	1,689	6	30,938	11	789
1981	7,996	21	7,290	19	13,137	34	6,044	16	1,734	5	2,049	5	38,250	24	923
1982	9,417	20	8,353	19	16,247	35	7,647	17	2,150	5	2,530	6	46,344	21	1,232
1983	11,059	21	8,461	16	17,190	33	9,585	18	2,224	4	3,730	7	52,359	13	1,405
1984	11,882	24	6,242	13	15,254	31	9,630	20	3,221	7	3,271	7	49,500	(6)	1,324

* Derived from bank calls.

Table P1-8 Serendipity Bank Capital-to-Loan Ratios*
(Periods ending December 31)

YEAR	OB	TB1	TB2	TB3	TB4	TB5	MEAN
1963	1: 8.2	1: 5.7	1: 6.7	—	—	—	1: 6.9
1968	1: 6.6	1: 7.2	1: 7.1	1: 5.3	1: 4.1	—	1: 6.1
1973	1: 6.3	1: 6.5	1: 7.6	1: 6.5	1: 8.5	—	1: 7.1
1978	1: 5.4	1: 7.0	1: 8.7	1:10.7	1: 7.5	—	1: 7.9
1979	1: 5.6	1: 7.6	1: 9.4	1:11.0	1: 8.5	1: 0.3	1: 7.1
1980	1: 5.9	1: 7.2	1: 9.8	1:10.9	1: 9.5	1: 4.8	1: 8.1
1981	1: 6.1	1: 8.0	1: 9.6	1:12.6	1:11.5	1: 7.4	1: 9.2
1982	1: 6.7	1: 8.0	1:10.3	1:11.0	1:12.4	1:11.8	1:10.0
1983	1: 6.2	1: 8.9	1: 9.7	1: 9.5	1:13.7	1:10.4	1: 9.7
1984	1: 5.9	1:12.3	1:12.0	1: 8.8	1:10.7	1:13.3	1: 9.7

*Ratios calculated from bank calls.

Table P1-9 Serendipity Banks Compared on Key Dimensions in 1984 (000)

	OB	TB1	TB2	TB3	TB4	TB5
Total assets	133,451	134,118	252,911	137,106	47,713	66,503
Equity capital	11,882	6,242	15,254	9,630	3,221	3,271
Total deposits	119,113	124,128	231,660	125,069	43,830	61,882
Capital-to-deposits	10.0	5.0	6.6	7.7	7.3	5.3
Loans	70,421	76,994	183,106	85,057	34,432	43,374
Equity-to-assets	8.9	4.7	6.0	7.0	6.8	4.9
Loans-to-deposits	59.1	62.0	79.0	68.0	78.6	70.1
Loans-to-capital	5.9	12.3	12.0	8.8	10.7	13.3
Time deposits	104,729	108,625	194,303	105,932	38,432	*
Demand deposits	14,384	15,503	37,357	19,137	5,397	*

*Not available because of missing data in final bank call in 1984.

This is in direct contrast to TB2, TB3 and TB5, each of which has been very aggressive in marketing its services. Some of Ourbank's competitors are not as prudent as they should be.

Close examination of accounts within Ourbank indicates that approximately 80% of its deposits come from about 20% of its customers. Many of these are accounts for retailers, manufacturing firms, service organizations and professional people. The cost-effectiveness of these accounts is very high. It is from these accounts that most of Ourbank's profits come year after year. On the other hand, about 20% of Ourbank's deposits come from about 80% of its clients. The cost-effectiveness of many of these accounts is much lower. In fact, some of these accounts maintain balances so low that service charges are routinely applied and even then some still lose money for Ourbank. Hence, Ourbank's management wants to focus on developing more accounts in the cost-effective categories.

Ourbank's management is also deeply troubled by the rising tide of bank failures nationwide. The fear is that as the number of failures increases, more and more people will become less trusting in banks in general. Since Ourbank is so solid, management is wondering what it can do to get that story to the market.

II

Ourbank's management has asked you to evaluate the extent to which the public has lost confidence in the banking industry and to suggest what Ourbank can do about it. You are, of course, expected to come up with some hard evidence.

You review the material from your analysis and supplement it with interviews with Ourbank officers. You talk with some colleagues in some of the competitor banks and with some friends in other markets. You find that they, too, are concerned about bank failures. You set out on a reading program, investigating journals and reports that may give clues to the best way to promote a bank and that also may carry articles on bank failures and public perceptions of them.

You finally arrive at a decision. You must have some empirical data on the market. You want to know how people in Serendipity feel about the safety of banks in general, and about Ourbank in particular. Since that means a survey, you decide that you want to do some market research (Ourbank has never done a market survey before), because the cost of getting additional information will be relatively small.

You report to management with these recommendations:

1. Authorize a consumer-attitude and marketing survey immediately.

2. Analyze the data and merge it with information already in hand.

3. Develop a marketing and promotional program based on this information.

After much study and deliberation, management gives you the green light, but only after Ourbank's board approves the project.

You contact a research firm and talk about what information you want and why. A deal is struck and work begins immediately on the construction of a questionnaire. With the firm, you decide early that it will be a telephone questionnaire, with an average interview length of under 10 minutes. It takes three meetings with management to finish a suitable set of questions. The questionnaire is then pre-tested and modified slightly; then a professional interviewing service is hired to administer the survey. Since you want to do some analysis beyond simple averages, you want the sample to be large enough to allow for cross-tabulations. Calculations indicate that 398 random interviews are necessary. Interviews are done from 4:40 to 8:30 P.M. Monday through Thursday. Because of some illness, about 30 interviews have to be done the next Saturday morning between 9 A.M. and noon.

All the data is entered into an IBM 3061 mainframe computer and subjected to a variety of analyses using SAS (Statistical Analysis System).

Some of the results of this work are shown in the following tables. No combined frequencies are shown because of space problems. However, each of the tables shows the results of how some cross-tabulations were made.

The first set of general questions to be resolved by the research dealt with consumer attitudes toward banking in general, toward banks in the community and toward the quality of services being given by banks in Serendipity.

Table P2-1 Perceptions of Respondents about Banks in General

ATTITUDINAL CONCEPTS	OUR BANK					THEIR BANKS				
	SA	A	N	DA	SDA	SA	A	N	DA	SDA
Banks today are more financially secure than they were five years ago.	6.2	40.0	15.5	37.7	4.4	2.8	33.9	18.4	40.7	3.9
Banks today are more cautious about lending money than they were five years ago.	8.8	66.6	11.1	11.1	2.2	18.1	53.2	15.5	12.1	0.8
Banks today have a better record of guarding deposits than they had five years ago.	6.6	37.7	40.0	13.3	2.2	3.4	43.9	31.1	19.8	1.7
I have more confidence in banks today than I had five years ago.	6.6	28.8	13.3	48.8	2.2	2.2	32.5	21.8	36.8	6.5
I am less concerned today with the safety of deposits in banks than I was five years ago.	4.4	44.4	20.0	31.1	—	2.8	32.6	18.7	41.7	3.9
I believe banks today are more financially stable than they were five years ago.	6.6	24.4	13.3	51.1	4.4	1.4	26.9	14.4	54.2	2.8
Laws and regulations are more adequate today to protect depositors than five years ago.	6.5	46.6	26.6	20.8	—	2.5	45.3	32.0	18.4	1.7
The general public has more confidence in banks today than it did five years ago.	4.4	26.6	8.8	51.1	8.8	1.7	18.7	13.3	59.3	6.8
It is more important for people to personally know their bankers today than five years ago.	11.1	71.1	11.1	6.7	—	13.8	55.2	15.0	15.8	—

Note: SA = strongly agree; A = agree; N = neither agree nor disagree; DA = disagree; SDA = strongly disagree.

Table P2-1 shows the responses to questions about banks in general. Responses from customers of Ourbank are on the left and those from all other banks are on the right. You can compare how Ourbank customers feel about each question with how customers of other banks feel. In general, Ourbank customers appear to be a little more "bank sensitive" than customers of the other banks. Ourbank customers seem to have a little more faith in the financial stability of banks; they believe banks are a little more cautious about lending than in the past; they are less concerned about the safety of deposits in banks; and they generally seem to have more confidence in banks in general. They are also more sure that people should personally know their bankers.

When the same questions are asked about their own bank, however, responses by customers of Ourbank appear to be about the same as those from customers of the other banks (see Table P2-2). This may be because respondents don't want to think they are dealing with a bank that may not be as dependable as it should be.

In general, however, it is clear from the data that people are concerned about banks and the safety of their deposits in them. The fears of Ourbank's management seem well founded. The question is, of course, what can Ourbank do about the situation?

Table P2-2 Perceptions of Respondents about Their Own Banks

ATTITUDINAL CONCEPTS	OUR BANK					THEIR BANKS				
	SA	A	N	DA	SDA	SA	A	N	DA	SDA
My bank today is more financially secure than it was five years ago.	6.6	35.5	44.4	13.3	—	5.1	37.6	47.5	9.0	0.5
My bank is more cautious today about lending than it was five years ago.	8.9	44.4	42.2	4.4	—	9.9	44.7	39.0	6.2	—
My bank has a better record of guarding deposits than it had five years ago.	6.6	46.6	46.6	—	—	4.8	36.9	53.6	4.5	—
I have more confidence in my bank than I had five years ago.	6.6	40.0	46.6	6.7	—	3.9	36.2	42.7	16.4	0.5
I am less concerned today with the safety of my deposits in my bank than five years ago.	6.6	42.2	40.0	11.1	—	3.4	28.3	39.9	26.0	2.2
I believe my bank is more financially stable than it was five years ago.	4.4	40.0	48.8	6.6	—	5.1	36.8	48.1	8.5	1.4
It is more important today for me to personally know my banker than it was five years ago.	8.8	44.4	28.8	17.7	—	11.6	42.4	30.0	15.3	0.5

Note: SA = strongly agree; A = agree; N = neither agree nor disagree; DA = disagree; SDA = strongly disagree.

In such a program as we hope to mount for Ourbank, it is necessary that we know clearly why customers choose a bank and what importance they put on those reasons. That is the substance of Table P2-3. Except in a few cases, there appears to be little difference between Ourbank customers and those of other banks.

Table P2-3 Frequency of Reasons Why Respondents Selected Their Banks

REASONS	OUR BANK*				THEIR BANKS			
	VI	I	SI	UI	VI	I	SI	VI
Ease of getting to bank from home	17.7	44.4	17.7	20.0	25.5	43.6	15.0	15.8
Ease of getting to bank from work	13.3	35.5	15.5	35.5	14.7	31.4	18.1	35.6
Interest rates on regular savings accounts	17.7	53.3	8.8	20.0	15.0	40.2	13.0	31.7
Interest rates on checking accounts	17.7	51.1	4.4	26.6	15.3	36.5	11.3	36.8
Interest rates on certificates of deposits or money market certificates	24.4	40.0	2.2	33.3	22.6	36.2	7.0	33.9
Interest rates on personal loans	28.8	42.2	2.2	26.6	24.9	39.3	5.6	30.0
Interest rates on commercial or business loans	8.8	37.7	6.6	46.6	15.3	23.2	8.2	53.2
Convenience of banking hours*	48.8	24.4	8.8	17.7	40.2	45.3	7.3	7.0
Convenience of branch bank	13.3	22.2	6.6	57.7	20.1	33.1	10.2	36.5
Convenience of automatic teller machines*	24.2	24.2	—	51.1	26.6	28.3	11.3	33.7
Convenience of drive-in tellers	37.7	40.0	8.8	13.3	33.9	43.6	11.6	10.7
Convenience of 24-hour depository	17.7	24.4	15.5	42.2	15.0	30.5	15.0	39.3
Quality of financial counseling and guidance*	8.8	51.1	4.4	35.5	17.2	36.2	16.1	30.3
Financial strength of the bank	51.1	44.4	2.2	2.2	47.3	42.2	5.9	4.5
Willingness to consider my financial needs fairly	24.4	68.8	4.4	2.2	37.3	47.8	7.6	7.0
Monthly statements from bank are easy to understand	55.5	40.0	2.2	2.2	47.5	44.1	5.6	2.5
Personally acquainted with an officer at the bank	15.5	44.4	2.2	37.7	16.4	32.5	15.5	35.4
Personally acquainted with other bank personnel	11.1	28.8	11.1	48.8	7.6	27.7	20.9	43.6
Variety of services available at the bank	20.0	64.4	4.4	11.1	23.2	52.6	17.2	6.8
Professional handling of loan applications	20.0	51.1	4.4	24.4	28.0	43.9	8.5	19.5
Safety of my deposits at this bank	66.6	28.8	—	4.4	55.8	37.1	4.5	2.5
Trustworthiness of bank officers	64.4	35.5	—	—	57.1	34.9	4.5	3.4

*Difference is statistically significant at <.05.

Note: VI = very important; I = important; SI = somewhat important; UI = unimportant.

The three that stand out most are statistically significant at the $<.05$ level. One is the convenience of banking hours. The reason for this is probably that Ourbank began to keep its lobby open on Thursdays until 8 P.M., a point many customers have commented on favorably. Another is the convenience of automatic teller machines (ATMs). While more than half Ourbank's customers don't place much importance on them, the rest consider the machines very important indeed. The fact that a little more than half don't consider the machines important is curious, also, because one of Ourbank's ATM locations is the most often used ATM in the entire state. The other major point is the value placed on the quality of financial counseling and guidance from Ourbank's officers.

Other important findings show that Ourbank customers place great importance on interest rates on personal loans, certificates of deposit, money market and regular savings accounts.

The financial strength of Ourbank shows up as important, as is the fact that our monthly statements are easy to read. Our customers seem to think that their deposits are safer here than customers believe to be the case at other banks, and

Table P2-4 Index of Reasons Why Respondents Selected Their Banks

REASONS	OUR BANK	THEIR BANKS
Trustworthiness of bank officers	364	345
Safety of my deposits at this bank	357	346
Monthly statements from bank are easy to understand	348	336
Financial strength of this bank	315	332
Willingness to consider my financial needs fairly	315	315
Convenience of banking hours	304	318
Convenience of drive-in tellers	302	300
Variety of services available at this bank	293	292
Interest rates on personal loans	273	259
Interest rates on regular savings account	268	238
Professional handling of loan applications	266	280
Interest rates on checking accounts	260	240
Interest rates on certificates of deposits or money market certificates	255	247
Personally acquainted with a bank officer	237	230
Quality of financial counseling and guidance	233	240
Ease of getting to bank from work	226	225
Convenience of automatic teller machines	222	247
Convenience of 24-hour depository	217	221
Interest rates on commercial or business loans	208	200
Personally acquainted with some bank personnel	202	199
Convenience of branch bank	191	236

our customers place more importance on the trustworthiness of our officers than do those at other banks.

An array of data like this, however, can be confusing. It is difficult to get a clear fix on what is most important and what is least important. Hence, you constructed Table P2-4, an index of the importance customers place on reasons they select a bank. The higher the index number, the greater is that item's importance.

It is gratifying that trustworthiness of bank officers and safety of deposits come out on top. Since Ourbank does not have a branch, although one is

Table P2-5 Perceptions of Quality of Services Given by Banks

TYPE OF SERVICE	OUR BANK*					THEIR BANKS				
	S	VG	A	BA	P	S	VG	A	BA	P
Ease of discussing financial needs with an officer	22.2	26.6	51.1	—	—	12.1	28.6	55.2	1.4	2.5
Availability of a loan officer	17.7	24.4	53.3	—	—	9.7	30.8	56.3	1.7	1.9
Adequacy of information on loans and interest	22.2	37.7	37.7	2.2	—	9.3	36.5	50.9	1.3	1.9
Interest or dividends paid on deposits or investments	17.7	24.4	57.7	—	—	9.0	30.0	58.3	1.7	0.8
Fairness of bank policies*	31.1	35.5	33.3	—	—	9.6	43.6	42.4	2.8	1.4
Efficiency of taking care of my banking needs*	48.0	48.8	6.6	4.4	—	22.0	50.7	23.5	2.5	1.1
Pleasantness of atmosphere at bank	46.6	37.7	15.5	—	—	29.1	51.5	16.7	2.2	0.2
Ease of applying for a personal loan	13.3	31.1	51.1	2.2	2.2	9.4	24.5	62.9	1.7	1.4
Knowledgeable handling of my financial needs	26.6	48.8	24.4	—	—	13.3	43.1	39.7	2.7	1.4
Reliable and accurate handling of banking transactions	37.7	46.6	13.3	2.2	—	23.2	50.7	21.8	2.5	1.7
Professional handling of loan applications	17.7	26.6	51.1	4.4	—	9.3	27.2	60.9	1.4	1.1

*Difference is statistically significant at <.05.

Note: S = superior; VG = very good; A = average; BA = below average; P = poor.

Table P2-6 Index of Quality of Services Given by Banks

TYPE OF SERVICE	OUR BANK	THEIR BANKS
Pleasantness of the atmosphere at my bank	431	407
Efficiency of taking care of my banking needs	424	390
Reliable and accurate handling of my banking transactions	420	391
Knowledgeable handling of my financial needs	402	364
Fairness of bank policies	397	357
Adequacy of information on loans and interest	380	350
Ease of discussing financial needs with an officer	371	346
Interest or dividends paid on deposits or investments	360	344
Professional handling of loan applications	357	342
Availability of a loan officer	353	343
Ease of applying for personal loan	351	343

under construction, we should not be disappointed that branch banking appears last in importance among our customers.

While these may be important services, one of the telling issues is the perception of the quality of these services as provided by banks. That is the subject of P2-5. Two items in this table stand out. One is that Ourbank customers perceive its policies as being fairer than customers at other banks perceive their banks' policies. Also, Ourbank customers seem to consider Ourbank more efficient in at-

Table P2-7 Frequency of Use of Services Offered by Banks

SERVICES	OUR BANK*							
	D	W	2M	M	2Y	1Y	E	N
Regular checking account	55.5	24.4	11.1	4.4	—	—	—	4.4
Commercial or business checking account	4.4	13.3	2.2	—	—	2.2	2.2	75.5
Checking account with interest	17.7	4.4	6.6	6.6	2.2	—	2.2	60.0
Certificate of deposit account	4.5	4.5	—	9.0	2.2	9.9	2.2	68.1
Money market checking account	2.2	2.2	—	4.4	—	—	2.2	88.8
Passbook savings account	—	—	4.0	13.3	4.4	4.4	6.6	66.6
Money market savings account	—	2.2	—	2.2	2.2	4.4	—	88.8
Automobile loan	—	—	—	16.6	—	5.2	11.2	56.7
Home improvement loan	—	—	2.2	—	—	2.2	2.2	93.3
Personal loan	—	—	—	—	—	13.3	11.1	75.5
Business loan	—	—	—	—	4.4	—	4.4	91.1
Construction loan	—	—	—	—	—	2.2	—	97.7
Estate planning services	—	—	—	—	—	—	2.2	97.7
Personal trust services	2.2	—	—	2.2	2.2	2.2	—	91.1
Drive-in tellers	11.1	28.8	28.8	15.5	4.4	2.2	2.2	6.6
Automatic teller machines	2.2	17.7	6.6	2.2	4.4	—	4.4	62.2
Buy or sell stocks or options	—	—	—	—	—	4.4	—	95.5
Buy or sell government or municipal bonds*	—	—	—	—	2.2	6.6	2.2	88.8
IRA or KEOGH retirement account	—	—	—	—	—	2.2	2.2	95.5
VISA or MasterCard account	2.2	4.4	2.2	11.1	—	8.8	2.2	68.8
Cashier's checks or money orders	—	2.2	6.6	6.6	2.2	26.6	17.7	37.7
Traveler's checks	—	—	—	—	13.3	24.4	13.3	48.8
U.S. savings bonds*	—	2.2	—	2.2	4.4	2.2	2.2	86.6
Foreign currency exchange	—	—	—	—	2.2	4.4	4.4	88.8
Direct deposit	—	6.6	13.3	17.7	—	—	4.4	57.7
Night deposit	—	—	11.1	13.3	5.5	2.5	7.6	11.3
Safety deposit box	2.2	—	—	2.2	8.8	13.3	2.2	71.1
Financial counseling and planning	—	—	—	—	2.2	4.4	6.6	86.6

*Difference is statistically significant at <.05.

Note: D = daily; W = weekly; 2M = twice monthly; M = monthly; 2Y = twice yearly; 1Y = once yearly; E = ever; N = never.

tending to customer needs. In terms of a rank order of quality, Table P2-6 provides an index for reference. This index shows that pleasantness of the atmosphere at Ourbank is tops. Other services are perceived in descending order, with ease of applying for a personal loan in last place.

Specific services offered by a typical bank are summarized in Table P2-7. These are rank-ordered via an index in Table P2-8. Probably the most important column is the one for "never." This gives you a quick clue as to the level of use.

| | | | | THEIR BANKS | | | | |
SERVICES	D	W	2M	M	2Y	1Y	E	N
Regular checking account	52.1	34.8	5.6	3.9	—	—	1.7	1.7
Commercial or business checking account	9.9	5.6	0.8	2.2	0.5	0.5	1.9	78.1
Checking account with interest	7.6	7.9	2.8	7.9	1.7	1.1	3.4	67.4
Certificate of deposit account	0.5	0.8	0.2	5.1	3.9	13.8	5.9	69.4
Money market checking account	0.8	1.1	0.5	4.2	1.4	3.6	2.5	85.5
Passbook savings account	1.1	4.5	3.6	15.5	8.5	6.8	7.0	52.6
Money market savings account	0.2	0.5	0.5	5.1	1.9	3.9	2.2	85.2
Automobile loan	0.2	0.2	5.6	—	0.2	5.1	15.5	72.8
Home improvement loan	—	—	0.5	—	0.2	1.1	5.1	92.9
Personal loan	0.2	—	0.5	5.1	1.9	7.6	9.0	75.3
Business loan	—	—	0.2	1.9	1.9	3.4	5.1	87.2
Construction loan	0.2	—	—	0.8	1.3	1.1	2.8	93.7
Estate planning services	—	—	—	0.2	0.2	1.7	1.4	96.3
Personal trust services	1.4	—	1.1	0.8	0.2	1.7	1.9	92.6
Drive-in tellers	7.6	48.0	12.2	13.6	5.4	1.9	1.4	9.6
Automatic teller machines	8.5	26.4	7.1	9.6	3.4	1.4	1.9	40.9
Buy or sell stocks or options	0.2	0.8	0.2	0.2	0.2	0.5	2.2	95.1
Buy or sell government or municipal bonds *	—	—	—	0.8	0.2	0.8	1.9	96.0
IRA or KEOGH retirement account	—	—	0.2	1.1	0.5	7.3	1.9	88.6
VISA or MasterCard account	1.1	4.5	2.2	7.6	1.7	1.7	2.8	78.1
Cashier's checks or money orders	0.2	0.8	3.4	7.0	12.1	25.5	10.2	40.5
Traveler's checks	0.2	—	0.2	1.1	6.2	30.8	9.9	51.2
U.S. savings bonds *	—	—	—	0.5	0.2	1.9	3.4	93.7
Foreign currency exchange	—	—	—	0.2	0.2	4.2	4.8	90.3
Direct deposit	0.2	7.9	11.3	16.7	1.4	0.8	3.1	58.3
Night deposit	1.7	2.8	4.5	7.3	4.8	4.2	3.4	71.1
Safety deposit box	—	0.8	0.8	5.6	5.6	8.5	1.7	76.4
Financial counseling and planning	—	—	—	0.8	3.4	9.6	3.9	82.1

* Difference is statistically significant at <.05.

Note: D ≐ daily; W = weekly; 2M = twice monthly; M = monthly; 2Y = twice yearly; 1Y = once yearly; E = ever; N = never.

The next most important column is the one for "ever." Since all these questions were asked from the standpoint of the last twelve months, anyone not using a service at least annually was also asked if they had ever used it.

Although this array of data is complex, Table P2-8 helps to clarify it. It is an index of the frequency of usage. As you might expect, activity in a regular checking account occurs most frequently and estate planning comes last. In terms of marketing specific services, this table may be of special use. If this table is compared to one showing which services are most profitable to the bank, then an agenda for promoting certain services would not be too difficult to construct.

In addition to these tables, other analyses not shown here support the following statements as statistically significant at the $<.05$-level.

Table P2-8 Index of Frequency of Use of Bank Services

SERVICES	OUR BANK	THEIR BANK
Regular checking account	701	719
Drive-in tellers	577	578
Checking account with interest	320	257
Direct deposit	282	282
Automatic teller machine	282	409
Cashier's checks or money orders	251	250
Commercial or business checking account	228	221
Certificate of deposit account	222	176
Visa or Mastercard account	217	188
Passbook savings account	204	262
Traveler's checks	202	198
Night depository	188	207
Safety deposit box	180	169
Automobile loan	155	152
Money market checking account	148	146
U.S. savings bonds	140	110
Personal loan	137	155
Money market savings account	137	144
Personal trust service	133	123
Financial counseling and planning	122	136
Buy or sell government or municipal bonds	122	107
Foreign currency exchange	120	115
Business loan	117	127
Home improvement loan	115	110
Buy or sell stocks or options	108	113
IRA or KEOG account	106	124
Construction loan	104	113
Estate planning	102	106

Ourbank Compared to TB3   Ourbank customers are less concerned about location and convenience than TB3 customers. Ourbank customers say information about loans and interest rates is far more adequate than customers at TB3. Customers believe that Ourbank is more efficient in attending their needs and that it handles financial matters more knowledgeably. Ourbank customers also attend to CD accounts more often but rely less on ATMs, and they are more likely to buy U.S. savings bonds or to buy or sell other government or municipal bonds.

Ourbank Compared to TB1   Customers at Ourbank see banking hours as far more convenient than TB1's customers see theirs. A branch bank is less important to Ourbank customers than to customers at TB1. Ourbank customers perceive banking policies as much fairer than those at TB1. And Ourbank customers believe more strongly that their financial needs are handled knowledgeably than at TB1.

Ourbank Compared to TB2   Customers believe that the convenience of banking hours at Ourbank is more important than at TB2. Automatic teller machines are less important to Ourbank customers than to those at TB2 and our customers are less likely to use them. And Ourbank customers are far less concerned about their deposits than customers at TB2.

Comparisons with TB4 and TB5 were made but some cells were so thin as to be statistically unreliable and are thus not used in this analysis.

With these data in hand, you can develop a plan and methods of implementing it.

III

This part of the writing project leads you through a series of steps in developing the writing portions of a complete campaign. It does this by assigning you tasks. You are asked to do these in the order assigned because, in some cases, the next task is built on the previous one. So take this part a step at a time.

Writing Task 1   Your first writing assignment is to write a backgrounder on the status of the banking industry today. The special focus in this backgrounder should be on the reasons so many banks are failing today. Two of the obvious reasons are the recent and current general economic conditions and bank deregulation. There are probably others, but you don't know exactly what they are or how important they may be. Review the purpose of a backgrounder, how to do it, then write it.

Writing Task 2   Write a report to the chief executive officer of the bank, outlining all of the publics of the bank. Identify and highlight the publics you consider the most significant and explain why.

Writing Task 3   Write a memo to all of the loan officers, describing how you propose to promote certain services and to which audiences. Ask for their ideas. And let them know that you want to discuss this topic with each of them personally.

Writing Task 4   The president of Ourbank is scheduled to address the Rotary Club three weeks from today. His topic is to be on the ailing banking industry. He wants to supplement the talk with some slides. Write the speech for him and develop a list of slides to illustrate his talk.

Writing Task 5   Write press releases for the local media about what Ourbank's president will say to the Rotary Club. You need pieces for one newspaper, three radio stations and one television station (not counting a cable system, which does not run local material).

Writing Task 6   Write a public relations plan that covers advertising and marketing questions for Ourbank. Since you have been staying in close contact with management and many discussions have dealt with a slogan for Ourbank, you and management decide together that Ourbank will be promoted with a slogan of "The Safe Place." This slogan will appear on all signs, in all ads and on all printed materials used by the bank. Review what should go into a plan. Then write the plan using the data from Parts I and II and your backgrounder in Writing Task 1.

Writing Task 7   Write a magazine feature article on how Ourbank plans to promote itself. This article will appear in the state's banking magazine. Describe any illustrative materials you want to send with the story.

Writing Task 8   Design and write a brochure about the bank's services. The copy should be heavy on information and light on persuasion, since it will be available in racks in the bank's lobby and at the new branch and at ATM sites.

Writing Task 9   Write the copy for a statement stuffer. The subject is on the high interest paid on checking accounts with interest. Use a graph or table to make clear how much interest customers can earn at different balance levels.

Writing Task 10   Write the copy for a newspaper ad that introduces the concept of "The Safe Place" as a slogan. Describe any illustrations that will go with it.

Writing Task 11   Write a thirty-second spot for radio on "The Safe Place." Be sure to specify special effects or music to make Ourbank memorable.

Writing Task 12   Do a ten-minute audiovisual slide show that will be lent on request to public schools. The primary audience for this show will be children in the fifth through the ninth grades, so keep it simple and to the point. The emphasis is on how a bank operates. Obviously, you will use Ourbank to illustrate your ideas.

Writing Task 13   Part of your communication plan calls for a monthly newsletter directed at the 20% of Ourbank's customers who account for 80% of the business. The newsletter will be two pages long, letter size, and it will be called "Money Matters." Its focus will be on economic conditions and issues that may affect interest rates, certain industries, investments and a variety of other areas. One of the senior vice presidents at Ourbank is a specialist in forecasting. She will provide you with the information. Design and write the first edition of "Money Matters."

Writing Task 14   You know, of course, that Ourbank has a branch under construction. In fact, it should be ready to open in about three months. Meanwhile, there is a serious move in the state legislature to return to no branching. Ourbank has made a large economic commitment to this construction (other banks in other markets are doing the same thing) and doesn't want to see the law changed again. So Ourbank's president asks you to write a position paper. Your position is to retain branch banking. This document will be the primary one that you and other officers of the bank will use to lobby legislators to retain branch banking.

A Final Word

Ourbank is obviously fictitious, but the data presented here is what you would encounter on the job. This project is similar to assignments you will handle when you get into the "real world." The point is this: It is better to make mistakes now than later. So deal with Ourbank as if it were real. Doing these tasks well will put money in the bank—not Ourbank—for you later.

Appendixes

Appendix A
Readability Formulas

Research in readability goes back at least to the 1920s. Early work identified various factors—like sentence length, word length, prepositional phrases—that affected the readability of prose.

In *What Makes a Book Readable*, published in 1935, William Gray and Bernice Leary discussed 64 different aspects of prose that seemed to affect reading difficulty. It would have been nearly impossible to devise a usable formula covering that many variables, so when readability formulas were developed, most emphasized two of the most important factors: sentence length and word length.

Dozens of formulas have been designed to measure readability. In 1959 George Klare identified 31 formulas and 10 variations, and he didn't cover all the different types of formulas. More formulas have been designed since then. Only a handful of these formulas are in general use, however. The three best-known formulas are those devised by Rudolf Flesch, by Robert Gunning, and by Edgar Dale and Jeanne Chall.

Flesch

The first formula to gain much notice was the one proposed by Flesch in the late 1940s. His formula is based on the average sentence length and the average number of syllables per word.

To use the Flesch formula, select 100-word samples at random from your text. Divide the number of words by the number of sentences to obtain an average sentence length (asl) expressed in words per sentence. Next count the number of syllables in the sample and divide by the number of words to obtain an average word length (awl) expressed in syllables per word. Then insert these values into the Flesch "Reading Ease" formula:

$$\text{Reading Ease} = 206.835 - (84.6 \times \text{awl}) - (1.015 \times \text{asl})$$

The resulting score should fall between 0 and 100; the higher the score, the easier the material is to read. A score in the 70–80 range is "fairly easy"; a sixth-grader could understand it. Scores below 50 are considered difficult reading. Scores below 30 are generally found only in scientific and technical journals.

When using the Flesch formula, count contractions and hyphenated words as one word. When counting sentences, count clauses separated by colons or semicolons as separate sentences.

Recognizing that there is more to easy reading than short words and sentences, Flesch devised a "Human Interest" formula that measures the degree of reader interest. It is not used as often as the reading ease formula. It is based on the number of personal words (pw) per 100 words and personal sentences (ps) per 100 sentences. Personal words include personal pronouns and any other words that are either masculine or feminine. Personal sentences are direct quotations, exclamations, questions—sentences that address the reader directly. The formula:

$$\text{Human Interest} = \text{pw}/100 \text{ words} \times 3.635 \\ + \text{ps}/100 \text{ sentences} \times 0.314$$

A score below 10 is dull; 20 to 40 is interesting; above 40 is very interesting.

Gunning

Gunning's formula is much simpler to apply than Flesch's. The "fog index," as Gunning calls it, measures reading difficulty rather than reading ease.

Gunning also counts words and divides by the number of sentences to find an average sentence length. But rather than counting syllables, Gunning's method is to count the number of "long words"—those of three syllables or more. He excludes from this count all proper nouns, verbs where the third syllable is an *-ed* or *-es*, and compound words made from two short words, like "manpower."

To apply the formula, take the average sentence length and add to it the number of long words per 100 words. Multiply the total by 0.4.

The resulting score is roughly equal to the grade level of difficulty. A score of 12, for example, indicates that an average high school senior should be able to read the material. In practice, no general audience magazine would rate above 12 on the Gunning index. *Time* magazine probably rates about 10, *Reader's Digest* would score about 9, and comic books would score around 6.

Dale-Chall

The Dale-Chall formula is more difficult to apply because it requires the use of a list of 3,000 words. Words on the list are known by 80 percent of fourth graders. [The list is included as an appendix to Gunning's book, *The Technique of Clear Writing*, rev. ed. (New York: McGraw-Hill, 1968).]

To use the Dale-Chall formula, select 100-word samples and determine the average sentence length (as with the Gunning and Flesch tests). Then count the number of words not on the Dale list. The formula:

average sentence length $\times$ 0.0496
+ words not on Dale list $\times$ 0.1579
+ 3.6365

Dale-Chall scores will typically be lower than Gunning scores for a given piece of writing. A Gunning index of 16, for example, indicates readability on the college graduate level; the same piece would score about 10 on the Dale-Chall test.

Keep in mind that readability scores do not reflect a "recommended" level of reading difficulty. They only indicate the readability level that an average reader (average seventh-grader, average high school senior, or whatever) is likely to understand. To make the reading *easy*, the writing level should be a couple of steps below the educational level of the intended audience. Rarely do popular magazines—even those read by college graduates—score higher than a high school senior readability level.

Other Readability Tests

A completely different type of readability test is Wilson Taylor's "Cloze" procedure. This test, first used in the early 1950s, was developed from concepts of Gestalt psychology. It tests readability by seeing how easily a reader can "fill in the blanks" when words are left out of a passage.

For example, readers might be given a passage with every fifth word deleted. From the context, the reader should be able to fill in some of the missing words. The more words the reader can fill in, the more readable the selection is.

This unique readability test has one major drawback: It can't be applied simply by making calculations. The prose must be tested on real readers, and those readers must be representative of the intended audience.

All readability formulas are approximations, because no single formula can cover all the variables that affect readability. With the increased use of computers, though, more complicated formulas may soon come into use. Computers can be programmed to calculate readability automatically when a sample of a story is typed in at a computer keyboard.

An early formula appropriate for computerized use is the Danielson-Bryan formula. It is based on the total number of characters (letters) per word and per sentence. The formula:

$$1.0364 \times \text{characters per word}$$
$$+ \, 0.0194 \times \text{characters per sentence}$$
$$- \, 0.6059$$

An even more elaborate formula has been devised by Danielson to measure the probable time period of prose. It has long been known that English sentences have, on average, become shorter over the centuries. Taking a random sample of novels published between 1740 and 1977, Danielson found several other variables that change with time, such as paragraph length (shorter now than in the past), presence of long words (less frequent now than in the past), and presence of "internal apostrophes" for possessives and contractions (more frequent now than in the past).

Using data from his sample of novels, Danielson produced a formula that would "predict" the publication date for a fiction selection. These predictions work with a fair degree of accuracy on fiction, but the formula in no way predicts publication year for nonfiction, since only novels were included in the original sample. However, any prose can be given a "stylistic year" rating by applying the formula. And while the formula is not a readability measure by design, "style year" scores show a very high correlation to readability scores obtained by standard formulas.

A computer program has been written to apply this formula, and tests show that a selection with a style year of 1900 or later rates "very readable" on standard readability tests. Style year scores of before 1850 are not very readable.

The formula, which must be applied to an integral number of paragraphs, is:

$$\text{Style year} =$$
$$1949$$
$$+ \, 36.41 \times \text{internal apostrophes per sentence}$$
$$- \quad 2.57 \times \text{words per sentence}$$
$$- \quad 2.92 \times \text{sentences per paragraph}$$
$$- \, 16.71 \times \text{long words per sentence}$$

Long words are defined as words with 10 or more letters.

Table A-1 Comparison of Readability Scores with Style Year

GUNNING SCORE (FOG INDEX)	GRADE LEVEL	STYLE YEAR
4	Fourth	1948
5	Fifth	1939
6	Sixth	1929
7– 8	Seventh–eighth	1916
9–10	Ninth–tenth	1897
11–12	Eleventh–twelfth	1879
13–15	College	1856
16 and up	College graduate	1838

Appendix B
Corporate Reporting
Requirements

B

Source: Reprinted with permission of Doremus & Company.

| Doremus & Company | **1984 Annual Report Checklist** |

The annual report is one of your company's most effective sales tools. The perception of your company is shaped to a major degree by what shareholders, analysts, customers, prospects and other audiences see in your report.

To help you produce the best possible annual report, Doremus & Company has compiled for the tenth consecutive year this checklist which will be helpful in planning, writing, design, and production of a successful annual report. We have included information and procedures that are required by the SEC, NYSE, AMEX, and NASD. In addition, there are other suggestions for enhancing the appearance and content of your report.

SEC Requirements

Audited Financial Statements
- ☐ Consolidated balance sheets (2 years)
- ☐ Consolidated statements of income (3 years)
- ☐ Consolidated statements of changes in financial position (3 years)
- ☐ Consolidated statements of shareholders' equity (or footnote disclosure) (3 years)
- ☐ Notes to consolidated financial statements
- ☐ Report of independent public accountants

Supplementary Financial Information
Selected quarterly financial data (2 years):
- ☐ Net sales
- ☐ Gross profit
- ☐ Income (loss) before extraordinary items and cumulative effect of any change in accounting policies
- ☐ Per-share data based upon such income (loss)
- ☐ Net income (loss)
- ☐ Disagreements on accounting and financial disclosure matters

Selected Financial Data for Five Years
- ☐ Net sales or operating revenues
- ☐ Income (loss) from continuing operations (in total and per common share)
- ☐ Total assets
- ☐ Long-term obligations and redeemable preferred stock (including capital leases)
- ☐ Cash dividends declared per common share
- ☐ Additional items that will enhance understanding and highlight trends in financial condition and results of operations

(Such data may be combined with the five-year summary information on the effects of inflation and changing prices if required by FASB 33)

Management Discussion and Analysis of Financial Condition and Results of Operations
Discuss financial condition, changes in financial condition and results of operations; provide other information believed necessary to an understanding of the Company's financial condition. Areas to be covered include Liquidity, Capital Resources and Results of Operations. Discussions of Capital Resources and Results of Operations may be combined whenever the two are interrelated.

Generally, the discussion shall cover the three-year period covered by the financial statements.

- ☐ Liquidity: Identify any trends, demands, commitments, events or uncertainties that will materially increase or decrease liquidity. If material deficiency is identified, indicate course of action to remedy situation. Identify and describe internal and external sources of liquidity, briefly discuss any material unused sources of liquid assets.

B continued

□ Capital Resources: Describe material commitments for capital expenditures as of end of latest fiscal period; indicate general purpose of such commitments and anticipated source of funds needed. Describe any known material trends, favorable or unfavorable, in capital resources. Indicate any expected material changes in mix and relative cost of such resources. Discussion shall consider changes between equity, debt and any off-balance sheet financing arrangements.

□ Results of Operations: Describe any unusual or infrequent events or transactions, or significant economic changes, that materially affected reported income from continuing operations. In each case indicate extent to which income was affected. Also describe any other significant components of revenues or expenses that would help to understand results.

The discussion should use year-to-year comparisons or any other format that will enhance a reader's understanding. Where trend information is relevant, reference to the five-year selected financial data may be necessary. Trends or uncertainties that may have material impact on sales or revenues and income must be described. Any events that will cause a material change in the relationship between costs and revenues (cost increases in labor or materials, or price increases or inventory adjustments) must be disclosed. If there are any material increases in net sales or revenues, provide narrative discussion of the extent to which such increases are attributable to price increases in the volume or amount of goods or services sold, or, to the introduction of new products or services.

Discuss the impact of inflation and changing prices on net sales and revenues and on income from continuing operations.

Industry Segment Breakdown for Three Years
□ Revenue (with sales to unaffiliated customers and sales or transfers to other industry segments shown separately), operating profit or loss and identifiable assets attributable to industry segments and geographic area, for three years. Classes of similar products or services, foreign and domestic operations, export sales.

Financial Reporting and Changing Prices Information
□ Five-year summary: effects of inflation and changing prices; may be combined with Selected Financial Data

Information on the Market for Common Stock and Related Security Holder Matters
□ High and low sales prices of stock for each quarterly period in last two years
□ Frequency and amount of dividends paid
□ Principal market(s) in which the company's securities are traded

Identity
□ A brief description of the company's business

Directors and Executive Officers
□ Name, principal occupation, title, employer's principal business

Litigation
□ Cite significant cases; include any in which civil rights, ecological statutes or ethical conduct of directors or executive officers are involved

Form 10-K
□ Offer of free copy of Form 10-K in annual report or proxy statement in boldface type (not required if annual report is incorporated by reference into the Form 10-K and is filed with the SEC in satisfaction of disclosure requirements)

B | continued

| Type-Size Requirements | ☐ Financial statements and notes—Roman type at least as large and legible as 10-point Modern; if necessary for convenient presentation, financial statements may be Roman type at least as large and legible as 8-point Modern; all type leaded at least 2 points |

| Distribution | ☐ Distribution of annual report to all stockholders, including beneficial owners underlying street names; analysts, brokers, press, etc. |
| | ☐ Annual report must precede or accompany proxy statement if proxies are solicited in connection with an annual meeting |

Significant Accounting Policies	*The SEC requires that these subjects be reported in accordance with generally accepted accounting principles:*
	☐ Principles of consolidation, summary of accounting policies, changes in accounting principles
	☐ Pensions: accounting and funding policies, changes and amendments, financial status
	☐ Income taxes and investment tax credit
	☐ Inventories: valuation method
	☐ Property, plant and equipment: depreciation policy
	☐ Lease commitments
	☐ Translation of foreign currency transactions
	☐ Reporting effects of changing prices and general inflation
	☐ Long-term debt agreements, short-term borrowings

Other Material Recommended by Doremus for Inclusion

Feature Items

☐ Front cover design to establish theme for report
☐ Financial highlights and table of contents
☐ Letter to stockholders and photographs of chairman and president
☐ Discussion of rate of internal growth
☐ Explanation of growth of production, market shares and industry trends
☐ Forward-looking information— projections of sales, income, earnings per share, capital expenditures, dividends, capital structure; corporate goals and objectives

The SEC's "safe harbor" rule protects companies from liability if such statements are made on a "reasonable basis" and in "good faith"; underlying assumptions, if disclosed, are also protected

☐ Significant effects of foreign exchange translations
☐ Regulatory climate and compliance actions including impact of wage and price standards
☐ Management report on internal accounting control
☐ Depth of management: training programs, promotion from within
☐ Financial strength: debt, profit-center control
☐ Marketing skills: sales force and technical service backup
☐ Production achievements: new equipment, unit cost control, list of facilities
☐ Research capability: scientific disciplines, achievements, programs
☐ Corporate policies: markets served, product development, acquisitions
☐ Regulatory climate
☐ Social responsibilities
☐ Political action programs

International Operations

☐ Sales: trends, percent of consolidated total, market share
☐ Taxes: local regulations, amount

☐ Foreign currency translation
☐ Earnings: equity interest
☐ Unrepatriated earnings

B continued

Five- or Ten-year Financial Summary (ten years preferred)	
☐ Sales	☐ Dividends declared or paid, total
☐ Cost of goods	☐ Per share
☐ Selling, general and administrative expenses	☐ Shares outstanding: average number (adjust for stock dividends and stock splits)
☐ Operating costs	☐ Number of shareholders
☐ Operating margin	☐ Price/earnings ratio range
☐ Other income	☐ Debt ratio
☐ Interest and other financial charges	☐ Total invested capital
☐ Pre-tax earnings	☐ Percent earned on average total invested capital
☐ Income taxes	
☐ Percent of pre-tax earnings	☐ Research and development costs
☐ Extraordinary items and discontinued operations	☐ Capital spending for plant and equipment
☐ Net earnings, total	☐ Depreciation
☐ Per share	☐ Number of employees—worldwide
☐ Earnings as a percent of sales	
☐ Percent earned on average shareholders' equity	

Miscellaneous

☐ Notice of annual meeting	☐ Graphs, tables and charts to illustrate key points in text
☐ Names and addresses of legal counsel, auditors, transfer agent, registrar, public relations or investor relations counsel	☐ Photographs to emphasize theme of annual report
☐ Disbursement of sales dollar	☐ Tabulation of company's divisions, locations, products and managers
☐ Company's rank: "Fortune," "Forbes," "Business Week"	☐ List of major distributors of company's products
☐ Market research orientation: total industry, competitors, market share	☐ Procedure for joining company's dividend reinvestment plan
☐ Economic environment orientation: U.S. and important foreign countries	☐ Procedure for stockholder participation in programs for the purchase of company's products
	☐ Stockholder profile or opinion survey questionnaire

Note

Following are the delivery requirements of the annual report to your shareholders based on where your securities are listed or traded.

NYSE 15 days before annual meeting; not later than 90 days after close of your fiscal year.
AMEX 10 days before annual meeting; not later than 120 days after close of your fiscal year.
OTC No delivery of annual report to shareholders is necessary unless there is an annual meeting for which proxies are being solicited. State laws governing corporate activities should be checked to determine how many days before your annual meeting the annual report must be delivered.

This is the tenth consecutive year Doremus & Company has produced its Annual Report Checklist. The material is current as of September 30, 1984. Companies must continue to be alert to changing requirements and guidelines. For example, the SEC has several proposals currently under consideration regarding industry segment and other interim financial reporting matters, management's "discussion and analysis," and off balance sheet financing disclosures.

Doremus Offices

Boston
535 Boylston Street
Boston, MA 02116
(617) 266-2600

Chicago
500 North Michigan Avenue
Chicago, IL 60611
(312) 321-1377

Los Angeles
10960 Wilshire Blvd.
Suite 1422
Los Angeles, CA 90024
(213) 478-3071

San Francisco
825 Battery Street
San Francisco, CA 94111
(415) 981-4020

New York
120 Broadway
New York, NY 10271
(212) 964-0700

Rockford
850 North Church Street
Rockford, IL 61103
(815) 963-1321

Washington
655 Fifteenth Street, NW
Suite 815
Washington, DC 20005
(202) 628-3440

Marketshare/Doremus
41 Madison Avenue
New York, N.Y. 10010
(212) 725-8400

Appendix C
Copyfitting

You need to fit copy accurately: (1) to determine how much space a given amount of copy will take when set in type, and (2) to determine how much copy to write to fill a predetermined space.

Occasionally both circumstances are important. If an editor has prepared copy and a layout showing space where copy is to go, some adjustment will usually be necessary. The copy will have to be cut (or lengthened) to fit the space or the layout will have to be redesigned to allow more (or less) space for copy, or both.

In either case the principles of copyfitting are the same.

Sizing Copy

To fit copy, an editor must know the type specifications. Among the things that must be determined are

1. The type face, type size, and amount of leading
2. A "characters per pica" count for the type face
3. The column width of the copy after being set in type
4. The total number of characters in the original copy

The total number of characters (letters and spaces) in the original copy can be precisely counted (in short copy) or estimated (in long copy). Precise counting is rarely used if the copy exceeds one typewritten page.

To estimate the number of characters in typewritten copy, first determine the number of spaces per line. (There are 10 spaces to the inch with pica typewriters; 12 with elite type.) If lines are typed unevenly, you will have to determine an average line length. One way to do this is to draw a straight line down the right margin so that half the lines go beyond your line and half don't reach it. Then measure the number of spaces from the left hand margin to the line you've drawn.

Once the average number of spaces (characters) per line is determined, simply count the total number of lines in the copy and multiply by the number of characters per line. For example, if each typewritten line contains 65 characters, and the copy has 50 lines, the total number of characters is 65 × 50 or 3250.

Partial lines should be counted as full lines, since space will appear at the end of paragraphs.

Once you've determined the total number of characters, you must determine the specifications of the type to be used.. The *type face* is simply the name of the style of type you are using—Times Roman, for example. The *type size* is measured in *points*—it takes about 72 points to make 1 inch. Type size in most general publications ranges from 8 point to 12 point.

Leading refers to the amount of space between lines of type. Sometimes type is set solid, that is, without leading. Often, to improve legibility, the type is leaded 1 or 2 points. This simply means that 1 or 2 points of space is added between each line of type.

Copy space on a layout is usually measured in *picas*—there are 6 picas to the inch. One pica of copy depth is equal to 12 points. Thus one line of 12-point type takes up 1 pica of copy space.

If the type is set solid—no leading—100 lines of 12-point type take up 100 picas, about 16⅔ inchs. The general formula for determining copy depth, then, is:

$$\frac{\text{lines of type} \times \text{point size (plus leading)}}{12} = \text{copy depth in picas}$$

Thus, if you used 10-point type with 1-point leading, 100 lines of type would be:

$$\frac{100 \times (10 + 1)}{12} = 91.7 = 92 \text{ picas}$$

Notice that if 10-point type is used, and is leaded 2 points, the number of lines of type is equal to the copy depth in picas.

The number of lines of type can be determined only after the width of each line is known. In other words, how many characters will each line contain?

Type books commonly give a "characters per pica" count for different type faces and sizes. Ten-point Helvetica, for example, has a characters-per-pica count of 2.4. If your copy space is 10 picas wide, then, the number of characters per line will be 24.

Sample Copyfitting Problems

Suppose you want to set the original copy—calculated at 3,250 characters—in 10-point Helvetica. The width of a column of type will be 14 picas. How many lines of copy will you have?

Step One: Characters per pica times line width in picas gives characters per line:
$$2.4 \times 14 = 33.6$$

Step Two: Total characters divided by characters per line gives number of lines:
$$\frac{3250}{33.6} = 96.4 = 97 \text{ lines}$$

Given 97 lines of 10-point type, and 1-point leading, what will the depth of the copy be when set in type?

Step One: Point size (plus leading) times number of lines gives depth in points:
$$(10 + 1) \times 97 = 1067$$

Step Two: Depth in points divided by 12 gives depth in picas.
$$\frac{1067}{12} = 89 \text{ picas}$$

If the copy had been 10-point leaded 2 instead of 1, the copy depth would have equaled the number of lines—97.

Suppose the layout is flexible. You have copy with 3,250 characters. Type face is 10-point Helvetica leaded 2. You want the length of copy when set in type to be 49 lines. How wide will the column of copy have to be?

Step One: Total number of characters divided by number of lines gives characters per line:
$$\frac{3250}{49} = 66.3$$

Step Two: Characters per line divided by characters per pica gives picas per line:
$$\frac{66.3}{2.4} = 27.6 = 28$$

The column width will have to be 28 picas. Finally, you are given a layout with columns 21 picas wide, and you have a depth of 120 picas. Copy must be written to fill the space. If you set your typewriter to provide a 60-space line, how many typewritten lines will be needed to fill the space? (Assume type will be 10-point Helvetica leaded 2 points.)

Step One: Characters per pica times line width in picas gives characters per line:
$$2.4 \times 21 = 50.4$$

Step Two: Characters per line times number of lines gives total characters:
$$50.4 \times 120 = 6048 \text{ characters}$$
(number of lines equals depth in picas because type is set 10 point leaded 2).

Step Three: Typewriter lines equals total characters divided by typewriter characters per line:
$$\frac{6048}{60} = 100.8 = 101 \text{ typewritten lines}$$

Appendix D
Public Relations Description

D

from: PRSA NEWSLETTER
Nov/Dec 1982

OFFICIAL STATEMENT ON PUBLIC RELATIONS

(Formally adopted by PRSA Assembly, November 6, 1982.)

Public relations helps our complex, pluralistic society to reach decisions and function more effectively by contributing to mutual understanding among groups and institutions. It serves to bring private and public policies into harmony.

Public relations serves a wide variety of institutions in society such as businesses, trade unions, government agencies, voluntary associations, foundations, hospitals and educational and religious institutions. To achieve their goals, these institutions must develop effective relationships with many different audiences or publics such as employees, members, customers, local communities, shareholders and other institutions, and with society at large.

The managements of institutions need to understand the attitudes and values of their publics in order to achieve institutional goals. The goals themselves are shaped by the external environment. The public relations practitioner acts as a counselor to management, and as a mediator, helping to translate private aims into reasonable, publicly acceptable policy and action.

As a management function, public relations encompasses the following:

- Anticipating, analyzing and interpreting public opinion, attitudes and issues which might impact, for good or ill, the operations and plans of the organization.
- Counseling management at all levels in the organization with regard to policy decisions, courses of action and communication, taking into account their public ramifications and the organization's social or citizenship responsibilities.
- Researching, conducting and evaluating, on a continuing basis, programs of action and communication to achieve informed public understanding necessary to the success of an organization's aims. These may include marketing, financial, fund raising, employee, community or government relations and other programs.
- Planning and implementing the organization's efforts to influence or change public policy.
- Setting objectives, planning, budgeting, recruiting and training staff, developing facilities—in short, *managing* the resources needed to perform all of the above.
- Examples of the knowledge that may be required in the professional practice of public relations include communication arts, psychology, social psychology, sociology, political science, economics and the principles of management and ethics. Technical knowledge and skills are required for opinion research, public issues analysis, media relations, direct mail, institutional advertising, publications, film/video productions, special events, speeches and presentations.

In helping to define and implement policy, the public relations practitioner utilizes a variety of professional communication skills and plays an integrative role both within the organization and between the organization and the external environment.

Index